Revolution & Counterrevolution in Nicaragua

Revolution &
Counterrevolution
in Nicaragua

EDITED BY

Thomas W. Walker
OHIO UNIVERSITY

Westview Press
BOULDER □ SAN FRANCISCO □ OXFORD

#23768843

The drawing on the paperback cover was created especially for this book by Leóncio Sáenz of Managua. During the revolutionary period, Sáenz was a frequent artistic contributor to *Nicaráuac, Pensamiento Própio*, and other Nicaraguan publications. In addition, his works hung in President Daniel Ortega's outer office and were featured in exhibitions around the world.

Copyright © 1991 by Westview Press, Inc., except for Chapter 15, which is copyright © 1990 by Peter Kornbluh

Published in 1991 in the United States of America by Westview Press, Inc., 5500 Central Avenue, Boulder, Colorado 80301, and in the United Kingdom by Westview Press, 36 Lonsdale Road, Summertown, Oxford OX2 7EW

Library of Congress Cataloging-in-Publication Data
Revolution & counterrevolution in Nicaragua / edited by Thomas W. Walker.
    p.   cm.
Includes index.
ISBN 0-8133-0862-3 — ISBN 0-8133-0863-1 (pbk.).
    1. Nicaragua—Politics and government—1979–
2. Counterrevolutions—Nicaragua.   I. Walker, Thomas W.   II. Title:
Revolution and counterrevolution in Nicaragua.
F1528.R49   1991
320.97285—dc20   91-18353
                                                                                     CIP

Printed and bound in the United States of America

The paper used in this publication meets the requirements of the American National Standard for Permanence of Paper for Printed Library Materials Z39.48-1984.

10   9   8   7   6   5   4   3   2   1

As before . . .

Lest history once again be written
by the rich and the powerful
at the expense of the poor

Contents

Preface

Books on revolution often leave much to be desired. The subject evokes strong emotions. As a result, cardboard portrayals of the revolutionaries as either flawless saints or bloodthirsty, conspiratorial devils flow off the presses almost as soon as an old regime is overthrown. And because important vested interests—international as well as local—are inevitably affected by revolution, deliberate disinformation or "black propaganda" (to use the CIA's term for it) becomes routine. Covertly funded propaganda books, articles, and op-ed pieces appear in the guise of scholarly or journalistic products. In addition, revolutions are so media marketable that they inevitably stimulate an outpouring of quick, often sensationalist, ahistorical, and ethnocentric journalistic efforts. Normally anecdotal in character, the latter rarely give the type of verifiable documentation essential for a scholarly understanding of the subject.

Even the well-trained scholar honestly interested in producing an objective overview of the revolutionary experience is faced with an almost impossible task. Because true revolution implies a rapidly evolving multifaceted process of social, cultural, economic, and political change, it is difficult for any one individual to keep abreast of everything that is going on.

Those are some of the factors that motivated me on four occasions to organize multiauthor efforts at documenting the Nicaraguan revolution. I reasoned that a team of scholars, each focusing on a discrete, manageable subject within her or his area of expertise, ought to be able to produce the type of comprehensive, yet accurate and well-documented, volume that is so often lacking in the study of revolutions.

I have had a scholarly interest in Nicaragua and the subject of revolution since long before the Sandinistas came to power in 1979. I spent the summer of 1967 in that country doing the research for my M.A. thesis, "The Christian Democratic Movement in Nicaragua," which was published under the same title in 1970. Because few U.S. scholars prior to 1979 had ever paid much attention to this seemingly obscure and unimportant ministate, my little monograph (which came out also in Spanish in Venezuela) made me, by default, one of only a handful of U.S. specialists on Nicaragua at the time.

When I accepted my current teaching position in 1972, I inherited a course on revolution in Latin America, which I have taught ever since. I have found that the give-and-take with bright students that one experiences in teaching any course has a marvelous way of honing one's analytical perceptions of, and piquing one's interest in, the subject of that course. This certainly was the case with my course on revolution in Latin America.

Though I was already at work on a concise introduction to Nicaragua—published as *Nicaragua: The Land of Sandino* (Westview, 1981; third ed., 1991)—the idea of organizing a team effort to document in greater detail the revolutionary reality of that suddenly very important ministate took shape almost immediately after the Sandinista victory. In fact, if I remember correctly, it occurred to me as I was hitchhiking into Nicaragua on the first Sunday after the Sandinista victory of July 19, 1979. Over time it resulted in two books on the revolution itself—*Nicaragua in Revolution* (1982) and *Nicaragua: The First Five Years* (1985)—and one on the U.S.-sponsored counterrevolution, entitled *Reagan Versus the Sandinistas: The Undeclared War on Nicaragua* (Westview, 1987). The purpose of this fourth volume is to tie the two strands together and provide a reasonably comprehensive contemporary history of both the revolution and the counterrevolution during the nearly eleven years in which the Sandinistas were in power.

Thomas W. Walker

ONE

Introduction

THOMAS W. WALKER

From the late 1970s through 1990 the tiny republic of Nicaragua was the focal point of inordinate attention by the U.S. government and, hence, the U.S. media. That a poor, underdeveloped country of only a few million people could command such attention from the world's leading superpower may seem—and probably was—absurd. But what was happening in Nicaragua was unusual. A traditional "pro-American" dictator, Anastasio Somoza Debayle, was overthrown on July 19, 1979, by a mass-based insurrectionary movement. That movement then proceeded to implement pragmatic but sweeping changes in social, economic, political, and foreign policy. As perceived by conservative policymakers in Washington, those changes were a threat and a challenge to U.S. hegemony in Central America, "our backyard." In less than two years, the United States would be engaged in an undeclared surrogate war against the upstart state. The U.S. obsession with Nicaragua would ultimately subside only in 1990 when—after the destruction of the Nicaraguan economy and the death of nearly 1 percent of the populace— a desperate Nicaraguan electorate would vote to end the revolutionary experiment and replace it with a regime endorsed and sponsored by the United States.

In order to understand what happened in Nicaragua in that period, it is necessary first to examine the history of revolution and counterrevolution in Latin America. In addition, the Nicaraguan experience of the 1970s and 1980s must be set in its historical and national context.

Revolution and Counterrevolution

As the term is commonly used by social scientists, "revolution" is a process of rapid social, economic, and political change, which normally results in a restructuring of the relationship between classes. Revolutions usually involve some physical violence and lead to a significant outflow of émigrés consisting of both individuals from the former privileged

1

class and others whose lives are disrupted by the turmoil of change taking place.

If one uses this definition in examining the history of Latin America, one quickly concludes that, contrary to popular belief, Latin America is not very revolutionary. Though extralegal changes in government such as coups d'état have been common in twentieth-century Latin America, few have led to any serious attempt at a reordering of social and economic structures. Generously, we might include seven cases in the revolutionary or proto-revolutionary category: Mexico, 1911–1940; Guatemala, 1945–1954; Bolivia, 1952–1964; Cuba, 1959 to date; Peru, 1968–1975; Chile, 1970–1973; and Nicaragua, 1979–1990. Of those real or would-be revolutions, five eventually died, were crushed, or were transformed into nonrevolutionary systems before significant social and economic change could be completed. As this book was going to press, the Nicaraguan revolution was in a state of dynamic limbo. Only the Cuban revolution was still unambiguously alive.

Given the low success rate of revolution in Latin America, one might wonder why insurgencies and other attempts to begin the revolutionary process were constantly taking place throughout the region. The answer seems to be that nothing else appeared to be working either, if by "working" one means producing an alleviation of the miserable condition of the majority poor of Latin America. There seems to have been something structurally wrong with most Latin American social, economic, and political systems, something that was causing the rich to get richer and the poor, poorer. Described as "dependency" by some scholars, the system plaguing Latin America was one in which the resources and means of production were controlled by, and benefited, a relatively few citizens who worked in symbiotic relationship with foreigners to produce products destined in large part for foreign markets.[1] This pattern was visible whether the political form was liberal democracy (Colombia and Venezuela from the late 1950s on), one-man dictatorship (Paraguay under Stroessner or Haiti under the Duvaliers), or military rule (Brazil from 1964 to the mid-1980s and Argentina from 1966 to 1983).

It would seem that the privileged classes, which dominated the media, controlled the military, and had the de facto backing of the United States, were simply unwilling to make the sacrifices necessary to redress the structural imbalances that were holding the majority in poverty. As long as that situation persisted, socially concerned nationalists would likely continue to risk their lives in insurrectionary activities aimed at bringing about revolutionary change, no matter how dismal the prospects for success.

It is clear that both revolutionaries and counterrevolutionaries learn from history and from each other. In the twentieth century, from the Mexican revolution through the Nicaraguan revolution, the tactics and strategies of both sides evolved considerably. Though I cannot discuss this dialectic process in detail here, I can give some idea of what I mean.

First, one can see the learning dialectic present in the evolution of twentieth-century techniques of rebellion and counterinsurgency. The Mexican revolution came to power in 1911 when conventional combat between pro- and antirevolutionary cacique-led armies resulted in an overall revolutionary victory. It was not until the late 1920s that Nicaraguan patriot Augusto César Sandino would develop—by trial and error—the classical techniques of rural guerrilla warfare. These included small hit-and-run attacks, ambushes, and the cultivation of friendly relations with the rural population.

Those techniques, adapted by Fidel Castro and Ernesto "Ché" Guevara in Cuba and given the name rural *foco* (focus) war, helped bring about the success of their revolt in 1959. However, the United States, learning from the Cuban experience, quickly began a program of counterinsurgency training and support for Latin American military establishments; that assistance helped foil several subsequent *foco* efforts, including ones by Ché in Bolivia and the Sandinistas in Nicaragua, both of which were crushed in 1967.

There then followed a brief flurry of interest in, and experimentation with, urban guerrilla warfare as advocated by Spanish ex-patriot, Abraham Guillén.[2] Involving selective assassination, propaganda, and sabotage, this technique was quickly discredited when major practitioners such as Carlos Marighela in Brazil, the Tupamaros of Uruguay, and the Montaneros in Argentina were destroyed by bloody U.S.-backed programs of urban "counterterror" implemented by the military regimes of those countries.

The 1979 victory of the Sandinistas was the product of a very pragmatic combination of rural and urban techniques with one new twist, the mass-based urban insurgency. Having taken stock of this experience, however, the United States refined the techniques of "counterterror" to block any repetition of what had happened in Nicaragua. In February 1980, for instance, U.S. Chargé d'affaires James Cheek instructed the governing Christian Democrats of El Salvador to institute what was euphemistically called "a clean counter-insurgency war," in which civil rights would be severely curtailed and Salvadoran security forces, already known for their savagery, would be accorded even greater leeway in dealing with "subversives." During the next decade, more than 70,000 civilians would be slaughtered by government security forces and associated "death squads," but in the long run El Salvador would be "saved"—at least for the time being—from a much-feared "leftist takeover."[3]

The learning dialectic is also present in what happened after revolutionary groups had come to power. On the one hand, revolutionaries

in this century learned a number of techniques for the consolidation
of power and the successful implementation of change. On the other,
counterrevolutionary forces—particularly the United States—perfected
techniques to destabilize revolutionary governments, make them appear
inept, and ultimately cause their downfall.

One of the things that revolutionary governments learned over the
decades was that if "revolution" is, indeed, to be "revolutionary," it
must immediately embark on social programs designed to improve the
human condition of the previously exploited majority. These would
include projects and legislation designed to advance public health,
education, housing, and equitable food distribution; agrarian reform;
the protection of rural and urban workers; and an effort to resurrect
and nurture authentic national culture. Such programs are important
not only for their intrinsic human impact but also because they provide
opportunities for popular participation and tend to build a social base
for the revolutionary system.

Another closely related lesson of history is that it is very important
to support and encourage the formation of mass or grass-roots organizations. Such neighborhood and interest organizations have a variety
of useful functions ranging from (1) providing the voluntary organizational
infrastructure and labor needed for the relatively inexpensive implementation of social programs; (2) facilitating the learning of new, more
socially responsible values; (3) serving as a vehicle for genuine democratic
grass-roots participation; (4) facilitating information and demand "feed-
back" from the people to their government; to (5) organizing vigilance
against inevitable counterrevolutionary activities. Where such organizations flourished (Cuba and Nicaragua), the revolutionary systems were
reinforced and invigorated—at least for a while. Where they were weak
or nonexistent (Bolivia and Peru), the revolutionary systems quickly
perished.

Moreover, revolutionary governments learned much about economics.
By the 1970s, the problem of dependency was painfully apparent to
most Latin American intellectuals. What was not clear was what to do
about it. On the one hand, the middle-class "revolutionary" governments
of Bolivia in the 1950s and early 1960s had turned to the West for
financial assistance and, hence, had been forced to accept and implement
the monetarist formulas of the International Monetary Fund. The
regressive social consequences of doing so had driven a wedge between
the revolution's potential social base and its middle-class leadership and
had led to a quick demise of that revolutionary experiment. On the
other hand, Cuba's forced isolation from the West and its radical turn
to a command economy had led to another series of problems, including
lack of innovation and low productivity. By 1979 it was clear that
although the problem of dependency could not be ignored, it would
have to be dealt with in new and creative ways.

Meanwhile, the forces of counterrevolution—notably the U.S. government—had been perfecting techniques for destroying revolutionary experiments. Some of the many devices were legal and aboveboard; others were not.[4] Covert devices—usually employed by the CIA—included planning assassinations; instigating dirty tricks; inventing and disseminating "black propaganda"; funding or bribing opposition groups (church, labor, press, party); training and arming surrogate native "rebel" forces; and carrying out selective acts of sabotage, often in the name of these "freedom fighters." More-overt activities took the form of official warnings or expressions of displeasure; diplomatic moves aimed at isolating the target regime; and a variety of devices designed to cause economic collapse (such as the cutting off of U.S. trade and aid relationships, pressure to restrict the flow of funding from multilateral lending agencies, the use of travel bans to curtail tourism).

Often the particular combination of techniques employed appeared to be chaotic, ad hoc, and poorly thought out. The amateurish and comical surrogate invasion of Guatemala in 1954 succeeded only through bluff and because the regular Guatemalan army was not loyal to the elected president. Having "succeeded" on that occasion, the United States then mounted the ill-fated surrogate invasion of Cuba in 1961. The latter failed, not, as some have argued, because President Kennedy refused to provide sufficient air cover, but because fewer than 2,000 surrogate troops—no matter how well armed or protected—simply cannot overthrow a mass-based revolutionary government.

By the 1980s, however, indirect strategies for the destruction of enemy regimes had undergone considerable refinement. Indeed, a whole school of thought concerned with "low-intensity conflict" had come into being and was very much in vogue among the cold war policy planners and advisers of the Reagan administration. The multifaceted low-intensity conflict employed against Sandinista Nicaragua will be described in great detail in Part 3 of this book.

Background

Located at the geographic center of Central America, Nicaragua is the largest country in the region. Even so, its 148,000 square kilometers of territory make it only slightly larger than the state of Iowa. And its population of 3.7 million (in 1989) was a scant 27 percent greater than Iowa's 2.8 million. Given Nicaragua's low population density, abundant natural resources (good land, timber, gold, petroleum), access to two oceans, and long-recognized potential as a site for a transoceanic waterway, one would expect Nicaraguans in general to be prosperous. In fact, however, when the Sandinistas overthrew Anastasio Somoza Debayle in 1979, the social conditions of the majority of Nicaraguans ranked that country with the two or three most backward of Latin America. The explanation for this apparent paradox lies in Nicaraguan history—one of the most unfortunate of the hemisphere.

Two major factors had combined to produce this situation: elite irresponsibility flowing out of a highly unequal social system and endemic foreign intervention or manipulation. The inegalitarian nature of Nicaraguan society has its roots in the Spanish conquest in the early sixteenth century. In contrast to events in neighboring Costa Rica, where the Spaniards either killed or expelled the Indians, the conquerors of Nicaragua drastically decimated, but did not completely destroy, the native population. As a result, in Nicaragua there was an underclass of nonwhites who could be used as virtual slaves in the income-concentrating economic activities of the European minorities. In Costa Rica, the Europeans had no ethnically distinct underclass to exploit. Thus, over the centuries, Costa Rica developed the relatively more egalitarian society that gave birth in the twentieth century to liberal democracy, whereas Nicaragua and the other Central American countries to the north—with which it shared sociohistorical characteristics—produced a chain of elite-run dictatorships. Although the natural resources of the country were exploited by the elite to produce export products to generate wealth for its members, the human condition of the bulk of the population actually declined as the country's rulers used law and brute military force to promote their already lopsided class advantage. In Nicaragua, the last of these income-concentrating regimes were those of the Somoza dynasty—Anastasio Somoza García (1937–1956), Luis Somoza Debayle and puppets (1956–1967), and Anastasio Somoza Debayle (1967–1979). By the time Anastasio Somoza Debayle (with a net worth estimated well in excess of U.S. $500 million) was finally overthrown, the poorer 50 percent of his country's people were struggling to make do on a per capita income of around U.S. $250 per year.

Parallel to, and often intimately connected with, this story of elite exploitation was a long experience of foreign intervention and meddling. During the colonial period, the Spaniards on the Pacific Coast and later the British in the Atlantic region exercised control over what is now Nicaragua. Although Spanish rule in the west came to an end in 1822, the British were finally expelled from the east only in the 1890s.

Decades before, the Americans had also begun meddling in Nicaraguan affairs.[5] In the 1850s, a U.S. filibuster, William Walker, briefly imposed himself as president of Nicaragua and actually won diplomatic recognition from Washington. Later, in 1909, the United States encouraged and assisted the minority Conservative party in overthrowing Liberal nationalist president José Santos Zelaya. Subsequently, to keep elite pro-American governments in power, U.S. troops occupied Nicaragua from 1912 to 1925 and from 1926 to 1933. In return, these client regimes signed treaties giving away Nicaragua's right to have its own transoceanic waterway (which would have meant competition for the U.S. canal in Panama) and relinquishing its claims to San Andrés and other offshore islands (which Colombia demanded in apparent compensation from the United States for its involvement in engineering the independence of the Colombian province of Panama in 1903). During the second occupation, the United States created the Nicaraguan National Guard to preserve pro-American stability. After the U.S. troops departed, the National Guard's first Nicaraguan commander, Anastasio Somoza García, wasted little time in creating a pro-American dictatorship, which, with abundant U.S. assistance, was to last until 1979. By the time the dynasty was finally overthrown, its National Guard—one of the most corrupt and exploitative military establishments in the hemisphere—was also the most heavily U.S.-trained in all of Latin America.[6]

Not surprisingly, the centuries-old themes of elite exploitation and foreign meddling produced numerous incidents of grass-roots or nationalist resistance. Several heroic Indian leaders resisted the Spanish conquistadores. Centuries later, in 1881, thousands of Indians lost their lives in the War of the Comuneros in futile resistance to the seizure of their ancestral lands by Nicaraguan coffee planters. In 1912, Liberal nationalist Benjamín Zeledón lost his life after leading an unsuccessful revolt against the U.S.-imposed Conservative regime. From 1927 to 1937, Augusto César Sandino led a long guerrilla campaign to liberate his country from both the U.S. occupiers and the client regime they had imposed. Though his effort was partially successful in that it forced the United States to withdraw its troops, Sandino—who had signed a peace agreement with titular president Juan B. Sacasa—was subsequently murdered by Anastasio Somoza's National Guard.

The final—this time successful—resistance began in the 1960s. It flowed out of the confluence of two political currents, one Marxist, the other Christian. The first of these was the Sandinista Front for National Liberation (FSLN), founded in 1961 by three young Marxists—Carlos Fonseca Amador, Tomás Borge Martínez, and Silvio Mayorga—who had broken from the Nicaraguan Socialist party (the local pro-Soviet Communists) because of frustration with the PSN's subservience to Moscow and its lack of nationalism. Modeling their revolutionary movement on the nationalist image and ideas of Sandino, the Sandinistas, as will be detailed in Chapter 4, spent the better part of two decades of painful trial and error developing the type of revolutionary strategy, a combination of rural guerrilla warfare and urban mass-based insurgency, that would ultimately topple the Somozas in 1979.

By the mid-1970s, as we will see in Chapter 8, the Sandinistas began to receive a great deal of support from a powerful grass-roots Christian movement. In the late 1960s, the traditionally conservative hierarchy of

the Latin American Catholic church had undergone an apparent transformation of purpose. Declaring a "preferential option for the poor,"
the Second General Conference of Latin American Bishops, meeting
in Medellín, Colombia, in 1968, had advocated the creation of ecclesiastical
base communities (CEBs), in which ordinary people would meet in
groups, discuss their social situation in light of the liberating message
of the Bible, and then take action by forming grass-roots interest groups
that could promote their dreams and demands for a better life and a
more just society. Most bishops apparently assumed that as the poor
majority became more self-aware and empowered, the privileged classes,
moved by Christian conscience, would respond to their just demands
not by violence but by making the concessions necessary to create better
societies. However, when the CEB movement began to gain momentum
in Nicaragua in the mid-1970s, the Somoza regime responded with the
standard tactics of "counterterror." CEBs were attacked and leaders and
members were tortured and killed. Accordingly, large numbers of
Christians came to the conclusion that armed rebellion was the only
way to rid Nicaragua of its unjust system. By the late 1970s, tens of
thousands of committed Christians had joined the Sandinistas—formally
or informally—in the effort to overthrow the Somozas. As will be
detailed in Chapter 4, huge mass-based insurrections took place in 1978
and 1979. Finally, after eighteen months of intermittent conflict known
as the War of Liberation, Somoza's army was defeated and the Nicaraguan
revolution came to power.

The War of Liberation had cost Nicaragua around 50,000 lives, or
approximately 2 percent of its people. In the United States, that would
be the equivalent of a loss of around 4.5 million people, or more than
seventy-five times the U.S. death toll in the entire Vietnam conflict.

Why had insurgency succeeded in Nicaragua, whereas it had failed
in so many other Latin American countries? The answer is complex.[7]
The presence of poverty and injustice, in and of themselves, is not a
sufficient explanation. They exist in many countries that have not
experienced revolutionary victories. Nor were innovative and pragmatic
guerrilla strategies, however important, the decisive factor. Other well-
organized insurrections have failed. No, what probably tipped the scales
was the personalization of oppression in the form of a particularly venal
dictator, Anastasio Somoza, an individual who was so disliked that he
actually united his countrymen in the pursuit of his overthrow. At the
same time, the presence of the human rights–oriented Carter administration in Washington was also fortuitous: Though Carter was opposed
to the Sandinistas and tried in a variety of ways to block their rise to
power, he was unwilling either to intervene directly or to back Somoza-
regime repression to the degree that his successors would back equally—
if not even more—repressive regimes in Guatemala and El Salvador.

The Sandinista Decade

Sandinista rule was inevitably controversial both at home and abroad. Through ardently nationalistic and in many cases deeply religious, most Sandinistas were also openly Marxist or Marxist-Leninist in that they found the writings of Marx and Lenin useful in understanding the history of Latin America. Consequently, they were automatically viewed with suspicion both by Nicaragua's middle- and upper-class minority, who feared the immediate imposition of a Soviet-style state and economy, and by foreign-policy makers in Washington, who were worried about the specter of a "second Cuba." Internally, those fears led to rapid class polarization, rumor mongering, and a notable lack of cooperation in the reconstruction effort on the part of the private sector. Internationally, especially after the election of Ronald Reagan in the United States, those perceptions produced a multifaceted program to destroy the Sandinista revolution, including a campaign of propaganda and disinformation depicting the government of Nicaragua as a grim, totalitarian Communist regime and an instrument of Soviet expansionism in the Americas. Although most of the allegations were either completely groundless or very nearly so, the U.S. mass media and most U.S. politicians of both parties (perhaps fearing to appear "naïve," "liberal," or "biased") rarely challenged the carefully cultivated conventional wisdom. Reagan's tactics for dealing with the Sandinistas could be criticized but not the administration's picture of the Nicaraguan regime itself.

For U.S. scholars who did research in Nicaragua during that period, the discrepancy between what was heard in the United States and what was seen in Nicaragua proved stark and frustrating. Far from being a coterie of wild-eyed ideologies, the Sandinistas usually behaved in a pragmatic and indeed moderate fashion. Although they were forced increasingly to rely on the Socialist Bloc for trade and aid, they did not impose a Soviet-style state or a Communist, or even a socialist, economic system. In fact, the FSLN was habitually criticized by many on the left in Nicaragua for channeling far too much of the country's scarce resources into programs aimed at winning the economic cooperation of private agro-industrialists. Especially during the first five years, the Sandinistas carried out innovative and highly successful social programs without inordinately straining the national budget. And contrary to the conventional wisdom, their performance in the area of human rights—though not flawless—would probably rank Nicaragua at least in the top third of Latin American states.

The Sandinistas enjoyed a number of political assets, but their power was not limitless. Their greatest asset was the fact that their victory had been unconditional. The old National Guard had been defeated and disbanded. The new armed forces were explicitly Sandinista—that is, revolutionary and popularly oriented. Moveover, the mass organizations created in the struggle to overthrow the dictator gave the FSLN a grass-roots base that dwarfed the organized support of all potential rivals. Finally, the new government enjoyed broad international support.

Nevertheless, the country's new leaders were well aware that their revolutionary administration faced certain geopolitical and economic constraints. The Soviet Union had made it clear that it was not willing to underwrite a second Cuba. Hard currency would not be forthcoming from that source nor would military support in the event of a U.S. invasion. Furthermore, unlike Cuba, Nicaragua was not an island. Its long borders were highly vulnerable to paramilitary penetration, and any attempt to impose a dogmatic Marxist-Leninist system would certainly have generated a mass exodus of people. In addition, the Catholic church was so important in Nicaragua and Catholics had played such a crucial role in the War of Liberation that the Sandinistas were neither inclined nor well situated to attack the Catholic traditions of their country.

But the most important factor affecting the character of the Nicaraguan revolution was the international *coyuntura* (historical setting and conditions) in which it took place. By the end of the 1970s, it had become clear that the authoritarian systems and command economies of the socialist countries were not working very well. Accordingly, the Sandinistas were determined from the start to avoid the dogmatic imposition of failed formulas. In fact, Daniel Ortega was essentially correct, if a bit immodest, when he asserted in a 1990 interview with *Paris Match* that "it is the Sandinista Revolution which invented perestroika." Recalling an April 1985 conversation with Mikhail Gorbachev, he commented: "At that time, he [Gorbachev] was not even talking about perestroika. For three hours I had explained the specific policies we were following in Nicaragua. . . . How, for example, we had distributed individual plots of land to peasants so that they would become landowners. He responded that . . . that was the right path to follow and that we, the Sandinistas, should absolutely avoid committing the errors that they, the USSR as well as the Eastern Bloc countries, had committed."[8]

The chapters that follow will examine domestic groups, institutions, and power; Sandinista government policy; the U.S.-orchestrated counterrevolution; and the search for peace. Some readers may be disquieted by the frankness with which certain shortcomings and flaws in the Sandinista revolution are discussed. Other may be disappointed that the overall picture of the Sandinistas is not one of demonic conspirators. So be it. This book was prepared in order to give the serious reader the factual foundation for a balanced understanding of an important and unusual revolutionary experience: its successes, its failures, and its ultimate reversal.

Notes

1. For further discussion of this matter, see John A. Booth and Thomas W. Walker, "The Crisis of Poverty and Its Causes," in their *Understanding Central America* (Boulder: Westview Press, 1989), pp. 8–14.

2. See Donald C. Hodges, ed., *Philosophy of the Urban Guerrilla: The Revolutionary Writings of Abraham Guillén* (New York: William Morrow, 1973).

3. Booth and Walker, *Understanding Central America*, pp. 123, 124.

4. For an introduction to the techniques, short of direct invasion, that the United States has employed in the past to destroy chosen enemies, see Philip Agee, *Inside the Company: CIA Diary* (London: Bantam Books, 1976); Richard H. Immerman, *The CIA in Guatemala: The Foreign Policy of Intervention* (Austin: University of Texas Press, 1982); Seymour M. Hersh, "The Price of Power: Kissinger, Nixon and Chile," *Atlantic Monthly* (December 1982), pp. 31–58; Victor Marchetti and John D. Marks, *The CIA and the Cult of Intelligence* (New York: Dell, 1975); John Stockwell, *In Search of Enemies: A CIA Story* (New York: Norton, 1978); U.S. Congress, Senate, Staff Report of the Select Committee to Study Governmental Operations with Respect to United States Intelligence, *Covert Action in Chile* (Washington, D.C.: Government Printing Office, December 18, 1975); and Armando Uribe, *The Black Book of American Intervention in Chile* (Boston: Beacon Press, 1974).

5. The best study of the 150-year history of U.S. interference in Nicaraguan affairs is Karl Bermann, *Under the Big Stick: Nicaragua and the United States Since 1948* (Boston: South End Press, 1986).

6. Richard Millett, *Guardians of the Dynasty: A History of the U.S.-created Guardia Nacional de Nicaragua and the Somoza Family* (Maryknoll, N.Y.: Orbis Books, 1977), p. 252.

7. John Booth addressed this question throughout most of the first part of *The End and the Beginning: The Nicaraguan Revolution* (Boulder: Westview Press, 1985), as do both Booth and I in much of our *Understanding Central America*.

8. Ortega, as interviewed by Pierre Hurel, "Ortega ne rend pas les armes," *Paris Match*, March 22, 1990, pp. 78–81.

PART I
Groups, Institutions, and Power

Authentic revolution implies a significant restructuring of the social configuration of power. Some groups lose relative power, and others gain. If taken in this light, what happened in Nicaragua from 1979 to 1990 was a real, though moderate, revolution. The political and economic strength of the previously dispossessed majority was increased considerably, but although the power of the privileged minority was reduced, it was by no means completely destroyed.

The chapters in this section are addressed to various aspects of power and interest groups in revolutionary Nicaragua. Chapter 2 explores the evolution of governmental institutions. Andrew Reding shows that the interim Government of National Reconstruction (1979–1985)—created by the Joint National Directorate of the Sandinista Front for National Liberation (FSLN)—and the first elected government (1985–1990) contained significant mechanisms for non-Sandinista input and for pluralism. Reding also describes the democratic way in which the 1987 constitution was drafted, debated, revised, and promulgated as well as the unprecedentedly open process in which Nicaragua held elections in both 1984 and 1990.

Other chapters in this section look at interest groups in revolutionary Nicaragua. Luis Serra (Chapter 3) describes the role of the grass-roots organizations (OPs) as vehicles of participatory democracy. He very candidly notes the tensions and conflicts that eventually arose between the interests of a besieged state and party, on the one hand, and the sectoral goals and needs of the OPs, on the other. Though damaged and weakened by these conflicting interests, the OPs, he feels, served "as important channels for the democratic expression of popular interest and for the resolution of . . . pressing problems." In Chapter 4, I examine the Nicaraguan armed forces; show how they contained the U.S.-organized contra war; and argue that, contrary to the U.S. conventional wisdom, the Sandinista military buildup of the 1980s was actually a restrained and frugal response to the contra war and the real threat of a direct U.S. invasion. Gary Prevost (Chapter 5) examines the FSLN as a ruling party, focusing on its history, philosophy, and organization. In Chapter 6, Eric Weaver and William Barnes present the kaleidoscopic history of opposition parties and coalitions and conclude that the victory of the U.S.-coordinated UNO coalition was less a triumph of democracy than the logical outcome of the U.S. program of low-intensity conflict. The last two chapters in this section deal with two crucially important interest groups, women and the churches. Patricia Chuchryk (Chapter 7) describes the difficult struggle and the mixed record of the movement for women's rights during the revolution. Michael Dodson (Chapter 8) outlines and explains the conflicting roles of segments of the churches in support of, or opposition to, the revolution.

TWO

The Evolution
of Governmental Institutions

ANDREW A. REDING

Following two years of popular insurrection, the revolutionary triumph of July 19, 1979, was absolute. Dictator Anastasio Somoza Debayle fled first to Miami and then to Paraguay, where he was later assassinated by Argentine extremists. His praetorian National Guard disintegrated. While officers were rescued by a U.S. government DC-8 disguised with Red Cross markings, soldiers fled for the borders.[1] Thousands were captured and imprisoned by a population outraged by the slaughter of tens of thousands of their fellow citizens.

Many of the government institutions that did not collapse outright were so thoroughly discredited by their collaboration with the dictatorship that they were abolished after the triumph. Such was the case with local government, the courts, and the congress, all of which had been little more than sinecures for the dictator's family, friends, and supporters.[2] So strong was the popular revulsion that even the buildings in which these institutions had been housed—most notably the National Palace—had to be converted to other uses. Only the portions of the legal codes that did not conflict with the new revolutionary decrees were allowed to stand, pending preparation of new laws.

Most government institutions had to be created anew, beginning with those essential to restoring order: a provisional executive authority, a new army and police force, and new courts. These initially constituted the aptly named Government of National Reconstruction. By spring 1980 the revolutionary government was able to install a rudimentary legislative body, the Council of State, which by the following year had begun the complex task of translating the revolution's commitment to political pluralism into a Law of Political Parties. After extended debate and negotiation, a broadly acceptable compromise was reached in 1983, setting the stage for development of an Electoral Law and elections in 1984.

With the election of a president and legislature in 1984, Nicaragua became a representative democracy, in which seven ideologically diverse

15

political parties began deliberations over a new constitution. After a two-year process that included broad public participation and international consultation, the new constitution was promulgated on January 9, 1987. The constitutional order was then completed over the next two years, with passage of a Law of Municipalities and a Law of Autonomy, creating local and regional democratic institutions, and with passage of a new Emergency Law, a new Law of Constitutional Safeguards (*Amparo*), and a new Electoral Law, setting the stage for the February 1990 general elections.

Lacking valid domestic models for institution building, Nicaragua devised its democratic structures and practices by combining elements adapted from progressive foreign models with its own innovations. In so doing, it produced several global precedents, among them formalization of an independent fourth branch of government to prevent electoral fraud,[3] establishment of open forums for citizen participation in the drafting of a constitution, and empowerment of the Supreme Court to enforce international human rights treaties in the domestic legal process.

The revolution's commitment to political pluralism and to popular sovereignty through free elections was put to the ultimate test with the Sandinista loss to the U.S. government–backed National Opposition Union (UNO) in the February 25, 1990, general elections. Contrary to the prognostications of U.S. pundits, President Daniel Ortega graciously conceded defeat to President-elect Violeta Chamorro, assumed the responsibility of leading the opposition in the National Assembly, and laid the way for the first peaceful transition of power in Nicaraguan history.

Provisional Government

Fundamental Statute of the Republic

In early 1979, as it became clear that the Somoza dictatorship was foundering after a year and a half of unrest and periodic popular insurrection, the FSLN formed a government-in-exile, the Governing Junta of National Reconstruction in neighboring Costa Rica. Though two of the members of the JGRN (newspaper publisher Violeta Barrios de Chamorro and businessman Alfonso Robelo) were selected to represent nonrevolutionary forces that collaborated in the overthrow of Somoza, there was never any question as to who held the balance of power. The other three members—Moisés Hassan, novelist Sergio Ramírez, and Daniel Ortega—were known either to belong to, or to sympathize with, the FSLN; and Commander of the Revolution Daniel Ortega, of the Joint National Directorate (DNC) of the FSLN, emerged as coordinator. It was a combination of forces that, if anything, understated the overwhelming popularity and military advantage of the Sandinistas at the time. The state of affairs was described in the Fundamental Statute of the Republic of Nicaragua, issued the day after the revolutionary triumph, which formally established the JGRN, "designated by the revolutionary movement" (i.e., by the DNC), and "substitute[d] for the National Guard of Nicaragua a new National Army . . . to be formed by the combatants of the FSLN . . . provisionally commanded by the military chiefs and leaders of the armed movement that put an end to the dictatorship."[4]

The fundamental statute also provided for an independent judiciary and for a "colegislative" Council of State, both to be named by JGRN. Accordingly, seven magistrates were appointed to the new Supreme Court of Justice on July 21, three Sandinista judges, three from other parties, and one unaffiliated. Yet agreement could not be reached on the composition of the Council of State. In June, the JGRN had made plans for a thirty-three member council with a similar balance of power. After the July victory, with the National Guard destroyed and U.S. plans for a multinational peacekeeping force rejected by the Organization of American States (OAS), the Sandinistas insisted on a council that would more accurately reflect their popular support. As the JGRN was sharply divided on the issue, the council remained in abeyance until April 1980, when both Violeta Chamorro and Alfonso Robelo resigned their seats. On May 2, the remaining Sandinista members of the JGRN approved the General Statute of the Council of State, and two days later a forty-seven-member council held its first session, with revolutionary forces enjoying a safe two-to-one margin. Having passed this roadblock, the JGRN named two members of the Conservative party (banker Arturo Cruz and Rafael Córdova Rivas, a close associate of slain *La Prensa* editor Pedro Joaquín Chamorro) to fill its two empty seats.

The dispute over the Council of State was a revolutionary watershed. From that point on, there was no mistaking the predominance of the FSLN and its agenda of fundamental social change over the mildly reformist preferences of much of the opposition. The Chamorro family, publishers of what had until then been Nicaragua's principal daily newspaper, was profoundedly affected. Violeta's resignation set off such a rift in the family that the newspaper ceased publication the following day. The impasse was not broken until five weeks later, when Xavier Chamorro, brother of the slain editor, cashed in his share of the enterprise and walked out with 180 (91 percent) of 197 workers, to found *El Nuevo Diario*, which maintained an independent position supportive of the revolutionary process. Xavier Chamorro's nephew Pedro Joaquín took over as editor of *La Prensa*, converting it into a sounding board for frustrated segments of the country's traditional elites as they coalesced into a counterrevolutionary opposition.[5] At this point the Catholic hierarchy, led by Managua Archbishop Miguel Obando y Bravo, likewise broke with the revolution, setting off a parallel division between the traditional church led by the bishops and an emerging grass-roots church led by revolutionary priests, nuns, and theologians. Soon the repercussions would extend to the defections of Edén Pastora, "Commander Zero," and Alfonso Robelo and the emergence of the armed counterrevolution, organized by the incoming Reagan administration in early 1981.

Fundamental Statute of Rights and Guarantees

Underlying the political confrontation was a conflict over the very purpose of government. Though many failed to realize it, the JGRN had laid out that purpose in the Fundamental Statute of Rights and Guarantees of the Nicaraguan People, issued on August 21, a month after the triumph. This remarkable document, comparable to the preamble of the U.S. Declaration of Independence and the Bill of Rights, incorporated, often verbatim, key provisions of the UN Covenants on Civil and Political Rights and on Economic, Social, and Cultural Rights, recognizing these as binding in the domestic legal order. But it went beyond that by placing enormous emphasis on the "right to life" (Article 5), described as "inviolable and inherent to the human person." The death penalty, established in Article 38 of Somoza's constitution of 1974, was abolished for all crimes, even in times of national emergency.

For the first time in the history of major social revolutions, the ancien régime was spared violent retribution. Thousands of national guardsmen were imprisoned and tried—under Somoza's own laws—for crimes committed against the population. But there were no firing squads, scaffolds, guillotines, or any of the other paraphernalia of terror associated with past revolutions. The motto of new Minister of the Interior Tomás Borge, himself a victim of torture in Somoza's jails, was "revolutionary generosity." Confronting a lynch mob gathering immediately after the revolutionary triumph, he asked, "to what end did we carry out this revolution if we are going to repeat what they [the National Guard] did?"[6] Beyond the proscription of capital punishment, Article 6 forbade "cruel, inhuman, or degrading treatment" and, like the constitution and laws of neighboring Costa Rica, established a maximum prison sentence of thirty years. That these rights could not be suspended in war or for treason contributed to the integrity and durability of the revolution, as none of the tools of terror were available to be turned on new classes of "counterrevolutionaries."

Thus far, there was little to which the opposition could object. But the revolution's conception of the right to life was comprehensive, encompassing rights to basic needs without which life could not in fact be sustained. Thus Article 33 of the statute established that "every person has the right to social security . . . to an adequate standard of living for oneself and one's family, which ensures health, well-being, and in particular, food, clothing, shelter, medical assistance, and necessary social services." Since these rights are recognized in the UN Covenant on Economic, Social, and Cultural Rights, it would have been impolitic for the minority on the JGRN to object. Moreover, such rights have generally been considered unenforceable in all but socialist and social democratic states. Yet the Sandinistas never disguised their identity as social revolutionaries. As sole surviving founder of the FSLN and leading articulator of Sandinista ideology, Tomás Borge scandalized the opposition by "the defense of human rights" with "the defense . . . of the right to life. . . . There can hardly be human rights in a country where children suffer from hunger . . . where children don't go to school . . . where children don't receive love, and love in practical terms is also bread and education."[7]

Such a commitment to the basic needs of the most vulnerable members of society entails reallocation of material resources from the wealthy to the poor. That means the right to property must be seen as a secondary right, conditional to fulfillment of every human being's "inviolable and inherent" right to life. As expressed in Article 27, "property, whether individual or collective, fulfills a social function, in virtue of which it may be subject to limitations in regards to ownership, benefit, use, and disposition, for reasons of security, public interest or utility, social interest, the national economy, national emergency or disaster, or for purposes of agrarian reform." The Sandinistas interpreted this as a mandate for profound social change, beginning with the Literacy Crusade of 1980.

Though this limitation on property rights was unacceptable to much of the opposition, there was no denying its conformity with the language of the principal international human rights treaties, which Nicaragua endorsed on March 12, 1980. Thus the Superior Council of Private Enterprise (COSEP) could resort only to tortured argumentation to suggest that an inviolable right to property was essential to the right to life: "If Man is deprived of the right to hold onto the product of his own effort, it is the same as depriving him of the right to make the effort; and depriving him of the right to make the effort to sustain his own life is the same as depriving him of the right to life, which is the fundamental right of Man."[8]

Although the Sandinistas' elevating the right to life over the right to property was distasteful to their opponents both within and outside Nicaragua, it nonetheless established much of the ideological common ground for the enduring alliance between Marxist and Christian Sandinistas. It was no coincidence that whereas Christian activists in other Latin American countries were coalescing around a "theology of liberation," Christian revolutionaries in Nicaragua (and elsewhere in Central America) preferred to emphasize a "theology of life," grounded in Gospel commandments to see to the basic needs of the neediest, as in Matthew 25. Correspondingly, Sandinista Marxists tended to set aside ideological orthodoxies in favor of a return to the empirical, more genuinely "scientific," method of Marx, deriving working hypotheses from the experience of efforts at revolutionary transformation. This enabled them to cast aside outdated observations on the church's role as the "opiate of the masses," as well as to realize that socialism properly understood required greater and freer democracy than capitalist alternatives that depend on the management of public opinion.[9]

Formal and Informal Government

The convergence of Sandinista ideology and revolutionary theology had immediate and lasting consequences for the development of the formal and informal structures and policies of the revolutionary government. From the beginning, both the Marxist and the Christian Sandinistas controlled key government ministries, even though U.S. analysts, viewing Nicaraguan reality through the prism of past experiences of global "communism," tended to misunderstand the motivations of the former group and to underestimate the significance of the latter.

Members of the nine-person Joint National Directorate (DNC) of the FSLN indeed held some of the prominent positions in the government. Daniel Ortega served as coordinator of the JGRN. His brother Humberto Ortega was made minister of defense (in charge of the army), while veteran Sandinista Tomás Borge became minister of the interior (in charge of police, state security, and prisons), with Luis Carrión as his deputy. That assured the DNC undisputed control of all armed forces, yet in practice only formalized the status quo following the collapse of the National Guard. DNC member Jaime Wheelock, author of a major study on the relationship between dictatorship and export monoculture, was named minister of agriculture. Henry Ruiz became minister of planning. After a short stint as president of the Council of State, the polemical and confrontational Bayardo Arce was replaced by Carlos Núñez. Arce was reassigned to the task of developing the FSLN party structure, as chairman of the three-member Political Commission of the DNC. The only member of the DNC who never assumed a government post was Víctor Tirado, a Mexican by birth.

Less noticed was the pattern of appointments of Christian Sandinistas to prominent policy-making positions in the government. Maryknoll priest Miguel d'Escoto was placed in charge of foreign policy as minister of the exterior, while fellow priest Edgard Parrales was dispatched to Washington as ambassador to the OAS. The sensitive position of minister of education, charged with developing policies that would profoundly affect the future of the revolution, was entrusted to Carlos Tünnerman, a former president of the National Autonomous University of Nicaragua

(UNAN) and a prominent Catholic layperson. When named ambassador to the United States in 1984, he was succeeded by Jesuit priest Fernando Cardenal, who had helped organize an ecclesiastical base community (CEB) in Managua's Barrio Rigueiro that had fostered such revolutionary leaders as DNC member Luis Carrión and Army Chief of Staff Joaquín Cuadra. Priest and poet Ernesto Cardenal, whose contemplative community on the Solentiname Archipelago in Lake Nicaragua had become a focal point of resistance to the dictatorship, was named minister of culture. Among other Christian revolutionaries appointed to top positions were Roberto Argüello, president of the Supreme Court, Reinaldo Antonio Téfel, minister of social security and welfare, Miguel Ernesto Vigil, minister of housing, and Emilio Baltodano, comptroller-general of the republic.[10] Even Tomás Borge would have to be counted in this group, both for his close links to the revolutionary priests and for his own proclivity to articulate public policy in terms of a "theology of life."[11]

Beyond the formal structures of government, revolutionary Christian institutes played a major role in interpreting developments through rigorous multidisciplinary (political, economic, legal, cultural, and moral) analysis, which at once fostered and helped frame internal debate within important segments of the policy-making elite. Prime examples included the Jesuit-run Central American Historical Institute, with its monthly magazine, Envío, and the Antonio Valdivieso Ecumenical Center, which published books, pamphlets, and the magazine Amanecer, in addition to weekly columns in El Nuevo Diario. The output and originality of these institutes far outpaced that of corresponding Sandinista party institutes and publishing houses, such as Editorial Vanguardia. Revolutionary Christians also produced some of the most provocative and best-selling titles of the government publishing house, Editorial Nueva Nicaragua, among them Ernesto Cardenal's four-volume The Gospel in Solentiname, and theologian Giulio Girardi's Faith in the Revolution and the Revolution in Culture.

The influence of the revolutionary Christian ethos on government policies was substantial. Nicaragua's social revolution was the first one to abolish the death penalty.[12] The Foreign Ministry set an international precedent for the peaceful resolution of disputes by submitting Nicaragua's armed confrontation with the United States to the compulsory jurisdiction of the World Court, whose Western-dominated bench voted twelve to three in favor of Nicaragua. Later, it would be the Christian Sandinistas in the National Constituent Assembly who would provide the margin of victory for an article incorporating major international human rights treaties into the Nicaraguan constitution, another global precedent. Since such achievements did not fit the image of "communist totalitarianism," they were generally ignored in the United States, and when noticed at all, they were dismissed as the clever and "pragmatic" posturings of "Marxist-Leninists" intent on deceiving public opinion. The reality was much simpler: Each of these initiatives was a logical corollary of the "right to life" ethos first expounded in the Fundamental Statute of Rights and Guarantees.

Revolutionary Transformations, Counterrevolutionary Reactions

Some of the other logical corollaries of the "right to life" ethos, however, mandated conflictive and controversial measures. To redirect a national economy designed to concentrate wealth in the hands of elites toward securing the basic needs of the majority, the Sandinistas planned to seize the "commanding heights" of the economy by nationalizing the banking system, the mines, foreign commerce, and the vast network of holdings of the Somoza family. In addition, they planned a land reform to distribute more equitably the primary means of production in a still largely agrarian society. Only in this manner, they argued, could the foundations of genuine democracy be laid.

Such broad transformations, however, have seldom been achieved through the protracted give-and-take of legislative processes; and timing was critical as the Sandinistas had to anticipate the mounting counterrevolutionary efforts of the Reagan administration with a series of faits accomplis. For this reason, the Council of State was initially designed as a merely "colegislative" body, able to advise the JGRN but unable to alter or reject legislation of its own. Unencumbered, the JGRN made use of its decree-making powers to issue a quick succession of revolutionary laws in 1981, including the Agrarian Reform Law, the Law of Cooperatives, and, in anticipation of reactions to these, the Law to Prevent and Combat Decapitalization and the Law of Social and Economic Emergencies. The enactment of these fundamental socioeconomic transformations marked a second revolutionary turning point. Although the government rapidly gained support among beneficiaries of land reform and of the formation of cooperatives, it just as rapidly alienated traditional elites, many of whom fled to Miami, slashed investment and production, or swung their support to the counterrevolution. By early 1982, armed counterrevolutionary incursions across the Honduran frontier began to inflict serious damage in northern zones.

The JGRN responded to these challenges with extraordinary measures. To counter the military threat, it imposed a State of Emergency on March 15, 1982. And to circumvent the exceedingly slow pace and more conservative tendencies of the regular courts, it created special courts with streamlined procedures and the participation of citizen-judges of known revolutionary sympathies. The People's Anti-Somocista Tribunals (TPAs), modeled on the earlier special tribunals that had tried captured national guardsmen, were formed in 1983 to try captured contras and suspected collaborators. Similarly, Agrarian Reform Tribunals were established to review confiscations and expropriations carried out by the Ministry of Agricultural Development and Agrarian Reform (MIDINRA, formerly the Ministry of Agriculture). Also in 1983, the Law of Military Service established Nicaragua's first universal draft. To many U.S. observers, these drastic measures seemed to confirm their worst fears of the Sandinistas, that they were dedicated Marxist-Leninists intent on consolidating a Cuban-Soviet totalitarian dictatorship. Part of the problem was cultural and linguistic. The JGRN was commonly referred to as the *junta*, a term that in English usage has come to be associated with dictatorship by cliques of Latin American generals. To compound the problem, the junta was readily confused with the Joint National Directorate (DNC) of the FSLN; and the honorific title "commander of the revolution" held by each member of the DNC, was widely believed to designate military rank, a misconception reinforced by the olive green guerrilla garb that members of the DNC, including junta coordinator Daniel Ortega, habitually wore in public. Yet not a single member of the junta ever held a military rank, and only three members of the DNC were ever in active command of military or police forces (Humberto Ortega, Tomás Borge, and Luis Carrión); of these three Humberto Ortega alone held military rank as general of the army (Tomás Borge declined a similar commission). As for wearing olive green, the Sandinistas saw it as symbolizing a vocation of ongoing struggle alongside the "great majorities" and distinguishing the revolutionary leadership from the traditional elites in their white, elaborately pleated *guayabera* shirts.

For a more accurate and illustrative historical parallel, one must look not to the military juntas of South America, but to the all-but-forgotten precedent in neighboring Costa Rica, where another civilian junta ruled for eighteen months in 1948–1949. The Costa Rican crisis had been mild by comparison with the one that gave rise to provisional government in Nicaragua. After irregularities in the 1948 presidential election there was a brief civil war, culminating in the triumph of social democratic forces led by José Figueres. To circumvent the legislature, which was dominated by Christian Democrats and Communists, Figueres suspended the constitution and established the Founding Junta of the Second Republic, with himself as its president. Armed with decree powers, he rapidly nationalized the banks and hydroelectric facilities and imposed a one-time 10 percent levy on all wealth valued above 50,000 colones. These were drastic measures: Until then, only Communist countries had nationalized their entire banking systems. Although the levy on wealth was ultimately revoked by his successor, Figueres also acted to abolish the army, extend voting rights to women, and form an independent Supreme Electoral Tribunal to prevent recurrence of fraud.[13] These bold reforms, together with others that followed, contributed to the extraordinary stability of Costa Rican democracy in the decades that followed, after constitutional authority was restored.

When, in a parallel with the later Nicaraguan case, the reforms led to an invasion of Costa Rica's northern zone by counterrevolutionaries backed by Nicaraguan dictator Anastasio Somoza García's National Guard, the Costa Rican junta suspended habeas corpus and created a censorship office. It also set up special courts: the Tribunal of Administrative Probity and the Tribunal of Immediate Sanctions, which judged the "political crimes" of adversaries; in neither case was there any right of appeal. Yet the Costa Rican junta took even more drastic measures against domestic opponents than did the Nicaraguan one. Teachers and other public servants whose loyalties were questioned were fired; and even before the counterrevolutionary threat materialized from the north, the junta banned Popular Vanguard (a Communist, but thoroughly constitutionalist, party that had won ten legislative seats in the previous election) and dissolved seventy labor unions, most for their Communist affiliations. Also unlike the Sandinistas, who periodically censored and suspended the opposition daily La Prensa, the Costa Rican junta permanently closed down both the Christian Democratic newspaper La Tribuna and the Communist newspaper Trabajo.[14] Even during the worst periods of national crisis, the Sandinistas showed greater respect for civil liberties and political pluralism than had their Costa Rican counterparts.

Representative and Constitutional Government

As in the earlier Costa Rican case, the Nicaraguan junta never wavered from plans to hold national elections. From the time it assumed power in 1979, the JGRN foresaw holding elections in 1985; this timetable was reaffirmed by DNC member Humberto Ortega on August 21, 1980, at the closing ceremony of the Literacy Crusade. In November 1981, a draft Law of Political Parties was submitted to the Council of State, with the intention of developing a regime of political pluralism that would be acceptable to most, if not all, opposition parties. Though discussion in committee was slowed by the State of Emergency proclaimed in March 1982, the draft law that was resubmitted to the plenum in November 1982 had been considerably enriched by dialogue, as reflected in its enlargement from fourteen to thirty-four articles. Over the following six months, the second draft was exhaustively renegotiated in a special committee, producing a third draft that was debated by the plenum, then finally approved on August 17, 1983.

The two-year process of debate and approval of the Law of Political Parties indicated a change in the role of the Council of State: Whereas it had been a mere consultative appendage of the JGRN, it became an embryonic legislature. This was deliberate. As the focus shifted from establishing revolutionary faits accomplis to institutionalizing democratic structures that would legitimate the new revolutionary order, there was a corresponding transition from executive fiat to a search for as broad a consensus as possible among the country's political forces. As reconstituted in 1981, the corporative Council of State had fifty-one members, representing Nicaragua's principal political parties, labor unions, business confederations, churches, the army, and other significant groupings. The very pluralism that had earlier made it inconvenient for such "revolutionary conquests" as enactment of land reform, now made it the ideal forum—and laboratory—for the development of representative democracy.

As finally approved, the Law of Political Parties established the right to form political parties "freely . . . without any ideological restriction whatsoever," apart from a prohibition on advocating the return of a Somoza-style dictatorship (Article 4). That right to form parties was made substantive by Article 2, which recognized the right of all such parties to contend for power, and by Article 20, which set some of the most lenient requirements for registering a party to be found anywhere: submission of a name, emblem, political platform, and names of a few dozen party officials. Control over party registration was vested in an independent National Council of Political Parties, composed of three members named by the Council of State, four elected by the National Assembly of Political Parties, and one appointed by the JGRN. Because the National Assembly of Political Parties, where each party had a single representative, was dominated by the opposition, this formula ensured political balance. Appeals could still be made to the Supreme Court. For the first time ever, Nicaraguan political parties had a secure legal foundation.

In February 1984, the Council of State began work on Nicaragua's first serious electoral law. The two previous laws (1951 and 1974) had merely sought to legitimate dictatorship by reserving one-third of the seats in Congress for the Conservative party; and the two preceding laws (Ley Dodds and Ley McCoy) bore the names of their U.S. authors, from the period of U.S. marine occupation.[15] In search of better ideas, special commissions visited the United States and five European and seven Latin American countries.

The Electoral Law, approved at the end of March 1984, revealed the outlines of the form of government that would emerge from the Nicaraguan revolution. To maximize pluralistic deliberation, a ninety-member National Constituent Assembly would be elected by proportional representation, with any party that gained a mere 1 percent of the national vote assured of at least one seat (in practice at least two seats because losing presidential candidates also would be seated in the legislature). Yet to maintain an effective executive power to secure and pursue revolutionary gains, a president and vice president would be elected by plurality, as in the United States. Contrary to predictions that the Sandinistas would copy Soviet or Cuban models, the Nicaraguan government was instead taking shape as a variant of the progressive Latin American model (epitomized by Venezuela and Costa Rica), which blends the U.S. presidential system with the European system of proportional representation.

To "guarantee and respect the popular vote," the Nicaraguans turned primarily to the Costa Ricans, Venezuelans, and Swedes for inspiration and advice. The Supreme Electoral Council (CSE), modeled on the independent electoral tribunals of Costa Rica and Venezuela, was established to supervise the upcoming elections, which were advanced to November 4, 1984. Mariano Fiallos, the widely respected president of the National Autonomous University of Nicaragua (UNAN), was named president of the CSE; two of the four remaining magistrates were designated by opposition parties. All participating political parties were guaranteed the right to equal shares of public campaign financing, to equal time on radio and television, and to have poll watchers present during registration, voting, and counting of ballots. The Swedish electoral commission provided technical assistance.

The 1984 Elections

Six opposition political parties chose to contest the elections. Three of these—the Communist Party of Nicaragua (PCdeN), the Nicaraguan Socialist party (PSN), and the Marxist-Leninist Popular Action Movement (MAP-ML)—were small parties to the left of the FSLN; they objected to Sandinista deviations from various versions of orthodox Marxism-Leninism. On the right, however, the situation was complicated by splits within the three principal political currents. Faced with the unprecedented prospect of an open electoral contest with a revolutionary party, some sought to gain political space by winning legislative seats, while others opposed participating in an election that would legitimate revolutionary power. Thus the majority factions of the Conservatives (Democratic Conservative party—PCD) and the Liberals (Independent Liberal party—PLI) decided to field candidates, as did the Christian democratic Popular Social Christian party (PPSC), the product of an earlier left-wing split from the Social Christian party (PSC). The only noteworthy party to abstain was the PSC, which united with the COSEP and tiny groups of dissident liberals and conservatives in the Nicaraguan Democratic Coordinator (CDN).

The Reagan administration had long called for elections in Nicaragua, as part of its program of "public diplomacy" (i.e., propaganda). Caught off guard by the Sandinista announcement of elections, the administration swung all its weight into efforts to sabotage them. In the first place, it maneuvered to have the CDN set aside its obvious choice for a standard-bearer—Adán Fletes, president of the PSC—in favor of Arturo Cruz. Cruz was selected not so much for his appeal to Nicaraguan voters as for his attractiveness to the U.S. Congress and public. As a longtime resident of Washington, Cruz spoke fluent English; as an international banker, he knew how to speak to those in positions of influence. Moreover, his past stints as member of the Nicaraguan junta and as ambassador to Washington afforded him some credibility abroad when he accused the Sandinistas of betraying the revolution.

As reported in the *New York Times* just days before the election, the Reagan administration had all along planned on having Cruz either refuse to participate in the election or withdraw at the last moment, alleging unfair conditions. In particular, Enrique Bolaños and other leaders of COSEP met repeatedly with CIA officials in Washington and San José, Costa Rica, during the spring and summer of 1984 to coordinate this abstentionist strategy. According to a senior official, "the administration never contemplated letting Cruz stay in the race, because then the Sandinistas could justifiably claim that the elections were legitimate, making it much harder for the United States to oppose the Nicaraguan Government."[16]

Instead, Cruz returned to Nicaragua to campaign against the elections. Seeking to take advantage of rights conferred on political parties contesting the elections, but without itself taking part, the CDN organized open-air rallies for Cruz. These were disrupted by Sandinista partisans, angered by what they saw as a brazen violation of the electoral law by forces they suspected of being stage-managed by the CIA. Though such charges were at the time ridiculed by the U.S. government, in April 1985 the *Wall Street Journal* reported that Cruz had secretly been on the payroll of the CIA.[17] (Years later, Cruz admitted to having received $6,000 a month for twenty-six months from the CIA and said he came to believe it "was a fundamental error" not to have participated in the elections.[18]) Cruz's major function during the campaign period was that of teaser and pro-abstention propagandist. Though the Sandinistas offered to extend the deadline for candidate registration and even to postpone the election itself in an effort to woo him into the electoral process, Cruz remained a noncandidate, denouncing what he claimed were inadequate conditions for a fair election.

With the exception of the disturbances around Cruz, the campaign proceeded virtually without incident. Banners, posters, and billboards for the seven contending parties sprang up throughout Nicaragua, in a riot of contrasting colors and clashing ideologies. Wartime censorship was relaxed, and candidates competed for votes in public gatherings and on nightly prime-time television. Despite the CDN's refusal to participate, voters were offered a range of choices as broad as those available in Western Europe, ranging from the Far Left to the PCD, whose platform coincided in many respects with that of the CDN, and some of whose candidates openly expressed sympathy for the armed counterrevolution. On November 4, 75 percent of the electorate exercised its right to vote (as opposed to only about half the electorate in the U.S. presidential election two days later), even though voting was not compulsory (as it had been in El Salvador). Foreign observers, among them former Costa Rican president José Figueres and official delegations from the Irish and British parliaments and from the U.S.-based Latin American Studies Association, concurred that the elections were clean and fair.[19]

Despite Reagan administration prognostications of Cuban-Soviet-style sham elections, the opposition made substantial inroads. Not surprisingly, the FSLN, as the party that liberated the country from dictatorship, obtained two-thirds of the valid votes cast, winning it the presidency and sixty-one of ninety-six seats in the National Constituent Assembly (NCA). The PCD came in second, with 14 percent; the PLI third, with 9.7 percent; and the PPSC fourth, with 5.6 percent. None of the Communist parties drew more than 1.5 percent of the vote; their combined total was 3.9 percent. Altogether, the opposition garnered one-third of the vote, and more than one-third of the representation in the NCA, ensuring it an active role in the drafting of the constitution (Table 2.1).

The Constitution

On January 10, 1985, Daniel Ortega was sworn in as president of Nicaragua and Sergio Ramírez as vice president. Two days later, the National Constituent Assembly was convened and elected Carlos Núñez to be its president. With these two inaugural events, the provisional government (JGRN and Council of State) was replaced by an elected government whose legitimacy rested not only on revolutionary logic but also on a broad popular mandate at the polls, combined with truly proportional representation for minority political currents.

This proportionality was respected at every stage in the development of the new democratic institutions. First, in the election of officers of the NCA, where FSLN deputy Leticia Herrera was made first vice president, PCD leader Clemente Guido second vice president, and PPSC leader Mauricio Díaz third vice president. In the frequent absences of Carlos Núñez (a member of the DNC) and Leticia Herrera (national director of the Sandinista Defense Committees), Clemente Guido presided over the sessions. In April, a Special Constitutional Commission was named to prepare the first draft of the new constitution. Again, care was taken to ensure proportionality: Of twenty-two seats, twelve went to the FSLN, three to the PCD, two each to the PLI and PPSC, and

Table 2.1   Nicaraguan Political Parties and the Constitutional Process

	FSLN	PCD	PLI	PPSC	PCdeN	PSN	MAP-ML	Null	Total
1984 election for National Constituent Assembly (NCA)									
% votes cast	62.3	13.0	9.0	5.3	1.4	1.3	1.0	6.7	100.00
% valid votes	66.8	14.0	9.7	5.6	1.5	1.4	1.0		100.00
% seats	63.5	14.6	9.4	6.2	2.1	2.1	2.1		100.00
Seats in NCA	61	14	9	6	2	2	2		96
Seats on Special Constitutional Commission	12	3	2	2	1	1	1		22
Number of NCA representatives who signed consitituion	61	10	6	6	2	2	0		87

Notes: One of the PCD and three of the PLI signers were alternates (suplentes), legally entitled to sign in the absence of their respective proprietarios.
FSLN: Sandinista party, PCD: Democratic Conservative party, PLI: Independent Liberal party, PPSC: Popular Social Christian party, PCdeN: Communist Party of Nicaragua, PSN: Nicaraguan Socialist party, MAP-ML: Marxist-Leninist Popular Action movement.

Source: Andrew A. Reding, "Nicaragua's New Constitution: A Close Reading," World Policy Journal 4, no. 2 (Spring 1987), p. 260. Reprinted by permission.

one apiece to the three Communist parties (Table 2.1). And again, Clemente Guido presided over sessions in the absences of Carlos Núñez.

As in the earlier case of the electoral law, there was little to be salvaged from Nicaragua's constitutional tradition, shaped as it had been by dictatorship and foreign occupation. The constitutional commission therefore initiated its work in summer 1985 by sending three official delegations on visits abroad to study the constitutional experiences of other countries. One delegation toured Western Europe, with stops in Sweden, Great Britain, France, West Germany, and Spain. A second, among whose members were the representatives of the Communist parties, went to the Soviet Union, Hungary, Poland, Bulgaria, and East Germany. The largest delegation concentrated on the more progressive countries of Latin America: Costa Rica, Peru, Venezuela, Argentina, Colombia, Panama, and Cuba. In April 1986, a fourth delegation was sent to the United States, where it took part in a three-day National Conference on the Nicaraguan Constitutional Process held at the New York University School of Law, along with political scientists, jurists, and law school deans from the very country that was waging war on Nicaragua.

The choice of foreign countries consulted by the commission reflected both the heterodox qualities of sandinismo and the multiplicity of political perspectives on the constitutional commission. Nowhere was this heterogeneity more apparent than on the question of human rights, where the Sandinista delegation itself split in three. The critical moment came on a motion by PCD deputy Eduardo Molina to incorporate three key international human rights treaties—the UN Covenants on Civil and Political Rights and on Economic, Social, and Cultural Rights and the OAS American Convention on Human Rights—into the text of the constitution. The motion was opposed by the Marxist-Leninist party (new name of the MAP-ML) and by doctrinaire leftists in the Sandinista delegation who objected to such treaty provisions as rights to peaceable assembly and to freedom of religion. It was also opposed by a second group of Sandinistas who feared that incorporating such treaties into the constitution could provide foreigners a pretext for intervention in Nicaraguan domestic affairs. Yet the motion received the wholehearted backing of a third group of Sandinista deputies, the revolutionary Christians, including El Nuevo Diario managing editor Danilo Aguirre, appellate judge Humberto Solís, former Nicaraguan Baptist Convention director Sixto Ulloa, and Social Welfare Minister Reinaldo Antonio Téfel. Their votes together with those of the PCD and PPSC provided the one-vote margin of victory to the motion. By the time the new article reached the plenum, it was approved unanimously, and a new international legal precedent had been established.

A further precedent was set when the first constitutional draft was submitted to the people. In March and April 1986, the Special Constitutional Commission distributed 150,000 copies of the draft, which was supplemented by a dozen televised debates between representatives of opposing parties. In May and June, citizens were invited to express their views in seventy-three open forums held throughout the country. About 100,000 Nicaraguans took part in these forums, which were broadcast live on radio. Highlights were also published daily in the newspapers and excerpted in nightly half-hour television summaries.

Fearing Sandinista orchestration, the PCD and PLI boycotted the forums. Their fear was understandable, in view of the past history of "popular consultations" in such one-party states as East Germany and Cuba, where draft constitutions written by Communist party politburos were subjected to very perfunctory modifications in well-controlled local forums. Yet Nicaragua was the first to try such a participatory process in a pluralistic setting.

The outcome defied all expectations, including those of the Sandinistas. Regardless of the calls for a boycott, Nicaraguans of all political stripes showed up and spoke out. Managuans demanded that their mayor be elected rather than appointed. Women, not satisfied with provisions for equal work for equal pay, paid maternity leaves, and day care for children, demanded an article guaranteeing equal rights between men and women.

On abortion, there was a profound split, as professionals in the middle classes and armed forces proposed legalization but were opposed by even larger numbers of pro-FSLN peasant women from Chontales and Río San Juan. All agreed, however, on the need for a right to family planning, including sex education and birth control, despite the opposition of Catholic bishops. On the Caribbean Coast, Miskitos insisted on rights to bilingual education and to traditional forms of landholding and sought to ensure that earnings from the exploitation of natural resources be recycled within the coastal region to finance its development. In the cities, workers demanded participation in the management of their enterprises. Christians in Condega sought an invocation of God in the preamble to the constitution, but Christians in Chinandega thought that would be an inappropriate breach of the separation of church and state. There were numerous demands that judges be non-partisan, and by a narrow margin, citizens favored assigning control of the budget to the legislature. To the consternation of those unfamiliar with Tomás Borge's stewardship at the Ministry of the Interior, employees of that ministry asked for an article to guarantee the rights of prisoners.[20] And so it went. With the exception of the controversial issue of abortion, virtually all the suggestions were incorporated in either the constitution or subsequent legislation. As a result of this popular input, Nicaragua's constitution of 1987 was second to none on the rights of women, native peoples, and prisoners.

In its final form, the constitution formalized the four-way separation of powers anticipated in the Electoral Law of 1984. A president, vice president, and legislature were to be elected every six years. The National Assembly was armed with the power of the purse, transforming it into a Western-style legislature. An independent comptroller-general of the republic, selected by the National Assembly from a slate of three nominees submitted by the president, was entrusted with vigilance over the budget and the uses of state property. Similarly, the seven magistrates of the Supreme Court of Justice and five magistrates of the Supreme Electoral Council were each to be selected for six-year terms by the National Assembly, from slates of three nominees submitted by the president. To enhance their independence, they would be irremovable during their terms. The Supreme Court was empowered to declare laws unconstitutional, and to compel the executive branch to respect human rights through issuance of writs of protection (*amparo*). Going a step beyond its Costa Rican and Venezuelan models, the Supreme Electoral Council was formally recognized as the fourth independent branch of government, whose authority in electoral matters would be final.

Persisting in their interpretation of the Sandinistas in the light of Cuban and Soviet communism, the U.S. government and right-wing opposition parties within Nicaragua objected that this constitutional delineation of powers was meaningless because it ignored the informal power structure centered in the DNC of the ruling party. Indeed, Bayardo Arce had continued as coordinator of the Political Commission of the DNC even as Daniel Ortega assumed the presidency of the republic in January 1985. Yet only months later, on August 3, 1985, the DNC abolished the Political Commission and transferred its authority to a new Executive Commission, whose membership included the ministers of the interior, defense, and agriculture and agrarian reform.[21] Daniel Ortega was named coordinator, Bayardo Arce vice-coordinator. By aligning executive authority in the party with executive authority in the government, the DNC resolved the potential problem of dual (and unconstitutional) authority.

The constitutional section on Rights, Duties, and Guarantees of the Nicaraguan People was, for the most part, lifted from the statute that had borne the same name. Again, Article 23 stated that "the right to life is inviolable and inherent to human personhood." Accordingly, capital punishment, torture, and other mistreatment were prohibited, and prison sentences were limited to thirty years. To give further substantive support to the right to life, Article 59 established an "equal right to health," Article 63 a right to "an equitable distribution of food," and Article 61 extended social security coverage to all Nicaraguans. Also in keeping with this life-first ethic, all forms of property were "subordinated to the higher interests of the nation" and declared to "fulfill a social function." Yet subject to this limitation, Article 103 recognized the "democratic coexistence" of five forms of property: public, private, mixed (public/private), cooperative, and communitarian, the latter being the traditional form of landholding on the Atlantic Coast. By Article 104, all forms of property would "enjoy equality before the law and in the economic policies of the State." Other articles recognized rights to information, free speech, and freedom of religion and prohibited prior censorship except in times of national emergency. All these rights were reinforced by the incorporation of international human rights treaties in Article 46.

Confronted with such a humane document, shaped by a year and a half of public deliberation, consensus building, and popular consultation, more than two-thirds of the opposition deputies joined the Sandinistas in signing the new constitution (Table 2.1). The only party to repudiate it was the Marxist-Leninist party, which saw it as a "bourgeois" betrayal of a workers' revolution. On January 9, 1987, the constitution was put into force formally in the presence of Peruvian president Alán García, who praised the Nicaraguans for demonstrating that it is possible to combine socialism with freedom and democracy.[22]

Regional Autonomy and Local Democracy

Arguably the greatest mistake made by the revolutionary leadership was its early treatment of ethnic minorities on the Caribbean (commonly called Atlantic) Coast. Almost completely isolated from the Spanish-speaking Pacific slope by mountains and rain forest, the coastal peoples had developed distinct cultures. They spoke different languages: English in the case of the black Creoles of Bluefields, on the southern coast; native dialects in the case of the Miskito, Sumu, Rama, and Garífono (black Carib) Amerindian populations, concentrated on the northern coast, along the Río Coco boundary with Honduras, and around the interior mining districts. They differed as well in their religious traditions: Whereas the Pacific was overwhelmingly Catholic, the Caribbean was predominantly Moravian (Protestant). Moreover, the very isolation and neglect of the Caribbean communities had for the most part spared them from the repression of the Somoza dictatorship. Failing to make proper allowance for these differences, the Sandinistas at first tried to extend mechanically institutions developed to answer the needs of the people of the Pacific slope to their Caribbean compatriots. That the revolutionaries were not ill intentioned was evident from the launching of a literacy crusade in coastal languages in August 1980. Yet the revolutionaries just as clearly did not understand coastal culture: They sought to impose an alien land reform on communities that had long ago devised their own more equitable forms of landholding, and they attempted to establish Sandinista Defense Committees where indigenous forms of community solidarity were rooted in an aboriginal past. Not surprisingly, coastal inhabitants resisted.

As tensions mounted, the situation deteriorated. In late 1980 and early 1981, the Miskito organization MISURASATA (Miskito, Sumu, Rama, and Sandinistas Working Together) prepared a document laying claim to one-third of Nicaraguan territory, including subsoil resources, based on continuous occupancy of such lands by native peoples since time immemorial.[23] Alarmed at what it interpreted as a secessional move, Nicaraguan State Security arrested MISURASATA leader Steadman Fagoth in February 1981, producing evidence that he had been a Somoza informant while a university student. In seeming confirmation of the charges, Fagoth joined former National Guard colonel Enrique Bermúdez's contra forces in Honduras after his release in May. Unfortunately, the government overreacted. At the same time that it jailed Fagoth, it imprisoned MISURASATA leaders Brooklyn Rivera and Hazel Law, against whom it had no evidence. Then after MISURASATA released its document in July, the government responded in August with a Declaration of Principles stating that "the natural resources of our territory are the property of the Nicaraguan people. The Revolutionary State, representative of the popular will, is the only entity empowered to establish a rational and efficient system of utilization of said resources."[24] The lines were drawn. Brooklyn Rivera left for Costa Rica, from where he organized armed resistance.

Yet even as the situation degenerated into regional guerrilla warfare, Miskitos like Hazel Law, backed by Moravian and other Protestant church leaders, prevailed on the government to reexamine its policies. Their efforts bore fruit in December 1983, when Atlantic Coast prisoners were released in a general amnesty. By late 1984, the FSLN had persuaded Hazel Law to run on its ticket for a seat in the National Assembly, and the Ministry of the Interior had launched negotiations with Brooklyn Rivera. The talks foundered on Rivera's demand for recognition of the "sovereignty" of the peoples of the Atlantic Coast and his corresponding insistence that talks be held outside Nicaragua, in the presence of international observers. The Nicaraguan government responded by announcing plans to consult coastal inhabitants themselves on what they would like in the way of "autonomy." As a gesture of goodwill, thousands of Miskitos who had been forcibly relocated from a war zone on the Río Coco were permitted to return in 1985. Autonomy commissions were then formed for the northern and southern coastal zones, and local facilitators were trained to conduct door-to-door surveys and organize town meetings designed to allow inhabitants to define the substantive content of autonomy. After two years of discussions at the local level, communities sent 210 representatives to a Multiethnic Assembly in Puerto Cabezas in April 1987 to hammer out a draft Autonomy Law for submission to the National Assembly.

The Autonomy Law was passed unaltered on September 2 and signed by President Ortega on September 7. Building upon the earlier constitutional recognition of Nicaragua as a "multiethnic" nation, the preamble stated (Section 5) that autonomy, "without intensifying differences," should "recognize differentiated identities as a foundation for national unity." In Section 7, the preamble addressed the earlier issue of contention: "Autonomy enables the effective exercise of the right of the Communities of the Atlantic Coast to participate in the design of means of exploitation of the natural resources of the region in such a way that the benefits are reinvested in the Atlantic Coast and the nation." Article 9, the most hotly debated of all in the Multiethnic Assembly, specified that such exploitation must respect traditional communal landholdings (already secured in the constitution), and that allocations of the proceeds from public lands must "benefit in just proportion" the inhabitants of the autonomous regions, "through accords reached between the Regional Government and the Central Government."

The most important innovation in the Autonomy Law was establishment of regional self-rule. Two autonomous regions were created: Atlantic North, with its capital in Puerto Cabezas, and Atlantic South, with its seat in Bluefields. Each was to have its own Regional Council, consisting of forty-five representatives elected for four-year terms. As genuine legislatures, they were authorized to raise taxes, prepare a budget, fix boundaries of local governments, subpoena regional authorities of

central government ministries, regulate the rational use and conservation of natural resources, and determine allocations of economic development funds. They were also empowered to select the regional executives, entitled regional coordinators. In this way, the peoples of the Atlantic Coast were enabled to secure their rights through their own democratic institutions. As National Assembly legislator Hazel Law noted in February 1989, the law set a precedent for the Americas, where Amerindians had heretofore been constrained to, at best, limited self-rule on reservations or in villages.[25]

Though regional self-rule was confined to the Atlantic Coast, local self-government was extended to the whole of Nicaragua by the Law of Municipalities, approved by the National Assembly on June 28, 1988. For the first time in Nicaraguan history, municipal councils, likewise guaranteed autonomy by the constitution, were to be elected by universal suffrage. Their members would serve for six-year terms. As specified in a subsequent electoral law, Managuans would be represented by twenty councilpersons, ten from the party that won a plurality, and ten assigned by proportional representation; other larger towns and departmental capitals would elect ten councilpersons, five by plurality and five by proportional representation; small towns would have five councilpersons, three from the party that finished first, and two from the party that finished second. The councils would in turn choose mayors from their ranks. In keeping with the constitutional definition of the form of government as a "representative and participatory democracy," each municipality was required to hold at least two town meetings a year, in order to involve inhabitants in the management of their own affairs.

Constitutional Laws

The constitution mandated the development of three laws with constitutional status, meaning that they would require the assent of 60 percent of the legislators in the National Assembly for passage, and that once approved, they would be considered part of the constitution. In summer 1988, the National Assembly turned its attention to the first of these, a new Electoral Law to regulate the constitutionally mandated general elections of 1990.

Design of the new law was influenced by the results of the 1984 elections and by the parliamentary and extraparliamentary complications to which they gave rise. The central political reality of Nicaragua was that of a country deeply polarized by revolution and counterrevolution. Yet that reality was distorted at an institutional level by the unity of the revolutionaries and disunity of their opponents. The opposition was deeply divided among more than a dozen political parties, many of which were themselves internally divided. In 1984 those divisions had prevented a concerted decision on whether or not to participate in the elections and likewise had prevented formation of a broad alliance. These divisions had been facilitated and accentuated by the Electoral Law, which guaranteed representation to any party obtaining as little as 1 percent of the national vote. The outcome was a splintered, relatively ineffectual, parliamentary opposition, which failed to satisfy its constituencies and, thereby, to give them a stake in the new political order. Without a more unified and effective opposition, it would be all but impossible to convert the counterrevolution into an effective and eventually loyal opposition by channeling dissent into the give-and-take of legislative negotiation.

In an effort to resolve these problems, the FSLN joined forces with the second-largest parliamentary delegation, the PCD, to alter the electoral rules. They agreed to make it more difficult for new parties to be formed, by requiring submission of lists of at least 980 officers distributed through every municipality in the country. They also made it more difficult for small parties to gain representation in the National Assembly, by raising the threshold from 1 percent to 5 percent of the vote (as in West Germany). In a further modification, public campaign financing and television and radio time were to be allocated among parties in proportion to the votes they had won in the last election (as in Costa Rica). Another innovation, objected to by the right-wing opposition parties, was a total prohibition on the receipt of campaign contributions from abroad.

Ironically, the U.S. government and its Central American allies condemned these changes designed to fortify the civic opposition as "antidemocratic," because the changes favored opposition parties that had participated in the last election (thus demonstrating independence from U.S. influence) over parties that had not. In an un-self-conscious assertion of the double standard, the United States further denounced the proscription of funds from abroad, even though such a prohibition is part of U.S. law (2 U.S.C. Section 441c). Even so, President Ortega agreed to compromise on these positions at the February 14, 1989, meeting of Central American presidents in Costa del Sol, El Salvador. In exchange for a commitment to amend the Electoral Law and advance the elections from November to February 25, he secured a commitment to demobilize the contras. As it turned out, the contras were not in fact demobilized until after the elections a year later (and even then only after the Sandinistas lost). Nevertheless, the National Assembly amended the Electoral Law in April. The 5 percent requirement for representation in the National Assembly was dropped, and opposition parties were granted equal time on radio and television. Although foreign campaign contributions were legalized, it was specified that these would have to be channeled through the Supreme Electoral Council, which would retain 50 percent of the contributions to fund expenses of running the elections. Public campaign financing would similarly be split, with

60 percent of the funds divided equally among all parties and the remaining 40 percent allocated to parties in proportion to the vote they had won in the last election. Though President George Bush persisted in portraying Nicaragua's Electoral Law as a "stacked deck against freedom," his characterization was contradicted by two studies prepared by the Library of Congress for the House Foreign Affairs Committee's Subcommittee on Western Hemisphere Affairs.[26] In one report, careful item-by-item comparisons exposed the similarities between Nicaragua's Electoral Law and those of Venezuela and Costa Rica, no great surprise in view of the fact that the Nicaraguans borrowed most heavily from the laws of those two countries.[27] The other report concluded that "the requirements to organize and legalize political parties [in the Nicaraguan Electoral Law] have been lowered to facilitate the formation of political parties; the opposition will have access to the media; public financing of campaigning is provided and foreign contributions are allowed. . . . Finally, the provisions on poll watchers allow close monitoring of the ballot counting by the opposition."[28]

The second of the constitutional laws to be passed by the National Assembly was the Law of Emergency, approved on October 5, 1988. It reiterated the constitutional provision that any State of Emergency declared by the president must be approved by the National Assembly within forty-five days and stipulated that the president must submit a full written account within forty-five days of its termination. In conformity with Article 46 of the constitution, it limited suspendible rights to those allowed under the UN Covenant on Civil and Political Rights and the American Convention on Human Rights and required due notification to the secretaries-general of the UN and OAS. The right of protection (amparo) would remain in effect for all nonsuspendible rights, as well as to require the personal exhibition of detainees (habeas corpus) to ensure that their rights to life and to decent treatment were being honored. Authorities would also be required to honor the Geneva convention on armed conflicts. Any affected individual would have the right of appeal to the immediate superior of the executing authority; and all authorities would be fully accountable and punishable for any abuses committed during a State of Emergency. Even though this was among the most liberal of emergency laws, legislator Ramón Arbizú of the PPSC nonetheless accused the FSLN of having copied Somoza's Martial Law. The charge was baseless, as that law contained none of the aforementioned safeguards and instead declared that if the powers delineated were insufficient to restore order, "the military authority may adopt new measures in accord with the situation," carte blanche, as it turned out, for slaughter of the civilian population.[29]

The Law of Constitutional Safeguards (Amparo) was passed by the National Assembly on November 16, 1988, and signed into law by President Ortega on November 21. It specified that any citizen could interpose the Recourse of Unconstitutionality against any law or decree within sixty days of when it takes effect. The Supreme Court of Justice would then have to reach a decision within sixty days of the filing. The court was also empowered to declare laws or decrees unconstitutional in the case of repeated appeals or writs of protection relating to particular legislation.

The law further specified that the Recourse of Personal Exhibition (habeas corpus) could be presented by any citizen on behalf of anyone, either in writing or verbally, on any day and at any hour, even during a State of Emergency. Local courts were instructed to respond immediately by designating an "executive judge" (juez ejecutor), who could be any citizen of "noted honesty and learning," but preferably a lawyer, to visit the detainee. The detaining authority was required to cooperate and to honor the decision of the executive judge immediately, even if it entailed freeing the prisoner. Failure to do so would result in a fine of up to one-quarter of the authority's monthly salary; any authority who failed to honor a subsequent court order would be fired. Should the offending official belong to the executive branch, the Supreme Court would notify the president, who would have twenty-four hours to enforce compliance. Should he or she not do so, the court would make the violation public and inform the National Assembly.

Most significant, there were numerous indications that the new constitutional order, including the quadripartite separation of powers, was taking root. The Central American peace accords led to derogation of the State of Emergency in February 1988. In February 1989, President Ortega submitted the national budget to the National Assembly for the first time. It was a draconian austerity budget, providing for substantial reductions in the size of the government bureaucracy, including the armed forces and police. As submitted by the executive, it would also have forced closure of forty-six courthouses, threatening the integrity of an already overburdened judicial system. In reaction, the magistrates of the Supreme Court appeared before the National Assembly to request restoration of the deleted funds. Their cause prevailed, spearheaded by a coalition of legislators from the PCD (Sergio Torres and César Augusto Castillo) and the revolutionary Christian wing of the FSLN (lawyers Danilo Aguirre and Humberto Solís). On a separate occasion, when the legislature was preparing the new electoral law, it invited President Mariano Fiallos of the Supreme Electoral Council to make recommendations. He proposed several changes in the draft, most notably that poll watchers be ensured admittance to the National Computation Center on election night as a further guarantee against tampering with returns; that party lists for the elections in the autonomous regions of the Atlantic Coast be headed by representatives of the primary local ethnic groups (e.g., Miskitos and Sumus in the north, black Creoles in the south), in order to guarantee simultaneous ethnic and political pluralism; and elimination of a prohibitive requirement that new political parties obtain signatures of 10 percent of the electorate. All his recommendations were incorporated in the legislation.

The 1990 Elections

Though national elections were originally scheduled for November 1990, as we have seen, they were advanced to February 25 as part of a package of agreements reached by the five Central American presidents at their February 14, 1989, meeting in Costa del Sol, El Salvador. The accords, the latest in a series intended to bring peace to Central America, centered on Nicaraguan pledges to move up the elections, amend the Electoral Law (as previously discussed), invite international election observers, and release most remaining National Guard prisoners, in exchange for a pledge from the other heads of state to demobilize the contras.

In the course of the next two months, the Nicaraguan government fulfilled each of its commitments. It advanced the election to February 25, amended the Electoral Law, and, setting a global precedent, invited the United Nations, the Organization of American States, and the Council of Freely Elected Heads of State (organized and led by former-U.S. President Jimmy Carter) to send official election observer teams to monitor the elections. It also freed 1,894 former national guardsmen, excluding only 38 accused of "crimes against humanity." Even so, and in keeping with a pattern of one-sided Nicaraguan compliance with regional agreements, no serious effort was made to demobilize the contras. Costa Rican President Oscar Arias's mild efforts to achieve compliance were effectively blocked by President Bush, who, while not a party to the accords, controlled the contra purse strings.

Yet Sandinista concessions did set the stage for the August 4, 1989, signing of a political accord between the government and seventeen opposition parties, including those that had boycotted the 1984 elections. Among other provisions, the government agreed to the release of some contra prisoners, suspension of the military draft during the electoral campaign, and amendment of the constitution to advance the next presidential inauguration from January 10, 1991, to April 25, 1990. In return, all the opposition parties agreed to participate in the 1990 elections and made a formal appeal to the other Central American presidents "to approve the plan for the demobilization . . . of the irregular forces located in Honduran territory," together with an appeal to "governments with interests in the Central American region [diplomatic language for the United States] to abstain from covert activities in the Nicaraguan electoral process." Three days later, at a summit meeting in Tela, Honduras, the Central American presidents approved a plan for an International Commission for Support and Verification

(CIAV), with representatives of the secretaries-general of the UN and OAS, intended to achieve demobilization of the contras by December 5, 1989. Again, although the Nicaraguan government suspended the military draft, released 457 detainees, and otherwise complied with the provisions of the agreement, the Bush administration persisted in blocking demobilization of the contras. The U.S. government likewise ignored the appeal to refrain from covert involvement in the electoral campaign. In addition to $7.5 million allocated by Congress for distribution to opposition groups in 1989, *Newsweek* reported that the CIA had secretly added an additional $5 million.[30]

Perhaps the most significant impact of U.S. funding was the influence it gave U.S. strategists in shaping a serious challenge to the FSLN. In a country as small and poor as Nicaragua, $12.5 million was an extraordinary sum, amounting to more than $7 per voter, where annual incomes only reach a few hundred dollars. No independent opposition party could hope to raise even a fraction of that amount. As such, the only viable electoral alternative to the FSLN would be whatever entity was favored with U.S. funds. Thus most of Nicaragua's opposition parties joined forces with the U.S.-backed Democratic Coordinating Committee to form the National Opposition Union (UNO). Those few that did not, among them the PSC, the PCD, the Liberal Party of National Unity (PLIUN), and the Movement for Revolutionary Unity (MUR), were marginalized and, with the exception of the MUR, failed to win a single legislative seat. In all, fourteen registered parties and political associations joined the UNO, creating an improbable and often volatile mix of Communists, Socialists, Social Christians, Liberals, and Conservatives, united only in their antagonism to the Sandinistas and their quest for shares of funding and political power.

The divisions within the UNO came to the fore in the selection of presidential and vice-presidential candidates. The four parties of the Democratic Coordinating Committee favored COSEP president Enrique Bolaños; another four parties, all of which had participated in the 1984 elections, favored Virgilio Godoy.[31] Neither seemed suited to mount an effective challenge to the popularity of Daniel Ortega. Bolaños was too closely associated with the Far Right; Godoy was known for an intemperate personality; and neither was acceptable to the parties backing the other. Instead U.S. embassy operatives were said to be quietly promoting the candidacy of Violeta Chamorro. Like Arturo Cruz, the U.S.-backed candidate in 1984, she had served on the revolutionary junta and could reinforce the theme of a revolution betrayed. It was also believed she could capitalize on popular reverence for her slain husband, after the fashion of Cory Aquino in the Philippines. Even her most obvious weakness, her lack of political experience and aptitude, paradoxically played to her advantage, as she had made few enemies. After three days and on the tenth ballot, Chamorro won the nomination on September 2. Her margin of victory was achieved with the support of the remaining parties in the coalition, combined with the swing votes of the parties that had originally backed Godoy. In exchange, Godoy was offered the vice-presidential nomination. Whatever Washington's precise role in the selection, there was no mistaking its satisfaction with the outcome. On November 8, Chamorro was invited to the White House to meet with President Bush, who used the occasion to signal Nicaraguan voters that he would end the commercial embargo should she win the election.

Despite U.S. obstruction of the demobilization of the contras and overt and covert involvement in the electoral campaign, the electoral process otherwise proceeded normally. On June 8, the National Assembly selected five magistrates for the Supreme Electoral Council from slates of nominees submitted by President Ortega. In accord with the Electoral Law, they chose a carefully balanced panel of two Sandinistas (former National University president Mariano Fiallos and former insurance executive Leonel Argüello), two members of opposition parties (cardiologist Aman Sandino of the PCD and businessman Guillermo Selva of the PLI), and one unaffiliated member (Rodolfo Sandino, dean of the University of Central America Law School). Mariano Fiallos was reelected president of the council by a no partisan vote of sixty-six to five. Throughout the campaign period, the council demonstrated its independence and professionalism by making almost every decision by consensus and by ruling in favor of the opposition more frequently than in favor of the government.

In October, an estimated 88 percent of the country's eligible voters (it was impossible to be precise for lack of a recent census) registered to vote, a proportion considerably higher than the 63 percent registration rate in the United States.[32] Throughout the last quarter of 1989 and into the new year, the UNO and the FSLN held numerous campaign rallies throughout the country, marred only by occasional scattered incidents of violence that appeared to be more a reflection of the degree of polarization than of conscious design by the leadership of either of the two principal political forces. By far the most serious violence came from the contras, who on October 21, ambushed army reservists on their way to register to vote, killing nineteen, and provoking President Ortega into terminating the government's unilateral cease-fire. In addition, the Christian observer group Witness for Peace documented cases of four Sandinista poll watchers and nineteen other FSLN campaign workers who were killed, wounded, or kidnapped by the contras during the electoral campaign period, fostering an atmosphere of terror that "effectively limited the Sandinistas' ability to campaign in many rural areas."[33]

With the exception of some of the more isolated rural areas, voters had ample exposure to the two major contending forces. Two of the

three daily newspapers (*Barricada* and *El Nuevo Diario*) served the
FSLN campaign, while *La Prensa* was the mouthpiece of owner Violeta
Chamorro. Radio exposure was relatively balanced, with twenty-four
of forty-four domestic radio stations in private hands, and twenty of
thirty-five news programs produced from an opposition perspective,
supplemented by other anti-Sandinista broadcasts beamed from stations
in neighboring Honduras and Costa Rica.[34] Only on television, whose
reach is far more limited than that of radio in Nicaragua, did the FSLN
enjoy a clear advantage derived from state ownership of both channels.[35]
Yet even there, the opposition, including smaller parties, was given
access to large segments of prime time for political advertising. In
addition, *Elecciones 90*, aired from 6 to 7 P.M. daily, provided a different,
and in many ways more interesting, political forum. Twice a week, it
featured formal debates between pairs of political parties; and three
times a week, it subjected a representative of one of the contending
parties to questioning by reporters of differing ideological tendencies.
Among its virtues, it submitted all political perspectives to challenge
and cross-examination and provided an opportunity for underfinanced
parties to present their case. The MUR, a nascent leftist party that
criticized the FSLN for bureaucratization and corruption, made the most
of the opportunity and ultimately emerged with the strongest third-
force electoral standing.

The elections were the most carefully watched in modern history.
Never before had a sovereign government invited the United Nations
to observe domestic elections officially.[36] The UN sent a team of 240
observers, headed by former U.S. attorney general Elliot Richardson,
and the Organization of American States fielded a delegation of 450.
Several dozen other foreign and international organizations, most notable
among them, the Council of Freely Elected Heads of State and the
European Parliament, contributed another few thousand. Dozens of
public opinion surveys, their results often contradictory, were conducted
and published by organizations of varying political sympathies. Finally,
the UN, OAS, FSLN, and UNO established parallel vote counting and
sampling networks, all of which confirmed the official results tabulated
by the Supreme Electoral Council.

The UNO won the elections by an ample margin of 55 to 41 percent,
gaining the presidency and majority control of the National Assembly.
Of the country's nine administrative regions, the FSLN won in only
two. It carried the sparsely populated Río San Juan (Region IX) by a
three-to-two margin and scraped a narrow win in Las Segovias (Region
I), a traditional bastion of *sandinismo* ever since Sandino himself
established his base there in the 1920s. In the traditionally conservative
stronghold of Boaco and Chontales (Region V), on the other hand, the
UNO triumphed by almost three to one. Other particularly rough areas
for the Sandinistas were the two newly formed autonomous regions on

the Caribbean Coast. In the mostly black, English-speaking, Atlantic South (Region VIII), the UNO won almost twice as many votes as the FSLN. In the Mískito region of Atlantic North (Region VII), on the other hand, the vote split three ways among the UNO, the Mískito organization Yatama, led by Brooklyn Rivera (and appearing on the ballot in the PSC column), and the FSLN, earning each a single deputy to the National Assembly. In the municipal races, the UNO won control of Managua and a little over three-quarters of the other towns, though the FSLN won León, the country's second-largest city and capital of Region II, Estelí, capital of Region I, San Carlos, capital of Region IX, and more than two dozen other municipalities.

From public opinion surveys and postelection consensus, it is clear that the Sandinistas were defeated on two issues: their inability to reverse the economic collapse brought about by nearly a decade of low-intensity warfare and economic embargo, the cost of which was estimated at $9 billion as of July 1989;[37] and their unwillingness to end an unpopular military draft prior to demobilization of the contras. A majority, wearying of scarcity and of loved ones in wheelchairs or body bags, voted for Chamorro because she promised to end the draft, and because she promised to conquer inflation within a hundred days, a promise rendered somewhat more credible by President Bush's pledge to lift sanctions should she win. Yet surveys also established that an overwhelming majority of Nicaraguans disapproved of the contras, and a narrower majority blamed the United States for the war.[38] Most Nicaraguans were tired of war and economic hardship, but by no means desiring a return to the prerevolutionary status quo.

Furthermore, U.S. characterizations of the election results as a landslide victory for the UNO were highly misleading in the Nicaraguan context. Unlike the winner-take-all electoral system in the United States, the Nicaraguan system of proportional representation guaranteed full representation of minority political currents, all but eliminating the landslide effect in the contest for legislative seats. Thus the FSLN won thirty-nine (or 42.3 percent) of ninety-two seats in the National Assembly, enough to preclude unilateral amendment of the constitution of 1987, for which its adversaries would need a minimum of fifty-six votes (60 percent). With fifty-one seats, the UNO fell considerably short of the mark, particularly since there remained only two independently held seats. One belonged to the PSC-Yatama; the other to the MUR, whose third-place showing, with 1.2 percent of the national vote, entitled presidential candidate Moisés Hassan to a seat.[39] A former member of the revolutionary junta and Sandinista mayor of Managua, Hassan had resigned from the FSLN a year earlier, disillusioned, he had said, by corruption. Now, with the FSLN in opposition, he was expected to vote with the revolutionary bloc in most instances. Thus even in the unlikely event that the UNO could hold its parliamentary bloc together in spite of ideological incongruities and personal rivalries, it would face an opposition bloc of forty deputies capable, at a minimum, of preventing it from reversing the most fundamental of the revolutionary changes of the preceding decade.

These political realities were implicitly recognized in the course of negotiations for the transfer of power. Representing the Sandinistas was General Humberto Ortega, minister of defense and brother of the president, whose designation underscored the urgency of implementing the Tela commitment to demobilize the contras. His counterpart was Antonio Lacayo, the politically moderate UNO campaign manager, whose selection by his mother-in-law Violeta Chamorro helped substantiate the latter's election-night pledge to be "president of all Nicaraguans." The negotiations culminated in the signing, on March 27, of the Protocol on Procedures for Transferring Presidential Powers. In tandem with President-elect Chamorro's appeal to the contras to lay down their weapons, the accord emphasized that demobilization by April 25 was "an essential element" to a peaceful transition. The signatories further agreed that beneficiaries of agrarian and urban land reforms would be secure in their holdings, and that expropriated landowners could be compensated. There would be no "revenge" or "reprisals" against those who had been associated with the outgoing government, and both parties agreed to respect the "moral and physical integrity" of all citizens.

Yet the very moderation of these agreements only enraged the Far Right. As April 25 approached, contra commanders defied Chamorro and imperiled the transition, vowing not to lay down their arms until Nicaragua had been purged of every trace of *sandinismo*. Responding to this challenge to the legal order, in her inauguration speech in Managua's baseball stadium on April 25, President Chamorro announced she would, for the time being, retain General Humberto Ortega as chief of staff of the armed forces and would personally assume the position of minister of defense. Though the decision was received with further hostility by the UNO right wing (it was bitterly denounced by Vice President Godoy, and by Minister of Agriculture–designate Jaime Cuadra, who later declined the appointment), as well as consternation in Washington, it secured the transition and offered tangible evidence of the new president's expressed desire for national unity and reconciliation.

Conclusion

As symbolized in the peaceful transfer of power on April 25, 1990, the new Nicaraguan polity had, eleven years after the revolutionary triumph, matured to the point where it could be characterized, in the words of its constitution, as "a representative and participatory democracy," with an explicit commitment to human rights, encompassing economic and social as well as civil and political guarantees. Contrary to predictions that the Sandinistas would emulate the Communist parties of Cuba and the Soviet Union, the FSLN broke virtually all ideological molds. It joined forces with revolutionary Christians; developed an ethos of profound respect for a broadly conceived right to life; interpreted socialism to require more, not less, democracy and political pluralism; and promoted expanded roles for international law and multilateral institutions in the realms of human rights, verification of elections, and peaceful resolution of disputes. Significantly, virtually all these achievements were inaugurated well before the emergence of *glasnost* and *perestroika* in the Soviet Union. It was this record of accomplishment that earned Nicaragua ongoing and enthusiastic diplomatic support and economic assistance from the social democratic governments of Sweden and Norway, even as it incurred the disfavor of a U.S. government obsessed with fears that demonstration effects could spill over into neighboring countries and destabilize "friendly," though repressive, regimes (as in El Salvador).

In his concession speech the morning of February 26, President Ortega emphasized the extent to which democratic process had become identified with the revolution:

In this historic moment, I believe the most important contribution we Sandinistas are making to the people of Nicaragua is guaranteeing a clean electoral process that heralds peace to our consciences and, like the sunshine on this 26th of February, illuminates the path toward the consolidation of democracy, of a mixed economy, of an independent Nicaragua, free of any foreign intervention. . . . As Sandinistas, we should all be proud to be opening a new path for Nicaragua, comparable to the one we opened in 1979.[40]

Notes

1. Christopher Dickey, *With the Contras: A Reporter in the Wilds of Nicaragua* (New York: Simon and Schuster, 1985), p. 55.

2. Through a deal worked out with the Conservatives, however, one-third of the seats in Congress, with attendant privileges, were reserved for that party, with the understanding that they would legitimate the dictatorship.

3. Though several other Latin American countries, among them Costa Rica and Venezuela, had earlier established independent electoral councils, none was elevated to the constitutional position of a fourth branch of government.

4. John A. Booth, "The National Governmental System," in Thomas W. Walker, ed., *Nicaragua: The First Five Years* (New York: Praeger, 1985), p. 30.

5. Nephew Carlos Chamorro had already become founding editor of *Barricada*, the FSLN-sponsored daily newspaper.

6. Andrew Reding, ed., *Christianity and Revolution: Tomás Borge's Theology of Life* (Maryknoll, N.Y.: Orbis Books, 1987), p. 26.

7. March 5, 1981, address, in ibid., pp. 46–47.

8. COSEP, "Declaraciones de Principios del Sector Privado," *La Prensa*, September 28, 1985, p. 3.

9. For more on this, see Giulio Girardi, *Sandinismo, Marxismo, Cristianismo en la Nueva Nicaragua* (Managua: Centro Ecuménico Antonio Valdivieso, 1986). The book was endorsed by Minister of Culture Ernesto Cardenal, and Minister of the Interior Tomás Borge attended a Centro Valdivieso ceremony in honor of the book and its author.

10. For more on this, see Teófilo Cabestrero, *Ministers of God, Ministers of the People* (Maryknoll, N.Y.: Orbis Books, 1983), and *Revolutionaries for the Gospel* (Maryknoll, N.Y.: Orbis Books, 1986).

11. See Reding, ed., *Christianity and Revolution*, pp. 96–107.

12. Although the Bolsheviks eliminated the death penalty upon assuming power in 1917, they soon restored it when confronted with counterrevolution.

13. Jorge Mario Salazar, *Política y Reforma en Costa Rica: 1914–1958*, 2nd ed. (San José, Costa Rica: Editorial Porvenir, 1982), pp. 142–151.

14. Ibid., pp. 154–158.

15. "Ley Electoral: Nuevo Paso Hacia la Institucionalización," *Envío* 3, no. 34 (April 1984), p. 5b.

16. "U.S. Role in Nicaragua Vote Disputed," *New York Times*, October 21, 1984, p. 12.

17. "Leading Anti-Sandinista Got CIA Cash, Sources Say," *Wall Street Journal*, April 23, 1985, p. 64.

18. "Ex-Contra Looks Back, Finding Much to Regret," *New York Times*, January 8, 1988.

19. Latin American Studies Association, *The Electoral Process in Nicaragua* (Austin, Tex.: LASA, 1984); "The Elections in Nicaragua, November 1984" (Irish Parliament, Dublin, November 21, 1984); "Report of the British Parliamentary Delegation to Nicaragua to Observe the Presidential and National Assembly Elections," (British Parliament, London, November 1984).

20. For a more detailed account of the open forums, see Andrew Reding, "By the People: Constitution Making in Nicaragua," *Christianity and Crisis* 46, no. 18 (December 8, 1986), pp. 434–441.

21. *Barricada*, August 4, 1985, p. 2.

22. Alán García, "America Latina no se rinde," *El Nuevo Diario*, January 10, 1987, p. 12.

23. Martin Diskin et al., *Peace and Autonomy on the Atlantic Coast of Nicaragua: A Report of the LASA Task Force on Human Rights and Academic Freedom* (Pittsburgh: LASA, 1986), p. 10.

24. Ibid., pp. 10–11.

25. Andrew Reding, "Nicaragua: Ten Years Later," *Christianity and Crisis* 49, no. 10 (July 10, 1989), p. 218.

26. *Washington Report on the Hemisphere* 9, no. 17 (May 24, 1989), p. 5.

27. Law Library of Congress, "Comparison of Electoral Laws in Chile, Costa Rica, Guatemala, Nicaragua, Paraguay, and Venezuela," May 1989.

28. Law Library of Congress, "Nicaragua: Amendments to the Electoral Law," April 1989, p. 9.

29. *El Nuevo Diario*, October 5, 1988, p. 8.

30. *Newsweek*, September 25, 1989, p. 4, and October 9, 1989, p. 47; the figure of $7.5 million in overt aid is the sum of $3.5 million supplied earlier

in the year and another $4 million allocated by Congress in the fall (*Washington Office on Latin America Election Monitor*, no. 3 (October 13, 1989), p. 5; Central American Historical Institute, *Nicaragua Election Issues*, no. 9 (February 12, 1990), p. 5.

31. "Los Candidatos," *Envío* 8, no. 97 (September 1989), pp. 11–14.

32. Curtis Gans, *Washington Post*, January 31, 1990.

33. Witness for Peace, *Hotline Special Report*, "Contra Compaign Violence, August 25, 1989–January 24, 1990." On January 1, 1990, contras killed two nuns (one a citizen of Nicaragua, the other of the United States) and wounded Catholic Bishop Pablo Schmidt in an ambush in the Atlantic North Autonomous Region (America Watch, *The New Year's Day Killings: A Report of an Investigation*, New York, January 28, 1990, 53 pp.).

34. Central American Historical Institute, "Is There Equal Access to the Media?" *Nicaraguan Election Issues*, no. 3, p. 4.

35. Following the UNO victory, the government hastily privatized the television stations, granting the license for one of the two channels to Herty Lewites, minister of tourism and newly elected FSLN delegate to the National Assembly.

36. Months earlier, in November 1989, the United Nations supervised elections in Namibia, which were won by the South West Africa People's Organization (SWAPO). Yet in this instance the elections were to transform a colonial holding into a sovereign state.

37. *Diez años en cifras*, (Managua: Instituto Nacional de Estadísticas y Censos), July 1989.

38. Sergio Bendixen and Rob Schroth for Univisión television, released November 14, 1989, and Stanley Greenberg and Celinda Lake for Hemisphere Initiatives (HI), released December 13, 1989:

	HI (%)	Univisión (%)
Image of contras		
Negative	57	65
Positive	10	20
Responsible for		
Nicaragua's problems		
U.S. government	47	57
FSLN	39	29

39. By the same electoral provision, Daniel Ortega won a seat in the National Assembly, with Sergio Ramírez as his alternate.

40. My translation, from *Proceso*, no. 696 (March 5, 1990), p. 44.

THREE

The Grass-Roots Organizations

LUIS HECTOR SERRA

No discussion of politics during the Sandinista revolution, or during the several years preceding it, would be complete or even make much sense without an examination of the grass-roots organizations (OPs). Created by the FSLN, the OPs were based in various distinct social sectors and groups: peasants, workers, urban neighborhoods, youth and children, and women. Before detailing the organizational structure and history of the OPs and reflecting on their contribution to the construction of a democratic system, it is necessary to examine their role in national development during the ten and a half years of the Sandinista revolution.

Grass-Roots Organizations in National Development

By 1989, the Sandinista OPs had an estimated membership of about 0.5 million adults: 125,000 peasants in the National Union of Farmers and Ranchers (UNAG), 120,000 workers in the Sandinista Workers' Federation (CST), 50,000 agricultural laborers in the Rural Workers' Association (ATC), 50,000 young people in the Sandinista Youth (JS), and 150,000 in the Community Development Committees (CDC—until 1988 they were called Sandinista Defense Committees [CDS]).

The growth of the OPs during the fight against Somoza and their consolidation after the triumph was a collective response to the common interests of given social sectors. In dependent countries where the state has a shortage of resources, grass-roots organizations fulfill an important role as voluntary promoters of a diverse range of activities for socio-economic development. In the case of Nicaragua, these actions contributed to an improvement in the living conditions of the lower classes and at the same time, created an understanding of participation and organization necessary to build a democratic system.

The Economic Role of OPs

At the economic level, the OPs contributed to the development of productive forces and changed the old relations of production under which the population labored. Labor unions and rural organizations stand out particularly in this regard. In the field of union activities, from 1979 on, the Sandinista Workers' Federation and the Rural Workers' Association pushed for a concept of unionism that would respond to the new character of the state and the destruction caused by the war. It was not just a matter of seeking immediate gains, such as increases in the nominal salary, but rather of contributing to economic reconstruction through higher labor productivity, improving working conditions, and raising living standards by enhancing the social salary. Thus, in order to avoid slowing production, collective bargaining would be substituted for strikes and walkouts. Not surprisingly, the opposition labor unions critized the ATC and CST for adopting such an approach.

The participation of workers in the management of enterprises was promoted through various mechanisms. At first there were Economic Reactivation Assemblies, in which production plans and worker complaints were discussed. Later, Councils of Production and Enterprise Committees were formed as permanent organs with participation by union and management representatives. More advances were made in the state enterprises than in the private sector. The approval of a worker-management law and the reform of the old labor code were measures pending for the second decade.

The Collective Agreements that were extended in these years, regulating the rights and obligations of both workers and employers, included the right of unions to have access to business accounting information and to approval of the production plan in the majority of cases. By 1989 nearly 2,000 Collective Agreements for individual businesses had been drawn up at the Ministry of Labor, and each year general agreements were negotiated for the harvests of coffee, cotton, and sugar. The terms of these agreements varied, depending on the financial situation of the business in question and the militancy of the unions involved.

One method of increasing production, a goal of the Sandinista unions during these years, was voluntary overtime by the Economic Brigades, which in 1987 and 1988 reported a national total of 2 million manhours. In 1989 there were 742 brigades mobilized by the CST, in which 42,000 workers participated.[1] The annual mobilization for the agroexport harvests was another effort of the OPs, which during the 1983–1984 harvest cycle, for instance, involved 38,000 students, farmers, and workers. A related matter was the issue of the length of the workday. It had diminished drastically in the early years to six hours, but by 1987 the ATC had reinstated the eight-hour norm in agriculture. The standardization of work, that is to say, the definition of each activity and its duration, would increase labor productivity and establish a just relationship between production targets and wages. Finally, the unions emphasized the conservation of resources and a movement for innovation—approximately 1,000 innovators were recognized in 1988—to meet the shortage of spare parts and machinery caused by the U.S. commercial boycott.

In the development of agricultural production, UNAG served as a means for the resolution of problems and as a channel of communication through which the anxieties of the producers could reach the authorities. UNAG encouraged agricultural reform through the formation of cooperatives, the distribution of land and titles, the organization of producers by category and by territories, and the creation of a rural supply network of Peasant Stores, with the help of foreign aid.

The rural cooperative movement constituted a key factor in the agricultural economy, with peasants working together to improve their living conditions. At the end of the decade there were 3,363 cooperatives for both production and services, with a total membership of 68,085 peasant families composed of 474,572 individuals (49 percent of the peasantry nationwide), who held 1,622,564 manzanas of land, or 21 percent of the country's farmland.[2] The cooperatives provided the rural population access to such basic state services as education, health care, housing, potable water, and electricity, as well as technical assistance and machinery.[3]

The OPs also played an important part in the distribution of staple products at accessible prices. Until 1988, when this area of commerce was decontrolled, Sandinista Defense Committees managed the sale and distribution of certain staples in urban areas through a census of the population and state authorization of expenditures. Labor unions promoted the creation of small stores in their factories and workplaces, and UNAG organized the Peasant Stores, beginning in 1985. By 1989, there were 202 Peasant Stores located in all parts of the country.

To improve the supply of staple foods to the workers and peasants, products and labor were exchanged directly. Thus in 1988, 202 unions experimented with direct exchange between industrial enterprises and rural cooperatives, which increased the revenues of both by eliminating intermediaries.[4]

Other activities worthy of mention were those of the Popular Health Workdays, dedicated to the prevention of disease and the promotion of public hygiene. The OPs provided the brigades that performed tasks organized by the Ministry of Health. In 1983, for example, 36,000 brigade members were involved in the fight against malaria, polio, and diarrhea. Equally noteworthy were the community development works—road repair, potable water projects, maintenance of irrigation canals, construction of community centers and parks—carried out for the most part by the CDS in the cities and by the District Committees (Comités Comarcales) in the countryside as well as by other nongovernmental organizations and religious institutions.

The OPs and Education

The OPs also worked persistently to improve the inadequate educational situation inherited from the Somoza regime in order to develop the knowledge, attitudes, and abilities necessary for economic development and for effective popular participation. During the 1980 Literacy Crusade 400,000 people learned to read and write; nationwide, illiteracy fell from 52 percent to 13 percent. The OPs also played an important role in the continuation of the Literacy Campaign through the Program for Adult Education, which in 1983 included 160,000 students who met daily in 19,100 Popular Education Collectives (CEP). This program enabled adults to complete their education; it employed practical and participatory consciousness-raising combined with a tangible transformation of the student's life. Sadly, the contra war and the resultant deteriorating economic situation seriously affected rural education: CEP membership dropped and the illiteracy rate in the rural cooperatives increased, reaching an estimated 30 percent in 1989. Even so, from 1988 on, as the war was waning, rural OPs participated in adapting curricula and writing adult education texts for use in rural areas.

The principal educational guidelines were established in 1981 in a national consultation organized by the OPs, in which more than 50,000 people participated. The results were synthesized and eventually enacted into law and incorporated in the national constitution.

At the same time, the OPs, to improve their organization and efficiency, established programs of empowerment for group members and leaders. The OPs helped to select participants for education programs, such as technical courses for workers, and recipients of scholarships to state institutions, including accelerated secondary education programs and university-level studies. Additionally, OP members who were Sandinista cadres benefited from courses offered by the FSLN to its members and aspiring members.

The OPs contributed to the repair and construction of schools, generally through voluntary labor with the state or other institutions providing the materials. The establishment of preschools and day care centers, which improved the morale of the female population, was undertaken mainly by labor unions. In 1989 the Women's Section of the ATC reported that there were sixty-nine rural day care centers, most located on state farms. Nevertheless, this number was far from sufficient to meet the actual need.[5]

The OPs' Role in Facilitating Communication with the Government

The grass-roots organizations also functioned to link the masses and the governmental authorities through diverse channels of direct communication, such as the assemblies "Face the People" or "Open Council," radio programs like "Direct Line" and "Contact 620," and the newspapers—as in the "Public Mailbox" section in Barricada. The assemblies provided the most common form of public discussion as well as a two-way channel of communication between the masses and the authorities; in reality they served as a medium of education and critical expression for the masses in an organized form to resolve collective problems. However, these assemblies had their limitations. Though complaints and demands that the authorities resolve existing problems abounded, there was frequently a lack of follow-up on the accords and promises made at the meetings. This was due in large part to the causes of many of the problems: inefficiency and bureaucracy, weak self-motivation at the grass-roots level, economic crisis, and war.

Cultural development through the formation of sports and artistic groups and through celebrations and traditional fiestas of the Centers for Popular Culture was another accomplishment, albeit limited, of the OPs. The grass-roots organizations tried to reinvigorate Nicaragua's rich traditional culture while offering other types of healthy entertainment to the common citizen. Some of the blame for the less-than-optimal success of the OPs in the area of culture must be shared by the Ministry of Culture—after early 1989, the Institute of Culture—which focused mainly on groups of professional artists.

The Role of the OPs in Defense

National defense against imperialist aggression—the preservation of national independence (a necessary condition for expanding popular participation)—was a major achievement of the OPs, most notably in the form of Civil Defense organized in urban neighborhoods, rural districts, and work and study centers. The objective of the Civil Defense was to limit the damage of catastrophes—whether of natural origin or the result of war—by organizing brigades to provide first aid and fire protection, supply provisions, and care for children and the aged. During the floods caused by Typhoon Aleta (1982) and the destruction of Hurricane Joan (1988) the Civil Defense acted to prevent needless deaths and assisted the injured and displaced. It is significant that, in both cases, though the physical damage inflicted on Nicaragua was greater than that suffered by other countries in the region, the loss of life was less. The reason would seem to be that Nicaragua had a greater emergency life-saving mobilization capacity than did its neighbors.

Especially during the height of the contra war, the OPs also organized Neighborhood Night Watch groups to combat delinquency and to control the activities of counterrevolutionaries not only in neighborhoods but also in work centers, schools, and rural communities. Though participation in the Civil Defense and in the night-watch groups declined after 1985, the OPs later organized the Voluntary Police as a form of grass-roots involvement in the control of crime. Also, in the rural cattle-raising areas, UNAG and the Ministry of the Interior promoted the formation of brigades to fight cattle rustling. And Sandinista Youth groups developed a program to change Managua street-gang members into productive young people willing to participate in military service and community development projects.

For defense, the Sandinista People's Militia—which will be discussed in greater length in Chapter 4—was a mass organization for the defense of the various regions of the country. By 1984 the militia had placed at least 300,000 citizens of various ages and both sexes under arms. In the countryside, the contras made cooperatives their main targets. By 1989, 5,352 cooperative members had been killed and 3,086 kidnapped; 1,326 houses had been destroyed; and 15,665 head of cattle destroyed.[6] Accordingly, the cooperatives made a great human and material sacrifice as the first line of the national defense.

When the militia was depleted as a result of the passage of the Military Service Law in 1983, OPs took over the task of recruiting militia members, helping the families of those mobilized for service, and communicating with the combatants. The Sandinista Youth was the primary force behind this work among students. Partly because of their efforts, nearly 50 percent of the young people who took up arms did so voluntarily. The JS also attended to the needs of militia members demobilized after service, providing such benefits as free access to transportation, movies, and theaters, educational scholarships, and preferential treatment in obtaining jobs and land. It is clear that most of the responsibility for defense fell to peasants and the young.

Participation and Organization

All the OPs were characterized by basically the same relatively simple type of organizational structure. First, there was geographical hierarchy of national, regional, municipal, and local entities. Second, within each entity, there was a permanent executive committee with executive power, a council with a consultative role and periodic meetings, and an assembly serving as the ultimate decision-making body. In the case of the small farmers and agricultural workers, organizational structures were formed for each category of production—coffee, cotton, cattle, and so forth. In

manufacturing, the workers formed unions for each branch of production—clothing, metallurgy, food processing, and so forth.

Participation of the Masses (Bases)

The statutes of the OPs state that membership is open to all individuals
whose social sector pertains to that of the organization, without regard
to sex, religion, or political ideology, except for those connected with
Somoza. This openness was sometimes restricted, in practice, owing to
ambiguous interpretation of the last clause. There were some cases
where dissent against the government or the political line of the FSLN
was considered a counterrevolutionary attitude and caused the expulsion
of individuals from organizations.

In quantitative terms, the membership in OPs was quite high, estimated
at 40 to 60 percent of the population in each social sector. However,
actual participation in the OPs' activities and a conscious identification
with the organization were considerably lower.

Membership in the OPs was automatic in many cases, stemming from
the deduction of union dues from a worker's salary, membership in a
cooperative formed by UNAG, or merely residence on a block or in a
building housing a CDS. A 1988 study showed that the primary
motivation to affiliate with an OP was economic, to improve one's living
conditions and defend one's interests.[7] Workers sought job security and
higher wages; peasants, access to land, credit, seed, fertilizer, tools, and
fair prices; rural dwellers, sufficient food and public services.

Active participation of the masses (bases) was generally expressed
through attendance at meetings, in voluntary unpaid labor on collective
projects, in preventive health campaigns, and to a lesser extent in the
night watches and defense and educational activities. The amount and
quality of participation were dependent on such factors as the charisma
of the leaders, the organization and planning of the projects undertaken,
and the benefits accruing to the participants.

The levels of participation varied historically and differed markedly
for each OP and each region of the country. Moreover, participation
varied within each OP, with higher rates of participation found, for
example, in unions in the state enterprises than in those in the private
sector. Among peasants, participation was much higher for persons in
production cooperatives (Sandinista Agricultural Cooperatives, CAS)
than for individual producers. In urban areas more participation occurred
in lower-class neighborhoods than in middle- or upper-class ones.

Suggestions for improving participation of the bases in the OPs
included closer ties between the leadership and the OPs, more discussion
and decision making on questions that affected the OPs, searching for
solutions to the problems about which the members felt most strongly,

and the development of a consciousness among the bases concerning the importance of organization.

The Linkage Between the Leadership and the Masses (Bases)

There were three levels of leadership in the OPs: (1) leaders of the masses, at the primary level (DBs); (2) intermediate leaders, at the municipal level (DIs); and (3) higher leaders, at the regional and national level (DSs). Generally leaders at the primary level were elected or recalled directly by a show of hands of the members of the OP in public meetings. These people, known as "natural leaders," usually earned the trust of the membership through personal qualities (honesty, comradeship, industriousness) as well as through their experience in defending the interests of their sector. Base leaders performed their duties voluntarily, without pay, while continuing to work in their normal occupations. Frequently, they had little time or energy to devote to their work in the OP. Accordingly, it was often true that few members of the OPs sought the responsibilities of leadership. There was normally a high turnover in these positions, particularly among women, because of their already double workload (household chores as well as outside employment). Furthermore, the primary leaders felt pressure from two directions: from the masses, to resolve urgently felt needs; and from their superiors, to meet the goals of the OP. In many cases the same primary leaders were members of several OPs and involved in many projects—a "human orchestra" expected to organize and push through many different tasks.

The naming and recalling of the intermediate leaders was less direct because the candidates for election to the posts were designated by the directorate of the OP and because only the primary leaders—not the membership as a whole—had a vote in such elections. In some other cases, intermediate leaders were employees contracted by the leadership directors or designated directly by the FSLN. Often there was only one candidate for a post, or candidates not affiliated with the FSLN were prohibited from running. In the blue-collar sector, the party, government, or FSLN-oriented unions employed various tactics to prevent delegates from other unions from running for leadership positions. These included military conscription and firings to get rid of workers who were activists for competing unions. In 1988, for example, in two publicized cases (in the MACEN and TOÑA enterprises) the CST used force to prevent the reelection of delegates from other unions, actions that were even criticized by other factions of the FSLN.[8]

At the regional and national level, the higher directors were named by the party authorities, although formal elections were held for candidates running unopposed, for example, UNAG in 1984 and CDS in 1988. Generally the higher directors had been strong supporters of the revolution from the beginning and enjoyed the backing of the intermediate and primary directors as well as the masses.

Directors at each level periodically gave reports at group meetings and assemblies. The directors spoke about the goals that had been achieved, plans for the future, and the political situation, without normally going into an evaluation of their own performance in the job or an accounting for funds used in carrying it out. As can be imagined, the masses exercised more control over the primary directors, openly criticizing them, than over the directors at the intermediate and higher levels.

Despite the collective organs and democratic procedures based in law, certain directors concentrated too much decision-making power in their own hands, thereby inhibiting the growth of new leadership and participation by the masses. This centralization of decision-making power does not necessarily entail using that power for personal ends; it can be an attempt to resolve collective problems rapidly and to push on to achieve goals. It is interesting to note that protests by the masses against the decision making of particular directors were not common except where there was also criticism of the content of decisions. The other aspect of this centralization is the masses' tendency to place their confidence in a personalized way in a natural leader rather than in formal structures.

The work of the OPs was structured on the basis of "annual lines" or "plans of action" for each organization. The annual plans, in turn, were broken into plans for shorter time periods. Theoretically, these combined the desires of the organization's membership with the general orientation of the FSLN for all social sectors. Each year the OPs held meetings to evaluate the past year's plan and to develop one for the following year.

In practice quarterly and monthly plans were sent down (bajados) from the national headquarters of each OP to the regional level, where the overall plans were adapted to the local situation and where local wishes were taken into consideration before the plans were sent to the lower levels. In general, there was a lack of understanding at the local level of the national plans and an underfulfillment of some resolutions, particularly those dealing with the concerns of women.

This vertical system for the transmission of goals and plans kept the masses and the primary and intermediate directorates dependent and relatively powerless, particularly in regard to the formation of work plans appropriate to actual conditions. Moreover this verticalization placed the local leaders in the difficult position of having to mobilize the masses for projects that did not originate with them, even though these projects might be in the masses' own long-term interest.

It is interesting to observe the reactions to verticalization that occurred, such as regionalism or the membership of an OP mobilizing to change the national plans. In some cases, orders that would be difficult to carry out in a particular area were simply ignored. In general local leaders had an attitude of "critical subordination" toward the higher levels of authority, while a more complacent attitude existed at the intermediate-level leadership—among functionaries often hired by the OP—regarding the directives of the higher leaders.

There were also signs that planning often resulted in only a vague guide to action. In reality, what predominated was "activism," where tasks were chosen at the last minute in response to specific local conditions. The OPs were often involved in projects not foreseen in the general plans, projects originated by the party and by diverse state and private institutions. The multitude of activities that fell to the local leaders and membership made it hard to comply with orders from above and contributed to a lack of follow-through, control, and evaluation of OP work plans.

Relations with the State and the Party

The capacity of the OPs to satisfy the interests of the social sectors they represented depended on both internal and external factors. Among the internal factors were the participation of the masses in the definition and execution of work plans, quality of the leadership, organizational efficiency, availability of resources, and the articulation of a coherent strategy on the part of each OP. External factors included the relationship among social forces, the capacity to influence decisions taken by the government and party, and the national economic and political conditions.

At the internal level, the OPs generally exhibited a capacity to express the concerns of their respective social sectors as well as to suggest possible solutions and actively participate in them. One limitation was the subordination of the specific demands of the masses to the general lines emanating from the party and the government (national unity, defense, production, or elections).

This subordination, understandable in the broad perspective of the survival of the revolution in the face of war and economic crisis, was not easily assimilated by the masses, which were more concerned with their own problems. This difficult contradiction diminished the legitimacy of the OPs, especially when an organization's goals went against the immediate interest of its membership. Examples include layoffs (compaction) supported by Sandinista unions, military conscription supported by the CDS, or the demand made by UNAG that its members sell basic grains to the National Foodstuffs Enterprise (ENABAS), even though its prices were low.

Externally, the concerns of the masses met with satisfactory answers in many cases because the relationship among social forces after 1979 favored workers and peasants and because party and state apparatus were receptive to the masses' demands. However, the character of the mixed economy, with the considerable economic weight and political power of the bourgeoisie and petite bourgeoisie, marked a clear limit to the demands of the popular sectors for a fairer distribution of resources and income.

Relations between the OPs and the state were ambiguous. On the one hand, OPs defended the government against the opposition, while, on the other, they criticized bureaucratic inefficiency and fought for a greater share of government resources vis-à-vis other social sectors. There were many instances where the OPs participated in the formation of state policies and projects affecting their interests, from the National Planning Council down to interinstitutional commissions at the municipal level. However, this participation was generally of a consultative nature, with the OPs being in a minority voting position in relation to the government's delegates.

Limitations on the technical and professional training of many OP leaders, the multiplicity of interinstitutional commissions, and the lack of channels for the exchange of information and investigation on the part of the OPs diminished their capacity to discuss and generate proposals. For this reason many projects for the public good were designed by government technicians, with the provision of voluntary labor reserved as the contribution of the OPs.

Despite these obstacles, the technical capabilities of the OPs advanced during the 1980s. For example, the Meetings of Fundamental Forces in early 1989 completed an economic analysis in which alternatives were suggested for the revitalization of the economy, some of which were adopted by the government.[9] It is true that the control of considerable material and human resources by government institutions often permitted them to act independently of the OPs, which suffered from shortages of such resources. However, this situation changed somewhat from 1988 on, with the reduction of the government's budget and foreign aid given to the OPs to pursue specific projects.

The direct participation of representatives of OPs in the national legislative power structure, as in the Council of State, ended in 1984; thereafter the OPs' participation was mediated through political parties. This change meant that the specific interests of the social sectors were subordinated to the dynamics of the political parties. Because of the party discipline of the FSLN, the constitution and the laws relating to political parties, elections, and local government were enacted. However, sectoral demands expressed by the membership of the OPs since the ouster of the Somozas were often relegated to the background. These included workers' demands for the revision of the Labor Code, farmers' desire for the harsher punishment of cattle rustling, and women's demands for the legalization of abortion and the prosecution of wife abusers.

From the start, the FSLN had been recognized by the principal OPs as the vanguard because of its successful fight against dictatorship and imperialism and because it founded and promoted the OPs themselves. The FSLN had three objectives in fostering the OPs: to promote popular participation in the resolution of the problems of each stratum of society, to develop a seedbed for revolutionary cadres to consolidate the party, and to mobilize the people in defense of the revolution.[10] The function of the FSLN as vanguard was to articulate the interests of each social sector within the framework of the Sandinista project in accordance with the characteristics of each political situation. The plan that the FSLN drew up annually for each OP was based on these principles.

One of the problems of this relationship between the OPs and the FSLN was that most of the directors of the OPs were also full or aspiring members (militantes or aspirantes) of the FSLN, thus giving them two roles, which, though theoretically separate, were often confused in practice, as revealed in the discourse of the OP directors. That blurring of roles tended, in turn, to affect not only the supposed openness and pluralism of the OPs but also their ability to attract non-Sandinista elements to their ranks. During electoral campaigns in particular (1984 and 1989–1990), party work took on the top priority for the Sandinista OPs, with other tasks being neglected.

The centralism and vertical structure of the FSLN (see also Chapter 5) made the question of participation in both the party and the OPs difficult to resolve.[11] Moreover, with the discipline and hierarchy of the party being more important than those of the OPs, the goals and orientations of the party's directors were given a higher priority than those of the OPs. Demand for autonomy on the part of the OPs surfaced on various occasions, but with unequal results: UNAG, for example, achieved more autonomy than the other OPs.

The party committees that exist inside the OPs assumed, in many cases, a role of discussion and resolution that theoretically competed with the organs of the OP itself, diminishing the possibility of their development. In addition, party cadres located in the OPs were frequently transferred to other jobs without regard to the opinions of the members or the debilitating effects on the organization. Dependency was worst in the JS because it was considered, more than others, to be a party organism—the principal nursery for the development of cadres. The low level of material and human support given the OPs by the FSLN, compared to that given party and state apparatuses, was an indicator of the low priority placed on these organizations. The central role given the state apparatus by the FSLN in the transformation of society carried a double risk. On the one hand, there was the possibility of the consolidation of a bureaucracy out of the control of the OPs. On the other, there was the danger that as a result of a free electoral system, another party with other objectives could take control of this strong apparatus, as happened in 1990.

Historical Development of the OPs

A historical overview of the OPs through 1990 reveals four stages with their own distinct characteristics. This is evident in spite of the fact that there was some continuity based on the principal founders of the OPs and on their relationship with the FSLN.

The First Phase:
Growth and Ascent (1977–1982)

Although the OPs had existed in an embryonic form in the decades preceding the revolution, especially the labor unions, it was during the insurrectional ground swell at the end of 1977 that the principal OPs were established. Thus, the OPs were a recent phenomenon, and the major impulse for their development came from the FSLN.

The United People's Movement (MPU), established by the FSLN in June 1978, brought together more than twenty student, worker, civic, and women's organizations and political parties of the left. In this first phase of rapid expansion, the OPs were characterized by their broad, pluralistic, and flexible organization in pursuit of a common objective: the overthrow of the dictatorship. They were constituted in the new structures of popular power that were attempting to resolve the basic problems confronting a population in the state of war.

As a social phenomenon in this phase, the anti-Somoza movement went through a period of explosive and dynamic growth that overwhelmed incipient OPs. Alan Touraine's three components of a social movement[12] were clearly present: (1) an enemy (the National Guard, Somoza, and his followers); (2) a collective identity (the people, or the popular sectors alienated from Somoza); and (3) a question in dispute (liberty in all of its manifestations and the right to life).

On July 19, when the old state apparatus fell, it was the OPs that assumed the basic functions of social organization and direction while the junta and the FSLN directorate tried to settle into their new roles and start the process of national reconstruction. The party itself had only recently been reunited. For example, while the peasants and farm laborers of the ATC assumed control of the haciendas confiscated from Somoza and his cronies and formed rural cooperatives, the Sandinista Defense Committees became the informal local authorities regulating the life of the population in urban neighborhoods.

After July 19 the three components of the popular movement began to undergo a gradual change, with the population optimistic about the collective mode. The "enemy" of the movement was identified with backwardness and misery and with the pro-Yankee bourgeoisie. The "questions in debate" were no longer life and liberty but rather improvement of the standard of living. The popular anti-Somoza "identity" began to be differentiated in class terms, and a portion of the bourgeoisie dropped out of the government early in 1980.

At this stage the Sandinista OPs were seen as institutions for the defense of the revolutionary project and as channels for participation and for the resolution of popular demands. Meanwhile the political parties, representing distinct social interests, languished as organizations, and the OPs became the principal democratic channels of the political system under construction.

In this phase the directorate of the FSLN emphasized the relative autonomy of the OPs and recognized their right to fight on behalf of the interests of their members with all means possible, such as "internal criticism, public criticism and the utilization of all the methods of communication, including the staging of demonstrations to demand the measures required to guarantee that your plans are heard."[13] In practice, the autonomy of the OPs, understood as "control over the fixing of goals and the taking of decisions,"[14] depended on the relative strength of the popular and bourgeois sectors, and on the attitude of the FSLN, which had assumed the role of arbitrator in class conflicts in order to continue the effort to achieve national unity, a mixed economy, and nonalignment. Its "arbitration" sometimes relied on coercive methods: In the name of national unity, the Sandinista OPs were sometimes involved in suppressing the Extreme Right and Extreme Left.

The autonomy of the OPs was demonstrated by the popular sectors' defense of their own interests, accomplished by direct action and by their representatives in the Council of State, in which OP representatives made up 44 percent of the members. A well-known example was the movement led by the Labor Coordinator of Nicaragua (Coordinadora Syndical de Nicaragua), formed late in 1980 by the ATC, CST, FO, CAUS, CGT, and CUS in a collective effort to control decapitalization of state and private enterprises.[15] This movement included strikes and plant takeovers that continued until August 1981, when a strict law against capital flight was approved by the Council of State. Moreover, peasant assemblies gathered small- and medium-scale farmers into UNAG to push for an agricultural reform that would be responsive to peasant interests. The assemblies helped attain recognition of the right to land in the July 1981 Agricultural Reform Law, a law that partially modified the emphasis on state ownership imposed by MIDINRA after 1979.

However, the beginning of the contra war and the declaration of a State of Emergency led to a curtailment of popular action for the redress of grievances and the suspension of the right to strike, to take over businesses, and to hold mass demonstrations. Thus the contra war ushered in a new phase in the development of the OPs.

The Second Phase:
Institutionalization (1982–1985)

In the second phase the social movements of women, youth, urban dwellers, workers, and peasants were crystallized into permanent and complex organizations within the context of war and the strengthening of the party and state apparatus. The social movements were institutionalized by statutes that defined the distinctive aspects of each organization; the political system established rules for their participation. Encompassing the popular movements within the framework of the statutes was a long-drawn-out and arduous process. The grass-roots representatives were formally elected or named and became more professionalized as spokespersons for the interests of their respective movements. Offices, emblems, celebrations of past events, heroes, slogans, hymns, and other rituals were institutionalized.

The OPs went through a dynamic common to all social movements: the building of an organization capable of a permanent and coherent defense of its own interests through representatives and leaders. However, the leaders tended to cling to office and to view the consolidation of the organization as an end in itself rather than a means of achieving the goals of the social movement. These phenomena, along with the lack of participatory experience and qualifications among the illiterate masses before 1980, contributed to the requirements that leadership positions be specialized and be filled by qualified individuals.

As a result the OPs were accused of bureaucratization; there were attempts to eliminate abuses of power and elect new directors. These periodic "assembly processes" were, on the one hand, an indication of the democratic intentions of some leaders and, on the other, a symptom of the recurrence of the same problems. For example, there was an electoral process in the CDSs in 1982 after public criticism by Commander Bayardo Arce against the abuses of power; a similar set of elections occurred in 1985 and again in 1988.

In this phase the state apparatus expanded in a disorderly fashion, reclaiming functions that had been initially assumed by the OPs, relegating the organizations to a consultative role and to the provision of voluntary labor for state projects. The regionalization effort of 1982 facilitated a decentralization of the state apparatus but did little to increase the participation of OPs in government decision making.[16] In sectors like the peasantry, there was great resistance to the new administrative divisions that followed a logic of planning alien to the cultural traditions of the countryside. In a parallel way, the FSLN was consolidating organically and expanding, for the most part with cadres from the OPs, thus diminishing the autonomy that the OPs had enjoyed in the first phase of party construction.

The authority claimed by the military in defense of the country also affected the OPs, for it involved their incorporation within defense plans. In the beginning this incorporation did not diminish popular participation because defense needs were met through OPs such as the People's Militias, Neighborhood Night Watch groups, and Civil Defense. However, from late 1983 on, with priority given to obligatory military service as defense needs grew, the OPs became channels for military recruitment. This changed the situation, particularly when coercion was used to levy recruits. Many leaders and members of OPs were absorbed into the military—by late 1984, 47 percent of those affiliated with the CST and 30 percent of the workers of the ATC.

The revival in 1984 of the moribund traditional political parties for the electoral campaign resulted in a partial eclipse of the OPs as channels of democratic participation. The FSLN used the Sandinista OPs during the campaign, thus reinforcing their connections to their founding party. Unlike in the corporative Council of State, there was no direct representation by the OPs in the directly elected legislative assembly that was inaugurated in 1985. As we have seen, groups were represented through political parties. In the 1987 constitution priority was given to the political parties over the OPs in a system that attempted to combine representative and participatory democracy.

The Third Phase:
The Decline of the OPs (1985–1988)

The factors that precipitated the decline of grass-roots organizations were the economic measures taken in 1985 in response to the crisis resulting from the war, the commercial and financial boycott, the deterioration of the terms of trade on the world market, and the political errors of the government. The economic adjustment and stabilization efforts of 1988 continued those of 1985, with a monetarist emphasis on attacking inflation and declining exchange rates and, at the same time, on promoting business profitability and exports. This political economy of survival meant a decontrol of prices and internal marketing channels, the elimination of subsidies for basic consumer goods, increased flexibility in salaries and wages, and reductions in government spending on defense, education, and health care.

For the popular sectors these measures meant a drastic drop in family income, to the limits of physical survival in many cases. If in February 1988, the basic salary of an agricultural worker was taken to be 100, by June its purchasing power was 60, and it had fallen to 16 by the end of July.[17] Food costs came to represent more than half the typical family's income in the popular sectors. Unemployment was expanding rapidly, beyond the absorption capacity of the informal sector, while the urban population seemed unwilling to seek work in the countryside, where a shortage of labor existed.

The situation of the peasants who had benefited from land reform was much better, since they had the capacity to produce food for their own needs and were receiving a larger share of consumer supplies and production inputs in addition to higher prices for farm products as a result of the decontrol of the market. Favorable to the rural sector, these policies were in part an attempt to deny the contras a base of support in the countryside.

All this implied that grass-roots organizations were less able than before to meet the material needs of their sectors and to mobilize their members. The latter found themselves increasingly absorbed in the struggle to feed their families. Because of this struggle, the solidarity and cooperation that had typified the early years was replaced by fierce competition for scarce resources. The OPs were caught in a cross fire between the pressure to meet the subsistence needs of their members and the demands of the government to encourage voluntary labor for defense and to justify austerity and the reduction of the work force. In this context, it was natural that participation in most OPs dropped off. The major exception was the farmers' organization, UNAG. Its membership among the midsized producers increased, a result of the activity of commissions and associations organized by product category, and the Peasant Stores initiated organizational advances.

An important factor in the deterioration of the social base of the OPs was the decomposition of the proletariat and the peasantry that resulted from the war and the economic crisis. From early 1982 on, 350,000 peasant families were displaced from war zones to more peaceful areas, either in new rural settlements or on the periphery of the cities in the urban informal sector. For the proletariat, the closing of businesses and the drop in real salaries pushed many workers into the service sector. In sum, the tendency of this phase—the subordination of the OPs to party and state in the context of war—had combined with the deepening economic crisis to create a clear decline in the popular movement.

The Fourth Phase:
The Challenge of Revitalization (1988–1990)

The military and political collapse of the counterrevolution, the negotiations between the government and the contra leadership, the change in administration in Washington, and the international pressure for peace in Central America created a new opening in 1988 that enhanced popular participation. Equally important, the stagnation of the OPs motivated the FSLN to make changes that would revitalize the popular movement.

The FSLN recognized that the vertical style of OP leadership, while perhaps appropriate in times of war, needed to be changed as the country apparently headed toward a postwar normalcy and that OP leaders should submit to elections. The CDS, for example, had national elections in 1988 to choose a new slate of leaders and held a series of meetings to discuss its problems and develop a new focus. The new idea was to transform the Sandinista Defense Committees into a Community Development Movement for the improvement of life in urban neighborhoods. A variety of modalities, including neighborhood commissions and Community Development Committees, designed to incorporate the natural leaders of a given area into the organization, made the movement more pluralistic. Some communities surveyed the population as a way of promoting a collective analysis of community problems and the search for solutions.

Setting aside party and recruitment tasks, the Community Development Movement placed top priority on community development projects, such as the campaign on behalf of children. This campaign included the development of community leaders, the publication of the rights of children as recognized by the United Nations, mass vaccinations, environmental hygiene, and the improvement of nutrition. Other actions undertaken by the movement included the deeding of urban lots and dwellings, the repair of streets and parks (assisted by municipal governments), and the emergency care and evacuation of populations during Hurricane Joan in October 1988. The community organizations also called for the reestablishment of price controls on some staple goods and demanded the establishment of a peasant market to cut out the middlemen between producers and consumers, an issue UNAG had complained about for years.

A widely publicized case involved the position taken by the community organizations in early 1989 with respect to the rise in the price of milk, the production of three distinct types of milk, and the inadequate control of milk quality. The result of this public protest was a massive drop in the consumer price of milk and a promise by President Daniel Ortega of a daily glass of milk for each child in school—a promise that proved to be impossible to fulfill.

The Sandinista Youth (JS) promoted an election process in all centers of secondary and higher education and drew up a plan of action based on demands made at mass assemblies throughout the country. At the university level, the JS, with 63 percent of the votes cast, won the elections, followed by the Social Christian youth, with 18 percent.

In the fourth National Sandinista Youth Assembly in April 1989, the most prominent themes were the inequality of women, the lack of attention shown to demobilized soldiers and to the graduates of foreign universities, and the complex of problems resulting from the economic crisis and the electoral process. The principal tasks defined in the assembly were defense, the fight against inflation, and the support of the FSLN's election campaign.

With respect to women's issues, it was decided to push for sex education and the legalization of abortion and to oppose the commercialization of beauty contests. Women were to be given greater access to high leadership positions; the JS National Executive Committee, for example, had been criticized for having no women members. Other tasks were to promote sports, recreation, and culture, to support veterans, and to assist in the campaign for children.

The priority of the JS was to continue its work in urban neighborhoods and with students. According to its national coordinator Ajax Delgado: "The Sandinista Youth must be a broad, flexible organization that integrates in its rolls the patriotic youth. It must be an organization of all the youth of Nicaragua."[18] However, despite these statements, it was still difficult for a young person not identified with the FSLN to work for an organization taking part in the electoral campaign of the FSLN. This contradiction, which was not compatible with the idea of an open and practical party, was common among all the OPs discussed here, not just the JS.

The Association of Sandinista Children (ANS) initiated a health campaign in 1988 to work on preventive measures and the reeducation of children at risk (street children and delinquents), vaccination campaigns, publication of the rights of children, and the denunciation of maltreatment of children. It also built playgrounds and promoted sports and cultural activities. The ANS was supported by 11,170 teachers and young people; they worked on this campaign in schools and neighborhoods, targeting displaced children and orphans from the war and hurricanes.

All the mass organizations reduced the number of their full-time paid staff in order to bring in new volunteer leaders, to avoid entrenched bureaucracy, and to reduce expenses. UNAG, for example, slashed its number of field organizers by half. Many of those let go returned to productive work in agriculture or were incorporated into the regional organizations if they had been elected to their positions. This renovation process permitted a change in the leadership of the OPs. At the same time, however, it brought with it problems such as the loss of experienced staff and the volunteer directors' limited time to meet the demands of the membership.

The winding down of the war also made it possible to organize and to hold meetings in the countryside without the fear of contra reprisals. Many displaced peasant families returned to their farms. In Nueva Guinea all but 240 of 960 displaced persons had returned by May 1989. Teachers, technicians, and the leaders of OPs were able to return to work in the rural areas as well.

During this period, Committees for Peace, with a broad representation of religious workers, politicians, and community leaders, were formed in the war zones. Their purpose was to promote the demobilization of those under arms and to create the conditions for peace. They became authentic channels for popular participation and the resolution of community problems. Don Martín Mendoza, a member of the Committee for Peace in a rural zone of Siuna, explained: "These committees watch over the necessities of the community: For example, we take care of the orphans and widows of the war, repair schools, or obtain seeds for planting time."[19]

In 1989, the UNAG, in order to consolidate its national organization and its participation in government negotiations, helped revive the rural cooperative movement. After a series of meetings had taken place in the 147 municipios (a local geographic and political entity in which rural and urban governmental functions are fused), Cooperative Councils were formed or revived at the municipio and regional levels. The councils studied the principal problems of their areas and drew up a program that included economic, organizational, and educational actions. Rejecting the model of quasi-governmental "cooperativism," UNAG again supported autonomy for the cooperatives and confirmed their constitutional right to participate in the formulation of agricultural policy.

In Region I, which includes the departments of Estelí, Madriz, and Nueva Segovia, a valuable experiment in "participatory investigation," with the goal of consciousness-raising at the community level and the promotion of grass-roots discussion of ways in which to improve local conditions, was carried out. In each community in this densely populated region a socioeconomic census was carried out; the census was collectively analyzed at public meetings, and the analysis led to plans for improving local living conditions. Regional development planning was addressed from the bottom up, from the communities to the municipio, and from the municipio to the regional level. For Manuel Morales, regional president: "The construction of grass-roots power has been a continuous apprenticeship; and now, with this experience, we can consolidate participatory democracy."[20]

Among women, too, participation once again became a priority. From 1987 on, the feminist movement organized a series of meetings to discuss the problem of getting the FSLN to issue a proclamation recognizing women's rights and condemning machismo and sexual discrimination. The Luisa Amanda Espinoza Association of Nicaraguan Women (AMNLAE) was reorganized to promote within each OP the work of consciousness-raising and the advancement of women. A special section on women's issues was created within each OP and female representatives were incorporated into the directorates of the OPs.

An example is the study done with 2,395 female peasants, industrial workers, and urban residents of Region IV, which resulted in a better understanding of the situation of women and in the development of a plan of action for each sector. These plans include collective projects to reduce housework (cafeterias for children and infants, mills for grinding corn), publicizing the proclamation on women's rights by the FSLN, and offering classes on sex education. Unfortunately, this program was not repeated in other regions.

The participation of agricultural workers was outstanding in the women's movement. Women constituted 30 percent of the members and directors of the ATC. In the ATC's 1988 national assembly women signaled their desire for equal pay for equal work, pre- and postnatal subsidies, and the fulfillment of production goals. The female workers promised to continue fighting to resolve the most pressing problems, such as low wages, a shortage of day care centers, inattention to occupational health and safety concerns, the lack of technical and sex education, maltreatment and discrimination against female workers, and the barriers to union leadership positions.

In February 1989 representatives of the 16,000 peasant women in UNAG celebrated their first national convention. After examining their problems, they produced a plan of action for the next two years that called for the incorporation of women as full members of the cooperatives, their inclusion on deeds as title holders to agricultural property, the granting of subsidies to pregnant women and those with newborns, construction of day care centers, and access to leadership roles and to technical training. Although the plan's execution was slow in some areas, prospects were best in the production cooperatives in concentrated settlements.

By the end of 1988, AMNLAE was supposed to have established electoral procedures at all levels for its directors and set its own bylaws. However, the FSLN's naming of a new national executive committee in May 1989, the postponement of the internal election process, and the imposition of a plan of action that subordinated the concerns of the members to Sandinista unity in the national elections signified a clear setback for the feminist movement.

The critical economic situation and government austerity policies set in motion in February 1988 severely limited grass-roots participation in organized labor. Struggling to curb inflation, lower the budget deficit, and promote exports, the government implemented measures that provoked a recession, resulting in the closing of many businesses, the loss of private-sector jobs, and a drastic reduction in the number of government employees. Workers engaged in many protests, strikes, and other actions in defense of their jobs and in favor of a minimum salary. These activities occurred where strong and independent unions existed or were wildcat in nature.

In June 1989, teachers struck for higher pay, without the authorization of their Sandinista union, the National Association of Educators of

Nicaragua (ANDEN). They also demanded transportation in rural areas, the decentralization of Ministry of Education, and efforts to improve working conditions and halt the exodus from the profession (in 1988 more than 30 percent of the nation's teachers quit their jobs). The FSLN accused the CIA and the opposition of fomenting the strikes and expelled two U.S. embassy staffers from the country. The Right responded by accusing the government of being the cause of the educational crisis. Finally the government arrived at an agreement addressing the demands of the teachers.

In other strikes the same phenomenon was observed: wildcat actions by members of a Sandinista union, ideological polarization, and negotiation with the government. For the workers the lesson was clear: Unless they resorted to force, the possibility of obtaining their demands was minimal. The large cotton and coffee producers used similar tactics in 1989, threatening to stop production to obtain their demands.

In this same period of economic crisis, a salary that would cover half the cost of a basket of twenty-four basic products (demanded by the CST) or the cost of a basket of eight products (the ATC's minimum) was yet to be approved by the government. The latter apparently evaluated such demands in the light of each enterprise's profitability and the negotiating power of its union. In June 1989, the coffee workers, in their negotiations with the producers over a new labor agreement, proposed a basic salary sufficient to cover the basket of eight products; as an incentive, a contribution of 50 percent in dollars toward projects for social betterment (stores, schools, latrines); and incentives for labor productivity.

Compaction (*compactación*), or cost reductions in state institutions and enterprises, was one battleground where the worker's movement made few gains. In the majority of cases, compaction, decided by the directors of the institution in question, resulted in the layoff of many employees, including union leaders and people "in conflict" with the bosses. In some cases, such as that of the metallurgical company METASA, unions participated in a general review of expenses in an attempt to improve the productive efficiency of the firm and to keep layoffs to a minimum. In some cases the CST and National Union of Employees (UNE) were successful in their demands for limits on expense accounts and executives' and technical cadres' perquisites as a cost-cutting alternative to the firing of workers, who had no employment alternatives.

The upsurge in land seizures in 1989 was another expression of popular mobilization outside the bounds of the OPs in response to the deterioration of living conditions. There were land invasions by poor peasants and unemployed workers—sometimes at the instigation of opposition unions—particularly in Regions II and IV, the most densely populated regions on the Pacific Coast. Though the government declared these invasions illegal, together with the UNAG and the ATC, it searched for a solution in cases where the demands were just.

The 1989 economic accord (*concertación*), promoted by the government between businessmen, labor, and the state, satisfied the interests of producers more than those of workers. This became clear at an April 1989 meeting of the government and agricultural producers, where a subsidy of 1 million cordobas per manzana was granted to cotton producers but where wage concessions were not made to workers. That same month, union leaders who met to analyze the politics of the accord concluded that it was necessary to make the union movement more independent of the parties and the state, to increase democratic participation in unions, and to push for the drafting of a new labor code.

Reflections on Popular Participation

During the ten and a half years of Sandinista rule there was undeniable development in grass-roots participation if seen in relation to the Somoza years. It was not always a steady upward growth, but rather a process involving many ups and downs and contradictions and limitations caused by the war, the economic crisis, and the inheritance of the past.

The contra war fundamentally limited the process of political democratization that began in Nicaragua in 1979. It is true that a prolonged situation of war acquires a logic of its own, and with that logic a unique structure in social relations and the realm of symbols. It perceptibly alters the implementation of the democratic socialist project in a revolutionary process such as that of Nicaragua.

This phenomenon, sometimes called the "militarization of political society," was reflected in the OPs. The involvement of these organizations in the war bespoke the preeminence of military concerns over activities designed to promote the interests of OP members. Organizational methods reflected the military logic of a vertical hierarchy and strict discipline. When the OPs ceased to respond effectively to their original objectives and began limiting the democratic and voluntary participation of the masses, membership declined. A clear contradiction appeared between the need to increase the OPs' support of the war effort and the OPs' need to maintain their voluntary character and to respond to the immediate needs of the masses.

The absorption of resources by the war also made it impossible to satisfy adequately the material needs of the population, particularly of the lower-income groups. To this privation were added the demands made by the war in the form of extra work and sacrifice. The economic situation negatively affected participation in the OPs. An extra dose of ideology was no substitute for basic necessities like food, clothing, and shelter.

On the one hand, in wars of national liberation such as that in Nicaragua, there is a need to establish a broad multiclass anti-imperialist front, as much for internal reasons (to join forces against the foreign army) as for reasons of international politics (to gain solidarity and support). On the other hand, in Nicaragua, the deterioration of the economic situation of low-income groups led some to question this broad unity and to demand more-equitable distribution of the scarce basic goods. Furthermore, the space for political discourse tends to narrow in times of war. The relative autonomy of ideological debate and the complexity of its dynamic gets lost, and any discrepancy is seen as a machination of the enemy.

I believe that another factor that explains dwindling grass-roots participation in Nicaragua is the reproduction of the social relations of subordination existing in the previous system. Although, in the final analysis, the Somoza regime was based on coercion, there also existed a hegemony of the dominant classes, a network of social relationships of a "paternalistic" or "clientelistic" nature. These relations of subordination, typical of rural societies, were established between the dominant and subordinate classes by means of a reciprocal system of rights and obligations that operated through the exchange of material and symbolic goods. This domination manifested itself in these hidden relations through personal linkages or relationships, for example, godparenthood (*compadrazgo*), friendship, and protection. These elements were still part of the traditional culture predominant in both rural and urban areas at the end of the first revolutionary decade.[21]

The old social relations possessed a profound inertia and tended to reproduce themselves in new forms as long as the underlying structural determinants were not modified. The paternalistic or clientelistic relations continued because there existed a distinct difference in access to resources, whether material, educational, or political. The shortage of technicians and professionals, typical where revolutions are developing, meant that a small group was carrying out research and planning and, in many cases, exercised state power that the popular sectors did not possess. This resulted in the planning of projects intended to benefit the people, but without effective grass-roots participation in the decisions that concerned them. The disparity in educational levels was offered as an excuse for this subordination.

In other areas of political and civil life, various arguments were made for the necessity of some form of subordination. Some political leaders felt that only they possessed the "revolutionary ideology" and the capacity to govern. Among some members of the bourgeoisie there was a belief that they were the only ones suited to the entrepreneurial activities necessary to develop the forces of production. Some of the ecclesiastical hierarchy thought that only they had the ability to interpret religious doctrine and represent God. Machos believed that only men had the intellectual and physical capacity to lead. And so it went.

It would be an error to see the reproduction of these relations as a result of conscious planning by the dominant groups. Rather they constitute a structural process in which the subordinate groups contribute equally to the continuation of these relations. Popular-sector attitudes of idleness, passivity, and "what do I care-ism" (yoquepierdismo)— associated with an undervaluation of their own capacities and with magical or fatalistic conceptions of social reality—helped reproduce these relations of subordination. In many cases, for example, political partic- ipation in the OPs was seen as an undesirable task compared to more attractive options such as engaging in sports, drinking, attending fiestas, or simply "hanging out."

The question of popular participation is based directly on the type of political system promoted by the Sandinista revolution. The FSLN project envisioned the construction of a democratic and pluralistic system that combined in an original form both representative and participatory models. A system of political parties freely competing for the votes of the citizens in periodic elections was advocated from the start (Chapter 2). At the same time, the participatory model could be seen in the direct intervention of the people in matters of collective concern, a task in which the OP played a fundamental role. In this way the FSLN attempted to overcome the limitations of both the so-called formal or liberal democracy and the so-called real or socialist democracy.

It is relevant to note that the question of democracy was limited to the political sphere, when history demonstrates that the reproduction of vertical relations in civil society (work, school, and family) in the process of transition to socialism has confounded the intent to democratize the state or party apparatus. By the end of the Sandinista administration, it was increasingly apparent that there was a need to enlarge the concept of democracy to include all aspects of social life, to define a type of social relationship where those affected by decisions participate equally in their making. In this task to build new social relations at every level, the OPs could play an irreplaceable role, straddling the frontier between political and civil society and built on a broad base that includes all the popular sectors.

Conclusions

During the Sandinista revolution, in spite of ups and downs and limitations, the grass-roots organizations served as important channels for the democratic expression of popular interests and for the resolution of the most pressing problems and adverse conditions brought on by the war, the economic crisis, and the inheritances of the past. Freedom of expression and organization had become a palpable reality. Though the contra war and the resultant economic crisis had created shortages in resources and personnel as well as pressures from both the party and the government that tended to reduce the size and limit the autonomy of the OPs, many people, in spite of everything, had learned to state their opinions, criticize, be informed about the policies of the government, and organize in collective attempts to attain satisfaction of their common needs.

There had also come into being a representative form of democracy typified, as noted in Chapter 2, by Western-style elections (1984 and 1990) through which public officials were chosen. Here too, as mentioned, there were contradictions and tensions between grass-roots participatory and more traditional representative forms of democracy. In 1985, the change from a corporative Council of State, featuring direct involvement of grass-roots organizations, to an elected National Assembly, in which parties rather than OPs played a central role, tended somewhat to diminish OP access to decision making and the public debate. Also, since national elections were essentially contests among parties, there was a tendency during campaigns for revolutionary leaders to let FSLN party interests eclipse those of the OPs. That problem existed during the 1990 elections just as it had in 1984.

Clearly, the most relevant vehicles for popular participation were those that exist in neighborhoods, rural and urban workplaces, schools, and in all areas of collective life. It was there that a truly democratic Nicaragua would be constructed, where the people could participate with equal rights and obligations in the decisions and actions that most affect their social life. There is no doubt that, during the little over a decade of Sandinista rule, enormous advances in political participation at the grass roots had taken place. By the same token, it is also evident that even had the Sandinistas won in 1990, there would still have been much to be done before equal participation by people at all social levels in the decisions affecting them could have been attained.

With the surprise victory of the U.S.-sponsored UNO coalition, the OPs were certain to face even tougher challenges in their roles as vehicles of grass-roots participation and articulators of popular interest. Facing a government that stood for other interests and parallel organizations that that government was creating, the OPs would have to respond effectively to specific base demands, displaying greater independence from the FSLN line, in order to sustain their memberships and the advances already obtained. However, what they had achieved and learned in their relatively brief history since the late 1970s was likely to ensure that the "playing field" of politics in the 1990s would be much more "level" than it had been under the Somozas.

Notes

1. Damaso Várgas, "Encuentro de Fuerzas Fundamentales," a speech to the CST, Managua, January 15, 1989.

2. UNAG, *Diagnóstico del Movimiento Cooperativo Agropequario*, Managua, September 1989.

3. UNAG, *Plan de Trabajo del Movimiento Cooperativo*, Managua, April 1989.

4. Lucio Jimenez, *Barricada*, September 19, 1988, p. 3.

5. ATC, "Informe de la 4a. Asamblea Nacional de Obreras Agrícolas." Managua, October 1988, p. 5.

6. Ibid.

7. M. Ortega, L. Serra, and R. Salazar, "El Proceso de democratización en Nicaragua." Managua: Itztani, 1988.

8. Carmén Herrera, "Gestión sindical sandinista: una discusión pendiente," *Pensamiento Propio*, 6, no. 55 (November 1988), pp. 15–18.

9. UNAG, ATC, y otros, "Pronunciamiento de las Fuerzas Fundamentales de la Revolución sobre la economía de Nicaragua," *Revista Nicaragüense de Ciencias Sociales*, 3, no. 5 (1989), pp. 70–93.

10. Carlos Nuñez, *Las Organizaciones de masas en la revolución sandinista*, Department of Political Education and Information, FSLN, Managua, 1980.

11. Bayardo Arce, *Adonde va el FSLN*, entrevista de D. Julius, Managua, Editorial Vanguardia, 1988.

12. Alan Tourain, *Le voix et le regard* (Paris: Seuil, 1978).

13. Nuñez, "Las organizaciones de masas."

14. J. Fox, "Grassroots Organizations vs. the Iron Law of Oligarchy," Research Note, Cambridge University, October 1987.

15. The Workers' Front (FO) is a union movement of the Left allied with the MAP-ML party. The Confederation of Union Action and Unity (CAUS) is aligned with the Communist party. The General Confederation of Independent Workers (CGT) is aligned with the Socialist party. The Confederation of Union Unity (CUS) is integrated with the coordinator of the right-wing opposition organizations.

16. Charles Downs, "Local and Regional Government," in Thomas Walker, ed., *Nicaragua: The First Five Years* (New York: Praeger, 1985), pp. 45–63.

17. ATC, Informe de la la 4a, Asamblea Nacional, p. 8.

18. *Barricada*, March 27, 1989, p. 3.

19. Don Martín Mendoza, as interviewed by the author on April 5, 1989.

20. Video: "Participación popular en las Segovias," Delegación de Gobierno, Estelí, January 1989.

21. François Houtart and Geneviève Lemercinier, "Managua: una cultura en transición," ponencia Congreso ANICS, Managua, August 1988.

FOUR

The Armed Forces

THOMAS W. WALKER

In mid-1985, during a lengthy interview with Nicaragua's interior minister, Tomás Borge, one member of a group of visiting scholars attempted to preface an intended question with the phrase, "When Salvador Allende came to power in Chile in 1970, . . ." Borge, the lone surviving founder of the FSLN, immediately interrupted—politely, but with obvious intensity of conviction: "Ah, but Allende never really came to power."[1] What Borge meant was that although the mildly revolutionary Allende was elected and formally inaugurated president, he, like most other chief executives in twentieth-century Latin America, would govern at least in part at the pleasure of an essentially conservative and insubordinate military establishment. Thus, on September 11, 1973, after being subjected to a multimillion-dollar campaign of economic and political destabilization orchestrated by the U.S. Central Intelligence Agency (CIA) and other U.S. government bodies,[2] Allende's experiment in democratic revolution was bloodily terminated by his country's own U.S.-trained military. Borge was keenly aware of this historical reality, and he, like the rest of the FSLN leadership, was determined from the start that Nicaragua's revolutionary armed forces would be loyal and subordinate to their country's revolutionary government.

The Origin of the Sandinista Armed Forces

The armed forces that were to provide internal security and defend Nicaraguan sovereignty during the Sandinista administration had their origin in the guerrilla and insurrectionary movement begun with the formation of the FSLN in 1961. The eighteen-year period in which the FSLN struggled to topple the Somoza dictatorship is roughly divisible into three subperiods: the *foco* stage, 1961–1967; the years of "accumulation of force in silence," 1967–1974; and the period of renewed armed struggle, 1974–1979.

During the first two subperiods, the FSLN never numbered more than a few dozen individuals. Inspired by the quick success of Cuban

77

revolutionary Fidel Castro and his handful of rural guerrillas in toppling the Batista dictatorship in the late 1950s, the Sandinistas at first embarked on a strategy of creating a rural guerrilla focus (*foco*) from which to harass the Somoza regime. This strategy—which also harkened back to that which their own national hero, Augusto César Sandino, had successfully employed against the U.S. Marines three decades earlier—ultimately failed. Somoza's National Guard, which, in the years following Castro's victory had received considerable U.S. training in rural counterinsurgency warfare, eventually surrounded and killed most of the FSLN's best cadres at Pancasán in 1967.

The survivors then adopted a practical strategy of "accumulation of force in silence." Until the mid-1970s, they would work to build grassroots support among the rural and urban poor while they waited for a more opportune moment to renew the armed struggle.

The final period of armed struggle began in December 1974 when FSLN commandos invaded the Managua home of prominent Somocista José María Castillo during a farewell party for the U.S. ambassador. They held a number of prominent Somocistas (the ambassador had left shortly before the operation began) hostage until the dictator agreed to pay a large ransom, release FSLN prisoners, and publish and broadcast an FSLN communiqué. This successful operation enraged the dictator, who conducted a reign of terror in the countryside that lasted until early 1977. Although most of the thousands of individuals killed were innocent peasants, Somoza's counterinsurgency effort did inflict some damage on the FSLN.

Smarting from these losses, the Sandinistas fell to arguing among themselves over tactics. Three "tendencies" soon appeared. One, the Prolonged Popular War (GPP) faction, advocated renewed rural *foco*-style guerrilla war. Another, the Proletarian Tendency (TP), argued for a lengthy effort to organize and mobilize the urban working classes. The third, known as the Terceristas, or Third Force, advocated an immediate combined urban-rural insurgency and an alliance with all anti-Somocista forces.

As it turned out, the Tercerista strategy emerged as the most appropriate for the times. The idea of a broad-based multiclass effort made sense. By the second half of the 1970s virtually every important group in Nicaraguan society—except for the Somozas, their business cronies, and the National Guard—was determined to see the dynasty end. Thus, from 1977 on, the Terceristas seized the initiative, forging alliances with important intellectuals, religious leaders, and even businesspeople. By late 1977, spectacular guerrilla operations were renewed, and in 1978, spurred on by the assassination of beloved opposition publisher Pedro Joaquín Chamorro, massive urban insurgency began.

The insurgencies came in three main waves: (1) isolated rebellions in Indian neighborhoods of Monimbó and Subtiava on the outskirts of the cities of Masaya and León early in 1978; (2) massive insurgency in a half-dozen major cities in September 1978 following the spectacular FSLN seizure of the Legislative Palace the previous month; and (3) the final insurrection of May through July 1979.

During the year and one-half prior to the "Triumph" of July 19 at least three important things happened to the FSLN. First, unity was achieved. The Monimbó and Subtiava uprising proved that the country was ripe for the insurrectionary strategy proposed by the Terceristas. By late 1978, informal unification had taken place. The following March a formal declaration of unity was made and a nine-man FSLN directorate (DNC), composed of three individuals from each of the three tendencies was created. That body would remain unchanged throughout the Sandinista administration.

A second important aspect of this period was that it was the time in which the Sandinistas perfected the technique of mass-based urban insurgency and eventually came to play the central role in it. The Monimbó and Subtiava uprisings, and even the September insurrections, had been largely spontaneous and uncoordinated. The Sandinistas recognized the potential of such insurgency, but they also came to realize that any final insurrection, if it were to be successful, would have to be much better coordinated and supported by FSLN cadre than had been the events of 1978. Accordingly, grass-roots organization, which had begun on a modest scale in earlier years, was accelerated with urgency in the year prior to the victory. Women's, students', and rural and urban labor organizations were strengthened, and Civil Defense Committees (CDCs, in the posttriumph period to be called Sandinista Defense Committees [CDSs] and after 1988, Community Development Committees [CDCs]) were created in neighborhoods throughout the country. The CDCs functioned as civilian support groups for insurgent forces during urban uprisings, providing food, first aid, safe houses, intelligence, and so forth for the armed FSLN cadre and the tens of thousands of young people (the "muchachos," or kids) who spontaneously joined them during the fighting.

By the time of the final insurrection in the summer of 1979, FSLN organization and grass-roots mobilization were impressive. The country was divided into six fronts (Northern, Southern, Eastern, Western, Central, and Internal [Managua]). Each front, with its own FSLN general staff, was assigned a specific battle plan complete with a time table for the achievement of objectives. In the end, it was superior organization and extensive grass-roots support that made it possible for the small insurgent forces to defeat the corrupt and demoralized, yet much more numerous and better-armed, National Guard.

The third important phenomenon of this period was a rapid increase in the size and quality of the FSLN army. At the time of the September

1978 uprisings, the regular FSLN armed force numbered only a few hundred. There were plenty of muchachos willing to fight, but they lacked training. In the ensuing eight months, however, thousands of these youth formally joined the FSLN. At clandestine training camps in the Nicaraguan countryside and other parts of Central and South America, they received both military training and political education. Among other things, they were taught the revolutionary ideals of the FSLN, including the idea that, in the new system, members of the armed forces would be the servants, not the masters, of the people. They were also taught to distinguish between the U.S. government, on the one hand, and U.S. citizens on the other. The latter were not to be held responsible for the sins of the former. In addition, they were admonished, urged, and, in most cases, convinced not to treat their vanquished enemy, the National Guard, with a spirit of cruel vengeance. A slogan I often heard ordinary FSLN foot soldiers proclaim during my short visit there in July 1979 was "Tenacious in battle. Generous in victory."[3] Thus, over an eight-month period of accelerated recruitment and training, a small guerrilla force of only a few hundred was expanded into a reasonably seasoned, unified, and politically aware military establishment of several thousand. After the triumph, the bulk of these men and women, in turn, would become the nucleus of the Sandinista armed forces

The Posttriumph Consolidation Phase: 1979 Through 1980

As the Sandinistas celebrated their victory on July 20, the day after their entry into Managua, they were aware that they enjoyed an advantage that some other revolutionary governments in the past—such as those of Allende in Chile in the 1970s and the Arévalo and Arbenz governments in Guatemala in the late 1940s and early 1950s—had not had: unambiguous command of a unified revolutionary military establishment. Somoza's National Guard had been defeated, and its surviving members had surrendered or fled the country. Nevertheless, the FSLN was also aware that it would be foolish to let down its guard. As one top official in the Foreign Ministry commented later, "History tells us there's never been a revolution without a counter-revolution, and, in the history of Latin America, there's never been a counter-revolution without the participation of the CIA."[4] Informed international specialists also were soon advising the Sandinistas not to be complacent. Less than six months after their victory, La Prensa, at the time still mildly supportive of the revolution, published an article by former CIA agent Philip Agee in which he described in prophetic detail how he thought the CIA would go about destabilizing and undermining their revolution.[5]

On a more tangible plane, the Sandinistas were disquieted by the fact that thousands of former troops from Somoza's National Guard were being housed, fed, and clothed (by some group or institution with considerable money—most likely the CIA) in camps in Honduras and that the government of that country, closely allied with the United States, was showing notable reluctance to break up these camps and resettle their inhabitants. It is likely also that the Sandinistas were aware, at least soon after the fact, that at the very moment of their victory, the CIA had sent a DC-8 jet, disguised with Red Cross markings, to Managua to fly some of Somoza's officers' corps to Miami.[6] Many of these individuals would later command the contra army. Therefore, although the Carter administration continued normal diplomatic relations with Nicaragua, choosing to employ a policy of co-optation rather than confrontation, and although the Sandinistas fervently wanted a continuation of such relations,[7] the latter knew that they could not automatically assume such a benign future. Thus, a major task confronting the new government during the final year and a half of the Carter administration was to build a security apparatus that could not only perform normal peacetime internal security functions but also provide some margin of safety against possible counterrevolutionary activity coming from within or beyond Nicaragua's borders.

The transformation of the small rebel armed forces and supporting muchachos into a regular, multibranched security apparatus was accomplished rapidly in the months following the victory. The major security institutions were the Sandinista People's Army (EPS), under the Ministry of Defense; the Sandinista Police (PS) and State Security forces, under the Ministry of the Interior; and the Sandinista People's Militias (MPS), under both Interior and Defense. The controlling ministries, in turn, were responsible to the FSLN Joint National Directorate and were headed by directorate members Humberto Ortega (Defense) and Tomás Borge (Interior).

As the reader will note, Nicaragua's new security forces were explicitly "Sandinista." The FSLN leadership had little use for the liberal myth that military establishments can—or even should—be politically neutral. Their experience and reading of history had taught them that, in Latin America at least, the armed forces are the instruments of class control— normally that of the privileged classes over the poor majority. They were determined that Nicaragua's new security forces would set that tradition on its head, guaranteeing and protecting the revolution and the rule of the poor majority. The adjectival use of Sandino's name in the title of the three major security institutions would underscore that determination.

From July 1979 through the end of 1980, the recruitment and training of security forces were emphasized. The victorious FSLN army, numbering around 5,000 at the time of the triumph, was expanded into a regular army of around 18,000; police and State Security forces numbered several thousand each, and the Popular Militia had an undetermined number of members.[8] Training included not only standard military matters, but also basic literacy (approximately 45 percent of the EPS had been illiterate in late 1979) and social and political awareness and responsibility. Considerable stress was placed on the goals and principles of the revolution and the need for security personnel to protect and support, rather than abuse and mistreat, their fellow citizens. To reinforce that training, cases of abuse of civilians by members of the security forces were rigorously investigated and disciplined. As a result, the behavior of security personnel toward civilians was usually quite respectful—a marked contrast to the situation that had existed in Nicaragua under the Somozas and that continued to exist in the rest of northern Central America throughout the 1980s.[9]

During this period, too, the urgent need to increase and standardize the weaponry of the Sandinista armed forces was addressed. The FSLN guerrillas had won the war with a hodgepodge of Western-made weaponry, much of it in deplorable condition. During the five days I spent in Nicaragua during the first week of the victory, I saw rebel soldiers armed with U.S. M-16s, Belgian FALs, Israeli UZIs and GALILs as well as an assortment of antique U.S. M-1s, hunting rifles, pistols, shotguns, and even some handmade weapons. (I saw no weaponry of Socialist Bloc origin.) Most of these, I later learned, had been captured in battle, liberated from the National Guard at the time of the victory, or acquired on the Western arms market (with the logistical help of Costa Rica, Venezuela, Panama, and Cuba). In November 1979, Vice Minister of Defense Luis Carrión commented on this problem: "The arms market is a difficult one. We are seeking favorable conditions in Europe, the Arab countries and the United States. Without doubt, the diversity of arms we are using at this moment is going to create problems; further on we will have to think about standardizing them which will mean discarding some. But our principal problem at this point in time is to acquire weapons of whatever type from whatever source."[10]

As it turns out, Sandinista decision making was simplified by the Carter administration: Although a joint report of the State Department and Pentagon recognized the inadequacy of Sandinista arms and urged that the FSLN request for U.S. assistance in standardized weaponry be favorably acted upon,[11] Carter, facing a cold warrior in the 1980 elections, chose the politically expedient course of turning down that request. In the long run, though they would receive some arms from France, Greece, the Arab countries, and elsewhere, the Nicaraguan government would come to rely primarily on Socialist Bloc sources. This fact, in turn, would become a major excuse for U.S. hostility.

For Third World countries, it is normal for advising and training to accompany arms transfers. The case of Nicaragua was no exception. Though the United States, while refusing to provide arms, did offer assistance in training, the Sandinistas declined such assistance: The United States had been the major source of training and advice for their vanquished enemy, Somoza's National Guard. Indeed, at the time of its defeat, the National Guard had been the most heavily U.S.-trained military establishment in Latin America.[12] Accordingly, although Nicaragua did accept some police-training assistance from Panama, most of its foreign military training ultimately came from the Socialist Bloc. Cuba provided hundreds of military advisers, and the Soviet Union and other East European countries sent a few dozen military technicians and security advisers. However, contrary to what the Reagan administration would later allege, these advisers did not play a central role in Nicaraguan military planning. In fact, in October 1988 at a CIA-funded conference on Nicaragua, Col. Alden M. Cunningham, U.S. military attaché in Managua during the Reagan administration, contended: "The EPS for the most part has planned and fought the counterinsurgency war itself. Soviet and Cuban advisors have been a major help, especially with key items of equipment, such as the HIND helicopter. The resistance [contras] on the other hand, cannot effectively take the field without U.S. support. If neither side had support, the Sandinistas would easily prevail."[13]

Besides the work of organizing, training, and equipping the Sandinista armed forces, the only other major military challenge faced by the Sandinistas during the Carter years was the initial task of imposing law and order as the old regime was replaced by the new. At first this task was made difficult by two factors: the continued presence in Nicaragua of renegades from Somoza's defeated National Guard and the ongoing armed activities of autonomous ultrarevolutionary or bandit groups. Though the National Guard renegades killed dozens of people during the first week after the victory, most guardsmen had surrendered or been killed within a month or so.[14] The ultrarevolutionaries and bandits were another matter. Heavily armed with automatic weapons that the National Guard had discarded on July 17, 18, and 19, these groups set out to "liberate" bourgeois property. They were a real scourge of the wealthier neighborhoods of Managua. At night in such neighborhoods, it was not uncommon to hear the staccato of automatic weapon fire (the ultrarevolutionaries or bandits), punctuated by the pop of a pistol (the owner), and then silence. FSLN command posts normally responded to telephoned requests for assistance, but sometimes it was too late. It was not until early 1980 that these groups were eliminated— some physically in battle, others by agreement to integrate themselves into the FSLN armed forces.[15]

The relatively minor problem of controlling organized counterrevo-lutionary activities during the Carter period was handled quite efficiently by the Ministry of the Interior and, particularly, State Security. Like the FBI in the United States, the latter maintained surveillance of potentially subversive groups and broke them up when they began to embark on subversive activities. For instance, on November 17, 1980, Jorge Salazar, head of the ultraconservative Union of Nicaraguan Farmers (UPANIC), was caught and killed in a shoot-out by State Security forces as he was allegedly meeting gunrunners to pay for arms to supply a nascent insurgent force.

Generally, however, the latter part of the Carter period was a time of peace, stability, and renewed hope for most Nicaraguans. During this time, the Sandinista armed forces were reorganized, modestly expanded, and reequipped to deal with the immediate security problems mentioned above as well as the historically predictable problem of foreign-backed counterrevolution. Nevertheless, the Nicaraguan armed forces were clearly defensive in nature and neither in manpower nor in armaments could they reasonably be considered to be out of line with the military establishments of other countries in northern Central America.

Defending a Country Under Siege:
1981 Through 1988

This situation changed radically with the election of Ronald Reagan in November 1980. The 1980 Republican party platform had explicitly "abhor[red] the Marxist Sandinist takeover" in Nicaragua. Advisers close to Reagan in the campaign and in the transition period had spoken of the need to turn back the Nicaraguan revolution. A Reagan transition team "fact finder" sent to Nicaragua shortly after the election had queried at least one prominent Nicaraguan businessman about how the United States could help them get rid of the Sandinistas.[16] In March 1981, a little more than a month after the Reagan inauguration, even the U.S. media were already carrying reports of Nicaraguan exiles in Dade County, Florida, and elsewhere engaging in paramilitary training for the "liberation" of their country—in open violation of U.S. law.[17]

The U.S.-sponsored low-intensity war, of which the contra effort would be the centerpiece, is amply described and documented in Chapter 15. Here I shall just note that by the end of 1981, the contras had already begun to carry out operations in Nicaragua. Their numbers would subsequently escalate from the 500 combatants originally deemed sufficient to do the job to more than 15,000 by the mid-1980s when the war reached its peak. Although that is not a large number in an absolute sense, Nicaragua is a very small country. Non-Nicaraguans can perhaps better understand the meaning of the contra invasion by visualizing a hypothetical, but proportionately equivalent, situation in which the United States were invaded across both borders simultaneously by over 1 million well-armed combatants backed by an infinitely more powerful hostile state. That would probably not be a large enough force to overthrow the U.S. government; but, considering that the Pentagon itself usually estimates that it takes 10 regular troops to contain 1 irregular combatant, it would be far more than enough to justify a sharply heightened concern about defense and national security.

But this was not all. To add to Nicaraguan fears, about two years into the Reagan administration, various foreign policy branches of the United States (CIA, Pentagon, Department of State) began an apparently well-coordinated campaign of "leaks" designed to create the false impression that Nicaragua was about to be invaded directly by the United States.[18] A very detailed Operation Pegasus, leaked late in 1983, called for an invasion early in 1984. Though Pegasus did not materialize, a similarly elaborate invasion plan for 1985 was leaked in 1984. The invasion leaks, in turn, were underscored and made credible by ever-escalating U.S. involvement in war games and training exercises in neighboring Honduras. As noted in Chapter 15, this psychological war—part of the overall strategy of low-intensity conflict—was apparently designed to cause the Sandinistas to panic and, in the name of national security, restrict civil liberties and divert public spending from popular and successful social programs into military preparedness. To some extent, it was successful.

Strengthening the Armed Forces

The major Nicaraguan response to the real and perceived threats being generated by the Reagan administration was to increase vastly the country's defensive capabilities in both personnel and arms. The overall size of the active-duty armed forces was increased significantly in step with the growing threat. The close relationship between threat and armed-personnel increase is illustrated even in otherwise somewhat misleading statistics in U.S. government publications. For instance, in *The Challenge to Democracy in Central America*, published by the Departments of State and Defense in 1986, the Sandinista "Military/Security" forces were depicted as having grown from 24,000 in 1980 to nearly 40,000 in 1981. Thereafter, they grew slowly to 46,000 by 1983, but leaped to 67,000 and 75,000 in 1984 and 1985, respectively.[19] It is significant that the first major jump came in 1981, the year in which Reagan came to power and Nicaraguan contras began training openly in camps in Florida and other parts of the United States. The second jump came in 1984, immediately after the late 1983 disinformation leaks concerning Operation Pegasus.

These figures appear to be inflated by the inclusion of Ministry of the Interior police and security forces and by simple exaggeration. Estimates taken from more reliable sources indicate that the size of the regular army (EPS) probably stood at between 13,000 and 18,000 in 1980; jumped quickly in 1981 to around 24,000, where it remained relatively constant until late 1983; jumped again to between 30,000 and 40,000 in 1984 and to between 60,000 and 75,000 in 1985 and 1986; and remained constant through the rest of the Reagan period.[20] The important point, however, is that whichever set of estimates one chooses to use, the dramatic jumps followed periods of sharply escalated threat.

Backing the regular army were a tiny air force and navy, somewhat larger police and state security forces of the Ministry of the Interior, and the Sandinista People's Militia, which a secret 1984 U.S. *Army Intelligence Survey* described as "poorly trained and ill-equipped" yet generally "effective against guerrilla [contra] activities."[21] Estimates of membership in the militia at any one time run from between a few tens of thousands to at least 100,000. The militia, though, were simply civilian volunteers (of both sexes and all ages over about twelve years) who could be mobilized in times of crisis to defend their community or region. Except when mobilized, they were not government-maintained members of the armed forces.

The importation of arms—especially of Socialist Bloc origin—also appears to have been dramatically stimulated by the external threat posed by the Reagan administration. Again, as in the case of the jumps in military personnel, the relationship can be seen even on a graph published in U.S. documents obviously designed to discredit the Sandinistas (see Figure 4.1).

Prior to the coming to power of Ronald Reagan, "no heavy Soviet weapons were approved [by the Socialist Bloc] for Nicaragua."[22] It was not until mid-1981, several months into the Reagan administration, that the first Soviet-built tanks were imported.[23] But even these World War II–vintage leviathans were apparently obtained not from the Socialist Bloc but secondhand from countries in the Middle East. Throughout 1981, Nicaragua attempted to obtain less–politically sensitive weaponry from non–Socialist Bloc sources. In December 1981, for instance, the Sandinistas actually reached a $15.8 million arms purchase agreement with France, only to have it subsequently torpedoed under U.S. pressure.[24] Thus, the dramatic escalation of arms imports from the Socialist Bloc that we see in Figure 4.1 as having begun in 1982 can be considered a temperate, delayed response to a serious threat that was by then a year old.

Though dramatic, the arms buildup was defensive in character. In an attempt to standardize weaponry, the EPS was given Socialist Bloc AK-47s and the militia received 1950s-vintage Czech BZ-52 ten-shot

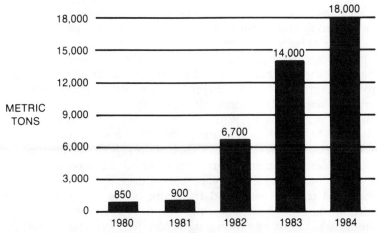

Figure 4.1   Soviet Bloc military deliveries to Nicaragua. *Sources:* Two white papers released by the U.S. Departments of State and Defense, *The Soviet-Cuban Connection in Central America and the Caribbean* and *The Sandinista Military Buildup* (Washington, D.C.: U.S. Government Printing Office, 1985), pp. 25 and 33, respectively. Also reproduced in Eldon Kenworthy, "Selling the Policy," in *Reagan Versus the Sandinistas: The Undeclared War on Nicaragua,* Thomas W. Walker, ed. (Boulder, Colo.: Westview Press, 1987), p. 174.

rifles. Eventually, since the "BZs" were obsolete in comparison with the weaponry carried by the contras, the militia were also issued AK-47s. By the late 1980s, the AK-47s in the hands of both the EPS and the MPS were being replaced by newer AK-Ms.

Heavy weaponry was also imported in large quantity. The Socialist Bloc tanks imported originally from the Middle East were followed in subsequent years by as many as 100 similar obsolete tanks imported directly from the Socialist Bloc. Though tanks had proved useful in Cuba in repelling the Bay of Pigs invaders two decades earlier, they were found to be of little use in counterinsurgency in the very different Nicaraguan setting. Instead, they were stored near major population centers such as Managua and deployed in moments of heightened tension with the United States as an apparent deterrent to direct U.S. invasion. Other armaments included patrol boats (the contras and CIA commandos frequently attacked by sea); several dozen Soviet-built helicopters, including more than a dozen MI-25 HIND D "flying tanks" (which proved of crucial importance in some of the pivotal battles against the contras in the mid-1980s); a wide variety of anti-aircraft guns and shoulder-held SAM 6 and 7 ground-to-air missiles (which subsequently downed a number of contra and CIA aircraft, including several cargo planes used to fly arms to the contras); a goodly supply of rocket launchers, howitzers, and mortars (which proved very effective in dealing with pockets of invading contras); a score of old fixed-wing aircraft (used mainly for troop and cargo transport); an assortment of Socialist Bloc trucks, and a variety of electronic equipment.[25]

In most respects these armaments and materials were adequate in dealing with the contras, served the function of raising the potential cost to the United States of a direct invasion, and roughly balanced the military hardware of Honduras. However, in air power, Nicaragua was at a distinct disadvantage. With a fleet of more than seventy Israeli-, French-, and U.S.-made war planes—including a squadron of U.S. F-5 jets—Honduras, even by the mid-1980s, had the biggest and most powerful air force in Central America, one that dwarfed and would continue to dwarf the half-dozen or so Korean War–vintage planes the Sandinistas had inherited from Somoza and the score of old Soviet cargo planes they were in the process of acquiring.[26] From early in the Reagan period, the Sandinistas talked of purchasing fighter jets. But the United States blocked a French sale in 1982 and threatened Nicaragua into not importing Soviet-built MIGs. Thus, Nicaragua faced a harsh dilemma: Whereas jet aircraft such as the MIGs would be crucially important in the event of a full-scale invasion, their importation might well trigger just such an attack.

Winning the War

It took the Sandinistas a few years to come up with an effective military strategy for dealing with both the immediate military problem posed by the U.S.-sponsored contra invasion and the seemingly very real possibility of an eventual direct U.S. invasion. The original strategy appears to have been to keep the regular army in or around the major urban areas to serve as a deterrent to invasion while, in effect, letting local militia deal with the contras. As a U.S. *Army Intelligence Survey* put it in 1984: "The best trained and equipped units have been deployed to posts in Managua and other major urban areas, while the less-trained militia and reserve units have been responsible for defending border areas from the contras. While this strategy has resulted in a dispro- portionate amount of Sandinista casualties, the most capable units are prepared to defend Nicaragua from a major offensive."[27]

Eventually, however, it became obvious that it was necessary to expand the regular army so that it could play a major role both as a deterrent against U.S. invasion and as a device for the ultimate defeat of the contras in Nicaragua's rural hinterlands. The growth in regular military personnel in 1984 documented above reflects the implementation of this strategy. The major device by which it was accomplished was the imposition of a national draft system, the Patriotic Military Service (SMP), late in 1983. All young men from seventeen to twenty-four years of age were to serve two years in the regular armed forces.

Though the SMP was never very popular, especially among the middle- and upper-class families, it proved quite successful in the long run. Most important, it allowed for a rapid expansion in numbers of active-duty personnel. The young, rigorously trained draftees became the muscle of new units that fought the contras in rural areas. In addition, the SMP had an important role in political socialization. All societies inculcate in their youth an array of national patriotic myths, heroes, and values. In the United States this is done via the organized activities of Brownies, Cub Scouts, Girl Scouts, and Boy Scouts, in the schools through the Pledge of Allegiance, civics classes, and so forth, and in early adulthood through military service itself. In revolutionary Nicaragua, SMP training was one device to help promote new values. In addition, the actual process of participating in, and sacrificing for, the defense of the homeland gave many draftees, if they did not already have it, a real stake in and commitment to the revolution. This was of considerable political importance because by the end of 1989, an estimated 170,000 young people—both rural and urban and of all social classes—would be veterans of the SMP.[28]

The strategy of deploying regular troops to confront the contras in the countryside actually began in the region of Jalapa, on the Honduran border, in June 1983, several months before the creation of the SMP.[29] However, the draft and the resultant expansion in the number of active-duty personnel allowed this strategy to become standard practice in the mid-1980s. In the period from late 1983 to 1985, new draftees were organized into twelve irregular warfare battalions (BLI), which from 1985 to 1987 "were augmented by approximately seventeen to nineteen light hunter battalions (BCLs) and forty-nine permanent territorial companies (COPETES)."[30] These new units were trained to take the war to the enemy in the countryside under very difficult conditions, and they proved to be very effective in doing so. Ironically, the Sandinistas apparently had borrowed much of their new strategy directly from U.S. Army counterinsurgency manuals and practice.[31]

By 1983, the Sandinistas had also hit upon a technique for further isolating the contras by accelerating land distribution and giving arms to the rural poor. From 1983 on, hundreds of thousands of AK-47s were passed out to civilians, mainly in rural areas. In addition, Agricultural Self-Defense Cooperatives were set up in rural areas affected by the war. Groups of peasants—many of whom had been displaced by the contra war—were given land, some social and technical services, and "AKs" with which to defend themselves and their new belongings. These folk, too, had come to have a stake in the revolution and a motive for defending it.

Another tactic was to deal flexibly with the enemy. Late in 1983, the government declared an amnesty program through which contras could lay down their arms and reincorporate themselves—without penalty—into civilian society. Over the years this policy produced a slow but important sapping of contra strength. Amnesty and flexibility were especially effective in dealing with indigenous contras on the Atlantic Coast, where a process of autonomy negotiations had also begun late in 1983. By the mid-1980s, groups of Mískito contras had shown interest in accepting amnesty but with one important condition; that they be allowed to keep their weapons after crossing the Río Coco to resettle in their traditional villages on the Nicaraguan side. The Sandinistas accepted the proposal, and in an ironic twist of history, hundreds of U.S.-trained and -equipped contras were soon incorporated into Nicaraguan government's security forces guarding the Río Coco region. Later, one of their commanders, "Comandante Ráfaga," would be named to the Sandinista list of candidates running in his region in the 1990 election.

A final tactic that helped turn the tide of the war was the decision to make occasional limited incursions into Honduras in "hot pursuit" of contras operating out of that territory. The policy had actually begun in the fall of 1982 when, in the words of the 1984 *Army Intelligence Survey*, the "Sandinista armed forces announced that border troops would be formally instructed to pursue contra bands into Honduras for approximately 1/2 kilometer. The Sandinistas considered this border area a 'no man's land' because of the official withdrawal of [Honduran] government personnel from the area."[32] The right of hot pursuit is enshrined in international law. Nevertheless, for the Sandinistas its use was risky because the United States, especially in the case of major incursions in March and December 1986 and March 1988, was quick to sensationalize each of these limited-objective operations into an "invasion" of Honduras, thus seemingly proving the long-term U.S. claim that the Sandinistas were out to subjugate their neighbors. Risky or not, the policy paid off. Almost immediately after the major Sandinista offensive, which culminated in the March 1988 incursion, the contras entered into peace talks with the Sandinistas in Sapoá, Nicaragua. These resulted in an eighteen-month period of reduced confrontation under a cease-fire unilaterally declared by the Nicaraguan government.

By the late 1980s, the various strategies and tactics that the Sandinistas had developed from 1983 on in their effort to win the war had borne fruit. The war itself, which had peaked in the mid-1980s, had diminished through 1987 and had all but evaporated when the Esquipulas peace process began to take effect in August of that year.

The Post-Reagan Period

A number of factors converged in 1989 to produce some interesting changes in the Nicaraguan armed forces. One of these, as detailed in

Chapter 12, was the harsh austerity program implemented by the government in its efforts to reverse the economic crisis. As part of this program, the military budget was slashed by approximately 30 percent.[33] This move was made safer and more palatable to defense-minded planners by a second phenomenon: the petering out of the contra war. A third factor, the warming of relations between the United States and the Soviet Union, led to another important change: the cutting off of Soviet arms transfers to Nicaragua, beginning early in 1989. An additional matter, the internal and international negotiations regarding the conditions and rules governing the Nicaraguan elections of 1990, led to yet another change; an agreement by the government of Nicaragua in August 1989 to suspend the SMP draft at least until after the elections. Thus, with the war all but over, Nicaragua in 1989 appeared to be headed back in the direction of a normal peacetime military posture. The only constraint on that trajectory was the possible continued existence of the contras, which, in turn, would depend on the will of the Bush administration. But it was hoped that a clear Sandinista victory in the elections of 1990, verified by a wide array of international observers, would make it virtually impossible for Washington to justify continued maintenance of the contras.

The surprise victory of the U.S.-backed candidate, Violeta Barrios de Chamorro, in 1990 elections proved to be a double-edged sword for the Sandinista armed forces. Whereas, on the one hand, it provided the final impetus for the disarmament and demobilization of the contras, on the other, it delivered the country's military apparatus into the hands of an openly anti-Sandinista administration that had vowed to de-Sandinize the country's military establishment. This situation created some tense and explosive moments during the final two months of the Sandinista government and the first months of the Chamorro administration.

The demobilization of the contras was an arduous process. At first, though both Violeta Chamorro and Daniel Ortega immediately called for the contras to lay down their arms, the latter refused to do so, arguing that they could not trust the Sandinista armed forces to respect their lives. Though ever since it began in 1983, the amnesty process had been highly successful, with virtually no incidents of government or civilian abuse of demobilized contras, the U.S. government and press were almost unanimous in echoing this contra concern. Accordingly, an elaborate process, supervised by the United Nations and the Organization of American States, was set into motion whereby the contras (without giving up their arms) were allowed to move into Nicaragua to designated "security zones," where they would eventually undergo demobilization. There they recruited additional troops, passed out additional arms and managed to build their force to around 20,000—a manpower level never before reached even during the height of the war. They then proceeded to violate one demobilization accord after another until the Chamorro government agreed to disarm many pro-Sandinista peasant cooperatives and set aside huge, relatively unpopulated areas of the country for conversion into "development poles," where the contras could, if they wished, settle and, with considerable government and international financial support, engage in economic activities ranging from farming to lumbering. Within those poles, police units composed of former contras would be the only security force present. In June 1990, with great fanfare, lavish words of praise from Chamorro, and the compliments and blessing of Cardinal Miguel Obando y Bravo, the contras signed demobilization papers, turned in many of their weapons, and dispersed either to their original homes or to the new development poles.

It was no secret that the contras as well as many of the members of peasant cooperatives had held back weapons. Indeed, late in June, former president Daniel Ortega commented—with obvious hyperbole—"Here, everyone has hidden arms."[34] However, Ortega, as well as other top Sandinistas,[35] the leadership of Chamorro government,[36] and representatives of the UN and the OAS peace-keeping forces,[37] expressed confidence that the war was over. As former vice president Sergio Ramírez put it: "There are problems [with the contras] but I would not say they are serious. Now the contra [effort]—as a military project—no longer exists."[38] And famous FSLN guerrilla leader Comandante Omar Cabezas commented, "We won peace at the cost of losing the government."[39]

But if the Sandinistas were willing to relinquish power in order to achieve peace, they were not eager to commit suicide, either politically or physically. Accordingly, although they recognized Chamorro's right to serve as the commander in chief of the armed forces and were willing to make significant concessions such as allowing the Interior Ministry (including the important State Security forces) to be dismantled, agreeing to have Chamorro take on the title of minister of defense, and accepting the disarmament of large numbers of peasant militia, they were unwilling to see a complete "de-Sandinization" of the armed forces. Their reluctance in this case was well founded. They felt they needed to retain some presence in the military in order to prevent a violent de-Sandinization of the country as a whole. They could not ignore the fact that in the recent history of Latin America, whenever U.S.-backed "national security" states had attempted to restrain or reverse the forces of change, their U.S.-supplied and -advised security forces and associated death squads had routinely engaged in what U.S. advisers euphemistically call "counterterror." These anti-Left programs had cost the lives of more than 150,000 civilians in Guatemala in the decades following the U.S.-engineered overthrow of elected reformist president Jacobo Arbenz in 1954, 50,000 Nicaraguans in the Somoza years, 75,000 Salvadorans in the 1980s, and tens of thousands of citizens each in Argentina, Brazil, and Chile in the period from the late 1960s through the early 1980s.[40]

At first, Chamorro seemed to understand Sandinista concerns. Within hours of her election, she called for the immediate disarmament and demobilization of the contras—seen by the Sandinistas as a potential nucleus for future death squads. In March she reached an accord with the Sandinistas in which she pledged to respect the integrity of the armed forces,[41] and, in April, though she appointed herself minister of defense, she nevertheless agreed to retain Humberto Ortega as head of the army for an indefinite period.

Once she came to office, however, things began to change. In June, a 50 percent reduction of the armed forces (from around 82,000 to 41,000), to take place within one year, was announced. That, in itself, was not alarming: In 1989, the FSLN had decided on such cuts, even assuming they would win the elections in 1990. Furthermore, the 41,000 would come largely in the area of draftees (SMP) and militia. The professional army would remain essentially intact.[42]

Later the same month, however, Chamorro announced that she hoped to demobilize the remaining 41,000, whom she called *militantes*. Nicaragua was "destined to become a country like Costa Rica, where there ought only to exist a small police force."[43] That "small police force" was already being shaped: A force of less than 10,000 was being increased by at least 50 percent through the recruitment of new troops, in some cases demobilized contras.[44]

As this was being written it was unclear how the issue of the armed forces would be resolved. Clearly, Chamorro's plans, if implemented, would violate not only the transition agreement but also the Nicaraguan constitution itself. Perhaps she had been speaking off the top of her head, expressing wish rather than hard intention. When questioned about the matter, Daniel Ortega expressed confidence that she would be restrained by the constitution.[45]

Myths and Distortions

Having traced what, from frequent and close observation, I feel to be the reality of Sandinista military history, it seems obligatory to make some parting observations about the abundant myths and distortions related to this matter. From the moment the Reagan administration came to office, it devoted tremendous energy and imagination in an attempt to demonize the Sandinistas in the eyes of the world and, especially, the U.S. public.[46] Distortions and complete fabrications regarding the Nicaraguan military were an important component of this propaganda campaign. Within a year, for instance, the Sandinista military was being depicted as a bloodthirsty gestapo, which among other things was committing "genocide" against Nicaragua's indigenous population. On one occasion, this dramatic, but largely groundless, charge was documented at a press conference by Secretary of State Alexander Haig with a grizzly photo that he claimed showed Sandinista troops burning heaps of bodies of Mískito Indians. To Haig's embarrassment, the *Gamma* photographer who had taken the photograph (of Red Cross workers disposing of corpses during the Nicaraguan insurrection several years earlier) soon went public to denounce the misuse of his work.[47]

On other occasions Sandinista limited-objective incursions into remote border regions of Honduras in hot pursuit of the contras were deceptively depicted as invasions threatening the Honduran government. On at least one occasion, in order to dramatize this interpretation, the U.S. embassy in Tegucigalpa arranged for reporters to fly to "the front" (actually nowhere near where the incursion had taken place), where suspiciously bloated corpses of Sandinista soldiers were displayed and depicted as "enemy" casualties that· had just then resulted from a heated battle between the Honduran government troops and Nicaraguan "invaders." Months later, a contra officer (who had in the meantime defected) explained to one reporter who had been present at that display that the corpses the press had been shown were actually of Nicaraguan soldiers killed not by the Hondurans but by the contras a couple of days before.[48]

The Reagan and Bush administrations also charged Nicaragua with developing a military establishment that far exceeded its legitimate security needs. To sustain that argument U.S. spokespersons and apologists often resorted to ingenious verbal sleights of hand such as that of lumping anyone in Nicaragua with access to a weapon—including hundreds of thousands of militia members, agricultural self-defense cooperative members, and so forth—under the category of "armed forces" or, even more deceptively, the Sandinista "army." Rarely did they discuss the much more modest size of the active-duty EPS, which, as noted above, would be considered inadequate by Pentagon standards.

Probably the most dramatic example of a deliberate and successful lumping of categories in order to create the impression of excessive Sandinista militarism occurred late in 1987. A high-ranking functionary in the Nicaraguan Ministry of Defense, Maj. Roger Miranda Bengochéa, had defected to the United States in October of that year. Given asylum and a reported "$800,000 from the U.S. government in rewards, resettlement assistance, and a contract for unspecified services,"[49] he was debriefed for over a month before being presented to the press. Miranda made a number of damning charges against his former colleagues, but the most dramatic was that even if the contra war ended completely as they expected, the Sandinistas intended to expand their military force to between 500,000 and 600,000 persons by the early 1990s. The impact of the Miranda revelations was sensational. Typical of most U.S. media coverage of the event, the *Washington Post* headlined: "Nicaragua Describes Major Arms Buildup: Defense Minister Projects Force of 600,000." Congress also reacted as apparently desired. A stalled contra aid bill was hastily passed before the members departed for Christmas recess. What was missed for a while, in all the commotion, was the crucially important fact that the stolen Sandinista planning document out of which Miranda and the U.S. government selectively drew their information, though it did indeed speak of people with access to arms numbering between 500,000 and 600,000, nevertheless stressed that the reason for somewhat increasing the number of arms available to civilians, militia, and reservists was to make possible a significant *reduction* in the size of the standing army.[50]

Finally, throughout the Reagan/Bush years, administration officials argued publicly that the real purpose of the Sandinista armed force was to commit aggression against other countries in the region. Yet while they were publicly stating this, they were receiving secret intelligence briefings and analyses that showed the opposite. In September 1982 the Reagan administration was embarrassed when a subcommittee of the House Committee on Intelligence issued a staff report criticizing U.S. intelligence performance in Central America and noting in particular that while U.S. intelligence services were publicly trumpeting Nicaragua's supposed offensive capabilities and intentions, there had been "classified briefings whose analytical judgments about Nicaragua's intentions were quite distinct from those that appeared implicit in the briefings on the buildup."[51] And the classified 1984 U.S. *Army Intelligence Survey* cited earlier said flatly that "the primary mission of the Nicaraguan Armed Forces is the *protection of the country from external aggression*, while also maintaining internal security and order during the consolidation of the Sandinista Revolution." Later, the same document reiterated that "regular activities by counterrevolutionary groups have made the *protection of the country from external aggression* the primary concern."[52]

These internal findings were also reinforced by those of important U.S. military experts such as Lt. Col. Edward L. King (U.S. Army, Ret.) who, after considerable field investigation, declared that "to believe seriously that the infantry-heavy, logistically weak Sandinista armed forces genuinely threaten Costa Rica, Honduras or El Salvador ignores the facts of geography, rational military tactics, military logistics, force structures and economics."[53]

Conclusion

During its incumbency, the revolutionary government had built a military force that was clearly defensive in character. That force had successfully defended the revolution against a two-pronged external threat. It had contained, and all but destroyed, the U.S.-sponsored contra insurgency while maintaining sufficient strength around strategic populated areas to dissuade the United States from staging a direct invasion such as those inflicted during the same period on Grenada and Panama. Furthermore, it did all of this without raising its active-duty armed forces even to the size that the U.S. Pentagon itself would ordinarily recommend to contain an irregular force threat of the size Nicaragua faced. This was accomplished by entrusting part of the responsibility of defending the nation to ordinary civilians.

As this was being written, the future of the Nicaraguan armed forces was unclear. In 1989, various factors had allowed or motivated cutbacks in the military. More had been planned by the Sandinistas had they won the 1990 election. Ironically, the surprise UNO victory in that election eventually made possible the demobilization of the contras. However, it brought to power a conservative, U.S.-sponsored government that quickly made significant changes in the armed forces and promised eventually to eliminate the army itself and to replace it with a "small police force," expanded through the recruitment of former contras. The pursuit of such an objective was almost certain to bring conflict and more bloodshed.

Notes

I would like to thank the Center for International Policy and the National Security Archive, both of Washington, D.C., for invaluable assistance in obtaining some of the U.S. government documents upon which this chapter is based.

1. Tomás Borge, as interviewed on June 26 by scholar-participants in the 1985 Latin American Studies Association Research seminar in Nicaragua.

2. See U.S. Congress, Senate, Staff Report of the Select Committee to Study Governmental Operations with Respect to United States Intelligence, Covert Action in Chile (Washington, D.C.: Government Printing Office, December 18, 1975); and Armando Uribe, The Black Book of American Intervention in Chile (Boston: Beacon Press, 1974).

3. I hitchhiked from the Honduran border to Managua on July 22 and left via the same route by bus and hitchhiking on July 26. My impressions of that historic period are recorded in "Images of the Nicaraguan Revolution," in Nicaragua in Revolution, Thomas W. Walker, ed. (New York: Praeger Publishers, 1982), pp. 81–91.

4. Alejandro Bendaña, Secretary General of the Nicaraguan Foreign Ministry, "The Sandinista Perspective on Central America," as presented in a symposium on "Perspectives on War and Peace in Central America" at Ohio University on November 5, 1988. For the text of all the speeches presented at that symposium see Perspectives on War and Peace in Central America, Sung Ho Kim and Thomas W. Walker, eds., Papers in International Studies (Athens: Ohio University Press, forthcoming).

5. Philip Agee, "El Plán de la CIA en Nicaragua," *La Prensa*, January 2, 1980, pp. 1 and 7.

6. Peter Kornbluh, "The Covert War," in *Reagan Versus the Sandinistas: The Undeclared War on Nicaragua*, Thomas W. Walker, ed. (Boulder, Colo.: Westview Press, 1987), p. 21.

7. See, for instance, Alejandro Bendaña, "The Foreign Policy of the Nicaraguan Revolution," in Walker, ed., *Nicaragua in Revolution*, pp. 319–327, and Sergio Ramírez, "What the Sandinistas Want," *Caribbean Review* 8, no. 3 (Summer 1979), pp. 24–27, 49–52.

8. For more detailed discussion of these matters see Stephen M. Gorman, "The Role of the Revolutionary Armed Forces," in Walker, ed., *Nicaragua in Revolution*, pp. 133–146.

9. The benign behavior of the police—most of whom did not even wear sidearms—occasionally put them into situations in which they were verbally and even physically abused by civilians unaccustomed to their new freedom. In 1981, for instance, I saw a uniformed security officer in a military vehicle in which I was traveling "given the finger" by another motorist after the former carelessly changed lanes without signaling. Such a gesture of disrespect might have been suicidal in the Somoza years. And on various occasions, such as the return to Managua of Miguel Obando y Bravo after his elevation to cardinal in 1985, Sandinista police patiently accepted jeers and stoning from provocateurs in opposition crowds rather than use the force necessary to contain the affronts.

10. Interview with Luis Carrión, "La guerrilla se transforma en ejército regular," *Cuadernos de Marcha 1*, January-February 1980, pp. 99–100, as quoted in Gorman, "The Role of the Revolutionary Armed Forces," p. 121.

11. Excerpts from State Department and Pentagon, *Congressional Presentation Document*, Security Assistance Programs, FY 1981, as reproduced in Robert Matthews, "The Limits of Friendship: Nicaragua and the West," *NACLA Report on the Americas* 19, no. 3 (May/June 1985), p. 24.

12. Richard Millett, *Guardians of the Dynasty: A History of the U.S.-Created Guardia Nacional de Nicaragua and the Somoza Family* (Maryknoll, N.Y.: Orbis Press, 1977), p. 252.

13. Col. Alden M. Cunningham, "The Sandinista Military: Current Capacities, Future Roles and Missions," a paper prepared for the conference on "Nicaragua: Prospects for a Democratic Outcome," sponsored by the Orkand Corporation (under contract with the CIA), October 12, 1988, Washington, D.C., p. 14.

14. During my short stay in Managua during the first week after the triumph, I witnessed one firefight with diehard guardsmen and heard several others from a distance. I also heard FSLN announcements on the radio that any former guardsmen caught sniping and committing acts of sabotage would be shot (*passar por el fuego*). During the entire first decade of the revolutionary government, this short-lived emergency measure was the only documentable example of official approval of an exception to the FSLN's immediate blanket abolition of the death penalty. Atrocities involving violation of the right to life carried out by individual armed forces officers or soldiers did occasionally take place, but the world's major human rights organizations were in agreement that they did not appear to be government sanctioned.

15. The largest semiautonomous armed revolutionary group was the People's Anti-Somocista Militias (MILPAS). According to Marvin Ortega, at the time a member of the MILPAS High Command, that organization, which at one point had controlled up to 2,000 troops, had played a central role in the fighting in and around Managua. Distrustful of the MILPAS's strength and its Maoist ideology, the Sandinistas moved within the first few weeks to round up its weapons, close its newspaper, El Pueblo, and jail some of its leaders, including Ortega. Nevertheless, rightly or wrongly, the banditry occurring in wealthy neighborhoods was routinely attributed to "the MILPAS" well into 1980. (Information from a conversation I had with Marvin Ortega in Ottowa, Canada, on October 7, 1989.)

16. From an extended conversation I had with businessman Antonio Lacayo, in March 1981. Lacayo, perhaps the country's wealthiest agro-industrialist and certainly no admirer of the Sandinistas, had been shocked by the "fact finder's" attitude.

17. Eddie Adams, "Exiles Rehearse for the Day They Hope Will Come," Parade Magazine, March 15, 1981, pp. 4-6.

18. Council on Hemispheric Affairs, press release, "Reagan Administration Taking Two Track Approach to Nicaragua: Talk Peace, Prepare for War," August 30, 1984.

19. Department of State and Department of Defense, The Challenge to Democracy in Central America (Washington, D.C.: Government Printing Office, June 1986), p. 38.

20. If anything, even these figures may be inflated. For instance, an initially secret, but subsequently released, Army Intelligence Survey of the Nicaraguan armed forces published in 1984 stated that "the EPS consists of approximately 30,000 troops." Department of the Army, United States Army Intelligence and Threat Analysis Center, United States Army Intelligence and Security Command, Army Intelligence Survey: Nicaragua, Volume 3—Armed Forces (U) (Washington, D.C.: Department of the Army, May 1984), p. 2-1. For other reliable information about Sandinista military strength see International Institute for Strategic Studies, The Military Balance, 1983-84 (London, 1983), p. 112, and The Military Balance, 1988-89 (London, 1988), p. 196.

21. Department of the Army, Army Intelligence Survey, p. 2-3.

22. Mary B. Vanderlaan, Revolution and Foreign Policy in Nicaragua (Boulder, Colo.: Westview Press, 1986), p. 277.

23. Department of State and Department of Defense, The Challenge to Democracy, p. 20.

24. Vanderlaan, Revolution and Foreign Policy, pp. 288-289.

25. Most of this information on arms is drawn from either personal observation or Jozef Goldblat and Victor Millan, The Honduras-Nicaragua Conflict Prospectives for Arms Control in Central America (Solna, Sweden: Stockholm International Peace Research Institute, 1984); Department of Defense, Soviet Military Power, 1984 (Washington, D.C.: Government Printing Office, 1984); or [Department of State], "Soviet Bloc Military Equipment Supplied to Nicaragua, July 1979–December 1988," typed photocopy [1989].

26. Goldblat and Millan, The Honduras-Nicaragua Conflict Prospectives, pp. 526 and 532; and Department of Defense, Soviet Military Power, 1984, p. 122.

27. Department of the Army, Army Intelligence Survey, p. 1-28.

28. This estimate was prepared by Lt. Col. Rosa Pasos, press officer for the Sandinista People's Army, at my request, on June 30, 1989.

29. Department of the Army, Army Intelligence Survey, p. 1-28.

30. Cunningham, "The Sandinista Military," p. 6.

31. Ibid. and Lt. Col. Edward L. King (Ret.), The Nicaraguan Armed Forces: A Second Look (Boston: Unitarian Universalist Committee, 1985), p. 8.

32. Department of the Army, Army Intelligence Survey, p. 1-28.

33. Interview with Lt. Col. Rosa Pasos, press officer for the Sandinista People's Army, June 29, 1989.

34. From a lengthy interview of Ortega by members of the 1990 Latin American Studies Association (LASA) Research Seminar in Nicaragua on June 30, 1990.

35. The LASA Seminar received such assurances in interviews with former vice president Sergio Ramírez (June 18, 1990), Comandante Omar Cabezas (June 19, 1990), Comandante Luis Carrión (June 25, 1990), Lt. Col. Rosa Pasos, chief spokesperson of the EPS (June 26, 1990), and Alejandro Bendaña, former general secretary of the Nicaraguan Foreign Ministry (June 26, 1990).

36. Numerous statements by Chamorro and her top aides, La Prensa, June 1990.

37. LASA interviews with Captain Gonzalo Gamboa of ONUCA, of the Military Observers of the United Nations for Central America (June 21, 1990), and Arturo Garzón, chief of the OAS International Commission of Support and Verification (CIAV-OAS) for the peace effort for Region I (June 21, 1990). Both interviews were conducted in Estelí.

38. LASA interview with Ramírez.

39. LASA interview with Cabezas.

40. For excellent discussion and thorough documentation of U.S. promotion of "counterterror" in two Central American states see Michael McClintock, The American Connection, Vol. 1, State Terror and Popular Resistance in El Salvador, and Vol. 2, State Terror and Popular Resistance in Guatemala (London: Zed Books, 1985).

41. From the LASA interview with Ramírez.

42. All the preceding information in this paragraph is from the LASA interview with Lt. Col. Rosa Pasos.

43. "Desarme Total, Presidenta Chamorro: Nicaragua será un país sin armas," La Prensa, June 27, 1990, pp. 1 and 12.

44. "Contras, nuevos policías: 150 desalzados a imponer la ley," La Prensa, June 28, 1990, pp. 1 and 12.

45. Conversation with Ortega.

46. For more detail see Eldon Kenworthy, "Selling the Policy," in Walker, ed., Reagan Versus the Sandinistas, pp. 159–181, and Thomas W. Walker, "Nicaraguan-U.S. Friction: The First Four Years, 1979–1983," in Kenneth M. Coleman and George C. Herring, eds., The Central American Crisis: Sources of Conflict and The Failure of U.S. Policy (Wilmington, Del.: Scholarly Resources, 1985), pp. 157–186.

47. Council on Hemispheric Affairs, press release, "Miskito Atrocity Stories Termed 'Grossly Exaggerated' and 'Groundless,'" March 5, 1982, p. 2.

48. Fred Kiel, United Press International News Director for Mexico and Central America, "Covering Central America," a paper delivered at an inter-

national symposium on "Perspectives on War and Peace in Central America," Ohio University, November 5, 1988.

49. From unidentified "congressional sources," as cited in Tom Kentworthy and Don Phillips, "U.S. to Give Defector $800,000," *Washington Post*, February 4, 1988, pp. A1 and A32.

50. The document in question is "Primary Guidelines for Functionally Improving, Strengthening and Equipping the Sandinista People's Army (SPA) for the Period 1988–1990 and Preliminary Guidelines for the Five-Year Period 1991–1995 (Diriangen I–Diriangen II)," typed copy dated October 1987. For a good expose of the Miranda revelations see Robert Parry, "Showtime for Major Miranda," *Nation*, January 30, 1988, pp. 126–128.

51. Staff Report, Subcommittee on Oversight and Evaluation, Permanent Select Committee on Intelligence, "U.S. Intelligence Performance on Central America: Achievements and Selected Instances of Concern," September 12, 1982, mimeographed, p. 43.

52. Department of the Army, *Army Intelligence Survey*, p. 1-5 (emphasis added).

53. King, *The Nicaraguan Armed Forces*, p. 9.

FIVE

The FSLN as Ruling Party

GARY PREVOST

The Sandinista Front for National Liberation (FSLN) carried out a political and military insurrection in Nicaragua for almost twenty years under extremely repressive conditions and with a cadre of only about 1,000. It achieved relatively few successes until just a few months prior to its decisive victory in 1979. During the period of Sandinista rule, 1979–1990, the government successfully resisted an insurgent force sponsored by the United States; at the same time, it carried out a program of significant social, political, and economic reforms. This chapter will analyze the evolution of Sandinista political philosophy as well as the growth of the FSLN as a party in power.

FSLN Philosophy

How could the political philosophy of the FSLN be characterized at the time the movement took power in 1979? To what degree did the FSLN shift its perspective during its ten years in power? In my judgment, the FSLN entered power as a vanguard, political-military organization that based itself on three pillars: Marxism (as interpreted by Lenin, Mao, Ho Chi Minh, and Carlos Fonseca), the revolutionary and class-conscious ideas and practices of Augusto Sandino, and the inspiration of the successful Cuban revolution. Studies of the Sandinista movement generally agree on the importance of these three primary factors, plus several secondary ones, particularly, liberation theology.[1] Attempts to place relative weights on the three pillars fail largely because of their complicated interaction. In the late 1980s Sandinista leaders, in their public speeches and official interviews, emphasized the connection to Sandino and downplayed the role of Marxism in their development. On the other extreme, opponents of the Sandinista revolution stressed the FSLN's connections to the Soviet Union and Cuba and to Marxist-Leninist ideas.[2] A more accurate assessment of the development of the FSLN's political philosophy would include a significant role for both

Sandino and Marxism, plus acknowledgment of the influence of liberation theology.

The leaders of the FSLN often stated that the philosophy of the revolution is embodied in three principles: political pluralism, a mixed economy, and nonalignment.[3] And in fact, when the Sandinistas were in power, .they put into practice the political philosophy that they enunciated.

Nicaragua's political pluralism could be seen in the legal existence of twenty-one political parties in addition to the Sandinistas and the right of these parties to function in the public arena and to put forward candidates in national and local elections.[4] This pluralism was visible in the debates and decisions of the Nicaraguan National Assembly and was spelled out in the Nicaraguan constitution, drafted by the assembly and effective in 1987. Although suspensions of civil liberties occurred during the 1980s, the Nicaraguan system actually showed considerable tolerance, given the fact that the country was under attack from a foreign power. The transfer of formal governmental power from the Sandinistas to the National Opposition Union (UNO) following the 1990 elections is further proof of the pluralist nature of the Nicaraguan system established under Sandinista leadership.

Nicaragua has a mixed economy. The leaders of the FSLN asserted that their adoption of a mixed economy was strategic, not tactical. They stated that they were not opposed to socialism in principle, but rather that socialism was impractical in Nicaragua and would not work. As a result, the Nicaraguan government's policy included both a considerable involvement of the state in the economy and a state partnership with the private business community to stimulate production. Sandinista economic policy was also quite flexible, exemplified by the shift toward small private farmers in the agrarian reform program and the government-imposed austerity program in 1988 (see Chapter 12).

The third principle of Sandinista revolutionary philosophy, nonalignment, refers to the foreign policy stance of the government, as both a guideline for foreign relations and a specific organizational affiliation. Less than two months after the new government was established, the leaders decided to join the Nonaligned Movement (NAM). That decision was natural because the revolution had origins in an anticolonial national liberation struggle, and the NAM, although it seeks to avoid hegemonic domination by any superpower, is not "neutral" but vigorously supports anticolonial struggles. Nicaragua was an active member of the organization for the entire decade of the 1980s and hosted a ministerial meeting in 1983. Moreover, the NAM proved to be an important source of support for Nicaragua in its struggle with the United States.

However, Nicaragua's concept of itself as a nonaligned nation was not limited to membership in the NAM. For Nicaragua, nonalignment meant having firm relations throughout the world, with the socialist countries, including both the USSR and the People's Republic of China; the developed capitalist nations, including the United States; and the rest of the Third World. With the important exception of the United States, Nicaragua under the Sandinistas was generally successful in pursuing this strategy (see Chapter 14).

Marxism-Leninism

Crucial to an analysis of the political philosophy of the FSLN is an assessment of the role of Marxist and Leninist ideas in shaping the political action of the Sandinistas. Bayardo Arce, in an interview, said that Sandinismo is the application of Marxism-Leninism to the Nicaraguan reality. In response to the question, "What is the difference between a Marxist and a Sandinista?" Arce replied: "In Nicaragua there needn't be a difference. A good Marxist is no more than a man who applies a scientific-social conception to a concrete reality. A Marxist in Nicaragua is necessarily a Sandinista."[5] However, Arce also noted that Sandinism's embrace of Marxist and Leninist ideas does not mean that Nicaragua emulates the Soviet Union, Cuba, or Vietnam. In 1983 Víctor Tirado, member of the Joint National Directorate, was explicit in acknowledging the debt of the Sandinistas to Marx and Lenin: "Marxism for the Sandinistas was a complete revelation. The discovery of a new world. . . . Through Marxism we came to know Sandino, our history, and our roots. . . . We value his writings as we do Lenin's, as a guide for action, as a creative instrument that must be continually recreated."[6]

It is clear that Marxist ideas were essential in the formation of the political ideas of the leading cadre of the FSLN, from Carlos Fonseca and Tomás Borge to Daniel Ortega and Jaime Wheelock. Fonseca was probably the most important in shaping the direction of the FSLN because he was the first of his generation to draw on the rich revolutionary experience of Nicaragua and link it with the international workers' and peasants' movement, particularly the Cuban revolution. Tomás Borge, reflecting on Fonseca's contributions, in a 1986 interview with the Argentine magazine *Crisis*, had this to say: "Fonseca was the first Marxist in Nicaragua, the most lucid Marxist. . . . He was a student of Marxism, not a student of manuals but of science. He was no stranger to the works of Mariategui [a Peruvian Marxist] nor world revolutionary experience."[7] In declaring Fonseca to be Nicaragua's first Marxist, Borge explicitly rejected the validity of the Nicaraguan Socialist party's avowed Marxism as being "mired in a policy of class collaboration, of support to the bourgeoisie and to U.S. imperialism."[8]

Despite the role of Marxism and Leninism in shaping the views of the FSLN leadership, it should not receive exclusive focus in a study of the Nicaraguan revolutionary experience. Arce, in another interview, credited two other historical currents as being essential to understanding contemporary Nicaragua: Christianity and nationalism. According to him, the convergence of three historical currents in Sandinism suggests that the revolutionary cadre of the FSLN came to the movement from different paths—some from a Marxist-Leninist, socialist inspiration, others from Christian activism, and others from a nationalist, anti-imperialist perspective—but all agreed on the program of the FSLN.[9]

Christianity

If we examine the issue of Christians in the FSLN, we find that there were basically three relevant types among them. (1) There were those who come from a Christian background (e.g., Luis Carrión) and who demonstrated sensitivity toward Christians and expressed Christian values but who eventually ceased to be practicing Christians.[10] (2) There were socially committed Christians, such as Tomás Borge and Ernesto Cardenal, who were members of the FSLN and who believed that Marxism and Christianity are fully compatible.[11] (3) A third type, represented by people such as Sixto Ulloa, a Baptist minister and member of the FSLN parliamentary delegation, was more in the mainstream of liberation theology. This group drew important ideas from Marxism but would clearly disagree with Ernesto Cardenal's statement that "to be a good Christian, you must be a Marxist."[12] All three of these groups existed within and around the periphery of the FSLN, providing much of its diversity and contributing to the vitality of debate. The Christian influence in the revolution could be found in the abolition of the death penalty, the generous attitude toward the members of Somoza's National Guard (including the release of the last National Guard war criminals early in 1989), the inclusion of several international human rights covenants within the Nicaraguan constitution, and the eventual political accommodation with the indigenous peoples of the Atlantic Coast. It should be noted that these influences contributed to widespread international approval of the Nicaraguan revolution.

Most important, the highly divergent paths that led people to the Sandinista movement meant that the FSLN did not follow the lines of a classic, Marxist-Leninist party as in the Soviet Union or Cuba. I have consciously referred to a Sandinista philosophy rather than ideology because there was very little "officialism" in Nicaragua under the Sandinistas. Sandinista philosophy continued to grow and evolve as the revolution faced new challenges. Probably the greatest challenge was the construction of a party to govern and lead the country.

The FSLN Party

FSLN leaders came to power in July 1979 after the party's brief, rapid rise to prominence. The organization was founded in July 1961 by Tomás Borge, Carlos Fonseca, and Silvio Mayorga. The FSLN had its roots in the long struggle against the Somoza family dynasty and the domination of the country by North American political and economic interests. The front took its name from Augusto César Sandino, the legendary Nicaraguan guerrilla who led the fight against the U.S. Marines and the Nicaraguan National Guard from 1927 until 1933.[13] However, Sandino alone did not shape the thinking of the founders of the FSLN. Besides Marxist ideas and the philosophy and practice of the Cuban Revolution, which heavily influenced Fonseca, he and Borge were also deeply impressed by the long history of armed resistance to North American dominance of Nicaragua, culminating in the assassination of the elder Somoza in 1956 by Rigoberto López Pérez.

In their early years, each of the founders of the FSLN was active in the Moscow-oriented, Nicaraguan Socialist party. Borge and Fonseca worked in its youth organization while they were students at the law school in León. Along with Marxism, Borge and Fonseca studied the history of Nicaragua's struggles against foreign domination. Most important, they became familiar with the ideas and actions of Sandino. Fonseca was inspired by his strong class consciousness and internationalism. Later Fonseca met Santos López, a veteran of Sandino's army, who became the living link between the revolutionary generations of Sandino and Fonseca.

In 1957 Fonseca traveled to the Soviet Union and wrote *A Nicaraguan in Moscow*, a positive, almost uncritical view of the Soviet model of socialism. By 1959, however, he had begun to be disillusioned by the reformist approaches of the PSN and to search for a new vehicle for change based in the methodology of armed struggle. Fonseca saw in the July 26th Movement in Cuba the playing out of the revolutionary traditions of Sandino. Castro's triumph also showed that victory was possible. As Borge said at the time: "The victory of the armed struggle in Cuba, more than a joy, was the lifting of innumerable curtains, a flash of light that shone beyond the simple and boring dogmas of the time. Fidel was, for us, the resurrection of Sandino."[14]

In the ensuing years Fonseca and Borge formally broke with the PSN; in July 1961 together with Mayorga, they formed the FSLN at a meeting in Tegucigalpa, Honduras. Under the strong influence of Ché Guevara and Sandino, the leaders of the FSLN proceeded to carry out a guerrilla warfare strategy. They invoked the *foco* theory of revolutionary warfare, based largely on the Cuban, and to a lesser degree on Sandino's, experiences. The FSLN sought to establish a primarily military base in the mountains of northern Nicaragua from which they could launch hit-and-run attacks against Somoza's National Guard. As happened with other *foco* efforts in Latin America at the time, the FSLN had very little success. However, unlike other groups, the FSLN learned quickly from its mistakes and by the mid-1960s was also doing significant political work in the urban areas. Nevertheless, after the organization's guerrilla units were largely defeated at Pancasán in 1967, the organization was successfully marginalized and shut out of Nicaraguan political life by Somoza's National Guard.

In spite of their often heroic efforts, there was almost no FSLN movement in Nicaragua in the early 1970s. Most of its cadre were dead, jailed, or in exile. The appeal of the FSLN remained strong in key sectors such as the students, but the actual membership of the party was a mere several dozen people. However, the catastrophic earthquake of 1972 and Somoza's brutal and corrupt response to it created important new opportunities for the opposition. The FSLN reemerged in dramatic fashion when, in December 1974, thirteen Sandinista commandos invaded an elite Christmas party and took several of Somoza's closest friends hostage. The FSLN succeeded in gaining the release of numerous political prisoners, including future president Daniel Ortega, and signaled to the country that they were again a force to be reckoned with. However, the wave of repression that followed the 1974 attack almost destroyed the FSLN's small guerrilla base, and the party lost many of its key cadre, including Carlos Fonseca, who was killed in 1976. Somoza did win a military victory over the FSLN in this period, but his repression severely undermined his political position at home and abroad.

Somoza's counterattack succeeded in dividing the beleaguered FSLN. The Prolonged Popular War (GPP) faction, led by Borge, favored the continuation of the long-term, rural-based strategy. In 1975, the GPP was challenged by the Proletarian Tendency (TP) group, under the leadership of Jaime Wheelock. Educated abroad and heavily influenced by the events in Allende's Chile, Wheelock argued in a more traditional Marxist sense that the Nicaraguan working class had grown strong enough to become the primary focus of Sandinista political work. In October 1975 the Wheelock group was expelled from the FSLN by the dominant GPP.

The Tercerista (insurrectionalist) faction emerged after the TP split. Led by Daniel and Humberto Ortega, the Terceristas argued that the time was right for tactical alliances with all those elements, including businessmen, that were moving into opposition to the Somoza regime. In 1977 the Terceristas began to implement their strategy and late that year formed Los Doce ("The Twelve"), a committee of prominent businessmen and cultural and religious figures. These people called for the resignation of Somoza and the inclusion of the FSLN in a provisional government. As the opposition to Somoza became widespread and social unrest grew, the FSLN, though still small in numbers, was at the center of resistance to the regime. In October 1977 Terceristas carried out a series of armed attacks on National Guard barracks; in August 1978 the FSLN seized control of the National Palace, extracted stinging concessions from the regime, and with crowds cheering them, flew out of the country.

In September 1978, a largely spontaneous national uprising that was put down brutally by Somoza ultimately turned into a political victory for the FSLN. By his actions Somoza demonstrated that he would leave office only by force. The FSLN, as the only Nicaraguan organization prepared to lead an armed insurrection, was thrust into the leadership of the opposition. Although for the September 1978 insurrection, the FSLN could muster no more than 150 armed cadres, between that event and July 1979, the FSLN trained and armed thousands of guerrilla fighters. In March 1979 the three tendencies formally merged. In May the FSLN commenced its final offensive, and by July it had achieved a total victory.

The destruction of the Somoza regime was total: The National Guard collapsed, as did Somoza's ruling Liberal Nationalist party (PLN). Therefore, the revolutionary coalition led by the FSLN could begin with a clean slate. The task the party faced was enormous: the organization of an entirely new state and military apparatus.

At the time of the triumph thousands of Nicaraguans considered themselves to be Sandinistas because they had taken up arms under FSLN leadership, but the party itself had perhaps 500 formal members.[15] The National Directorate of the FSLN decided soon after the triumph to embrace the Leninist concept of a party of limited membership, systematically incorporating only the most committed revolutionary individuals.[16] Throughout the ensuing decade the FSLN described itself— in virtually every document—as a vanguard organization. The usual context of the term is a description of FSLN militants who have led heroic struggles against seemingly insurmountable odds. This flavor is captured in a quote from Dora María Téllez, a Sandinista leader and former guerrilla commander, soon after the overthrow of the Somoza dynasty:

Sandinismo is our national identity. And it is more than that. There are a few men and women who at a given moment in history seem to contain within themselves the dignity of all the people. They are examples to all of us. And then, through the struggle the people as a whole reclaim the strength and dignity shown by a few. That's what Sandinism is to the Nicaraguan people. It is our history, our heroes and heroines, and our people's struggle and victory.[17]

Such a historical stance, taken throughout the long guerrilla war, is consistent with the political-military structure of a primarily guerrilla army, a small, disciplined, and clandestine organization. These characteristics, which typified the FSLN for its first eighteen years, fit quite well with the model articulated in Lenin's *What Is to Be Done*. My task is to analyze to what degree the FSLN has shifted its form of organization since assuming power in July 1979. To answer that question, it will be necessary to describe how the party is currently structured, how it recruits its new members, and how it relates to the other institutions of Nicaraguan society.

Joint National Directorate

The Joint National Directorate has retained its dominant position in the FSLN since the final offensive against Somoza. Its membership of nine was determined in early 1979 when the three factions of the organization came together to form a united front. There is no official or unofficial account of how the nine commanders of the revolution were selected for their positions, but nonetheless they are Daniel and Humberto Ortega, Víctor Tirado (Terceristas); Tomás Borge, Bayardo Arce, and Henry Ruiz (GPP); and Jaime Wheelock, Carlos Núñez, and Luis Carrión (TP). Although there was a great expansion in the membership of the FSLN and much restructuring of the organization at most levels, the National Directorate remained a consistent player throughout the first ten years, with the same membership in 1990 as in 1979. Not all its members had equal weight and prominence over the years, but all remained highly active and there were no defections or purges. Such a record of stability is not common in revolutionary Third World organizations and, in my opinion, is an indicator of the level of both flexibility and unity within the Sandinista Front.[18]

Unfortunately, little can be said about the functioning of the Joint National Directorate. At its meetings, which were apparently quite regular, deliberations were secret. Only final decisions were made public. If differences existed within the directorate, as is likely, they were not known to the outside world. However, given the stability of this leadership, it is plausible to speculate that the differences were manageable and pragmatic, not differences of fundamental principles.

What insight we do have on the functioning of the directorate comes from an interview with Jaime Wheelock published in 1983 under the title *Nicaragua—The Great Challenge*. In response to a question on the functioning of the body, Wheelock stated:

> We have achieved a collective function in which the National Directorate is the leader and each one of us has more or less the same weight. ... Similarly, there is no opinion that could be imposed through external conditions, through the weight the opinion might have, but rather the opinion imposes itself through absolute logic. ... Our opinions are formed as the opinions of a collective. In this way it is harder to be mistaken. ... The experience that we have from all these years is that with rare exceptions, the National Directorate always arrives at consensus. The

system of voting has been an exceptional procedure, and when, in rare opportunities, we reach a vote of five to four, we consider that there is no consensus and we return to discussing the problem.[19]

The Joint National Directorate was officially the highest decision-making body of the FSLN, and its decisions were final and authoritative. Unlike many political organizations that entrust the highest decision-making authority to a periodic, elected national congress, the FSLN did not have such a body. When the structure of the party was formalized in 1980, an official communiqué stated, "The National Directorate is the supreme leadership body and central authority of the FSLN and of the Sandinista People's Revolution."[20] In 1985 an FSLN statement on party organization reiterated the language of the 1980 communiqué describing the authority of the directorate.[21]

In keeping with the collegial style of leadership, the directorate never named a party general secretary. Instead the members of the directorate divided responsibilities in the state and party among themselves. For example, Humberto Ortega became minister of defense and Tomás Borge became interior minister. Jaime Wheelock became head of the agrarian reform program and Henry Ruiz, minister of planning. This arrangement led to what Dennis Gilbert called "rule by a college of caudillos, each with its own minions."[22] Observers noted that the *comandantes* in government tended to surround themselves with members of their own pre-1979 party factions. There is no significant evidence that this form of rule led to major problems, but the Joint National Directorate did declare that "overcoming divisiveness and feudalism" was a basis for the 1985 party reorganization.[23]

The 1985 party reorganization created a five-member executive committee of the directorate, which replaced the smaller Political Commission formed in 1980. The members of the executive committee were Daniel and Humberto Ortega, Wheelock, Arce, and Borge; Daniel Ortega, in addition to becoming president of Nicaragua, was named coordinator of the newly created body. The powers of the committee were strictly circumscribed: It was declared to be solely an administrative body with "none of the attributes" of the directorate.[24] Bayardo Arce, the vice-coordinator of the new body, retained his position as coordinator of the daily activities of the party's central apparatus. In the years immediately after 1985, it did seem that the authority of the full directorate was diminished. Naturally, Daniel Ortega's daily contact with state affairs increased his weight in decision making, but not to the point of reducing the authority of the directorate.

Below the Joint National Directorate there were four levels of party organization: (1) in the national center, the departments of the directorate and the Sandinista Assembly; (2) regional party committees; (3) zonal party committees; and (4) base committees, consisting of party members in workplaces, neighborhoods, or military units.

Sandinista Assembly

The closest thing in the FSLN structure to a party congress was the Sandinista Assembly. As delineated in the 1985 reform structure, the assembly consisted of not more than 105 members. Its role was to advise the Joint National Directorate; it was to meet at least once a year, usually in June. According to an August 3, 1985, communication of the Joint National Directorate: "The Sandinista Assembly is a consultative organ of the party which supports the National Directorate in making the most important decisions of the Revolution."[25] The wording of the description was crucial. The Sandinista Assembly was an important body, but it was not intended for day-to-day administration, and it was clearly subordinate to the Joint National Directorate, which appointed the assembly members and called it into session. The assembly, which had no existence independent of the directorate, was intended to be a sounding board and a pulse taker. The 105 members in 1985 represented a cross section of Nicaraguan society, including not only party functionaries and government officials (who were numerous) but also cultural figures and professionals.[26] Membership in the Sandinista Assembly was clearly one of the highest honors that could be achieved by a Sandinista.

Departments of the Directorate

Beyond the Sandinista Assembly there were numerous other important organizational structures of the FSLN, codified in the August 1985 reorganization. Seven auxiliary departments of the Joint National Directorate were established, with approximately 600 employees: Office of the Secretariat, Department of Organization, Department of Public Relations and Mobilization, Department of Political Education, Department of International Relations, the Department of Finance, and the Institute for the Study of Sandinismo. These institutions, although hampered by a lack of resources, were at the heart of the effort to organize the FSLN into a strong and consistent force in Nicaraguan society.

The Office of the Secretariat had the responsibility of overseeing the work of the other six departments of the Joint National Directorate and the regional apparatus of the party. The Department of Organization was responsible for overseeing the structures of the party at all levels, determining what political assignments were to be given to each member of the party, and recruiting new members to the organization.

It was not easy to be a member of the FSLN. The formal position of the party was that it wanted to recruit the "best workers [and] best peasants," provided that they were interested in the party and willing to subject themselves to its discipline and the responsibilities of membership.[27] The FSLN had two types of members, aspiring militants and militants. A person could gain candidate stature, as an aspiring militant, only through recommendation by an FSLN base committee and approval by zonal and regional party offices. Normally, an aspiring militant had to wait between a year and eighteen months before gaining full party membership. During that time the respective candidates would assess whether they were ready for party membership and the party organization would do likewise. Full membership had to be ratified at all levels of the organization. The overall picture of FSLN recruitment has been chaotic. As we saw, at the time of the revolutionary triumph in 1979, virtually anyone who had participated in the insurrection, at least tens of thousands of people, considered themselves to be Sandinistas. However, as we have seen, the FSLN leadership decided that the FSLN would remain a cadre party—an organization of limited and selective membership. Nevertheless, the party between 1979 and 1981 allowed a process of growth called absorption, not recruitment. Many people were brought without much care or thought into the organization. After 1981 the process became more systematized and the organization grew steadily from 2,000 in 1981 to 12,000 in 1984 and to 20,000 in 1987.[28] With the 1987 membership, the FSLN militants were only about 0.7 percent of the Nicaraguan population, much smaller than vanguard organizations such as the Cuban or Soviet Communist parties. In the wake of the 1990 electoral defeat the party leaders announced their intention of making the FSLN a mass party.

The Department of Public Relations and Mobilization was headed by Carlos Fernando Chamorro, editor of the FSLN newspaper, *Barricada*, the country's largest-circulation daily. This department also oversaw the Sandinista radio and television programming and a wide-ranging publishing program, which during the period of the confrontation with the United States, brought out numerous pamphlets and position papers in English explaining and defending positions of the Nicaraguan government. In that sense it was very much responsible for presenting the Nicaraguan revolution to the outside world. Although the scope of these institutions has probably diminished since the FSLN lost state power, they are likely to remain crucial to the efforts of the Sandinistas in the opposition.

The Department of Political Education ran the internal education for the members of the party, mainly by organizing schools for the cadre and setting their curricula. As of the end of 1989 there was one national cadre school and six regional ones. Courses ranged in length from one to three months. Those who attended were released from their regular political and work assignments in order to concentrate on their studies. Selection for the schools, which were open only to full members of the FSLN, was a high honor. The curricula varied, focusing on Nicaraguan history, the writings of Sandino, Marxist theory (including Lenin), and political economy.[29]

The Department of International Relations was responsible for relations with all political parties that chose to deal with the FSLN, ranging from Communist to Social Democratic, Christian Democratic and Liberal parties. This department also oversaw the work of a nongovernmental organization, the Nicaraguan Council for Friendship, Solidarity, and Peace (CNASP), which worked with grass-roots organizations in more than fifty countries, groups that provided Nicaragua humanitarian and technical assistance in a variety of fields.

The Department of Finance oversaw the financial matters of the organization, and the Institute for the Study of Sandinismo fostered the study of the life and writings of Augusto Sandino and the later founders of the FSLN. In the late 1980s the focus of the latter institution, renamed the Nicaraguan Historical Institute, was broadened somewhat. However, this department was not accorded the kind of resources and attention as the other organs.

In addition to the national institutions, the FSLN also had three other levels of organization—regional, zonal, and base or local. The regional structure of the FSLN corresponded to the governmental division of the country into six regular regions and three special territories in the Atlantic Coast area. There was a regional committee for each region, made up of no more than ten members. Subordinate to the regional committees were zonal committees, often covering an entire city or part of a large city. Finally, the FSLN was made up of hundreds of base committees. Each member of the FSLN, except those with national or regional tasks, was a member of a base committee. As with most vanguard parties, these units were usually based on the workplace: in the factories, on state and cooperative farms, in the army, and at the universities for example. Initially the neighborhood base committees were the most common form used, but at other times the workplace committees came to be dominant.[30] At the base level of the party, recruitment, education, and carrying out the directives of the Joint National Directorate were the key tasks.

Party Democracy

A definite assessment of party democracy within the FSLN was not possible as this was being written, but it is possible to make some preliminary judgments and set the framework for a more conclusive judgment. As the description of party structures indicates, there was considerable concentration of power within the Joint National Directorate. It was the highest decision-making body of the party. The more representative Sandinista Assembly, although important within the political life of the FSLN, had only an advisory role and was clearly subordinate to the National Directorate. In addition, because the Sandinista Assembly met only infrequently, even its function as an effective sounding board for initiatives developed within the directorate was reduced. Also, the lack of a formal congress structure limited the democracy of the FSLN: There was no formal manner for rank-and-file members of the party to have direct input in formulating the party's program. The rank and file lacked an opportunity to elect representatives to higher bodies, who would be charged with setting the party program for a defined period of time.

There were rumblings of dissent from within the FSLN over the tendency of the National Directorate to issue top-down commands and expect immediate compliance from the base. As a result, in April 1988 long-time FSLN leader and mayor of Managua, Moisés Hassan, quit the party. Hassan told a *New York Times* reporter that it was virtually impossible for anyone outside of the Joint National Directorate to influence decisions.[31] Hassan emerged in the 1990 election as the presidential candidate of the Movement for Revolutionary Unity (MUR), a party that ran on a platform accusing the Sandinista party of moving to the right and betraying its revolutionary heritage.

The rumblings of discontent within the party were magnified by the February election defeat. As no FSLN leaders apparently had considered electoral defeat possible, the disaster revealed that the party cadre had begun to lose touch with the people in the neighborhoods and within the workplace. It also appears that the separation of the FSLN from certain sectors of the population was exacerbated by the election campaign itself. The reliance of the FSLN on a relatively high-cost and personalistic campaign may have seemed incongruous to many poor Nicaraguans, given the condition of the country ravaged by years of war and economic decline. Specifically, the handouts of imported presents—clothes, toys, emblems—during Sandinista rallies contrasted with the country's poverty.[32] The overly optimistic Sandinista slogan, "Everything's going to be better," did not appeal to many Nicaraguans, who saw a continued contra war as a more likely future.

The election defeat opened up a new phase in the development of the FSLN party, and a process of change began almost immediately after the election. "Nobody planned it. By the time they realized it, people were discussing the cause of the defeat on their own initiative."[33] This comment by a member of the FSLN Regional Committee in Managua indicates that change was under way: The ranks of the FSLN may have been willing to accept a largely top-down structure during the years of state power, but that was no longer the case. Spontaneous discussions began almost immediately and laid the groundwork for an extraordinary meeting of the FSLN Assembly in mid-June 1990. The assembly decided to convene the first-ever congress of the FSLN in July 1991. The planning process was to take place in three stages. First there would be open discussion of all issues; then discussion of written documents submitted by party members and ultimately the election of delegates to the congress. The third stage would be the congress itself, where the elected delegates would act on the resolutions for future party activity and choose the leadership, including the Joint National Directorate. Resolutions adopted at the assembly publicly acknowledged serious shortcomings within the FSLN, including lack of attention to unorganized sectors of society, the appointment of officials from outside an affected district for lengthy terms, the ostentatious life-styles of some party officials, and the failure to dismiss obviously corrupt officials.

Although the future of the party was not certain some definite trends were emerging as this went to press. All party leaders were publicly pointing to victory in the 1996 elections as the key to the redemption of the FSLN. This electoral emphasis in a country where revolutionary and counterrevolutionary politics had dominated seemed to indicate that the FSLN was headed in a social democratic direction. A motion to seek membership in the Second International was tabled at the 1990 Sandinista Assembly, but such a shift might be inevitable, particularly in light of events in Eastern Europe.

Notes

1. See Carlos Vilas, *The Sandinista Revolution* (New York: Monthly Review Press, 1986), pp. 13–48; John Booth, *The End and the Beginning: The Nicaraguan Revolution* (Boulder, Colo.: Westview Press, 1985), pp. 272–273; Thomas Walker, ed., *Nicaragua: The First Five Years* (New York: Praeger Press, 1985), pp. 22–24.

2. For a sophisticated but ultimately anti-Communist treatment of the Nicaraguan revolution and the FSLN, see David Nolar, *FSLN: The Ideology of the Sandinistas and the Nicaraguan Revolution* (Coral Gables, Fla.: Institute for Interamerican Studies, 1984).

3. For example, see the 1984 electoral platform of the FSLN reprinted in Bruce Marcus, ed., *Nicaragua: The Sandinista People's Revolution* (New York: Pathfinder Press, 1985), pp. 313–327.

4. Registered and legal political parties in Nicaragua as of 1989 were the Sandinista National Liberation Front (FSLN), Democratic Conservative party (PCD), Independent Liberal party (PLI), Popular Social Christian party (PPSC), Communist Party of Nicaragua (PCdeN), Nicaraguan Socialist party (PSN), Marxist-Leninist Popular Action movement (MAP-ML) plus fourteen others legalized since the 1984 elections.

5. Gabriel Invernizzi, et al., *Sandinistas* (Managua: Editorial Vanguardia, 1986), pp. 11–12.

6. Víctor Tirado, "Karl Marx—The International Workers' Movement's Greatest Fighter and Thinker," speech reprinted in Marcus, ed., *Nicaragua: The Sandinista People's Revolution*, p. 105.

7. Interview with Tomás Borge, *Crisis* (Argentina) reprinted in *Militant*, November 14, 1986, p. 9.

8. Ibid.

9. Arce interview, *Excelsior* (Mexico), June 25, 1987.

10. Interview with Luis Carrión, *Nuevo Diario*, December 26 and 27, 1986.

11. Andrew Reding, *Christianity and Revolution: Tomás Borge's Theology of Life* (Maryknoll, N.Y.: Orbis Books, 1987).

12. Interview with Sixto Ulloa, Managua, January 20, 1987.

13. For full treatments of Sandino's life and ideas, see Gregorio Selser, *Sandino* (New York: Monthly Review Press, 1981), and Donald Hodges, *The Intellectual Foundations of the Nicaraguan Revolution* (Austin: University of Texas Press, 1986).

14. Tomás Borge, *Carlos, The Dawn Is No Longer Beyond Our Reach* (Vancouver: New Star Books, 1984), p. 28.

15. Interview with Julio Pérez, Political Secretary, FSLN Department of International Relations, Managua, January 23, 1987.

16. Ibid.

17. Dora María Téllez, quoted in Margaret Randall, *Sandino's Daughters: Testimonies of Nicaraguan Women in Struggle* (Vancouver: New Star Books, 1981), p. 53.

18. In contrast to the unity of the FSLN, the Grenadian revolutionary movement, the New Jewel Movement, was destroyed by an intraparty coup in October 1983 headed by Bernard Coard. The coup led to the assassination of Prime Minister Maurice Bishop and the defeat of the New Jewel Movement by a U.S. invasion. Also, the Salvadoran revolutionary movement was severely divided at many points of its history; those divisions led to the assassination of a Salvadoran revolutionary leader in Managua in 1985.

19. Jaime Wheelock, *Nicaragua: The Great Challenge* (Managua: Alternative Views, 1984), pp. 12–14.

20. FSLN-DN, "Communicado," *Barricada*, September 10, 1980.

21. FSLN-Secretaria de la Dirección Nacional (SDN), "Communicado," *Barricada*, August 4, 1985.

22. Dennis Gilbert, *Sandinistas* (New York: Basil Blackwell, 1988), p. 47.

23. FSLN-SDN, "Communicado."

24. Ibid.

25. Ibid.

26. Ibid.

27. Pérez interview, January 23, 1987.

28. Ibid.

29. Ibid.

30. Ibid.

31. Stephen Kinzer, "Sandinista Will Do It His Way," *New York Times*, May 8, 1988.

32. Carlos Vilas, "What Went Wrong," *NACLA Report on the Americas*, June 1990, p. 14.

33. Carlos Gallo, FSLN deputy, quoted in *Barricada International*, July 14, 1990.

SIX

Opposition Parties
and Coalitions

ERIC WEAVER & WILLIAM BARNES

Prior to the fall of the Somoza regime in 1979, Nicaraguans had never seen a large well-organized political party of any kind and had never experienced a free, competitive political process among opposing political parties. By the opening of the campaign for the February 1990 general elections, the Nicaraguan political panorama was characterized by a large, well-organized governing party, the Sandinista Front for National Liberation (FSLN), surrounded by approximately two dozen opposition parties.[1]

In the decade following its 1979 revolutionary triumph, the FSLN underwent a remarkable evolution: from a relatively small political-military "vanguard" organization to a much larger and more internally complex governing party that led in creating a new constitutional order and twice submitted itself to open, competitive elections. When the FSLN lost the 1990 elections, it cooperated in a peaceful transition of power, subsequently becoming the major opposition force within the political system it had founded. Never before had a regime that came to power through armed struggle evolved so rapidly. This evolution is all the more remarkable because it occurred in a society with no previous democratic tradition and in the face of crippling external aggression.

The two dozen opposition parties that existed in 1990 spanned the political spectrum from far left to far right, with the more significant parties best described as center-right to center-left. Prior to late 1989, none of those parties could compare with the FSLN in self-development or maintenance of organizational unity. Rather than cohering and expanding, opposition parties had splintered dramatically since the overthrow of Somoza. In 1989, about half of those opposition parties were nothing more than factions made up of a few leaders and their coteries of personal associates.

In late 1989, with the help of carrots and sticks from Washington, the loose opposition coalition known as "the fourteen" managed to turn itself into the National Opposition Union (UNO) electoral alliance. UNO included all but one of the nine or ten right-wing parties (splinters of Nicaraguan conservatism, liberalism, and Christian democracy), plus the center-right Independent Liberal party (PLI), the centrist Conservative National Action (ANC—a recent split from the Democratic Conservative party), the center-left Nicaraguan Socialist party (PSN), and the Communist party (PCdeN). Besides UNO, one right-wing party, four center/center-left parties (from the conservative, liberal, and social Christian traditions), and three left-wing parties ran separate national campaigns. The Mískito organization Yatama fielded candidates on the Atlantic Coast.

Despite the impressive election victory of UNO candidate Violeta Barrios de Chamorro, the 1990 campaign actually confirmed the relative weakness of opposition political parties as institutions. The UNO coalition was racked by feuding throughout the campaign (to the point where public recriminations, shoving matches, and fistfights sometimes broke out among prominent UNO leaders). As a result, UNO relied on Chamorro's personal image to coalesce voter dissatisfaction with economic catastrophe and the legacy of eight years of war. There was no evidence that the constituent parties had any particular popular strength in themselves, nor were there indications of movement toward unification among parties representing splinters from the same tradition.

This extreme splintering of the traditional party system began in the 1950s and accelerated substantially after mid-1984. Analysts typically blame the latter acceleration on FSLN meddling and/or the personalism, pettiness, and incompetence of opposition politicians. Such explanations are superficial. More important factors are the historical underdevelopment of Nicaraguan political culture, the Nicaraguan political parties' traditional organizational and strategic weaknesses, and the destructive impact of United States policy on efforts to institutionalize a new system. In addition, there were always real differences among opposition groups about how best to respond to the revolutionary transformation of Nicaragua.

Underdevelopment of Politics
and Parties in Nicaragua

Prior to World War II, two traditional political groupings, the Liberals and Conservatives, dominated Nicaragua.[2] These parties served primarily as vehicles for a series of caudillos and upper-class families who competed for power throughout the nineteenth and early twentieth centuries.

Liberalism in Nicaragua represented authoritarian efforts at national integration, economic modernization, and integration into the world economy, but lacked any element of populism or humanitarian progressivism. By the end of the nineteenth century, Conservatives differed with Liberals only on particular issues of economic policy, educational policy, and church-state relations. But this did not lessen the intensity and bitterness of factional fighting.

The United States shifted support from one party to another, depending on its momentary interests. When Liberal nationalist José Santos Zelaya approached Germany and Japan about building a Nicaraguan canal, the United States supported a Conservative uprising against him in 1909. In 1927, the United States shifted back to the Liberals when it became clear they had wider support than the Conservatives among the upper and middle classes and offered a greater likelihood of long-term stability.

The weight of U.S. support was decisive, and Liberals and Conservatives alike eagerly looked to the United States for assistance in unseating their rivals. The first notable exception was the Liberal general Augusto César Sandino, one of the very few leaders prior to the 1970s to reject U.S. involvement firmly and to attempt to incorporate the popular classes into politics.

The United States created the National Guard (GN) in the late 1920s as a replacement for the U.S. Marines. In the mid-1930s, guard commander Anastasio Somoza García, a Liberal, used the GN to seize control of the Nicaraguan government. The GN assumed responsibility for virtually all public functions, including national radio, telegraph, postal service, immigration, and internal revenue. All public institutions not directly controlled by the National Guard were dominated by Somoza's cronies from the Liberal Nationalist party (PLN). In reality, there were no genuinely "public" institutions. Both the GN and the PLN operated purely as personal instruments of the Somoza family and its entourage. The Conservatives were virtually excluded. Thus, under the Somozas, Nicaragua remained a society not only without any democratic traditions but also without any experience of well-organized politics, any substantial inclusion of the mass of the population in public life, or any history of sustained, organized expression of nationalism.[3]

The Emergence of Political Activism and New Parties

In 1950, Somoza García succeeded in co-opting key Conservatives, who agreed to the "pact of the generals," which gave one-third of the congressional seats and public appointments to the Conservatives in exchange for supporting the system. The Liberal and Conservative parties remained inert, with no ideological or organizational development. Their monopoly of the realm of party politics eroded gradually as groups began splintering off to form new parties.

In 1944, the Independent Liberal party (PLI) was founded to oppose Somoza García and the PLN. The Christian Democratic group, National Union of Popular Action, formed in 1948, the anticollaborationist Young Conservative movement appeared in 1952, and the Social Christian party (PSC) was founded in 1957. Though the PLI and PSC developed some level of organization in the major cities, no progress was made toward building mass followings. Opposition politics continued to be dominated by prominent personalities, individual actions, and what amounted to political clubs.

Frustration with stymied electoral politics gave way to armed actions by PLI and Conservative party activists in 1954, 1957, and 1959. In 1956, Rigoberto López Pérez, a PLI militant, assassinated Somoza García, who was succeeded as president by his older son, Luis Somoza Debayle. When dissident Conservatives gained control of their party and boycotted the 1957 and 1962 elections, Luis Somoza encouraged the creation of the National Conservative party (PNC) to maintain the appearance of electoral opposition.

In addition to the bourgeois parties, several working-class parties emerged. In the early 1930s, the Nicaraguan Workers' party emerged and was suppressed. In 1944, the Nicaraguan Socialist party (PSN) was founded; it eventually developed a small base among urban workers. Alongside these parties, the Sandinista Front for National Liberation (FSLN) was formed in 1961 by former militants of the PLI and PSN. From the beginning, the FSLN eschewed electoral politics in favor of armed struggle and the building of a clandestine support and political education apparatus. It remained small until the late 1970s.

Rapid economic growth in the 1960s, government investment in infrastructure, and five years of Luis Somoza's minimal social welfare/ public service programs created a measure of social stability. Opposition politicians continued to switch loyalties among various political factions and to bicker among themselves. Relatively skillful co-optation by Luis Somoza induced some politicians to collaborate with the regime. This pattern broke down when Anastasio Somoza Debayle assumed power in 1967, after a rigged election and the death of Luis following a heart attack. Anastasio moved to reassert the political monopoly of the Somoza family and quickly abandoned co-optation in favor of coercion.

The 1970s—Rising Popular Activism and Organization

At the beginning of the 1970s, opposition to Anastasio Somoza Debayle's reelection, barred in theory by the constitution, gave way to a deal with Conservatives that gave them 40 percent of congressional and government posts. As a result, the Conservative party divided into four pro- and anti-Somoza factions.

With the Conservative party splintered and largely discredited, the Social Christian party (PSC) appeared to gain support among the middle class, students, and some workers and from the Church. However, it failed to overcome ideological and strategic indecision and to reach out effectively to the popular classes. As a result, university students moved to the left, and the Student Revolutionary Front (FER) supplanted the Christian Democratic Front leadership of student governments in the early 1970s.[4] In 1976, leftists abandoned the PSC because of its refusal to acknowledge the legitimacy of armed struggle and formed the Popular Social Christian party (PPSC).

The Left was also splintered during the first half of the 1970s. In the PSN, younger, more militant activists pushed aside the old Stalinist leadership in 1967, and the latter went on to form the Communist Party of Nicaragua (PCdeN) in 1970. Two far-left groups split off from the FSLN in the early 1970s to form the Popular Action Movement (MAP) and the Revolutionary Workers' party (PRT). The FSLN itself divided into three factions in the mid-1970s.[5]

As the 1970s progressed, the corruption and repression of the Somoza regime increased, and revulsion toward the regime grew in all sectors not directly linked to it. During the mid-1970s, sectors of the middle bourgeoisie and the technocratic middle class tried to establish a moderate alternative to Somoza by founding a variety of groups, fronts, and organizations. The business organization COSEP began to become somewhat political, and Pedro Joaquín Chamorro founded the umbrella group Democratic Union of Liberation (UDEL) in 1974. But as with the PSC and PLI, this moderate tendency remained strategically indecisive and oriented toward eliciting support from the United States rather than toward mass organizing.

In the face of popular and activist frustration with the continuing political stagnation and ineffectiveness of political parties, new types of social activism and political organization proliferated. The most important of these were urban student organizations and various expressions of liberation theology, particularly base communities among the rural and urban poor. Disgust with the government's inability to respond to the 1972 earthquake, and with the government corruption and Somocista profiteering in its wake, greatly accelerated such developments. An increasingly large proportion of such new organizations moved into alliance with the Sandinistas, as the Tercerista faction of the FSLN, which advocated the formation of a broad opposition front, rose to preeminence over the period 1977–1978.

Building alliances with, and encouraging the radicalization of, the proliferating student, religious, and peasant organizations while also maintaining contact with middle-class moderates was the heart of the Tercerista strategy. Additionally, in the late 1970s, the FSLN organized or gained influence within such mass organizations as the Association of Women Confronting the National Problem (AMPRONAC), the Civil Defense Committees (CDC) (renamed the Sandinista Defense Committees [CDS] after the triumph), and the Rural Workers' Association (ATC). These organizations represented important nonparty political institutions organized to meet the needs of the rural and urban population during the final months of the insurrection. The FSLN viewed them as the basis of a new type of "popular democracy" that would allow the people to participate directly in the political process rather than indirectly through political parties.[6]

During the period 1974–1978, UDEL and other representatives of the moderate tendency played a substantial role in opposition politics, but they never won significant support from the richest sectors of the bourgeoisie or from the United States. They remained organizationally fragile. In their political competition with the FSLN, none of the traditional opposition political parties, nor any of the new, modern middle-class political organizations, were able to build comparable alliances or organizations among the popular classes. Nor did they have any strategy for doing so. Over the course of 1978 and early 1979, the Broad Opposition Front (FAO), successor to the UDEL, foundered in the face of the increasingly insistent popular demand that not only Somoza, but the GN and the entire Somoza political apparatus as well must go. The FSLN, its three factions reunited around the Tercerista strategy, established hegemony over the proliferating student and religious groups radicalized by the Somoza repression.

By the spring of 1979, virtually all sectors of opposition to Somoza had coalesced around the FSLN's insurrectionary strategy, and anti-Somoza moderates were confronted with the choice of joining with the FSLN or being swept away. As the sun rose on July 19, 1979, Nicaraguans confronted not only the sudden removal of a long-lived dynastic dictatorship but also the total collapse of the entire apparatus of government. The army, the state bureaucracy, the courts, and most civil institutions were gone. In this unexpected political vacuum, new political lines were drawn between revolution and counterrevolution.

1979–1981 Revolutionary Honeymoon

In the initial euphoria of victory, virtually all social sectors that did not flee joined in the revolutionary government.[7] But important elements retained widely differing expectations about the future course of the revolution. Violeta Chamorro, owner of *La Prensa* (and soon to be a prominent critic of the Sandinistas), participated in the first government junta, along with subsequent contra leader Alfonso Robelo and FSLN members Daniel Ortega, Sergio Ramírez, and Moisés Hassan. Upon the resignations of Chamorro and Robelo in 1980, Arturo Cruz (the proposed 1984 rightist presidential candidate) joined the junta along with longtime Conservative party leader Rafael Córdova Rivas.

The triumph of the FSLN's unorthodox politics left the traditional political parties in disarray. The provisional legislative body of the new government, the Council of State, reflected the relative weakness of the political parties and the relative strength of the mass organizations that had backed the FSLN in the fight against Somoza. Although all political parties then in existence had representatives in the Council of State, many other political organizations were also present. Mass organizations such as the CDS, the ATC, and even the army all had direct representatives in the council. It was clear that traditional politicians and political parties would not predominate.

As it became clear that the FSLN was serious about its efforts to effect fundamental economic and political changes, traditional political forces that had been marginalized or thrown into upheaval by the revolution began to regroup. From the beginning, three ideological positions emerged. On the right were forces opposed to the revolution, which sought its overthrow. Composed of extreme rightists who fled to Miami and private-sector groups inside Nicaragua, they cooperated with U.S. military efforts to overthrow the revolution instead of forming serious political parties to advance their positions within the revolution.

A second bloc was comprised of political parties that generally supported the revolution but opposed many of the FSLN's specific policies as well as (what they saw as) the FSLN's partisan appropriation of Sandinism and of the popular organizations. Known collectively as the "patriotic opposition," these parties ranged from the extreme left to the center-right and worked within the revolution to advance their positions.

The patriotic opposition was divided between those who urged a radicalization of the revolution and those who advocated moderation. To the left of the Sandinistas were the Communist party (PCdeN), the Marxist-Leninist Popular Action Movement (MAP-ML), and the Revolutionary Workers' party (PRT), all of which argued for radicalizing the revolution by vastly expanding land reform, expropriating the mixed economy, closing political space to "bourgeois" parties, and creating a dictatorship of the proletariat.

To the immediate right of the FSLN were parties in formal coalition with it (the Patriotic Front), including the Popular Social Christian party (PPSC), the Nicaraguan Socialist party (PSN), and the Independent Liberal party (PLI). In addition, the Democratic Conservative party (PCD) shared the general political perspective of the Patriotic Front, although it never formally was part of it.

Although the members of the Patriotic Front and the PCD had programmatic differences with the FSLN, they generally supported the

FSLN political program and strongly opposed U.S. intervention. They supplied government ministers, ambassadors, and Supreme Court Justices. Prior to mid-1984, they remained closely identified with the FSLN. Lacking their own concrete programs, these parties found it difficult to establish clear, independent political identities. In effect, they came to stand for the abstract goal of a broader, nonpartisan, and more effective implementation of the FSLN program—without being able to offer concrete ideas about how that might be accomplished.

From 1979 through 1983, the patriotic opposition had little opportunity to exercise any political influence. The United States and its allies on the right were dedicated to reversing the revolutionary process and had no interest in lending legitimacy to that process by recognizing some forms of participation in it. For its part, the FSLN focused on mobilizing Nicaraguan nationalism, legitimizing the "logic of the majority,"[8] institutionalizing mass participation through the mass organizations, and mobilizing the country to meet the military threat posed by the United States. Because the patriotic opposition opposed the U.S. strategy, it felt constrained to support the FSLN. At the same time, opposition leaders denounced the harsher provisions of the war-fostered State of Emergency and bitterly resented the resulting restrictions on their activities.

The 1984 Elections

The December 4, 1983, initiation of the first postrevolutionary electoral process began a new phase of political development in Nicaragua.[9] Coinciding with the growing contra war, it opened a non-military arena of political struggle. The elections also signaled a break with the "popular democracy" model, which had been based on increasing the direct political role of the mass organizations. As formal participation in the elections was limited to political parties, the focus of debate and activity began to shift away from the role and character of mass organizations toward the terms and conditions on which political parties would operate and contest the elections.

The political panorama during the 1984 campaign reflected the existing three major blocs. The pro-U.S. Right was formally organized into the Nicaraguan Democratic Coordinator (CDN). At the beginning of 1984, the CDN was composed of three political parties, the Social Christian party (PSC), the Social Democratic party (PSD), and the Constitutional Liberal party (PLC). In addition, three small trade unions and the private business association COSEP participated in this grouping. They were later joined by the National Conservative party (PNC). Only the PSC had a significant popular base or national organization. COSEP and the PSD leaders close to La Prensa dominated the CDN.

The CDN was identified by the Reagan administration and the U.S. media as "the opposition" and given virtually exclusive media attention in the United States. As its (prospective but never actually declared) presidential candidate, the CDN chose Arturo Cruz, an international banker who had lived outside the country for most of the previous twenty years, and who was briefly a member of the government junta and then ambassador to the United States in 1980–1981. Cruz had good contacts in Washington, a good media image, and a good reputation among Nicaraguan Conservatives.

The CDN pursued a brinksmanship electoral strategy, coupling ever-escalating demands for concessions from the FSLN with threats to abstain from the elections. At first, the CDN demanded advancing the date of the elections, which were scheduled for 1985. When the elections were rescheduled for November 1984, the Right denounced this as a FSLN maneuver to deprive the opposition of enough preparation time.[10]

The FSLN gradually agreed to most CDN demands for reforming the electoral process. In July 1984, the emergency law was modified to restore freedom of travel, freedom to organize, and freedom of the press. In August, habeas corpus and the right to strike were restored and the Electoral Law was modified to add PPSC and PCD representatives to the Supreme Electoral Council and guarantee the opposition more free media time and funding.[11] After each FSLN concession, the CDN raised new demands. Finally, negotiations with the contras emerged as the essential precondition to CDN participation in the election. The FSLN refused to meet with the contras.

The CDN strategy of constantly attacking the fairness of the electoral procedure and ultimately abstaining from the electoral process allowed the Reagan administration to attack the Nicaraguan election as a "Soviet-style sham." The CDN, by abstaining from the elections and denouncing them as "unfair," ultimately contributed to the administration's efforts to obtain more military aid for the contras. Though Cruz personally was equivocal, and some elements of the PSC wanted to participate in the election, COSEP and other rightist elements and the Reagan administration never intended that the CDN actually take part. According to Robert McCartney of the *Washington Post*, "Opposition leaders admitted in interviews that they never seriously considered running in the November 4 election but debated only whether to campaign for two months and then withdraw."[12]

The second electoral bloc in 1984 was the grouping of political parties in the Patriotic Front (PPSC, PLI, PSN) plus the PCD. All participated in the electoral process, supported nationalist anticontra positions, and opposed the Reagan administration's policy of intervention. Although the PLI pulled out of the Patriotic Front in February 1984 in order to position itself for the election, the PPSC and PSN initially intended to participate as part of the Patriotic Front coalition with the FSLN.

The PCD chose longtime Conservative leader Clemente Guido as its presidential candidate and coupled a nationalist, anticontra position with the vague promise to administer the revolution more competently than the FSLN and with greater respect for private property and the Church. Guido energetically denounced the CDN's abstentionism, arguing that "abstention was a vote for the FSLN."

The PLI chose Virgilio Godoy as its candidate. Godoy had served as labor minister until February 1984, when he resigned in order to run for president. The PLI platform initially differed little from that of the PCD or the Patriotic Front parties. As the campaign progressed, Godoy's attacks on the FSLN became more virulent. In late October, with the encouragement of the U.S. embassy, Godoy announced that he had come to share the views of the CDN and would abstain from the elections. But the ballots had already been printed and the Supreme Electoral Council declared that it was too late to withdraw as a candidate legally. Godoy subsequently assumed a seat in the National Assembly (as the defeated presidential candidate of a party receiving more than the minimum vote).

In contrast to the CDN, which tried to undermine the electoral process, the four centrist parties had difficulty differentiating themselves ideologically from the FSLN. For example, all four supported the revolution's most basic principles, nationalism and the logic of the majority, and the three pillars of the FSLN program, a mixed economy, political pluralism, and nonalignment, but each defined these in vaguely different ways. Each party supported the agrarian reform but claimed to have a better method of managing it. Extensive interviews with the leaders of each party in August 1984 demonstrated that none of the parties had clearly defined its political differences with the FSLN beyond general statements of FSLN incompetence, sectarianism, and excessive partisanship.[13] In place of programmatic political debate, the centrist parties offered abstract ideals on the one hand and complaints about the unfairness of the political process itself on the other.

All parties complained of an unfair FSLN media advantage, FSLN harassment of their supporters, and superior FSLN financial resources. None of the parties organized extensive campaigns, limiting themselves instead to principal cities, radio, television, and a few poorly attended rallies. Although the center parties expressed reservations about the fairness of the process, they did not, with the exception of the Godoy faction of the PLI, withdraw from the campaign.

On the left, the PCdeN and the MAP-ML continued to tout their radical vision of the revolution while accusing the FSLN of being social democratic rather than revolutionary. The MAP initially opposed holding elections, arguing that they gave the bourgeois parties too much space. The PRT abstained from the election.

The FSLN, by contrast, offered a comprehensive, if general, political program. As part of its promise to solidify "popular power," the FSLN invited the mass organizations to nominate members to stand as candidates on the FSLN slate even though they were not members of the FSLN. It promised to continue its efforts to achieve economic and social justice. It also met with the opposition parties almost continuously throughout the campaign to respond to their complaints about the process.

Although there has been debate about the degree and significance of FSLN "abuse" of the power of incumbency during the election campaign, most independent observers agreed that registration and voting procedures were scrupulously implemented and that there was no sign of fraud, misconduct, or significant intimidation on election day. With an estimated 75.4 percent turnout nationwide, the results provide the first survey of the political complexion of postrevolutionary Nicaragua.

Although the results confirmed that the FSLN was by far the dominant political force in the country, the more interesting fact was that despite their virtual invisibility outside Managua and a few other major cities and despite their inability to set forth a program or organize a campaign, the PCD, PLI, and PPSC together accounted for 27 percent of the total vote (29 percent of the valid ballots). This demonstrated that despite five years of intense political mobilization, traditional political affiliations remained relatively strong.[14]

A second revelation was the insignificance of all options to the left of the FSLN. This confirmed FSLN claims to represent the only meaningful revolutionary alternative.

A more difficult question is the level of support for the other clearly defined political pole, the pro-U.S. counterrevolutionary position. This is of particular importance because the U.S. media and the Reagan administration insisted that this sector was the only real opposition. The few serious studies available suggest that if CDN candidate Arturo Cruz had remained in the race, he probably would have received between 10 percent and 30 percent of the vote, costing the FSLN six to twelve assembly seats.[15]

Less clear is the ideological significance of the vote. On the most general level, the vote manifested strong popular support and appreciation for the accomplishments of the first years of the revolution, for the FSLN's championing of nationalism and the logic of the majority, and for the FSLN's stand against U.S. interference and counterrevolution.

It is virtually impossible to gauge the vote's implications for other more particular aspects of the FSLN program, such as its mode of institutionalizing mass participation and land reform, its reorganization of the legal system, educational system, and mass media. All parties, including those in the CDN bloc, voiced vague support for land reform and the three basic tenets of the revolution. This suggests that the

Sandinista revolution had changed the terms of debate in Nicaragua, and that Nicaraguans generally supported the outline of the revolutionary project.

However, the 1984 elections represented a watershed in the institutional development of the revolution. From the mid-1970s through 1983, the FSLN had focused on institutionalizing mass participation based on mass organizations. By opening political space to opposition parties, the elections displaced the mass organizations from the center of Nicaraguan politics. Henceforth politics shifted from a radical, if undefined, vision of popular democracy to a more conventional Western-style democracy based on political parties.

1984–1986: Counterrevolution and the Constitution

The Right's Strategy: Delegitimize the Government

Despite the strong showing of popular support for the FSLN at the polls, the United States and its rightist allies continued (indeed increased) their efforts to overthrow the revolution. In October 1984, the contras launched the first of a new series of offensives emphasizing civilian rather than military targets, and the war escalated sharply. The FSLN fielded its newly trained and equipped counterinsurgency battalions, developed a sophisticated counterinsurgency strategy, broadened the scope of the land reform, and mobilized broad popular support for defending national sovereignty against U.S.-backed forces. By late 1985, the contras' capacity to threaten the revolution militarily had been destroyed. However, the war continued to devastate the Nicaraguan countryside and disrupt the economy until the March 1988 Sapoá cease-fire agreement.

As the war escalated, the United States and its rightist allies continued to eschew efforts to build political parties or participate in the civic political arena in favor of counterrevolution. The pro-U.S. Right inside Nicaragua, led by the CDN, played an important role in the Reagan administration's war effort by denouncing the Sandinista-led government as a "totalitarian dictatorship" and openly lobbying for contra aid. The Reagan administration pointed to such groups as proof that Nicaraguan "democratic opposition forces" supported U.S. policy and contra aid.[16]

An important part of the CDN strategy was its effort to delegitimize the new political system, particularly the National Assembly. On March 2, 1985, the CDN and the Nicaraguan Democratic Force (FDN) contras issued a joint "Document on National Dialogue of the Nicaraguan Resistance" in San José, Costa Rica. This document denied the legitimacy of the recent elections, called for new electoral laws, new elections, and a transitional government with CDN and FDN participation.[17] The

CDN/FDN document set the political tone for the pro-U.S. opposition. CDN members regularly denounced the FSLN and the other parties participating in the National Assembly. Both the CDN and the contras were given extensive, favorable coverage in *La Prensa* and the U.S. media, which echoed the view that the FSLN had not been legitimately elected.

However, the CDN relied for political leverage on its association with the United States and the contras rather than on its own organizing efforts. As a result, the CDN political parties as institutions sacrificed what little relevance they enjoyed during the 1984 election campaign. Because the CDN political parties had abstained from the election itself, they did not have seats in the National Assembly and could not participate in drafting the constitution. Incapable of effective party building, their spokespeople used their party affiliations primarily to lend credibility to their statements to the U.S. media by implying that they enjoyed significant popular support.

The actual work of generating popular support for the pro-U.S. opposition was left to the rightist newspaper *La Prensa* and the Catholic church hierarchy, in particular to Cardinal Miguel Obando y Bravo.[18] *La Prensa* and the Church hierarchy issued a steady stream of anti-FSLN statements publicized in the United States. Obando and other bishops repeatedly denounced alleged government human rights abuses and the military draft, remaining silent about contra attacks on civilians. Bishops traveled to the United States to meet contra leaders, wrote opinion pieces in U.S. papers, and testified in Congress in support of contra aid.

However, no effort was made to organize discontented Nicaraguans into the CDN parties or to offer concrete suggestions for new national policies. *La Prensa* and the Church hierarchy helped gain support for contra aid in the U.S. Congress but failed to build an organized base of pro-U.S. opposition inside Nicaragua. In early 1986, the Nicaraguan government closed the Church-run Radio Católica after it broadcast appeals to resist the draft. Following the June 1986 U.S. congressional approval of $100 million in military aid to the contras, the Nicaraguan government barred Monseñor Bismarck Carballo from returning to Nicaragua and expelled Bishop Pablo Antonio Vega.

The expulsions revealed the political weakness of the Church. Although the government's action provoked strong reaction in the United States, there was no organized public opposition to the move inside Nicaragua. Subsequently, the Vatican stepped in, took control of Church-state relations, reduced tensions with the FSLN, and ended the Church's overt pro-U.S., procontra leadership role.

The government also closed *La Prensa* after the 1986 contra aid vote. Although this action provoked an outcry in the United States, there was little reaction inside Nicaragua. *La Prensa* editors confidently pre-dicted that the FSLN could not resist for more than a few weeks pressure to reopen the paper. When *La Prensa* finally did reopen in September 1987, it was in order to comply with the requirements of the Esquipulas peace accord, signed in August 1987, not because of any internal political pressure.[19]

Despite enormous media exposure in the United States and strong support from the Reagan administration, the pro-U.S. forces inside Nicaragua failed to organize an active anti-Sandinista political base inside the country. They based their strategy of legitimizing continued U.S. support for the contras on the assumption that the United States would eventually oust the FSLN. Once it became clear that the FSLN would defeat the contras militarily and that the United States would not intervene directly with its own forces, the Right's hope of assuming power by aiding counterrevolution was shattered. The collapse of this strategy eventually led to a split in the Right between diehards who refused to participate in civil politics under any conditions and those who slowly began to take advantage of the available political space.

Writing a Constitution in the Midst of War

The centrist parties adopted a different strategy. Rather than try to overthrow the system, they chose to attempt to influence its evolution. Clemente Guido of the PCD articulated this position in a January 1985 interview in which he argued that the elections had institutionalized a new, if somewhat imperfect, political system of separation of powers. Guido stated that he was not afraid that the FSLN majority would enable it to dominate the National Assembly because parliamentary dynamics require that minorities be taken into account. He denounced collaboration with the contras and reiterated his commitment to a vaguely defined Western democratic structure with an emphasis on social justice.[20]

Virgilio Godoy vacillated between Guido's position and that of the CDN. He argued that the National Assembly should be viewed as a caretaker government while a new structure was created to make way for early elections. He participated sporadically in the process of drafting the constitution.[21] In September 1986, Godoy's rightward drift led to a split in the PLI, with at least one-third of the party organizing a formal faction, the "Movement for Unity and Democracy of the PLI" (which then became a separate party, the Liberal Party of National Unity, PLIUN, in 1988).

The ground rules of the debate between the FSLN and the patriotic opposition were set in October 1984, on the eve of the elections. The FSLN held a marathon series of talks with the participating opposition parties at which an agreement was hammered out on the framework of postelection politics. The opposition parties publicly committed themselves to defending the revolution and national sovereignty and agreed to define the contra war as outside intervention rather than civil war. In exchange, the FSLN publicly committed itself to political pluralism within the revolution, continued democratization, broad civil liberties, access to the state media by opposition parties, and the depoliticization of the Sandinista Defense Committees.[22]

For the patriotic opposition, the FSLN's compliance with the terms of the agreement became the bench mark of FSLN commitment to democratization. Thus, when the FSLN reimposed the State of Emergency in October 1985 at the height of the war, many opposition politicians joined the Right in condemning the decree and temporarily withdrew from the National Assembly. The Supreme Court, including FSLN-allied justices, unanimously condemned the decree. Within days, the FSLN softened its terms, and many of its harshest provisions were never enforced.[23] Ultimately, most politicians (with the notable exception of Virgilio Godoy) returned to the constitutional debate.

At the outset of the debate, it became clear that there was broad agreement among all parties in the National Assembly on guaranteeing basic civil liberties, abolishing the death penalty, protecting women's rights, and promoting agrarian reform while protecting private property. However, the debate revealed that none of the parties, including the FSLN, had a clear vision of how the government itself should be structured.

Initially a fundamental conceptual difference separated the FSLN from the centrist parties. The FSLN traditionally supported a concept of power it called "participatory democracy." The FSLN argued that people would participate in government via their membership in mass organizations such as the Rural Workers' Association (ATC), the National Union of Farmers and Cattlemen (UNAG), or the Sandinista Workers' Federation (CST).

According to this concept, representative democracy through political parties alienates most people from government by forcing them to mediate their demands through a party composed of varying political forces and directed by professional politicians. Under "participatory democracy," people send representatives from their mass organizations directly to government bodies, and their interests are not mediated by political leaders seeking to balance the demands of all sectors (including middle classes and elites) in a political party.[24]

Although theoretically attractive to many on the left, creation of an electoral structure to implement participatory democracy appeared impossible and was strongly opposed by the participating opposition.[25] The 1984 election among political parties alone signaled the abandonment of any attempt to implement the concept. The FSLN provided for some electoral participation of the mass organizations by allowing them to name candidates, including non-FSLN members, to the FSLN slate. The FSLN ultimately accepted a more traditional Western-style representative structure, with legislative, judicial, and executive branches, although it maintained its ideological commitment to the logic of the majority and the principle of mass participation in political life.[26]

Once the basic outline of the new political system was determined, the debate turned to the distribution of power among the branches of government. The FSLN favored a strong executive, while the opposition parties favored a strong legislature, for obvious reasons. This debate focused on control of the budget, presidential power to declare a State of Emergency, and presidential reelection. Ultimately, a compromise was worked out by which the legislature was given the authority to approve or reject a budget proposed by the president, except in time of war. The FSLN insisted on presidential reelection and power to declare a State of Emergency.

A second debate focused on the nature and role of the Sandinista People's Army (EPS) and the popular militias. All opposition parties argued that the EPS was a "party army" loyal to the FSLN rather than a "national army" loyal to the nation. They feared that an FSLN-controlled army might block a future opposition electoral victory and argued that FSLN control of the army allowed it to indoctrinate a large segment of the nation's youth.

The opposition demanded that the army be separated from FSLN control and its name changed. They also called for disbanding the militias (viewed as party dominated). The FSLN, arguing that all armies are political, rejected the charge that the EPS had a sectarian character and argued that the militias served a valuable role in mobilizing the population for national defense. Ultimately, the FSLN ceded very little, agreeing only to a clause that the EPS is a "national army" subordinate to the constitution.

Although the FSLN held enough assembly seats to impose its draft constitution outright, it compromised on many issues. Seventy-five percent of the constitution was passed unanimously. However, the FSLN imposed its views at several key points. The constitution was adopted in January 1987 and signed by eighty-three of the National Assembly's ninety-six regular members (see Chapter 2).

The Political Failure of Opposition Parties in the Mid-1980s

Despite their prominent role in drafting the constitution, the participating opposition parties were unable to capitalize on this process to build a major public presence. This was due both to the overwhelming impact of the war and to internal weaknesses of the parties themselves.

The primary political conflict in Nicaragua was between the FSLN and the Reagan administration and contras. The center and left opposition parties watched this conflict from the sidelines. The Reagan administration and the internal rightist forces considered them Sandinista puppets. They were cut off from access to U.S. support, the U.S. media, and *La Prensa*. However, because the focus of the conflict with the United States was primarily military and diplomatic and not political, the participating opposition had no role in the actual confrontation with the United States, which was conducted by the FSLN and the EPS.

The main priority for the Nicaraguan population was the war and its consequences. The participating opposition could do little to assist the average citizen in securing basic necessities, to protect peasants from contra attack, or to meet the needs of families whose sons were mobilized to fight the contras. It watched from the sidelines as the FSLN directed the war effort and attempted to meet the needs of the people.

In addition, the opposition parties focused on long-term structural questions such as political pluralism, civil liberties, and media access. Although their efforts will affect the development of the Nicaraguan political system in the long run, they made few political inroads within a population militantly opposed to the contras and struggling to cope with the daily impact of the war. Organizationally, the opposition parties remained weak. They failed to mount major organizing efforts and offered no substantive policies and programs for dealing with the economy. Although the FSLN interfered with their political activities at times, they failed to seize political opportunities open to them.

Nevertheless, the patriotic opposition's participation did result in the adoption of a Western-style electoral government with a degree of separation of powers and a Western-style legal system. This confirmed the decline of the mass organizations as direct participants in the political process and guaranteed a space for political parties.

The opposition parties ratified the general principles of nationalism and the logic of the majority, and the three strategic pillars—a mixed economy, political pluralism, and nonalignment. But the constitutional debate brought none of the parties any closer to defining precisely how these principles translate into concrete policies. As in the election campaign of 1984, they all focused on the rules of the game rather than its substance. What exactly each party stood for and how it differed from the others remained unclear.

Central America Peace Process
Revives the Opposition

Once the constitution was drafted, the National Assembly reverted to the day-to-day task of political debate and policy review, and the patriotic opposition lost its leverage over the FSLN. Under the strong presidential system Nicaragua adopted, running the government was largely up to the executive, even more so in time of war. Since the war continued to dominate life, the patriotic opposition was once more relegated to the sidelines of the main political struggle between the FSLN and the counterrevolution.

With new elections not scheduled until 1990, the opposition parties had nothing to focus on and fell to squabbling among themselves. Splits and new parties emerged at a dizzying pace. The seven participating and five abstaining parties in 1984 fragmented into twenty-three parties by early 1989, as cliques and personalities scrambled for control of foreign funding. U.S. government efforts to prevent the parties from developing or maintaining any kind of working relationship with the FSLN administration also contributed to the process (the United States would provide the funds for factions to set themselves up as separate parties if those factions would agree to reject any such relationship).

Unable or unwilling to concentrate on the tedious task of building a mass base, the parties fractured over quarrels between those who believed in exercising opposition within the revolution and those who sought support from the United States. Intransigence was rewarded with U.S. money and support while conciliation was isolated as the United States played its traditional role of kingmaker.

According to an unidentified PLI member:

> It is a tradition for many center-right political figures in Latin America to find out what the [U.S.] Embassy wants, and then position themselves in hopes that the Embassy will choose them as its instrument. The tradition is so strong for some people that it is almost instinctual. The disadvantage of such a tradition is that it provides no incentive for parties to go out and organize, and instead provokes infighting among party leaders who vie for access to U.S. or Western European sponsors and funds.[27]

The parties were pulled from this back eddy by an external event— the Central American peace process. Beginning in December 1986, Costa Rican President Oscar Arias promoted a peace plan that called for democratization in Nicaragua in exchange for ending the contra war. This development gave a new role to the opposition parties because they were given a voice in evaluating whether or not the FSLN was meeting its commitment to "democratize" the country. Under the terms of the August 1987 Esquipulas accords, the opposition political parties participated in the National Reconciliation Commission, which was set up to supervise "democratization," thus regaining a measure of the influence they had enjoyed during the writing of the constitution. The issue of democratization provided a new political focus for the opposition.

The peace process began to break down the prevailing three-bloc political division. By 1987 the strategic defeat of the contras was clear, and sectors of the counterrevolutionary Right began to recognize the necessity of taking advantage of the political space that existed inside Nicaragua. In early 1987, the CDN's Social Democratic party (PSD) and Social Christian party (PSC) began cooperating with members of the patriotic opposition to establish a position on democratization.[28] In August 1987, the Nicaraguan government signed the Central American peace accords and accelerated the relaxation of the remaining restrictions on opposition political activity and media. Gradually additional opposition forces joined the political process, and after the March 1988 Sapoá cease-fire agreement between the FSLN and the contras, virtually all rightist forces began to participate, including groups of amnestied contras.

Despite their new role, the parties continued their fractious divisions. They were unable to agree on the meaning of "democratization" or to develop a unified slate of candidates for the reconciliation commission. When the work of the commission bogged down, the FSLN offered to allow all political parties and groups, registered and unregistered, to participate in national dialogue.

A key problem for the opposition as a whole was that it could not agree whether the system merely needed reform or whether the whole system was illegitimate and must be scrapped. The initial agenda of the dialogue was establishing the ground rules for holding Nicaragua's first-ever elections for municipal government, overall electoral laws and procedures, and laws governing political parties. The opposition, under the influence of rightists and the United States, responded with demands for seventeen substantive reforms of the recently passed constitution.

The FSLN, anxious to institutionalize the new system, did not reject the reforms outright but refused to consider them as part of the national dialogue. It insisted that reforms to the constitution could only be considered by the National Assembly according to the procedures established by the constitution. Since the Right held no seats in the assembly, it rejected this position and began to use the reform issue as a weapon against democratization. In December 1987, the entire opposition refused to continue the dialogue with the government without an agreement first on constitutional reforms.

This impasse was broken when it became clear that the Central American presidents did not consider constitutional reforms essential to democratization. In private meetings with opposition figures in late 1988 and early 1989, Oscar Arias and newly elected Venezuelan President Carlos Andrés Pérez told them not to expect outside support for constitutional reforms. More significantly, both Pérez and Arias told the opposition leaders that given the reforms undertaken by the FSLN, the parties could no longer credibly blame their weakness and disorganization on "FSLN totalitarian tendencies." Rather, Pérez and Arias insisted that it was now up to the parties to organize and act as real political parties.[29] In February 1989, President Ortega made an agreement with the other Central American presidents by which the 1990 election was moved ahead ten months and the Nicaraguan government committed itself to further negotiations with the opposition on the issue of electoral law reform.

For the first time, some of the more thoughtful opposition leaders began to examine their own organizational weaknesses instead of looking for excuses. In April 1989, PPSC leader Luis Humberto Guzmán told the *Los Angeles Times*:

> The Sandinistas have no peacetime vision to offer the country. Without the war, they will find it harder to explain their failures. . . . [But] look at us. Here we have four Social Christian factions, four liberal parties, three conservative parties and four Marxist groups against the Sandinistas. Instead of organizing the people, many of those parties have been waiting in vain for the Contras to win or the United States to invade. Now the Sandinistas are starting their campaign, and we are paralyzed.[30]

But elements of the Right continued to be intransigent.

In early August, Daniel Ortega called for a new round of national dialogue on the upcoming election. All parties participated in a thirty-six-hour marathon negotiation, which produced further government concessions to the opposition and an agreement by all opposition parties to participate in the election and to call for the demobilization of the contras by December 5. Rightist opposition leaders were said to be incredulous that their representatives in the negotiations had signed the accord. Apparently the FSLN and the participating opposition had created a momentum that carried the Right along virtually against the latter's will.

The 1990 Campaign

In the 1990 campaign, the distinctions among the three political blocs blurred to the point of disappearing. Patriotic opposition parties to the left and right of the FSLN joined with counterrevolutionary rightists to form the National Opposition Union (UNO). CDN parties that abstained in 1984 joined parties from the patriotic opposition to form coalitions that attacked both UNO and the FSLN. New forces to the left of the FSLN also emerged.

The 1990 campaign featured twenty-three parties, ten presidential candidates, and several formal or informal electoral coalitions. Nevertheless, the race quickly boiled down to a contest between the UNO, led by Violeta Chamorro and Virgilio Godoy, and the FSLN, headed by Daniel Ortega and Sergio Ramírez. The UNO comprised thirteen political parties, spanning the political spectrum from the ostensibly Marxist-Leninist Communist Party of Nicaragua (PCdeN) to the extreme rightist National Conservative party (PNC).

UNO's vague platform made it difficult to tell whether if victorious, it would reverse the revolution or merely modify it. The UNO platform did not call for outright counterrevolution, but it questioned basic policies of the revolution. It called for reviewing the confiscation of non-Somoza family land even if the prior owners had been Somocista collaborators. UNO also pledged to convert all titles issued under the land reform to outright ownership of individual parcels, paving the way for renewed land speculation and concentrated landownership.

UNO planned to restructure the Sandinista Popular Army to deprive it of its "partisan" character, with the implicit goal of converting it into a force willing to enforce whatever rollback of Sandinista policies a UNO government might mandate. It also planned to end the draft and abolish the National Unified Health System in favor of an unspecified "National Health System."[31]

The platform represented a compromise between center-left elements of UNO and rightists who advocated a more radical and complete repudiation of revolutionary policies. On the stump, UNO candidates attempted to portray their platform as a return to the "original" revolutionary program of 1979 "betrayed" by the FSLN.

Immediately after their victory at the polls, UNO leaders, including Violeta Chamorro, pledged reconciliation and an end to confrontation, hinting caution in moving to undo the revolution. However, statements by UNO leaders such as Virgilio Godoy called for revenge against the FSLN, leading many to fear that UNO intended nothing less than counterrevolution. UNO's rhetoric indicated that while the revolution had shifted the terms of the debate sufficiently far to the left that no one dared advocate its complete rollback, forces seeking to repudiate the entire system were nevertheless strong in UNO.

Divining the balance of political forces inside UNO was difficult. During the campaign the leftist forces appeared to have little influence. Financial and other resources seemed to find their way primarily into the hands of rightist and center-right elements (many of which had been receiving money from various U.S. sources ever since 1984). The hardest-line right forces were also weak, having suffered a major defeat when Chamorro and Godoy were nominated over COSEP's Enrique Bolaños. Nevertheless, to keep the rightists inside UNO, they were given prominence on its National Assembly candidate lists. As a result, rightists—many with a history of links to the Somoza regime—appeared on the list of UNO National Assembly candidates far out of proportion to the social or political weight of their political organizations.[32]

UNO's ability to eclipse all other opposition forces was due in no small part to the enormous U.S. financial backing that it (or its components) received. Although the exact amounts are unknown, it is clear that the United States poured money into the right and center-right sectors of UNO. Between 1984 and 1989 the National Endowment for Democracy alone committed $5.2 million to opposition forces that eventually became part of UNO, which amounts to $3.05 per voter.[33] It is estimated that the CIA contributed an additional $15 million. Various organizations linked to UNO also received $5.9 million from a congressional package approved in October 1989.[34]

In addition, UNO was able to capitalize on dissatisfaction with the economic situation and the widespread desire for peace. Ironically, because of La Prensa's de facto cooperation with the U.S. strategy of embargo and contra war, Violeta Chamorro could make a credible promise to the voters to end the embargo and bring peace, whereas the FSLN, which had doggedly resisted the United States, could not.

In contrast to UNO's counterrevolutionary message, the FSLN's platform consciously echoed the themes of its 1984 program. It promised to consolidate peace and the democratic process via political pluralism, strengthen the mixed economy, deepen the agrarian reform, protect disabled veterans, back autonomy for the Atlantic Coast, and defend national sovereignty and nonalignment. The FSLN argued that with the decline of the contras and the consolidation of democracy through the elections, social conditions would improve because foreign assistance would increase and government resources would be diverted from military spending.[35]

However, the FSLN campaigned hard on the theme that the U.S.-backed war rather than the economy was Nicaragua's most pressing problem. The FSLN pointed to UNO's heavy U.S. financing, to UNO's refusal to explicitly condemn contra violence, and to the presence of ex-Somocistas on UNO's candidate lists as proof that UNO was simply a new form of U.S.-sponsored counterrevolution.

Opposition leaders who campaigned outside UNO were largely marginalized. People such as Eduardo Molina and Clemente Guido (PCD), Rodolfo Robelo (PLIUN), Mauricio Díaz and Erick Ramírez (PPSC and PSC), and Moisés Hassan (MUR) led their parties in separate electoral campaigns. In addition, one of the few non-Miskito contras who ever had much popular support, Edén Pastora, drew substantial crowds for the PSC-PPSC alliance.

All these groups rejected UNO's close reliance on the United States and argued for a nationalist policy based on social welfare for all, while at the same time sharply criticizing the FSLN for its perceived sectarianism and corruption. These center to center-left parties presented some relatively detailed proposals for addressing Nicaragua's current economic, social, and political problems. Despite their long political involvement and commitment, all these figures—with the exception of the MUR's Moisés Hassan—failed to obtain the minimum votes necessary to seat their presidential candidates in the National Assembly.

Conclusion

Prior to the mid-1970s, no political force had ever made a serious, sustained effort to build democracy in Nicaragua. Neither the states nor the forces of opposition were seriously interested in or capable of such efforts. The U.S. government never made a serious effort to encourage or pressure the Somoza regime toward democracy until 1978. Starting in about 1974, serious efforts emerged from a number of sectors of Nicaraguan society. The U.S. government ignored or opposed all of these until 1978. It was the FSLN that organized these various efforts into an effective challenge to the Somoza dictatorship, opening the way to meaningful democratization. Whatever the "original intentions" of the Sandinista "founding fathers," it is historical fact that the struggles and achievements of the Sandinista movement from the mid-1970s to the end of the 1980s created the conditions for real democratization.

Opponents of the Sandinistas claim that the 1990 election, and democratization more generally, took place only because of the Reagan administration policy of unrelenting military and economic pressure on Nicaragua. The FSLN was simply forced to give in. Such claims ignore the pattern of events inside Nicaragua throughout the 1980s and the fact that, historically, regimes facing such external pressure have closed political space to their opponents. By contrast, from the beginning, the FSLN regime granted substantial political space to all but the openly seditious opposition parties, inviting opposition participation in and influence over the institutionalization of a new political order. The political interaction between the FSLN and those elements of the opposition that accepted this invitation, although not without problems, was far more genuine and constructive than any politics conducted under any previous Nicaraguan regime. The fact that some of the opposition politicians who took part in this process ended up joining with the hard-line opposition for the 1990 campaign, and that those who ran separate campaigns did very poorly in the elections, should not obscure the contribution that years of interaction between the FSLN and the participating opposition made to democratization. Nor should the role of the hard-line opposition and the U.S. government in the 1990 electoral defeat of the FSLN allow those forces to claim credit for democratization in Nicaragua.

UNO's electoral victory did achieve Washington's goals of unseating the FSLN, defeating uncompromising Nicaraguan nationalism, and bringing back into power leaders who know their place in the U.S. backyard. That, however, is not the same thing as promoting democracy.

Notes

1. The term *party* is used loosely to include factions and splinters that so defined themselves.

2. The principal sources for the historical discussion are Isabel Dumas, *Presentacion de los Partidos Politicos en Nicaragua de 1979 a 1986* (Managua: CRIES, 1987); Elia María Kuan and Trish O'Kane, *Nicaragua: Partidos Politicos y Elecciones Febrero 1990* (Managua: CRIES, Cuadernos de Trabajo, December 1989); and John Booth, *The End and the Beginning: The Nicaraguan Revolution* (Boulder, Colo.: Westview Press, 1982).

3. For the history of an isolated working class progressive strand within Nicaraguan liberalism, and of the attempts of the first two Somozas to coopt this strand, see: Jeffrey L. Gould, *To Lead as Equals: Rural Protest and Political Consciousness in Chinandega, Nicaragua, 1912–1979* (Chapel Hill: University of North Carolina Press, 1990).

4. Pedro Joaquín Chamorro said of the student movement in Managua: "70% of them are Marxists, about 25% are *social-cristianos*, and the remaining 5% are nothing at all. For these youngsters, to be a Conservative or a Liberal is like going out in the tropical sun wearing a bowler hat." Quoted in George Black, *Triumph of the People* (London: Zed Press, 1981), p. 84.

5. See ibid.

6. Central America Research Institute, *Central America Bulletin*, November 1986 and November 1984; and Gary Ruchwarger, *People in Power, Forging a Grassroots Democracy in Nicaragua* (London: Bergin and Garvey, 1987).

7. The primary sources for this discussion are Central America Research Institute, *Central America Bulletin*, November 1984 and November 1986; and Thomas Walker, ed., *Nicaragua in Revolution* (New York: Praeger, 1982).

8. On the "logic of the majority," see Jose Luis Coraggio and George Irvin, "Revolution and Democracy in Nicaragua," *Latin American Perspectives* 12, no. 2 (Spring 1985); "Towards a New Constitution," *Envío* 4, no. 53 (November 1985), pp. 7b–9b; and Jose Luis Coraggio, *Nicaragua: Revolution and Democracy* (London: Allen & Unwin, 1985).

9. Except where specifically noted, this section is based on Central America Research Institute, *Central America Bulletin*, November 1984.

10. The CDN demands included: (1) separation of party and state, (2) end of confiscation of private property and the draft, (3) end of the State of Emergency, (4) amnesty for political and common criminals, (5) freedom of religion, (6) the right to strike, (7) judicial autonomy, (8) allowing appeals to the court for violations of the Fundamental Statute and the Statute of Rights and Guarantees, and (9) dialogue with the contras.

11. Central American Historical Institute, *Update* 3, no. 29 (September 4, 1984).

12. *Washington Post*, July 30, 1984. See also *New York Times*, November 5, 1984, November 14, 1984, and November 17, 1984.

13. Central America Research Institute interviews with Clemente Guido (PCD), Domingo Sanchez (PSN), Mauricio Díaz (PPSC), and Virgilio Godoy (PLI). All interviews were conducted in August 1984.

14. In August 1984, FSLN campaign party spokesperson Giaconda Belli told the Central America Research Institute (CARIN) of examples of FSLN peasant organizers who intended to vote either conservative or liberal because, despite their militancy in the FSLN, they associated the traditional parties with elections. CARIN's own informal voter surveys also conducted in August 1984 indicated that among the less-educated and poorer classes, most party candidates apart from those of the FSLN, PCD, and PLI were unknown even in Managua.

15. Universidad Centro Americana, Encuentro, no. 35 (September-December 1988), pp. 13-21; and Daniel Wolf, "Falling Off the Bandwagon: Electoral Politics and the Scope Available to Loyal Oppositions in Nicaragua," paper presented at the Latin American Studies Association Convention, New Orleans, March 1988.

16. Central America Research Institute, Central America Bulletin, February 1985.

17. Central American Historical Institute, Update 4, no. 8 (March 25, 1985).

18. See "The Emergency and Cardinal Obando," Envío, November 1985, pp. 14a-17a.

19. Central America Research Institute, Central America Bulletin, December 1986. The Right no doubt retained or even expanded somewhat the 10-20 percent of the voting-age population that we estimate to have supported the CDN in 1984. However, no efforts were made to mobilize that support beyond a few poorly attended rallies.

20. Envío, January 1985.

21. Central American Historical Institute, Update 4, no. 16 (March 31, 1985).

22. The text of the agreement is reprinted in the appendix to Coraggio, Nicaragua: Revolution and Democracy. See also Central American Historical Institute, Update, November 1, and December 12, 1984.

23. For contrasting views on the 1985 reimposition of the State of Emergency, see "Behind the State of Emergency," Envío, November 1985, and the articles by Abraham Brumberg in the Spring and Summer 1986 issues of Dissent.

24. Central America Research Institute, Central America Bulletin, November 1986 and November 1984; and Ruchwarger, People in Power.

25. At an April 1986 conference on the Nicaraguan constitution at New York University Law School, leaders of the PCD, PPSC, and the left faction of the PLI emphasized that the constitution must establish a system of representative government on the Western, parliamentary model rather than attempt to institutionalize FSLN theories of popular democracy. They stated, "Socialism and participatory democracy are not yet on the agenda since we've only recently left fascism and have yet to build a democratic political culture." In response, FSLN representatives argued for integrating popular democracy into the representative/parliamentary model but were vague as to how this might be done. For an extended discussion of this FSLN view, see Jules Lobel, "The Meaning of Democracy: Representative and Participatory Democracy in the New Nicaraguan Constitution," University of Pittsburgh Law Review 49, no. 3 (Spring 1988).

26. In an interview on March 7, 1989, Rogelio Ramírez, FSLN assembly delegate and legal adviser to the FSLN National Assembly delegation, told CARIN that the concept of participatory democracy as it had been articulated up to that point would have led ultimately to a corporatist state reminiscent of the "national socialist conception of society."

27. Central American Historical Institute, *Update*, June 30, 1987.

28. At the same time some PSD members left to join the contras.

29. CARIN interview with Western diplomat, Managua, March 1989.

30. *Los Angeles Times*, March 6, 1989.

31. "Programa de Gobierno de la Unión Nacional Opositora," Kuan and O'Kane, *Nicaragua: Partidos Políticos y Elecciones Febrero 1990*.

32. *Barricada*, October 9, 1989, and October 12, 1989.

33. An equivalent level of funding in the 1988 presidential campaign in the United States would have been $305 million, based on an estimated voting population of 100 million.

34. Hemisphere Initiatives, *Nicaraguan Election Update #2: Foreign Funding of the Internal Opposition*, October 16, 1989.

35. Kuan and O'Kane, *Nicaragua: Partidos Políticos y Elecciones Febrero 1990*.

SEVEN

Women in the Revolution

PATRICIA M. CHUCHRYK

During the ten and one-half years of the Sandinista revolution in Nicaragua, progress in the area of women's rights was uneven. Legal rights and guarantees improved significantly, but the counterrevolutionary war of the mid-1980s and the economic crisis of the late 1980s severely limited the state's capacity to improve the material conditions of women's lives and to challenge the patriarchal structure and ideology of Nicaraguan society. As early as 1969, the Sandinista Front for National Liberation (FSLN) incorporated gender equality into its program for social change and social justice. The FSLN strategy, however, focused on increasing the participation of women in productive activities and thus often ignored issues related to women and reproduction. The mobilization of men for defense, especially from 1983 to 1986, substantially reduced the national budget available for social programs that could ease women's double burden. Yet that mobilization facilitated the entry of women into postsecondary education and typically male jobs; thus it helped break down the traditional gendered division of labor. And although the labor force participation and union membership of women increased dramatically during the revolution, they continued to be concentrated in lower-paid, lower-skilled jobs, and union leadership continued to be dominated by men.

The rate of women's participation in armed combat during the insurrection was the highest of any Latin American revolutionary movement. But this level was not sustained, and the numbers of women in the armed forces declined substantially after 1979. The conventional view is that women mobilize politically during periods of crisis and return to their traditional roles once the crisis subsides. The extent to which recent Nicaraguan history accurately reflects this view has important implications for the continuing struggle to eliminate the oppression of women.

One of the most important mass organizations in Nicaragua was the Luisa Amanda Espinoza Association of Nicaraguan Women (AMNLAE) named for the first woman combatant to die in the struggle to overthrow

Somoza. It was responsible for many of the gains in women's rights, especially in the area of legal reform. Yet credibility problems, identity crises, and ideological uncertainty constrained AMNLAE's ability to promote the change in values and attitudes required to sustain structural transformation.

In light of these contradictions, an examination of women and the Sandinista People's Revolution must be guided by three questions: What difference did the revolution make to the material conditions of women's lives? What improvements were made in the area of women's rights? In what ways, and how successfully, did the revolutionary government challenge those structures and ideologies that underpin and reinforce patriarchal and capitalist gender relations?

Women's Mobilization Before 1979

There was little in women's collective history and experience in Nicaragua to prepare the society for the role women were to play in the revolution. Although it has been reported that women fought together with Augusto César Sandino in the late 1920s and early 1930s, their numbers were so few that they are hardly ever mentioned.[1] Women had no history of activism in trade unions or political parties, and during the early years in the FSLN's history, few women were actively involved. Haley pointed out that at first the FSLN had a practice of not admitting women.[2] Moreover, FSLN attempts in the 1960s and early 1970s to organize women were largely unsuccessful.[3]

In September 1977, the Association of Women Confronting the National Problem (AMPRONAC) was formed. Organized to draw greater numbers of women into the struggle against the Somoza dictatorship, it initially focused on human rights issues; in particular it denounced human rights violations perpetrated by the National Guard and offered support to mothers of the detained and disappeared.[4] Thus it attracted women of all social classes.[5] Although AMPRONAC was not a feminist organization, its original nine-point platform included two demands specifically related to women: equal pay for equal work and the elimination of the commercialization of women's bodies (e.g., prostitution, sex-objectification in advertising).

By mid-1978, the organization had clearly declared itself in support of both women's and national liberation[6] and had more or less incorporated a critique of women's oppression.[7] By promoting a new image of women as political actors, it began to challenge the traditional view of women as essentially outside the realm of politics. Reasonably successful in mobilizing women, AMPRONAC had 8,000 to 10,000 members by July 19, 1979.[8] In one writer's evaluation: "AMPRONAC's strategy of raising women's concerns to create a mass political movement was successful. It helped overthrow the dictatorship, developed feminist demands later met by the new government, and gave women a sense of confidence in their ability to influence national events. It also changed the nature of the national liberation struggle from one in which women were merely helpmates to one in which they were fighting on their own behalf."[9]

During the liberation struggle, the FSLN offered women the opportunity to take on roles from which they had been excluded in Nicaraguan society. At the time of the triumph, approximately 25 percent of FSLN combatants were women,[10] among them many distinguished as combat officers, including Comandantes Doris Tijerino, Dora María Téllez, and Mónica Baltodano. But many of the women's roles were extensions of what had traditionally been defined as women's work.[11] They provided emergency medical care, hid weapons, passed information, provided food and shelter, made uniforms and explosives, organized safe houses and neighborhood defense, and cared for the children of those in the underground.[12]

Although women were adept at using and manipulating machismo to their own political advantage, they were also particularly vulnerable to the brutality of the National Guard. Few women captured by the guard, for example, escaped repeated rape.[13] Women involved in the anti-Somoza struggle also had to confront the sexist attitudes of their husbands and comrades-in-arms. According to numerous reports, family conflict was a frequent consequence of women's political participation.[14] Husbands and fathers often opposed the involvement of their wives and daughters.

In a paradoxical way, motherhood mobilized many Nicaraguan women. The role of mother, which defined the exclusive social destiny of the overwhelming majority of women and was greatly revered in Nicaraguan society, contrasted sharply with the mothers' inability to protect their children from the brutal excesses of the dictatorship. This contradiction served to galvanize many women into participating in activities in support of the armed struggle against Somoza.

Initially, attempts to mobilize mothers were not necessarily intended to politicize women as women. As Haley pointed out, in the early years, "the political activist was simply an outward disguise assumed by the traditional mother."[15] It was only with the emergence and success of AMPRONAC that "the role of mother [become] a disguise for the militant."[16] Contradictory social processes served both to reinforce women's traditional role as mother and to reconceptualize the apolitical mother as the revolutionary (or combative) mother. As one writer suggested, "the horrors of the dictatorship unintentionally gave birth to a tradition of revolutionary motherhood in Nicaragua."[17]

Nicaraguan women, particularly those who were mothers, were not strangers to hardship, suffering, and resourcefulness in the struggle for survival. Family instability[18] and "paternal irresponsibility," combined with economic insecurity and poverty, required that many mothers assume total financial responsibility for the support of their families. According to many observers, it was precisely the difficulty under Somoza to meet their economic and social responsibilities that explains women's considerable involvement in the insurrection and, later, in defense of the revolution.[19] This involvement, in turn, began to break down traditional stereotypes, especially among the guerrilla fighters. It also encouraged the growth of awareness among women of their oppression and, perhaps most important, the development of their self-esteem and self-confidence as political persons.[20] Logically, this led to a daily-life conflict between women's conception of themselves as women (mothers) and their emerging conception of themselves as political subjects.

This contradiction between politicizing motherhood by glorifying it and not politicizing women outside of their role as mothers surfaced many times and in many ways throughout the Nicaraguan revolution. It is probably the key to understanding some of the constraints that limited the ability of the Sandinistas to advance in the area of women's rights and women's emancipation.

AMNLAE and Legislation

After the triumph of the insurrectionary forces on July 19, 1979, AMPRONAC became AMNLAE, and its first strategy was to push for legislative reform. It was relatively successful, for the Sandinista government moved quickly to legislate equality between men and women. In September 1979, the Statute of Rights and Guarantees established the legal equality of men and women. Other legislation introduced in the first three years of the revolution prohibited the use of women as sexual objects in advertising, permitted women to adopt children, guaranteed the equality of all children whether or not they were born in formalized unions, prohibited the advertising of infant formula, and gave women the right, on the same basis as men, to hold title to property in the cooperatives of the new agrarian reform. A legal concept found in most Latin American societies, *patria potestad*, which granted fathers fundamental rights over children without making them financially responsible for them, was eliminated in Nicaragua in 1982 and replaced by a law that makes mothers and fathers equally responsible for the care of their children. A nurturance law, also introduced in 1982, "obliges both parents to guarantee their children food, clothing, health care, housing and education, and demands familial solidarity with all dependent family members: children, the elderly and the handicapped."[21] Furthermore, this law required that all members of the family share in domestic labor. But as several interviewees noted, it is difficult to legislate changes in attitudes, values, and behaviors marked by centuries of patriarchal relations between men and women.

Other indications that the state was serious in its commitment to incorporate women into the political process included AMNLAE's representation on the Council of State, which was formed by the FSLN in May 1980 and comprised representatives of twenty-nine organizations.[22] In September 1979, the state created the Women's Program, which later became the Women's Government Office, attached to the Office of the President. An Office for the Protection of the Family was created as part of the Nicaraguan Institute of Social Security and Social Welfare (INSSBI) in 1980, and in 1983 the Women's Legal Office was created to assist women with legal difficulties and to educate them with regard to their rights.[23]

The Defense of the Revolution

From 1979 to 1983, AMNLAE's first priority was to involve women in the defense of the revolution, considered a precondition for their emancipation. The group emphasized the need for women to participate in all aspects of the revolution, including the mass organizations, as well as production. It advocated improvements in living conditions, especially in the areas of health care, housing, and the provision of basic food stuffs. But AMNLAE lacked a clear sense of direction during these first years.[24] It seemed to duplicate the efforts of other mass organizations in which women participated (for example, the Rural Workers' Association and the Sandinista Defense Committees). Accepting the assumption that women are pillars of the family and thus of Nicaraguan society, AMNLAE gave priority to its work with the Mothers of Heroes and Martyrs, an organization of the mothers of those killed by the National Guard and later of those killed by the counterrevolutionaries. Consequently, this focus on women's traditional roles inhibited the development of an analysis and political strategy based on a critique of those roles.

Many of those involved in AMNLAE were members of the FSLN and threw themselves into party work.[25] One of the major criticisms of AMNLAE during this period was that decisions were made at the top levels of the organization to be carried out by women in the base. Another criticism was that AMNLAE's position on participation in the productive life of the country as a precondition for women's liberation, a position identical to that of the FSLN, precluded an analysis of women's oppression in the reproductive sphere. There were also internal debates about the mission of AMNLAE.

Women in the Productive Sphere

Integrating women into production is probably the area in which the Sandinista government was most successful, partly because women's labor was necessary to reconstruct an economy looted and destroyed by the Somoza dictatorship. Although in 1977 women constituted 28 percent of the economically active population (EAP), relatively high for Latin America,[26] there were few jobs available to them. Domestic service, street vending, prostitution, and work in the informal sector accounted for most women engaged in paid labor. Limited industrial development, concentrated landownership, and an agricultural sector dominated by export production created high unemployment and underemployment, high rates of rural-urban migration, job insecurity, and low wages, all of which created problems more acute for women than for men.[27]

In 1989, women were 45 percent of the EAP,[28] as high or higher than the female labor force participation rate in most industrialized countries. In the late 1980s, 37 percent of the industrial labor force, 35 percent of the salaried agricultural labor force, and 45 percent of the seasonally employed were women.[29] Eighty-four percent of market vendors,[30] 80 percent of health workers, 74 percent of teachers,[31] and 65 percent of those employed in the informal sector[32] were also women.

The increase in women's labor force participation and the passage of laws that established equal pay for equal work, protection for pregnant workers, and access to subsidized child care did not mean that employment discrimination had been eliminated. The traditional gendered division of labor remained relatively unchanged during the years of the Nicaraguan revolution. Women still tended to be segregated into lower-paying, sex-stereotyped jobs. They continued to be exclusively responsible for child care and domestic labor and thus worked many more hours than did men. They occupied few management positions and received less-than-equal pay for work of equal value. And although the number of child-care centers increased from 8 prior to the revolution to 248 by 1982, 128 of which were located in the rural areas,[33] in no way did they meet the need for such services. The Sandinistas, however, were not solely responsible for the lack of development of child-care centers. The escalation of the contra war as well as the U.S. trade embargo dramatically decreased the availability of resources for such development.

Many Nicaraguan social scientists have drawn attention to the contradictory impact of the war and of the economic crisis during the period 1983 to 1987.[34] The state had no choice but to make defense its top priority. While the men were mobilized in national defense, women took over their jobs. This resulted in feminization of the labor forces both in industry and agricultural work.

An important study, undertaken cooperatively by two research centers, the Center for the Investigation and Study of the Agrarian Reform

(CIERA) and the Center for Labor Studies (CETRA), and the agricultural workers' union (ATC), documented this feminization process in tobacco, cotton, and coffee production.[35] Based on a survey of 800 salaried female workers, the study specifically found that women came to represent an increasing number of agricultural workers, that the traditional gendered division of labor in agricultural work was beginning to break down, and that women, normally concentrated in the temporary or seasonal labor force, began to be salaried workers for an increasing number of months during the year. For example, in 1980–1981 women were 32 percent of the workers in cotton and 28 percent of the workers in coffee; by 1984–1985 these figures had increased to 56 percent and 41 percent respectively.[36] In tobacco in 1984–1985, women were 76 percent of permanent workers and 63 percent of temporary workers.[37] This study also found that there was greater feminization of the agricultural labor force in the state sector (40 percent of the workers) than in the private sector (27 percent).[38] The scarcity of male labor during this period required that women perform jobs traditionally reserved for men. But this study also found that women tended not to occupy decision-making positions within the enterprise, and that both management and male union officials continued to carry traditional beliefs and stereotypes about women's inappropriateness for certain kinds of work.[39]

Furthermore, most women continued to be responsible for child care and domestic labor, which severely limited their ability to take on the training and education required for some of the traditionally male jobs. "The fundamental effect [of the double day] is the reinforcement of their subordination and, in spite of the fact that the sexual division of labor is breaking down, the hierarchical relations between men and women in the reproductive sphere remain unchanged."[40] Only 8 percent of the women left their children at child-care centers, although many indicated that they would like to do so if such services were available. Most women had to rely on another woman, usually an older daughter or another family member, to care for their children while they were working outside the home. Despite the legal right to maternity leave, the study found that especially in the private sector, pregnant women were not being hired and maternity leave did not exist in practice.[41] A majority of women in the sample believed that men and women should share domestic responsibilities,[42] a strong indication that to some extent the attitudes of the women had changed to accommodate their new roles and responsibilities in production.

In the late 1980s, women constituted 40 percent of the membership of the ATC, representing over 10,000 women.[43] The CIERA/ATC/CETRA study found that 89 percent of the women in the sample attended union meetings, but as the authors were quick to point out, attendance did not necessarily indicate active participation.[44] The traditional sexual division of labor reproduced itself in the union, and responsibilities in the reproductive sphere made it impossible for women to turn their double day into a triple day.[45] Interestingly, the authors of the study also suggested that the union had not assumed its responsibility to motivate women to participate in such a way that women would feel that it was their organization too.[46] But by 1987, it appeared that this had begun to change.

In 1984 the ATC, with the assistance and support of AMNLAE, was the first organization to establish a Women's Secretariat. One ATC (woman) leader expressed the need for the organization to incorporate more women into leadership positions, to focus more on attacking the double day rather than on integrating women into production, and to address the particular demands of women workers.[47] Included in the concerns raised by women of the ATC at its second national assembly in 1986 were demands for increased social benefits like child care, maternity subsidies, collective laundry facilities, children's cafeterias, increased spaces for women in technical and union training programs, and the integration of more women in union leadership.[48] A major issue debated at this conference was that of work quotas. The women argued that they should have the same norms as men even though the men were not participating in household work. To suggest that women accept lower work quotas on the basis of the double day would only ideologically and structurally reinforce their exclusive responsibilities in the domestic sphere.[49]

The ATC made great inroads in the struggle for women's emancipation. Throughout the country it was well known for its feminist positions and its attempts to integrate gender-specific with class-based demands. From 1987 on, the ATC argued strongly that the issues normally considered "women's" issues, like child care and family planning, were social issues and therefore should not be "ghettoized."[50]

The laws on agrarian reform made it quite clear that women shared with men the right to hold title to land and the right to full membership in the cooperatives. In 1986, there were 2,745 registered cooperatives, and by the end of 1987, they worked 21 percent of the agricultural land in Nicaragua.[51] There was at least one woman member in approximately 44 percent of all cooperatives. Though the proportion of women members rose from 6 percent in 1982 to 7.3 percent in 1986,[52] only 19 percent of all cooperatives had more than 10 percent women.[53] A 1989 CIERA study based on the life histories of peasant women suggested that the traditional sexist attitudes that continued to thrive among peasants were in part responsible for the marginalization of women in the cooperative movement.[54]

In the urban industrial sector the situation was similar to that found in the agricultural sector. A 1989 study based on a sample of 250 women workers in the textile and garment-making industries, conducted by the

Nicaraguan Women's Institute, used much the same methodology as the CIERA/ATC/CETRA study and, not surprisingly, documented many of the same findings.[55] The study attempted to identify the obstacles to the promotion of the equality of women in both production and society as well as the concrete manifestations of continued discrimination against women in employment. Occupational segregation and unequal pay; exclusion from the better jobs, including management positions; stereotyped sexist attitudes; the absence of technical training programs for women; and discrimination against pregnant women were the norm for women working in the industrial sector.[56] Domestic responsibilities contributed to occupational segregation and women's inability to advance in their jobs.[57] Only 7 percent of the sample had their children in child-care centers, but the majority would have liked to.[58] Eighty-six percent believed that men and women should share household labor.[59] On the basis of these data, the authors of the study made an important point: "The value attributed to the woman-mother in our society is plagued with contradictions; because on the one hand, maternity is highly valued, yet on the other, pregnant women and women with small children are discriminated against in paid labor."[60]

In January 1987, one-third of the 158,000 workers associated with The Sandinista Workers' Federation (CST) were women, but they tended to be excluded from leadership positions. Women workers were characterized as dependent, submissive, docile, obedient, emotional, and unfit for leadership, and, unlike the ATC, the CST tended to view sexual harassment and other issues of particular concern to women as "women's issues."[61] In 1987, the CST formed a Women's Secretariat, but the federation seemed to have been unable to make the same progress as the ATC.

Domestic service continued to be a major occupation for women, accounting for 25 percent of the female labor force, and domestic servants continued to be the least protected of all workers.[62] Shortly after the FSLN victory in 1979, domestic servants met with FSLN leaders and organized the National Union of Domestic Servants. They were reasonably successful in their demands for a ten-hour work day, double pay for holidays and overtime, a minimum wage, and the right to six months severance pay in the case of unjust firing.[63] As Ruchwarger pointed out, however, the Sandinista goal of abolishing domestic service[64] was not even a remote possibility: "The plight of the domestic workers traps [the] Nicaraguan economy in a double bind. Without the domestic services these women provide, thousands of other Nicaraguan women would be unable to leave their homes to work. . . . Without other alternatives, women will continue to seek domestic employment. Thus far, neither the legislation that calls for men to share housework nor the new child care centers have had any effect on the demand for domestic workers."[65]

It must be kept in mind that the dual problems of economic scarcity and threat of war made it extremely difficult to develop the infrastructure necessary to advance the cause of women's rights. The economic crisis seemed to have hit women the hardest.[66] The feminization of poverty had deepened.[67]

The Reproductive Sphere

> To be a poor woman in Nicaragua in the 1970s, after thirty or more years of dependent "development," meant to expect to live to be about fifty. To be poor and female meant a three out of ten chance of never attending school and becoming one of every two over the age of ten who remained functionally illiterate. To be poor also meant to end childhood and adolescence abruptly at or shortly after puberty with a first pregnancy, usually outside of wedlock. To be a woman, aged 34, meant having reached advanced middle age. In the rural areas, such a woman could expect to have been pregnant an average of eight times, although only three or four of her children would still be alive. The vast majority would [have] responsibility for maintaining the household.[68]

One of the major difficulties with a strategy of integrating women into production when there is neither political will nor resources to alleviate women's domestic burden is that productive roles simply are added to reproductive roles.[69] The lack of resources to socialize household labor and for child-care centers, the absence of family planning and sex education, the continued influence of the Roman Catholic church, and the state's pronatalist policy all served to reinforce the traditional view of women as reproducers relegated to the private sphere of the family. Despite legislation, paternal irresponsibility—husbands abandoning and not financially assisting their families—continued to account for a high rate of female-headed households. In 1986, 48 percent of Nicaraguan families were headed by women; 60 percent in urban areas.[70] Eighty-five percent of single mothers were employed in the paid labor force.[71] Figures available in 1989 suggested that 42 percent of all Nicaraguan women were in their childbearing years.[72] In addition, machismo, traditionally measured by the number of children a man has fathered (not necessarily by the same woman), remained relatively unchanged, even in the late 1980s.[73]

Although the law had been changed to protect women and children and to guarantee the equality of men and women in marriage, the experience of women in marriage continued to reflect old patterns. Some aspects of the 1904 Civil Code had not yet been changed. For instance, a woman was still obligated to live at her husband's domicile. Only women were penalized for adultery, and the law defined the conditions under which women were permitted to remarry after divorce.

These antiquated notions of a particular morality for women coexisted, for example, with the divorce legislation introduced in 1988, which allowed both men and women to petition for divorce.

Other examples demonstrated the stranglehold that old patterns had on new ideas. In 90 percent of the divorce cases that came to the attention of the Women's Legal Office (OLM) between 1983 and 1986, wife battery was given as the reason for divorce.[74] And even though there was an emerging awareness that domestic violence was not socially acceptable, there was still no law specifically prohibiting it. Not surprisingly, an OLM study completed in 1986 found that law enforcement officials (police, lawyers, judges) continued to view the problem of domestic violence through the filter of traditional patriarchal values.[75]

Probably one of the more significant achievements of the Nicaraguan revolution was the politicization of domestic and sexual violence, that is, the entry of these issues into the realm of public discourse. But in 1989, AMNLAE was still—unsuccessfully—proposing to draft legislation that would overturn the laws that viewed sexual crimes as private crimes and required that the victim, rather than the state, press charges.[76]

One of the most contentious issues to emerge during this period was abortion. Although the police had stopped prosecuting women for abortion within a year of the FSLN victory, it was still a criminal offense, and efforts to decriminalize it were unsuccessful. Consequently, abortion continued to be the major cause of maternal death.

In a study conducted at the Berta Calderón Hospital for Women in Managua, of the 809 patients who "confessed" to having had an abortion, 61 percent were between the ages of twenty and twenty-nine, 74 percent were in stable relationships, 86 percent had some education, 64 percent were housewives, 76 percent had previous pregnancies carried to term, and 55 percent were not using any form of contraception.[77] In the absence of family planning programs and a comprehensive program of sex education, women continued to be victimized by their reproductive capacity.

The state's pronatalist policy exacerbated this problem. Women were exhorted to reproduce for the revolution and in 1987, President Ortega publicly declared himself against abortion: "One way of depleting our youth is to promote the sterilization of women in Nicaragua . . . or to promote a policy of abortion."[78] Women activists, although they did not deny the need for population replacement, suggested that women's right to choose, under social conditions designed to facilitate that choice, would be more appropriate than compulsory motherhood.[79] The debate subsided during the most intense years of the contra war, but it reemerged later, and in 1990, at the time of the FSLN electoral defeat, it was still unresolved. Clearly, the FSLN had fallen short of its commitment to women's emancipation in the area of the family and reproductive rights.

AMNLAE, the FSLN,
and Women's Political Mobilization

In October 1987, fifty-four Nicaraguan women, from various organizations and sectors, arrived in Taxco, Mexico, to participate in the
Fourth Latin American and Caribbean Feminist Encuentro. The participation of so many Nicaraguans was unprecedented in the history of
these conferences.[80] In the following discussion, I try to explain the
process that led to the participation of the Nicaraguan women's movement,
traditionally loath to describe itself and its activities as feminist, in a
Latin American feminist conference.

In the first three years after the FSLN victory, AMNLAE had focused
on legislative reform, national reconstruction, involving women in the
health and education campaigns, and in production.[81] The major difficulty
it experienced was coordinating its work with that of other mass
organizations. In 1983, with the escalation of the U.S.-financed counterrevolutionary war, efforts were shifted to national defense. When
the state moved to implement conscription, AMNLAE argued (unsuccessfully) in the Council of State that the draft should apply equally
to women. Although women were exempted from obligatory military
duty, they were permitted to form voluntary battalions. At this time
AMNLAE also increased its work with the mothers of conscripted men
and the Mothers of Heroes and Martyrs. AMNLAE's view was that in
the absence of intensive political work with these women, they could
easily be co-opted by the Right.[82] Gender-specific demands were, for
the most part, abandoned. According to one Nicaraguan social scientist,
many women were starting to become frustrated and disillusioned with
the organization, and by 1985, reproductive issues, such as abortion,
domestic violence, and family planning, began to be incorporated into
public discourse.[83]

One of the areas in which AMNLAE's organizing efforts were very
successful was in the open meetings to discuss first the draft of the
new Nicaraguan constitution. Thousands of women participated in these
meetings, which took place throughout May and June 1986. They were
concerned about issues such as women's economic dependence on men,
divorce, compulsory motherhood in the absence of legal and safe abortion,
violence against women, job training and protections for pregnant workers.
But as one observer pointed out: "The most radical proposals from the
cabildos [public town hall meetings], even those with apparently broad
support, did not make it to the second draft [of the Constitution]. This
is true, for example, of the Constitutional right to abortion, which
received support all over the country."[84]

The Nicaraguan constitution of 1987, however, did have a number
of guarantees that represented significant advances for women. Using

gender-inclusive language, the constitution eliminated obvious discrimination. For example, the age of majority was defined as sixteen without regard to sex (unlike the constitutions of many Latin American countries in which the age of majority is defined differently for men and women). Article 27 established equality before the law. Articles 70–79, dealing with family rights, defined the "absolute equality of rights and responsibilities between the man and woman."[85] Article 82 guaranteed equal pay for equal work, and Article 109 emphasized that "the state shall promote the voluntary association of peasants in agricultural cooperatives, without sexual discrimination."[86] These constitutional provisions clearly represented significant accomplishments on the part of AMNLAE.

For years the FSLN thinking on women had been ambiguous and traditional, focusing on the involvement of women in productive activities. The Sandinistas tended to glorify motherhood, encourage women to have babies, and reinforce rather than question women's traditional roles. Indeed they had difficulty imagining women except as mothers.[87] Although it is important that women's work in the home become socially recognized as valuable work, it is also important that it does not become defined as exclusively women's work. Yet in a now-famous speech, Tomás Borge, a member of the Sandinista Joint National Directorate, asked: "How can we not guarantee that a woman can be *both a mother and a worker, both a mother and a student, both a mother and an artist* . . . both fulfill all the tasks the revolution demands of her and at the same time fulfill the beautiful work of a *self-sacrificing, capable and loving mother?*"[88] In the same speech, Borge also spoke about the new "Sandinista courtesy and chivalry of man unto woman" and explained that women are weaker than men and thus need to be treated with special consideration.[89] Women—meaning mothers—by sacrificing their sons and daughters, were viewed as heroic defenders of the revolution.[90] On very few occasions had the FSLN confronted the issues of reproductive rights, the double day, or machismo.

By 1986, AMNLAE leadership began to reevaluate critically the organization's role in the Nicaraguan revolution. The issue was whether AMNLAE should be a broadly based social movement or an organization. A product of the efforts of many women political activists, the FSLN's Proclamation on Women, presented at AMNLAE's third general assembly on March 8, 1987, settled the debate. But the proclamation did not totally refute the FSLN's traditional and conservative view and in places seemed to imply the exclusivity of women's roles in the reproductive sphere; for example, it proclaimed: "We will struggle so that women can fulfill their maternal function and their family responsibilities under ever-improving conditions and in a way that these responsibilities do not become insurmountable obstacles to their own personal growth and development."[91]

The document did, however, mark an advance in the position of the FSLN. It raised issues beyond those related to production. It addressed women's access to jobs traditionally held by men, machismo, paternal irresponsibility, and domestic violence. Women's "problems" were defined as social issues, and its discussion of private-sphere concerns provided a starting point from which to begin to break down men's resistance to change.[92] Nevertheless, the FSLN reaffirmed its pronatalist policy and continued to publicly ignore the issue of reproductive rights, in part due to the fear of a religious backlash should they declare themselves in favor of women's right to a legal and safe abortion.[93]

The proclamation also articulated AMNLAE's reorganization. Rather than continue to duplicate the work of other mass organizations as well as compete for members, AMNLAE would encourage women to participate in their own sectors, such as the CST, ATC, and Sandinista Youth (JS), and offer support to the various women's secretariats. The FSLN proclamation argued that women must construct their demands on the basis of their needs and experiences in the sectors in which they work. Some criticized this as "integrationist," arguing the potential danger that women's interests would become diluted and ignored if subsumed within sectoral interests and demands. At the time of the FSLN electoral defeat in 1990, it was too early to tell what the effects of this reorganization might have been.

Structurally, AMNLAE was "deprofessionalized" and democratized. The number of full-time paid staff was decreased, and decision and policy-making shifted into the hands of the different constituencies represented. Replacing the previous board of directors, there was a new advisory board, consisting of representatives of the women's secretariats of various sectors, elected by newly constituted national assemblies within those sectors. These included the teachers' union (ANDEN), the Federation of Health Workers (FETSALUD), the farmers' association (UNAG), the National Confederation of Professionals (CONAPRO-Heroes and Martyrs), the ATC, and the CST.

Until the late 1980s, when strong organizations representing sectoral interests began to take initiatives somewhat independently, AMNLAE *was* the women's movement in Nicaragua. With the restructuring, however, AMNLAE's traditional hegemony with regard to the women's movement diminished. The women's secretariat of the ATC, for example, rejected AMNLAE's top-down "preachy" style and argued for a women's movement that would penetrate and be incorporated into all of the sectors.[94] The women's secretariat of CONAPRO–Heroes and Martyrs, in existence only since 1987, organized first a national conference, then an international conference on women and legislation—both of which were huge successes.

After 1987, AMNLAE's work focused on four areas: economic survival, child care, women's dignity ("the creation of a strong family with mutual respect between men and women"), and sex education.[95] A 1988 "plan of action" listed peace and dignity, rights for women workers, domestic violence, shared domestic responsibilities, political participation, legal reform, sex education, and the elimination of myths and prejudices as the key issues around which to mobilize women. Many Nicaraguan women observed that, by 1988, AMNLAE's program was essentially a feminist one, with the notable omission of the issue of sexual preference.[96] Amalia Chamorro, for example, a sociologist from the Central American University, argued that the period 1988–1989 marked the transformation of AMNLAE into a truly revolutionary feminist movement.[97] Indeed, one could hear the word *feminism* much more than ever before in the history of the Nicaraguan revolution; this is remarkable, given the fear and suspicion some had that the women's movement was separatist. In the Proclamation on Women, the FSLN reaffirmed the classic Marxist position that feminism is divisive, as well as the misconception, prevalent in Latin America, that feminism is a struggle against men rather than a struggle against patriarchy: "We reject those tendencies which propose the emancipation of women as a result of a struggle against men and as a struggle exclusive to women, since this kind of position divides the people and distracts them from their fundamental tasks."[98]

Historically, the FSLN had provided AMNLAE with institutional support. The links between the party and the movement were not organic, and the direction of the flow of influence was not always clear. For a time, many of the women in AMNLAE were party members and appeared to carry the party's positions on issues into AMNLAE. On the other hand, it was clear that AMNLAE's structural transformation long preceded the FSLN proclamation that formalized it, suggesting that AMNLAE leaders might have played a fundamental role in the FSLN positions articulated in the proclamation. In 1989, one of the unresolved internal debates within AMNLAE had to do with the extent to which the organization should remain independent of the party and the state. Many argued that considerable distance and autonomy were required so that AMNLAE could truly pressure the state to embark on a more comprehensive series of reforms. With what force, for example, would AMNLAE be able to present its petition for the decriminalization of abortion if its ties to the FSLN were too close?

The FSLN was criticized for treating women's issues as secondary[99] and for making its commitment to women's emancipation a conditional one.[100] As Molyneux pointed out in 1985, "It is clear that the FSLN was able to implement only those parts of the program for women's emancipation that coincided with its general goals, enjoyed popular support, and were realizable without arousing strong opposition."[101] Further, the Sandinista goals of democratic pluralism and a mixed economy had a contradictory impact. A substantial private sector, on which the economy had to rely heavily, tended to be less likely to comply with legislation requiring, for example, equal pay or maternity subsidies—and the state was less likely to enforce it. Democratic pluralism permitted the powerful and fully entrenched Roman Catholic church to oppose, among other things, family planning, sex education, contraceptive technology, abortion, and changes to the divorce laws.[102]

At the time of the FSLN victory in 1979, women constituted 38 percent of FSLN membership. By 1987, this had decreased to 24.3 percent.[103] In 1989, there were still no women in top FSLN leadership roles and only three of the thirty-two who held the top rank in the military hierarchy were women. Women held 31.4 percent of the leadership positions in government,[104] and approximately 15 percent of the members of the National Assembly elected in 1984 were women, including its vice president. The Supreme Electoral Council organized in 1989 to supervise the 1990 elections had five members, one of whom was a woman.

Women's participation in the military experienced a decline after 1979: from 25 percent of the insurrectionary forces to between 8 and 10 percent of the Sandinista People's Army only one year later.[105] In 1986, women constituted 20 percent of the Ministry of Defense, but most of them occupied administrative positions.[106] By 1989, women were only 6 percent of the permanent army.[107] In 1985, women were 45 percent of the Sandinista Police Force[108] and the chief of police was a woman, Comandante Doris Tijerino.

The majority of those who participated in the Sandinista Defense Committees as well as the overwhelming majority of those involved in the literacy campaign and in the ongoing health campaigns were women.[109] And whereas only 4 percent of all employed women were professionals (only 1 percent on the Atlantic Coast), 40 percent of the membership of CONAPRO-Heroes and Martyrs were women.[110]

In the area of education, women's situation improved significantly during the period 1979-1989. In the time of Somoza, only 21.3 percent of women aged thirteen to eighteen attended secondary school and 11 percent of those aged nineteen to twenty-four attended postsecondary institutions.[111] In 1981, 1984, and 1986 respectively, women were 38.2, 45, and 50 percent of those enrolled in higher education. Before 1979 there were no women in agricultural, industrial, or civil engineering educational programs, but by 1983, 11 percent of agricultural engineering students and 35 percent of industrial and civil engineering students were women.[112]

These figures all indicate that to a great extent, the Sandinista People's Revolution had been reasonably successful in involving and integrating women. But eleven years was not a long enough time to overcome centuries of marginalization and oppression.

Conclusion

What difference did the revolution make to the material conditions of women's lives? There is no doubt that the conditions in which the overwhelming majority of Nicaraguan women lived improved dramatically. In the area of social programs and social welfare, the Sandinistas excelled. They established a universal health system with increased and decentralized facilities.[113] Health care and education were defined as basic human rights. More schools were built, especially in the rural areas. The illiteracy rate was reduced from 50 percent or more to 15 percent. Social welfare and social programs were improved and expanded. But as Molyneux argued, women shared in these benefits with men not because of gender but rather because of their class position.[114]

What improvements were made in the area of women's rights? Clearly women gained the most in the area of legislative reform. New laws abolished gender discrimination in work and family. The new constitution established a structural and ideological framework within which the women's movement could press for further change. Women activists used the law as a tool to promote the emancipation of women, recognizing the need to at least establish legal equality. But at the time of the FSLN electoral defeat in 1990, there was still a huge gulf between the theory of equality (the law) and practice. Laws dating back to 1904 Civil Code still needed to be changed. The absence of legislation dealing with rape and domestic violence, as well as the decriminalization of abortion, remained unresolved issues.

In what ways, and how successfully, did the revolutionary government challenge the structures and ideologies that underpin and reinforce patriarchal and capitalist gender relations? Machismo, sexism, and patriarchy were, and are, deeply rooted in Nicaraguan society. What had taken centuries to entrench would not disappear in little more than ten years. Although they did not wage a campaign against sexism[115] or develop a comprehensive challenge to traditional gender roles, the Sandinistas did at least provide an ideological framework to support those who did. The counterrevolutionary war and the economic crisis made it difficult for them to allocate the resources necessary to build the infrastructure that would make women's emancipation possible.

Attitudes and values did not keep pace with socioeconomic change. Women appeared to be developing new consciousness of women's capabilities, but men were not, and general social awareness of gender discrimination appeared to be minimal. Indeed, in 1989, there were attempts to rescind the law prohibiting the sexual objectification of women in advertising and there was a renewed interest in beauty contests among Sandinista youth.[116]

Whatever its shortcoming, the Sandinista revolution succeeded in ways unknown in other socialist countries and under very difficult circumstances. What would be required in the future would be a strong, autonomous feminist movement and the development of a political strategy based on a feminist critique of women's oppression. In ten and one-half short years, Nicaraguan women had written a new chapter in their collective history—a chapter that represented a "leap of a thousand years."[117] This history cannot be rewritten.

Notes

The research for this chapter was conducted with the financial assistance of the University of Lethbridge Faculty Research Fund. I would like to thank Thomas Walker and Harvey Williams, organizers of the Latin American Studies Association Seminar in Nicaragua, for facilitating contacts in Nicaragua, and Eva Ligia Méndez, of the federation of professional associations (CONAPRO-Heroes and Martyrs), for assistance in organizing the interviews, which were conducted during June and July 1989.

1. Two of the sources consulted reported only that women fought with Sandino (Alicia Gordon, Christa Berger, and Pilar Lacerna, "Nicaragua: Somos Millones," *Revista Fem* 4 [13], March-April 1989), p. 39; and Margaret Randall and Linda Yanz, *Sandino's Daughters: Testimonies of Nicaraguan Women in Struggle* [Vancouver: New Star Books, 1981], p. iv). Eileen Haley pointed out that while there is some evidence that there were women in Sandino's army (primarily old photographs), Sandino himself only mentioned the support roles that women played ("Nicaragua/Women/Revolution," *Hecate* 9 [1], 1983, p. 83). Runyan mentioned a women's battalion called Choir of Angels (Anne Sisson Runyan, "Nicaragua Is to Feminism As the U.S. Is to Patriarchy," *Atlantis* 13 [1], Fall 1987, p. 149), but no source was provided.
2. See Haley ("Nicaragua/Women") for an excellent discussion of women's political involvement in Nicaragua from 1961 to 1979.
3. Gary Ruchwarger, *People in Power: Forging a Grassroots Democracy in Nicaragua* (South Hadley, Mass.: Bergin and Garvey, 1987), p. 45.
4. Magda Enriquez, "We Women Learned What We Were Capable of Doing," in *Nicaragua: The Sandinista People's Revolution—Speeches by Sandinista Leaders* (New York: Pathfinder, 1985); José Luis Coraggio, "Social Movements and Revolution: The Case of Nicaragua," in David Slater (ed.), *New Social Movements and the State in Nicaragua* (Amsterdam: CEDLA, 1985); Norma Chinchilla, "Women in the Nicaraguan Revolution," *Nicaraguan Perspectives*, no. 11, Winter 1985/86. Lea Guido, one of the founding members, disagreed with most reports and argued that AMPRONAC was not limited to human rights issues (cited in Randall and Yanz, *Sandino's Daughters*, p. 4).
5. Two accounts suggest that AMPRONAC was primarily a middle-class organization. See Heather Crowell and Barbara Levy, "What Difference Does a Revolution Make? A Marxist and Feminist Analysis of Women's Struggle for Human Development in Revolutionary Cuba and Nicaragua," paper presented at the Annual Conference of the Canadian Research Institute for the Advancement of Women, Quebec City, Canada, November 13, 1988, p. 15. Ruchwarger pointed out that the founders of AMPRONAC were bourgeois

and middle-class women and that working-class women viewed the organization with suspicion (*People in Power*, p. 48). But Chinchilla ("Women in the Nicaraguan Revolution," p. 19) and Gordon, Berger, and Lacerna ("Somos Millones," p. 40) argued that AMPRONAC was multiclass; Haley ("Nicaragua/Women," p. 98) suggested that it was composed primarily of poor women and grandmothers who had no other avenue for political activity.

6. Ruchwarger, *People in Power*, p. 49.
7. Haley, "Nicaragua/Women," p. 98.
8. Chinchilla, "Women in the Revolution," p. 19.
9. Ruchwarger, *People in Power*, p. 51.
10. Most writers suggest that women made up at least, or perhaps more than, 30 percent of all combatants. See Jane Deighton, Rossana Horsley, Sara Steward, and Cathy Cain, *Sweet Ramparts: Women in Revolutionary Nicaragua* (London: War on Want and the Nicaraguan Solidarity Campaign, 1983), p. 50; Catherine Gander, "Nicaraguan Women at War: Part 1," *Canadian Dimension* 19 (6), January-February 1986, p. 27; Hermione Harris, "Nicaragua: Two Years of Revolution," *Race and Class* 23 (1), 1981, p. 18; Maxine Molyneux, "Mobilization Without Emancipation? Women's Interests, the State, and Revolution in Nicaragua," *Feminist Studies* 11 (2) Summer 1985, p. 227; Lynn Silver, "Nicaraguan Women Organize to Defend the Revolution," *Intercontinental Press*, October 1979, p. 980; Harvey Williams, "Revolution or Reform: The Role of Women in Nicaragua," *Proceedings of the Pacific Coast Council on Latin American Studies* 14 (2) Fall 1987, p. 24; and Randall and Yanz, *Sandino's Daughters*, p. iv. Haley ("Nicaragua/Women," p. 81) and Stephen M. Gorman ("The Role of the Revolutionary Armed Forces," in Thomas Walker [ed.], *Nicaragua in Revolution* [New York: Praeger, 1982], p. 123), however, documented the figure as 25 percent. And Carlos Vilas implied that women's participation in direct combat was minimal: "More than in direct combat, women's participation seems to have taken place fundamentally in support tasks" (*The Sandinista Revolution* [New York: Monthly Review Press, 1986], p. 109).
11. Haley discussed the way in which the distinction between the role of "cadre" and the role of "collaborator" reflected the traditional gendered division of labor ("Nicaragua/Women," pp. 88–89).
12. Vilas, *The Sandinista Revolution*, p. 109; Chinchilla, "Women in the Nicaraguan Revolution," p. 19; Haley, "Nicaragua/Women," p. 97; and Elizabeth Maier, *Nicaragua, La Mujer en la Revolución* (Mexico City: Ediciones de Cultura Popular, 1980).
13. Interview data.
14. Randall and Yanz, *Sandino's Daughters*; Haley, "Nicaragua/Women"; Ruchwarger, *People in Power*; Norma Chinchilla, "Women in Revolutionary Movements: The Case of Nicaragua" (Working Papers on Women in International Development, Michigan State University, no. 27, 1983); and "The Nicaraguan Family in a Time of Transition," *Envío*, no. 34, April 1984.
15. Haley, "Nicaragua/Women," p. 100.
16. Ibid., citing Maier, *Nicaragua, La Mujer en la Revolución*.
17. "Becoming Visible: Women in Nicaragua," *Envío* 6 (78), December 1987, p. 19.
18. Social scientists historically have tended to regard the Nicaraguan family structure as relatively unstable, given the significantly high proportion of female-

headed households. See, for example, Sterner Ekern, *Street Power: Culture and Politics in a Nicaraguan Neighbourhood* (Bergen, Norway: Bergen Studies in Social Anthropology No. 40, 1987); "Women in Nicaragua: A Revolution Within a Revolution," *Envío*, July 1983; and "The Nicaraguan Family," *Envío*, April 1984. As a feminist sociologist, I do not subscribe to the argument that the absence of a male head of the household necessarily suggests family instability. Indeed, mother/child(ren) families in Nicaragua and other parts of the world are very stable.

19. Randall and Yanz, *Sandino's Daughters*, p. vi; Haley, "Nicaragua/Women," p. 84; Chinchilla, "Women in Revolutionary Movements," p. 6; Hermione Harris, "War and Reconstruction: Women in Nicaragua," in Olivia Harris (ed.), *Latin American Women* (London: Minority Rights Group Report No. 57, 1983), p. 19; Gary Ruchwarger, *Struggling for Survival: Workers, Women and Class on a Nicaraguan State Farm* (Boulder, Colo.: Westview Press, 1989), p. 76.

20. Chinchilla, "Women in Revolutionary Movements," p. 16; Susan Ramírez-Horton, "The Role of Women in the Nicaraguan Revolution," in Walker (ed.), *Nicaragua in Revolution*, p. 152; Ileana Rodríguez, "Obstáculos a la promoción y aplicación de la 'Convención sobre la eliminación de todas las formas de discriminación contra la mujer': Caso de Nicaragua," Ministerio de la Presidencia, Oficina de la Mujer, Managua, February 1987, p. 7; Roser Sola and M. Pau Trayner, *Ser Madre en Nicaragua: Testimonios de una Historia No Escrita* (Managua: Editorial Nueva Nicaragua, 1988).

21. Ruchwarger, *People in Power*, p. 192.

22. Luis Serra, "The Sandinist Mass Organizations," in Walker (ed.), *Nicaragua in Revolution*, p. 98.

23. Amalia Chamorro, "La Mujer: logros y límites en 10 años de revolución," *Cuadernos de Sociología* (Universidad Centroamericana), no. 9-10, January-June 1989, p. 122.

24. Ramírez-Horton, "The Role of Women," pp. 154–155.

25. Milú Vargas, "A Self-Critical View," *Cayenne* (Toronto), 3 (1), Winter 1987, p. 18.

26. Rodríguez, "Obstáculos," p. 13.

27. Williams, "Revolution or Reform," p. 21.

28. AMNLAE, *Podemos!! Las mujeres nicaragüenses a 10 años de revolución* (Managua, 1989), p. 20.

29. Ibid. The original sources for these figures are not provided.

30. Rodríguez, "Obstáculos," p. 15.

31. AMNLAE, *Podemos!!*, pp. 15, 20.

32. "Becoming Visible," p. 20.

33. Chamorro, "La Mujer," p. 120. Data on child-care centers are confusing. For example, Molyneux stated that by 1984, there were forty-three child-care centers, which accommodated about 4,000 children ("Mobilization Without Emancipation?" p. 240). These figures are consistent with those in a 1983 *Envío* article that stated that by 1983 forty-four child-care centers had been constructed, serving 3,368 children, only 0.5 percent of all those aged 0–5 ("Women in Nicaragua," *Envío*, p. 5c). Ruchwarger, however, stated that by the end of 1985, 80,000 children were receiving some kind of child care, but it is not clear whether or not he is referring to institutionalized child care (*People in Power*, p. 194).

34. Chamorro, "La Mujer"; Paola Pérez Alemán and Pamela Díaz, "10 años de investigaciones sobre la mujer en Nicaragua: 1976–1986" (Managua: Oficina de la Mujer, 1986); Paola Pérez Alemán, Diana Martínez, and Christa Widmair, *Industria, Género y Mujer en Nicaragua* (Managua: Instituto Nicaragüense de la Mujer, 1989). This point was also made repeatedly in the interviews.

35. CIERA, ATC, and CETRA, *Mujer y Agroexportación en Nicaragua* (Managua: Instituto Nicaragüense de la Mujer, 1987), p. 17.

36. Ibid., pp. 18–19.

37. Ibid.

38. Ibid., p. 24.

39. Ibid., pp. 56–57, 60–62.

40. Ibid., pp. 55–56.

41. Ibid., p. 91.

42. Ibid., p. 55. Only 17 percent of the sample did not think men should participate in household tasks.

43. AMNLAE, *Podemos!!*, p. 20.

44. CIERA, ATC, and CETRA, *Mujer y Agroexportación*, p. 102.

45. Ibid., p. 115.

46. Ibid., p. 117.

47. Clara Murguialday, "Women Agricultural Workers in Nicaragua," *Cayenne* (Toronto), 2 (4), Fall 1986, pp. 15–16.

48. The list of eight resolutions is reproduced in Ruchwarger, *Struggling for Survival*, pp. 81–82. See also Gary Ruchwarger, "Childcare and Cafeterias: Rural Women Organize for Equality," *Nicaraguan Perspectives*, Summer 1988.

49. Interview with ATC activist.

50. Ibid. and Sofía Montenegro, "Many Are Called and Few Are Chosen," *Cayenne* (Toronto), Fall 1987, p. 15.

51. Mignone Vego, Lucía Aguirre, and Paola Pérez Alemán, "Mujer Campesina y Organización en Nicaragua: Participación Productiva sin Participación Social?" *Revista Nicaragüense de Ciencias Sociales* 3 (5), 1989, p. 59.

52. Ibid.

53. Williams, "Revolution or Reform," p. 27.

54. CIERA, *La Vida Cotidiana de la Mujer Campesina* (Managua: Centro de Investigación y Estudios de la Reforma Agraria, 1989). This was also suggested in the interview data.

55. Pérez, Martínez, and Widmair, *Industria, Género*.

56. Ibid., p. 57. On this latter point of discrimination against pregnant women, 35 percent of the sample were required to present a medical certificate verifying they were not pregnant in order to get their present job and, in other cases, had to prove that they did not have young children.

57. Ibid., p. 63.

58. Ibid., p. 82.

59. Ibid., p. 78.

60. Ibid., p. 88.

61. Ibid., pp. 96–97.

62. Ruchwarger, *People in Power*, p. 202.

63. Ibid., pp. 202–203, and "Las domésticas: Una lucha que apénas comienza," in AMNLAE, *Las mujeres Nicaragüenses y la revolución* (Managua: n.d.), p. 31.

64. "Women in Nicaragua," *Envío*, p. 8c.

65. Ruchwarger, *People in Power*, p. 203.

66. Paola Pérez Alemán, "Crisis Económica y Mujer en Nicaragua: Ajustes a Nivel Familiar" (Managua: Instituto Nicaragüense de la Mujer, 1989).

67. Pérez, Martínez, and Widmaier noted that in 1981 for every 100 men in the poorest stratum of society in Managua, there were 354 women (*Industria, Género*, p. 18).

68. Ramírez-Horton, "The Role of Women," p. 148.

69. Molyneux, "Mobilization Without Emancipation?" p. 229.

70. Gander, "Part 1," p. 25.

71. Ibid.

72. Interview data.

73. Ekern, *Street Power*.

74. AMNLAE, *Oficina Legal de la Mujer* (Managua, 1986), p. 5.

75. Oficina Legal de la Mujer, *Aportes al análisis del maltrato en la relación de pareja* (Managua: AMNLAE, 1986), p. 36–44.

76. AMNLAE, *Boletín Quincenal*, no. 12, February 1989; "Women's Rights and the New Constitution: Town Meeting Discusses Abortion, Rape, Housework and Equal Pay," *Intercontinental Press* 24 (15), July 28, 1986, p. 465.

77. *Documentos Sobre la Mujer*, no. 6, January/March 1989, pp. 34–36.

78. Quoted in Maxine Molyneux, "The Politics of Abortion in Nicaragua: Revolutionary Pragmatism—or Feminism in the Realm of Necessity?" *Feminist Review*, no. 29, 1989, p. 114. In this article, Molyneux provided an excellent analysis of the abortion issue in Nicaragua.

79. Interview data. See also Marie Lorenzo and Linda Yanz, "Abortion in Nicaragua: The Debate Begins," *Cayenne* (Toronto) 2 (4), Fall 1986.

80. See Nancy Sapporta Sternbach, Marysa Navarro, Patricia Chuchryk, and Sonia Alvarez, "Feminism in Latin America: From Bogotá to Taxco" (forthcoming in *Signs: A Journal of Women in Culture and Society*) for a discussion of the implications of the strong Central American presence at the Fourth Latin American and Caribbean Feminist Encuentro.

81. "Becoming Visible," p. 21.

82. Chamorro, "La Mujer," p. 130.

83. Ibid.

84. Jeff House, "Democracy in Nicaragua: Making the Constitution," *Canadian Dimension* 20 (7), December/January 1986/87, p. 43.

85. *The Constitution of the Republic of Nicaragua* (Printed in Canada by Friends of Nicaragua by Authority of the National Assembly of Nicaragua), p. 15.

86. Ibid., p. 19.

87. See Joanne Passaro, "Conceptualizations of Gender: An Example from Nicaragua," *Feminist Issues* 13, Fall 1987, for an insightful analysis of FSLN discourse on women.

88. Tomás Borge, "Women and the Nicaraguan Revolution," in *Nicaragua: The Sandinista People's Revolution*, p. 53 (emphasis added).

89. Ibid., p. 55.

90. *El FSLN y la Mujer en la Revolución Popular Sandinista* (Managua: Editorial Vanguardia, 1987), p. 28.

91. Ibid., p. 37.

92. "Organizing Women: Rural Women Challenge AMNLAE," *Cayenne* (Toronto), Fall 1987, p. 13.

93. Molyneux, "The Politics of Abortion," p. 117.

94. "Organizing Women," pp. 10, 12.

95. "Becoming Visible," p. 26.

96. Interview data.

97. Chamorro, "La Mujer," p. 134.

98. *El FSLN y la mujer*, p. 34.

99. Montenegro, "Many Are Called."

100. Maxine Molyneux, "Women," in Thomas Walker (ed.), *Nicaragua: The First Five Years* (New York: Praeger, 1985), p. 17.

101. Molyneux, "Mobilization Without Emancipation?" p. 245.

102. Ibid., p. 244; Chamorro, "La Mujer," pp. 133-134.

103. "Becoming Visible," p. 19. The figure for 1983 was 22 percent ("Women in Nicaragua," *Envío*, p. 4c), so this could be seen to represent a marginal increase from 1983 to 1987. However, the 24.3 percent figure was also used in a 1989 AMNLAE publication, which suggests that these figures should be used cautiously.

104. "Becoming Visible," p. 19.

105. Gorman, "Role of Armed Forces," p. 123.

106. Catherine Gander, "Nicaraguan Women at War: Part 3—Military Defense," *Canadian Dimension* 20 (3), May 1986, p. 26.

107. Interview with Lt. Col. Rosa Pasos, press officer for the Sandinista Popular Army, LASA Seminar in Nicaragua, June 29, 1989.

108. Catherine Allport Charoula, Cristina Biaggi, and Gail Ellen Dunlop, "Women Demand Rights in Nicaragua," *New Directions for Women*, May-June 1985, p. 11.

109. AMNLAE, *Podemos!!*, p. 15.

110. Chamorro, "La Mujer," p. 126.

111. Ruchwarger, *People in Power*, pp. 197-198.

112. AMNLAE, *Nació en la lucha* (Managua, 1986).

113. This brief discussion of social welfare programs is drawn from Williams, "Revolution or Reform," pp. 24-25.

114. Molyneux, "Mobilization Without Emancipation?" p. 248.

115. Ruchwarger, *People in Power*, p. 179.

116. Chamorro, "La Mujer," p. 135.

117. Interview.

EIGHT

Religion and Revolution

MICHAEL DODSON

The Nicaraguan revolution took place in a regionwide setting of rapid economic modernization and severe political instability. It also occurred at a moment of energetic renewal in religious life when impressive church growth was taking place in Central America. Religion and politics interacted strongly, with important consequences for both.

This chapter argues that religious change affected politics in the Sandinista revolution in three ways. First, religious change took place most intensely at the popular level of society. During the decade from 1968 to 1978 a prophetic reading of the Bible led Christians at the bottom of the social hierarchy to challenge the existing structures of power. Those dates span the period from the 1968 meeting of the Council of Latin American Bishops (CELAM) at Medellín, Colombia, to the beginning of Nicaragua's popular insurrection. In that period Christians, especially at the grass-roots level, affected the course of political change by providing religious justifications for political struggle and by mobilizing sectors of the churches to participate in the uprising against Somoza.

Second, during the first decade of revolutionary rule in Nicaragua, factors that complicated the relationship of religion to politics arose, introducing new strains into church-state relations. These stresses affected primarily the Roman Catholic church, which became deeply divided over the revolution. The divisions that emerged in this period were grounded both in political ideology and in theological principles and attitudes. One sector of the church, which came to be called the "popular church," identified strongly with much of the revolutionary process. Other sectors, notably key members of the Catholic hierarchy and one faction within the Pentecostal churches, opposed the revolution, whereas some individuals identified with the armed counterrevolution.

Third, the Sandinista revolution, despite its Marxist characteristics, actually created conditions that fostered dynamic church growth in Nicaragua. Much of this growth was among Evangelical (Protestant) churches, especially those with a Pentecostal flavor. The contra war, aggressive mission efforts by conservative U.S.-based churches, economic hardship, and internecine conflict in the Catholic church all seem to have contributed to this phenomenon.

The Post-Medellín Decade

The Second Vatican Council (1962–1965) stimulated renewal in Roman Catholicism throughout Latin America. In keeping with the spirit of Vatican II, Latin America's bishops gathered in Medellín in 1968 to open their church to the world. They did so in a highly critical, what we might call "prophetic," way, by denouncing the pervasive poverty and exploitation present in their societies, pledging that the Church would side with the poor in their struggle for a better life. However, a severe shortage of native priests made it difficult for the Church to "go to the people." One solution was to encourage more foreign priests to enter Latin America; another was to broaden the role of religious women and the laity. In Nicaragua these improvisations had considerable impact. For example, the Catholic mission society, Maryknoll, supplied numerous priests and religious to Nicaragua (and elsewhere in Central America) from the late 1960s on. These pastoral workers helped to organize the marginal poor, and they publicized internationally various acts of Somocista repression in the years prior to the insurrection. Maryknollers collaborated with other clergy and religious to establish the network of ecclesiastical base communities (CEBs), which integrated the poor more actively into church life during the 1970s.

Before CEBs were created in Nicaragua, the rural and urban poor had never participated in local community organizations. Even though CEBs were primarily religious in their aims, they helped to fill a gap in Nicaragua's political life by enabling poor people to meet, discuss common problems, and develop a sense of group interest and even a measure of political identity. CEBs were a training ground for catechists who would teach others the principles of Catholic faith and also for a new type of religious lay leader called "delegate of the Word." In Nicaragua "delegates" were typically campesinos or persons from poor barrios who were entrusted with a broad pastoral responsibility. Perhaps their principal role was to organize and lead Bible study and group reflection, often focusing on the gospel message in relation to their own suffering. Since delegates shared in the daily life of the people, they formed a valuable link between the poor and the magisterium of the Roman Catholic church. The spread of delegates and CEBs created a network of poor people at the grass roots who could mobilize themselves politically in the right circumstances. During the 1970s, Somocista repression and loss of authority, together with Sandinista mobilization of the populace at the grass roots, created such circumstances.

The political impact of CEBs and delegates can be illustrated by the example of Estelí, a city that played a vital role in the insurrection. The first CEBs in Estelí were formed under the direction of a Colombian priest in 1972.[1] The local bishop approved the initiative but did not take a direct role himself. Initially the program centered on married couples, who attended weekly meetings for Bible study and discussion of personal or family problems. Little by little a more prophetic and community-oriented focus took shape.

In December 1972 an earthquake destroyed downtown Managua, which induced a flood of emergency aid to pour into Managua from all over the world. The extreme corruption of the local officials who managed this relief effort deepened public antipathy toward Somoza's regime. The Sandinista National Liberation Front (FSLN) began to establish contacts with potential opposition groups across the country. By 1975 the FSLN had established strong links with Christians active in the CEB movement in Estelí. When political repression increased during 1976-1977, CEB members took part in grass-roots resistance organized by the FSLN.

Just prior to the insurrection, CEB activists in Estelí helped to found local Civil Defense Committees, which became Sandinista Defense Committees (CDS) after 1979. When a contingent of Sandinistas came to Estelí in April 1978 more than 9,000 people from the city mobilized to support them in initial clashes with the National Guard. Subsequently, more than fifty CEBs in and around Estelí took part in preparations for the September 1978 insurrection. During the final insurrection the following summer, this network of mobilized Christians played a key role in defending Estelí against what they called the "invasion" of the National Guard. Participants later noted that the Christian contribution was made without much direct supervision from the Sandinista Front. As one person put it, "We took arms not to kill but to defend our young people."[2]

The experience of Estelí was repeated in many parts of Nicaragua. Because of this support, the FSLN came to power aware that the Roman Catholic church, particularly its grass-roots organizations, had contributed vitally to the success of the insurrection. One priest reported that in Estelí a majority of the youth who took up arms for the FSLN were members of the Christian communities.[3] The result was an unusual but powerful process of mutual influence. Catholic activists at the grass-roots acquired a strong political consciousness from their participation in the Sandinista-led insurrection. They entered the revolutionary period with strong links to the FSLN and a favorable disposition toward the impending changes in society. For a political movement whose leaders had a strong Marxist orientation, the Sandinistas displayed an unusually open and pragmatic approach toward the Catholic church and a strong respect for religious faith. This attitude, too, was firmly rooted in the concrete experiences of the insurrection.

Almost immediately upon taking power, the FSLN asked several prominent Nicaraguan priests to accept important positions in the new government. Not only had these priests played significant roles in the insurrection,[4] but they also had skills that were in short supply in Nicaragua. Their acceptance of the government's invitation, however, led to a situation that deepened into serious conflict over the years, at times severely damaging church-state relations. In effect, a competition developed between the FSLN and the Catholic hierarchy over the commitments and participation of the Catholic faithful in the CEBs and other popular programs. Traditionally the Church had its strongest ties among the middle and upper classes in Nicaragua. As was seen, following Medellín strong new links were forged among the popular classes. However, the Church was not accustomed to thinking in class terms, considering itself to be above partisan politics and its mission to transcend class lines. The revolution put great pressure on this self-image. The new religio-political consciousness of the poor demanded a more prophetic disposition from the Church hierarchy, a demand that was reinforced by the rapid consolidation of a Sandinista government pursuing the "logic of the majority."[5] In reality, many associated with the popular church movement seemed closer to the FSLN than to the bishops and more traditional clergy. For their part, the bishops were cautious about the revolution, no doubt aware that previous Latin American revolutions had been hostile to the Church. To make matters worse, a counterrevolutionary movement soon developed within a sector of the Nicaraguan elite, and it appealed to Catholic church leaders for support.

In summary, by means of the popular insurrection the Catholic church was politicized in a manner that created broad unity of purpose among Nicaraguan Christians, especially at the grass roots, thereby adding a religious sanction to revolutionary political action. Once a revolutionary government was in power, the religious arena was re-politicized in a way that exacerbated divisions both in the body politic and in the Church.

Growing Church-State Conflict

The political struggle against the Somoza dictatorship was strengthened by the multiclass alliance that closed ranks against the regime after February 1978.[6] The opposition movement was broad based ideologically, ranging from conservative social elites and members of the business class to peasants responding to the populist, nationalist appeal of the FSLN. However, the Sandinista Front led the uprising militarily and organized much of the popular participation. Because the regime's collapse had left the nation in chaos and the insurrection had left the economy in ruins, it was necessary to begin the process of reconstruction immediately and to pursue it vigorously.

Before the final victory was achieved, a coalition government reflecting some of the social and ideological diversity noted above had already been formed. But in 1979 real power in Nicaragua lay with the Sandinistas, who were committed to radical changes in society. They set about energetically to accomplish that end, introducing land reform, setting up literacy and health-care programs aimed at the poor, and nationalizing the banking system. These policies served two broad purposes. First, they sustained and harnessed the popular energies that had been mobilized by the insurrection, holding the promise of the better life for which the people had sacrificed so much. These programs were the people's reward, indeed their right from a popular democratic and revolutionary point of view. To achieve this agenda, popular energies were organized through a panoply of popular organizations that played a vital role in Nicaraguan nation building over the next decade. These organizations (discussed in Chapter 3) were linked to the second broad goal of the Sandinista program: to consolidate the FSLN's political authority within the revolution. This strategy for rooting political authority in popular groups affected church-state relations deeply because it generated a competition between secular and religious hierarchies over the allegiance of the so-called popular church.

During the 1970s a great strength of the Roman Catholic church was its institutional diversity and flexibility, which permitted the development of a "theology of liberation" and the spread of dynamic Christian communities at the grass roots. The decentralized, spontaneous, and popular character of this movement enabled it to grow and mature despite political repression. However, as the FSLN set about to consolidate the revolution, and its own power within it, these same qualities of the popular church alarmed the Catholic hierarchy, which was determined to preserve the integrity of the institutional church as the bishops understood it. The hierarchy tried to restrict Church participation in the revolutionary process, thereby precipitating conflict between Church and state and within the Church itself. These conflicts weakened the Church's potential to shape the building of a new society in Nicaragua.

Several examples can illustrate these developments. In November 1979 the Catholic hierarchy published a pastoral letter that praised the CEBs and popular participation in the revolutionary process, while also acknowledging the legitimacy of FSLN leadership. At the time this letter seemed to indicate solid Church support for the revolution. In fact, however, the bishops were suspicious of Sandinista ideology, which they assumed would be hostile to Church interests, and they were reticent

about Christian participation in the popular organizations. As it happened, efforts to mobilize such participation were already under way.

In August 1979 a group of Catholic priests and Protestant pastors
active in CEB work set up the Antonio Valdivieso Center (CAV).
Named for a sixteenth-century bishop who had defended the rights of
indigenous peoples in Nicaragua, the center's aim was to encourage
Christian participation in the many tasks of the revolution. The CAV
began publishing materials that articulated a theology of popular struggle
and organized workshops to train pastoral leaders at the base from that
perspective. Their agenda coincided closely with that of the FSLN, and
it soon proved to be incompatible with that of the bishops, who saw
active Church involvement with the revolutionary process as a political
manipulation of the Church.

Within a year the incipient break between the Catholic bishops on
the one hand and the FSLN and its Christian supporters on the other
had become real. The precipitating event was the formation of the
Council of State in spring 1980. Elites who were ideologically opposed
to the Sandinista agenda and feared a further consolidation of the
FSLN's power envisioned the council as a counterweight to Sandinista
influence. They argued for a body of thirty-three seats, designed so that
middle- and upper-class interests would be strongly represented. However,
an alternative plan fostered by the FSLN was adopted, expanding the
council to forty-seven seats and increasing popular-sector participation
vis-à-vis that of elite groups. This decision caused the first open split
within the coalition that had closed ranks with the Sandinistas during
the insurrection and led to the formation of a domestic opposition that
became militantly anti-Sandinista in the following years. Two prominent
non-Sandinista members of the ruling junta resigned over this issue,
and weeks later the bishops abruptly called upon all the priests serving
in the government to resign their offices.

Altogether nine priests were affected, three of whom occupied cabinet-
level positions. The priests called for dialogue with the bishops, but
continued to carry out their ministerial duties. Eager to retain their
services, the FSLN sent a special commission to Rome to obtain the
Vatican's approval. The issue simmered for a year, creating tensions and
ill will on both sides. Finally, in June 1981, the bishops again called
publicly for the priests' resignation, stating that the priests would be
penalized under canon law if they refused. They also declared that the
CAV and other similar religious organizations that promoted participation
in the revolution had "neither the approval nor the recommendation
of the Episcopal Conference."[7]

In the short run, pressure from the bishops did not yield resignations
from the priests in government, nor did it cause the CAV and other
popular-church groups to cease their support of the revolution. When

the Vatican refused to intercede, a compromise was reached allowing the priests to continue in office but preventing them from exercising the sacerdotal office. This controversy seemed to convince some of Nicaragua's bishops that the Church hierarchy was destined to lose authority in a revolutionary society. They saw within their own church the specter of a "parallel magisterium," a religious authority to rival that of the bishops themselves. That concern was exacerbated by their sense that the FSLN was intent on marginalizing the Church by filling all existing social space with its own programs and ideological symbols.

Henceforth the hierarchy became more openly critical of the government. Simultaneously they applied pressure on priests working with CEBs or with government programs. In the Managua archdiocese numerous priests were transferred out of parishes where they had established strong ties with the base.[8] These actions precipitated a decline in the vitality of CEBs. At the same time, Archbishop Obando y Bravo was promoting a more charismatic current within the archdiocese and giving renewed emphasis to the traditional *cursillos de cristiandad* (short courses in Christian faith), which represented an otherworldly and socially conservative form of worship. These programs appealed primarily to middle- and upper-class Catholics.

The Role of External Actors

The tensions that developed between church and state in the early years of the Sandinista revolution were heightened by external actors that sought to influence events in Nicaragua. Two of the most important such actors were the Vatican and the U.S. government. I will comment briefly on the pope's visit to Central America in March 1983 and then discuss the growing contra war and its impact on church-state relations and intrachurch conflict.

Pope John Paul's approach to the situation in Nicaragua was foreshadowed in a letter he sent to the Nicaraguan bishops on June 20, 1982. In that letter he raised the issue of a "people's church," saying that it represented an illicit "rupture" of church unity and usurpation of hierarchical authority.[9] This was the perspective he brought with him to the country on March 4, 1983. The pope celebrated mass in Managua's 19th of July Plaza before a crowd of nearly half a million people. The theme of his homily was church unity, and his aim apparently was to stand firmly with Nicaragua's bishops against what he viewed as the rebellious, schismatic tendencies represented in a "people's church." John Paul II focused so narrowly on this issue of authority and obedience that he disregarded the fervent desire of many in his audience to hear words of sympathy for Nicaragua's suffering and loss in the contra war. Ignoring a group of bereaved mothers whose fallen sons had been buried just days before, the pope proceeded to lecture and criticize, referring to the idea of a people's church as "absurd and dangerous."[10] In response, people in the crowd began to chant "we want peace," angering the pope, whose stern and distant manner only alienated his audience further. The mass was concluded in a tense atmosphere that was highly charged emotionally and ideologically.

Far from fostering the unity he sought, the pope's visit to Nicaragua only aggravated the institutional crisis in the Catholic church. The pope had correctly identified a problem—how to accommodate the diverse theological currents and pastoral experiences that made up the Nicaraguan church. But his authoritarian solution clashed with the reality of a society in which traditional authorities were being challenged on all sides. Moreover, by insisting, in effect, on unquestioning loyalty to Archbishop Obando y Bravo, he seemed to endorse a partisan political stance, inasmuch as Obando was openly opposed to the Sandinistas and more and more identified with the counterrevolution.

The other major external actor seeking to influence the Nicaraguan revolution was the government of the United States. In November 1981, President Reagan signed National Security Decision Directive Number 17, which authorized the CIA to spend nearly $20 million to create a 500-man paramilitary force to "interdict supplies" allegedly being sent by the Sandinistas to guerrillas in El Salvador. Recruiting and training took place in the United States and in southern Honduras, near the Nicaraguan border. The United States also funded the creation of Mískitos, Sumus, and Ramas (MISURA), an organization of Mískito Indians that could be integrated into the armed anti-Sandinista force that was being established. In a series of military actions called "Red Christmas," MISURA attacked villages and destroyed bridges along the Río Coco. In a two-month period more than sixty persons were killed, including Sandinista soldiers and Nicaraguan civilians. As a result, the government decided to relocate the Indians from the border areas to camps in the interior of the country, where they could be better protected. After the people were moved out, Sandinista troops burned crops in order to prevent them from being utilized by the contras.

In early February 1982 the Nicaraguan bishops issued a stinging criticism of the Sandinistas' relocation of the Mískitos, accusing the government of serious human rights violations.[11] These accusations occurred at about the same time that U.S. Secretary of State Alexander Haig was making similar charges, backed up with what later proved to be false evidence. The FSLN was deeply angered by the bishops' statement and, in reply, pointed out that the hierarchy had refused a government invitation to send representatives to visit the area during the relocation. Although this conflict eventually played itself out, its pattern was to reappear in the years to come. The bishops, most prominently Archbishop

Obando, were quick to see intended abuses in Sandinista policies, while the FSLN grew suspicious of the hierarchy's motives, which they saw as increasingly coincident with the hostile attitudes and aggressive actions of the Reagan administration.

As the war heated up, the government mobilized the populace for defense. Initially the Sandinistas relied extensively on the popular militias, but by early 1983 the size of the contra army and the extent of destruction it was able to inflict on the Nicaraguan countryside, much of it aimed at the government's most important social programs, convinced the FSLN that regular army units should be expanded rapidly. By August 1983 the front had prepared a Law of Patriotic Military Service and submitted it to the Council of State. While the proposed law was still being debated, the hierarchy issued another pastoral letter; this one suggested that Nicaraguans who did not share the Sandinista ideology could refuse military service on the grounds of "conscientious objection."[12] Leaving aside the merits of that position, it should be noted that it was widely seen as a gratuitous intervention by religious authorities into the political arena. Indeed, even many Catholics considered it a provocation, for it adopted a position more common to Protestantism and it did so before the final shape of the law was even known. The letter's message and tone implied that the Catholic hierarchy considered the Sandinista government to be illegitimate.

At that point in the war, no bishop had condemned any atrocity committed in contra attacks, even though gross abuses were well documented. Then, in spring 1984, the bishops issued a pastoral letter on the subject of reconciliation. Ironically, the letter attacked the government for promoting "materialistic and atheistic education" and criticized Catholics who supported the government for abandoning "ecclesiastical unity" and surrendering to "a materialistic ideology." The bishops argued that the causes of Nicaragua's problems were "individual sin" and "political ambition and abuse of power." They made no reference to the CIA mining of Nicaraguan harbors in the preceding weeks, referred to the contra war as a "civil war," and urged the Sandinista government to begin a dialogue with the contras.[13] Far from promoting reconciliation, this pastoral letter only increased the estrangement between the Sandinistas and the Church hierarchy.

Division Within the Roman Catholic Church

In early 1984 the contra war dominated Nicaraguan life. The continuing deterioration of church-state relations has to be seen against that background, as does the growing division within the Catholic church. Pressured by the war, the Sandinistas decided to advance their timetable for elections, which had originally been projected for 1985. Voter registration was scheduled for the first week of August, with the election itself to be held November 4, 1984. External media coverage of the eight-month-long electoral process focused primarily on the issue of whether the Nicaraguan Democratic Coordinator (CDN), a small coalition of right-wing parties allied with COSEP and *La Prensa*, would agree to run their candidates. In the end the coalition chose not to do so, claiming that conditions for free elections did not exist. Instead the CDN urged other Nicaraguans not to participate, and its position was openly endorsed by Archbishop Obando and by Bishop Pablo Vega, then president of the episcopal conference.

Less visible than these extensively reported events were two other happenings of great importance to the Church. On the one hand, there was the voter registration drive that occupied Nicaraguans through much of the summer. A massive grass-roots effort was undertaken simply to make effective registration possible. People were mobilized at the barrio level all over the country. Then, in the first week of August, more than 90 percent of the populace were successfully entered on the voter roles, many for the first time in their lives. Church people at the base were instrumental in the success of this project.

During this same period, Nicaraguan state security produced evidence that a member of the Catholic clergy was involved in setting up an internal front aimed at overthrowing the government by violent means. Rather than arrest the priest, officials of the Ministry of the Interior asked that he remain on the grounds of the papal nuncio while the investigation was completed. Instead, Archbishop Obando intervened, declaring publicly that the priest was innocent of any potential charges and suggesting a government frame-up. Defying State of Emergency laws, Obando led a public demonstration in support of the priest. The government responded by expelling ten foreign priests who were working in the Managua archdiocese, some on projects funded by the Citizens' Committee for the Pro-Democratic Forces in Central America (PRODEMCA), a U.S. government-backed organization.[14]

At one level, then, churches and individual Christians throughout Nicaragua were carrying on their daily activities unhampered by government interference. This was, in fact a period of dramatic church growth in the country. Three new bishops had been ordained since 1979, and more than two dozen new religious orders had entered the country. The number of Protestant churches had also grown sharply and the distribution of Bibles had increased tenfold. The Catholic church retained great influence in the field of education, where it continued to operate more than 170 schools, which enjoyed substantial government subsidies.[15] In July a Catholic priest, Father Fernando Cardenal, was appointed minister of education.

At another level, however, the Catholic church was deeply embroiled in the most explosive political conflicts facing the country. Several bishops were openly identified with the armed opposition. As the expulsion of the ten priests demonstrated, the bishops' clashes with the government adversely affected the Church's ability to carry out its religious mission.

By the end of 1984 Nicaragua was truly in the eye of a storm. The reelection of Ronald Reagan as U.S. president led to intensified efforts to destabilize and overthrow the Sandinista government. Not only armed conflict but also a propaganda war raged in Nicaragua, and the religious arena was a focal point for waging the ideological struggle.

The Church and the Propaganda War

In May 1985 Archbishop Obando y Bravo was appointed to the College of Cardinals, an honor that took many Central Americans by surprise and led to much speculation about the pope's motives. Moreover, opponents of the Nicaraguan revolution were quick to see political significance in the move because it increased the prestige of one of the FSLN's most visible domestic critics. Costa Rica's rightist newspaper *La Nación* called it a "magisterial political attack."[16]

This interpretation was reinforced by Cardinal Obando's own actions. The first mass he celebrated after receiving the cardinal's hat was in Miami before an audience consisting largely of Nicaraguan and Cuban exiles, including top leaders of the contras. Talking with reporters, Obando acknowledged a political role, saying, "I do not object to being identified with the people who have taken up arms."[17] Both the contras and the domestic opposition began referring to him as the "cardinal of peace."

During summer 1985 Cardinal Obando made an extensive pastoral tour of Nicaragua, in close coordination with the right-wing opposition parties. At each stop the cardinal stressed his message that peace could be achieved in Nicaragua only if the Sandinistas agreed to a dialogue with the contras. During this period, the Catholic radio station carried frequent appeals that young men resist the draft. Furthermore, the U.S. Congress approved aid to the contras and the Reagan administration imposed a complete economic embargo on Nicaragua.

In the face of this mounting external aggression and deepening internal division, the Nicaraguan foreign minister, Father Miguel d'Escoto, took a temporary leave from his post to inaugurate *el ayuno por la paz,* or "the fast for peace." Like Cardinal Obando, he too was attempting to mobilize public opinion. As Father d'Escoto put it, "We Christians have been unwilling to risk our lives to bring about the conditions for real sisterhood and brotherhood, and to do so nonviolently."[18] The fast triggered a strong response among the popular sectors. In mid-July 6,000 members of CEBs from all over Nicaragua met in León to endorse the fast and discuss ways of furthering the initiative at the grass roots. At the same time, statements of support and solidarity came from episcopal conferences and church leaders all over Latin America and the United States. However, there was no show of support from the Nicaraguan hierarchy, the more conservative members of which probably saw d'Escoto's fast as a purely political act on behalf of the FSLN.

Despite years of rhetoric about reconciliation, at the end of 1985 both Nicaraguan society and its Roman Catholic church were deeply divided along ideological lines. The division and hostility within the Church were vividly illustrated in spring 1986, as was the damage that ideological commitments could inflict upon the Church's capacity to carry out its religious mission. In February Father d'Escoto launched the Gran Viacrucis, or extended Stations of the Cross, a pilgrimage from Jalapa, a town near the Honduran border that had twice resisted strong contra attacks, to Managua. D'Escoto was using the Viacrucis, a popular religious celebration in Nicaragua, to speak prophetically to the need for peace. His aim was to mobilize religious sentiment at the grass roots in order to demonstrate the depth of Christian support for the "Sandinista position on peace."[19] He also sought to pressure the Nicaraguan hierarchy to acknowledge that the contra war was an aggression against Nicaraguan sovereignty. At the culminating act of celebration in Managua, d'Escoto accused Cardinal Obando of being an accomplice in the people's suffering and directly challenged him "to speak in the name of the God of Life, of Love, and of Peace."

There was no reply from Cardinal Obando. He and Bishop Vega had another agenda. As Father d'Escoto was walking the Gran Viacrucis, Bishop Vega was in Washington taking part in meetings sponsored by the Heritage Foundation, aimed at marshalling support for the Reagan policy toward Nicaragua. While in Washington, Vega charged the Sandinistas with religious persecution and endorsed contra leaders Arturo Cruz and Adolfo Calero as true "democrats." In May Cardinal Obando published an editorial in the *Washington Post* that questioned the legitimacy of the Sandinista government and denied that the contra war represented "a direct attack by the United States on our country."[20] In early June Bishop Vega visited Washington at the request of PRODEMCA, again making statements that appeared to endorse the contra cause, statements that were repeated by President Reagan in his appeals for congressional approval of contra aid. The House of Representatives approved that aid on June 25. Shortly thereafter Bishop Vega bitterly criticized the Sandinistas in a news conference, suggesting that a U.S. invasion was inevitable. This was the last straw. On July 4 the Nicaraguan government expelled him from the country.

The Evangelical Presence in the Revolution

Prior to the revolution, Evangelicals were a small religious minority in Nicaragua. Moravians predominated on the Atlantic Coast, while mainline mission churches from the United States, such as Baptists and Episcopalians, were found in Pacific Coast areas. Several Pentecostal churches, including the Assemblies of God and the Church of God, rounded out the picture. Altogether Evangelicals were only about 5 to 7 percent of the population. Historically these churches were dependent on the mother churches abroad and, due to comity arrangements among Protestant missionaries, were not in competition among themselves. They were welcome in Somoza's Nicaragua but did not grow rapidly. With a few key exceptions, Evangelical leaders and their churches stayed out of the insurrection and viewed the Sandinista triumph with concern and uncertainty.

That sector of the Evangelical community that did take an active role in the insurrection developed its anti-Somocista orientation after the 1972 earthquake. Under the leadership of a Baptist physician named Gustavo Parajón, Evangelicals set up a relief program to aid the homeless. Initially conceived as a temporary organization, this Evangelical Committee to Aid the Destitute, later called Evangelical Committee for Aid to Development (CEPAD), soon evolved into a Protestant development agency with a long-term commitment to grass-roots development. Out of CEPAD grew pastoral meetings for Protestant leaders that focused on the role of Evangelicals in a repressive society. According to one leader, these meetings caused a spiritual and organizational "explosion" in the Evangelical churches.[21] By the time of the insurrection, CEPAD had created more than two dozen local committees across the country, which worked closely with campesinos and often in ecumenical cooperation with Catholic groups. This grass-roots presence brought CEPAD into direct contact with the oppressions of the Somocista system, just as the CEBs served to educate the country's Catholic priests. After the failed insurrection of September 1978, CEPAD worked with Catholic groups to supply food and medical care to the rebels. Shortly after the Sandinista victory, a meeting of 500 Evangelical pastors issued a declaration thanking God for the victory over Somoza and pledging themselves to assist in the new government's programs to benefit the people of Nicaragua.[22]

By and large the sector of Nicaraguan Protestantism represented by CEPAD remained true to its commitments during the first decade of the revolution. Those Evangelicals were an effective religious presence in the revolutionary process because they maintained and even enlarged their development efforts, but not in ways that competed with Sandinista programs. They saw their goals as congruent with those of the government. CEPAD carefully guarded its credibility within the Evangelical community while strengthening its ties at the grass roots. Theologically CEPAD was progressive, but within the mainstream of Protestant thought. Its sociopolitical stance was compatible with the revolution.

CEPAD continued to work in rural development projects but also took on an educational role, sponsoring workshops and retreats and setting up educational groups in the workplace. CEPAD leaders described their stance as one of critical support for the revolution. They vigorously preserved their religious identity, firmly challenged the government when they thought its policies were wrong or its officials had committed abuses, but also accepted the fundamental legitimacy of the revolution. In this way CEPAD provided a strong link between Evangelicals and the Sandinista revolution. CEPAD also publicly and systematically opposed the contra war, calling it "a war imposed on us by the U.S. government that has brought terror and suffering to the countryside."[23] After signing the Central American peace accords in August 1987, President Ortega appointed Parajón to serve as the "distinguished citizen of the republic" on the National Reconciliation Commission, chaired by Cardinal Obando.

At somewhat the other end of the Evangelical spectrum from CEPAD was a broad and growing stream of Protestantism known as Pentecostalism. One result of the revolution was that many of the Pentecostal churches lost their pastors and their ties to U.S. churches when pro-Somoza missionaries abandoned the country. New leaders emerged who were free of some of the theological baggage, especially the vehement anticommunism, that the U.S. missionaries had carried with them. As one writer recently said of them, "These denominations are taking on a native life of their own, and are now largely self-sustaining and self-reproducing entities, with their own special relation to social class and the Nicaraguan revolution."[24]

Indeed, unlike the Cuban revolution, which produced a sharp decline in church activity across the board, the Nicaraguan revolution was an incubator for the dramatic growth of an infant Evangelical movement, particularly of the Pentecostal variety. In the first decade of the revolution these churches, or sects, as they are sometimes called, flourished in the same social milieu that gave rise to CEBs and their prophetic brand of theology within Roman Catholicism after Medellín. They were also CEB-like in that they stressed Bible study, sought God's personal guidance, and tried to live the principles of religious faith on a daily basis. This sort of Evangelicalism spread dramatically in Nicaragua after the triumph, especially in the poorest urban barrios of Managua and among landless peasants. In fact, their numbers more than doubled in the first six years.

One persuasive explanation for this level of Pentecostal growth is that the theology that undergirded it was highly congenial to the social reality of the marginal people among whom it flourished. This was true not so much in the sense of Lalive d'Epinay, who argued that a millenialist religion appeals to those for whom life on earth is hopeless.[25] While these groups certainly did live at the margin, they also existed in a society where the political discourse esteemed the poor and urged them to aspire to a better life. Nor did the Sandinista government interfere with their religious practice. Those who embraced the Evangelical faith lived ascetic, responsible lives and worked hard. Such behavior certainly was congenial to the revolutionary government, which espoused these very qualities. Daniel Ortega and other FSLN leaders had frequent contacts with Nicaragua's Evangelicals, and it is fair to say that, on the whole, this relationship improved and became solid at the same time that the Sandinista relationship with the Catholic hierarchy soured and broke down. The contra war and severe economic hardship discouraged the bishops and the middle- and upper-class Catholics who rallied around them, while these conditions only seemed to encourage the growth of Evangelicalism.

Thus, at the end of a decade of revolutionary rule at least eighty-five Evangelical denominations and sects were doing religious work in Nicaragua. The proportion of Protestants in the country had increased from 5 percent to 15 percent of the population. More than half the Protestant denominations were active members of CEPAD. However, as already indicated, the most rapid growth was among Pentecostal groups. Membership in the Assemblies of God, for example, grew from 8,500 in 1980 to more than 60,000 by 1987. In all, Pentecostals constituted nearly 85 percent of all Evangelicals in Nicaragua at the end of the 1980s.[26]

The Search for Peace

The summer of 1986 was a high point of U.S. pressure on Nicaragua. Simultaneously, and partly as a consequence, it was a low point of church-state relations and internal church unity. As we have seen, the Roman Catholic church got involved in the revolution initially for its own fundamentally religious reasons. During the period of national reconstruction, when deep changes in society were being carried out, the Church was subjected to conflicting pressures by a variety of self-interested actors. Among these actors were the FSLN, which appealed to members of the clergy to lend their skills to the revolution, and the CELAM and the Vatican, which pressured the Nicaraguan hierarchy to avoid all schismatic tendencies within the Church by discouraging the so-called popular church from identifying too closely with the revolution. There were also the political parties and groups of the opposition, which, as they became increasingly hostile to the revolution, were increasingly reliant on the Roman Catholic church as their only point of access to a potentially broad-based popular following. In this respect the Church became an arena of intense competition between two deeply opposed political movements, competing for the loyalty of Nicaragua's poor majority. The other major actor was, of course, the United States. Despite Cardinal Obando's claim to the contrary, the United States deeply influenced events in Nicaragua through the contra war. Indeed, until the signing of the Esquipulas peace accords in August 1987, the contra war was the primary vehicle of opposition, thereby usurping the natural development of a loyal opposition in the new Nicaragua. To the degree that Catholic church leaders became important figures in this opposition, they became, in effect, instruments that could be used to carry out U.S. policy. That policy was to overthrow the Sandinista government.

This profound politicization of the Church after the triumph of the revolution weakened the former in important respects. Neither the hierarchy's vision of a Church indifferent to the revolutionary project and obedient to hierarchical authority nor that of the popular church, which granted the popular sectors greater autonomy and integrated Christians into the revolutionary process, could be fully realized. The prospect of a church united under the authority of the bishops diminished at the same time that CEBs also declined, or had to survive and function under the tutelage of priests who worked quietly at the margins of a church whose leaders were deeply suspicious of them.

Only an end to the contra war seemed sufficient cause to alter this unhealthy situation. In that same summer of 1986 the Vatican began working toward that end. A new papal nuncio arrived in Managua shortly after Bishop Vega's expulsion. His most urgent mission was to reduce tensions between the Church hierarchy and the government, while also promoting a reduction of hostilities between Nicaragua and the United States. The nuncio immediately distanced himself from the positions taken publicly by Obando and Vega, urging Catholics to obey the laws of Nicaragua and calling for a resumption of the church-state dialogue that had been suspended in fall 1985.[27]

The Iran-contra scandal, which became public in November 1986, opened the door for peace efforts in Central America that had hitherto been thwarted by U.S. pressure. Following the lead of Costa Rican president Oscar Arias, the Central American nations concluded a peace agreement in August 1987 that called for demobilization of the contras and the establishment of conditions for reconciliation and democratization throughout the region.[28] In order to comply with the peace accords, the Sandinista government created the Nicaraguan National Reconciliation Commission and appointed Cardinal Obando to chair it. This move was designed to show the government's good faith but also aimed at weakening ties between the Church hierarchy and the contras. Effective leadership on Cardinal Obando's part required him to transcend the partisan loyalties of the preceding years. In the face of declining U.S. commitment to the contras, this strategy appeared to work. Church-state tensions diminished considerably once the Central American peace accords were in place. In March 1989 the Sandinistas permitted the exiled clergy to return to Nicaragua and also authorized Radio Católica to incorporate news broadcasts into its programming.

As a decade of Sandinista rule came to a close, relations between the government and the Roman Catholic church had once again become "correct," if not cordial. From the Church's point of view, that policy was dictated by the need to protect the Church's institutional interests, including the ability to carry out its pastoral mission. In this regard the Catholic church in Nicaragua had lost ground in the 1980s, but not because of religious persecution by an atheistic government. Rather, it had lost ground to a vigorous onslaught of Pentecostal evangelization that was still winning converts to the gospel of Christ after ten years of Sandinism.

Notes

1. Author interview in Estelí, February 1980.
2. Author interview in Estelí, February 1987.
3. Author interview in Estelí, February 1980.
4. Two of the priests, Miguel d'Escoto and Fernando Cardenal, had been members of "The Twelve," a group of intellectuals that was instrumental in unifying opposition to Somoza in the late 1970s.
5. The phrase "logic of the majority" was widely used in Central America during the 1980s. I first encountered it in an interview with Xabier Gorostiaga, S.J., a Panamanian economist working in Nicaragua. The interview took place in Managua in July 1982.
6. The key date was actually January 10, 1978, when Somocista gunmen assassinated the popular editor of La Prensa, Pedro Joaquín Chamorro. See John A. Booth, The End and The Beginning (Boulder, Colo.: Westview Press, 1982), pp. 157–161.
7. "Comunicado pastoral de la conferencia episcopal de Nicaragua," Iglesia de Nicaragua: Tiempo de discernimiento y de gracia, Movimiento Internacional de Estudiantes Católicos (Pax Romana)–Juventud Estudiantil Católica Internacional (MIEC-JECI), no. 25 (July 1981), pp. 13–15.
8. Numerous examples are provided in Michael Dodson and Laura Nuzzi O'Shaughnessy, "Religion and Politics," Thomas W. Walker, ed., Nicaragua: The First Five Years (New York: Praeger, 1985), pp. 134–135; and Manzar Foroohar, The Catholic Church and Social Change in Nicaragua (Albany: State University of New York Press, 1989), pp. 204–211.
9. "Leamos 'La Carta del Papa,'" Conferencia Episcopal de Nicaragua, June 29, 1982.

10. For a fuller account of the papal mass in Managua see Jorge Cáceres et al., *Iglesia, Política y Profecía: Juan Pablo II en Centroamérica* (San José, Costa Rica: Editorial Universitaria Centroamericana, 1983), pp. 30–45.

11. Michael Dodson, "The Politics of Religion in Revolutionary Nicaragua," *Annals, AAPSS*, no. 483 (January 1986), pp. 36–49.

12. "Conferencia episcopal sugiere 'objeción de conciencia' Nadie puede ser obligado a tomar armas por un partido," *La Prensa*, September 1, 1983, p. 1.

13. "Pastoral Letter on Reconciliation from the Nicaraguan Bishops," trans. U.S. Department of State, April 22, 1984, pp. 3, 6, 7.

14. Author interview in Managua, July 1984.

15. Howard Heimer, "Is There Religious Persecution in Nicaragua? An Open Letter to the American People," Ecumenical Committee of U.S. Church Personnel in Nicaragua, September 21, 1984, Mimeo., p. 8.

16. Quoted in Pablo Richard, "The Church of the Poor in Nicaragua: July 1979–April 1986," Mimeo., p. 4.

17. Connor Cruise O'Brien, "God and Man in Nicaragua," *Atlantic Monthly*, August 1986, p. 51.

18. Author interview in Managua, January 1987.

19. O'Brien, "God and Man in Nicaragua," p. 64.

20. Miguel Obando y Bravo, "Nicaragua: The Sandinistas Have 'Gagged and Bound' Us," *Washington Post*, May 12, 1986, p. A15.

21. Author interview in Managua, February 1980.

22. "Declaración de los 500," II Retiro interdenominacional de pastores evangélicos de Nicaragua, October 5, 1979, Mimeo.

23. "Pentecostals in Nicaragua," *Update* 6, no. 8 (March 10, 1987), p. 2.

24. Roger N. Lancaster, *Thanks to God and the Revolution* (New York: Columbia University Press, 1988), p. 104.

25. Ibid., p. 110.

26. "Pentecostals in Nicaragua"; and Lancaster, *Thanks to God*, p. 103.

27. "In the Eye of the Hurricane," *Envío* 5, no. 63 (September 1986), p. 11.

28. Under the terms of the Esquipulas peace accords the Sandinista government agreed to advance the timetable for 1990 elections and to permit extensive international monitoring. In return, the contras were to be demobilized and disarmed. The Sandinistas fulfilled their part of the agreement, holding elections, which they lost, on February 25, 1990. As of late June 1990 the contra army had been demobilized, but throughout Nicaragua there was much speculation that many of the contra weapons had not been turned in.

PART II

Government Policy

The real measure of a revolutionary government is whether it works effectively and quickly to implement changes that improve the condition of the common citizen. The chapters in Part 2 look at government output and behavior under a variety of headings: social programs, agrarian reform, cultural policy, economic planning, human rights, and foreign policy. One generalization that emerges from these chapters is that the significant changes in government policy effected by the Sandinista revolution were implemented in a pragmatic and humane fashion. Another is that although the government was able to improve the lot of most Nicaraguans during the first few years of the revolution, many of the social programs and other positive aspects of Sandinista government policy were severely damaged—directly or indirectly—from the mid-1980s on by the U.S.-sponsored contra war and related programs of destabilization.

The chapters on economics and foreign policy give an indication of the difficult practical context in which domestic policy was being implemented. Joseph Ricciardi (Chapter 12) offers lengthy and frank criticism of many aspects of Sandinista economic planning and behavior, but he also points out that "relentless foreign military and economic aggression, in addition to nature's own unkindness of flood in 1982 and hurricane in 1988," made it extremely difficult to govern. Harry Vanden (Chapter 14) argues that although Nicaragua was able to develop a "fresh, unique, and independent" foreign policy of nonalignment that helped "protect the revolution from a very hostile U.S. policy for more than a decade," it failed to garner sufficient external support to offset the economic damages done by U.S. policy or to bring an end to the contra war.

In light of the mammoth economic problems faced by the country in this period, one might have expected Sandinista social accomplishments to have been quite meager. In fact, the revolution achieved quite a lot. Chapter 9, by Harvey Williams, on social policy and Chapter 11, by Eduardo Baumeister, on agrarian reform show that the Sandinistas succeeded in implementing a variety of important changes for the better. Some, such as the agrarian reform, were not as revolutionary as might have been desired. Most were negatively affected by external aggression. But the changes were significant. And some, such as the use of traditional folk medicine as a component of health care, described by Kirsi Viisainen in Chapter 10, showed the capacity of the revolutionaries to adapt creatively to extreme economic exigencies.

Finally, it is interesting to note, as Michael Linfield does in his study of Sandinista human rights policy (Chapter 13), that the Nicaraguan revolution was able to implement important changes and withstand major external aggression without severely and unduly restricting human rights. "Judged from the standpoint of a country at war, Nicaragua's human rights record under the Sandinistas was," in Linfield's words, "in full compliance with the standards imposed by international human rights treaties. Its record . . . compared favorably with that of many Western European nations and even that of the United States in time of war."

NINE

The Social Programs

HARVEY WILLIAMS

The Nicaraguan revolution was a "popular revolution" in the sense that it depended upon the participation of a broad political base to achieve the overthrow of the Somoza regime, in that the benefits of the revolution were to be widely distributed, and in that it required a high level of support from the masses. The FSLN government had to acknowledge the importance of the vast number of marginally employed urban and rural poor and to incorporate them into the revolutionary process. The goal of the revolutionary process was to produce social justice, which could not be accomplished without significant social change. This change in turn could be realized only through broad-based popular participation, encouraged and supported by the government.

One should understand the concept of "social justice," as it was used in Nicaragua. Social justice meant more than mere economic growth, or even distributive justice, concepts that were seen as too restrictive and that did not address the fundamental problems of the capitalist economic system.[1] Rather, "social justice refers to the *structure* and *policies* of a society, to its political, legal, economic and social institutions."[2] It went beyond the satisfaction of material needs to address nonmaterial, human needs, which "include the needs for self-determination, self-reliance and security, for the participation of the workers and citizens in the decision-making that affects them, for national and cultural identity, and for a sense of purpose in life and work."[3] Gustavo Gutiérrez called this kind of development "*a total social process*," or what "we would prefer to call liberation."[4] In Nicaragua, although there was some resistance from the more conservative elements, there was general acceptance of the need to go beyond the mere removal of Somoza and his closest supporters. Maintaining the same system while changing the leadership—Somocism without Somoza—was not to be tolerated.

The first public document of the revolutionary government made explicit the commitment to social as well as political and economic change. It specifically pledged the government to develop policies to promote the improvement of the quality of life for all Nicaraguans and outlined objectives in health, education, welfare, housing, and other areas.[5] Later policy statements of the government reaffirmed these goals and defined the role of the government not as "a handout agency for the people but rather one of coordinating and giving technical assistance to the independent efforts of the people."[6]

In development, the change from an economic approach to an emphasis on providing social requisites—from "trickle down" to "basic needs"— shifts the focus of effort to the poorest sectors of society. But this shift is frequently only a matter of expediency. "The nongovernmental, anti-bureaucratic approach is born of frustration. It argues that the public agencies are more likely to absorb than distribute resources."[7] Although the poor are seen as the beneficiaries of change, it is usually a top-down process, which emphasizes private property and commerce.[8] People are viewed as the objects of the development process.

That is not the meaning of popular participation in the revolutionary process. In that context, "*participation* refers to an active process whereby beneficiaries influence the direction and execution of development projects rather than merely receive a share of the project benefits."[9] The people become the subjects, rather than the objects, of change. The influential Brazilian educator Paulo Freire referred to this as "consciousness raising" (*concientización*), wherein "subjects meet in cooperation in order to transform the world."[10] Their role will be "not pseudo-participation, but committed involvement."[11] Gutiérrez, who drew frequently upon Freire's work, provided this interpretation: "In this process . . . the oppressed person rejects the oppressive consciousness which dwells in him, becomes aware of his situation, and finds his own language. He becomes, by himself, less dependent and freer, as he commits himself to the transformation and building of society."[12]

Within the revolutionary process, the government played a key role. The government sought to substitute the "traditional paternalistic prin-ciples of Government" with "participation, both individual and collective, of all Nicaraguans."[13] In this people-centered approach, the government strove to build "linkages between the people, bureaucrats and inter-mediaries in project choice, planning and implementation."[14] Freire stressed the need to organize. But he noted the difference between the traditional elites, who organize *against* the people, and the revolutionary leaders, for whom "organizing means organizing themselves *with* the people."[15] At the same time, he warned against the temptation to manipulate the people, to become the new oppressors: "The leaders— in spite of their important, fundamental, and indispensable role—do not own the people and have no right to steer them blindly toward their salvation."[16] In the revolutionary process, government involvement should be characterized by two-way communications.

During the years between the triumph of the people over the Somoza regime and the election victory of the National Opposition Union

(UNO), the government, led by the FSLN, made tremendous progress toward meeting the needs of the masses through the development and implementation of programs in the social sector. Both within Nicaragua and internationally, the accomplishments of four key program areas— health, education, welfare, and housing—were acknowledged as significant, even by critics of the revolution. These achievements were the result of a combination of flexible and pragmatic planning on the part of the government and of mobilization, involvement, and commitment on the part of the masses.

Nicaraguan social policies and programs during the ten years of FSLN governance fall into four time periods. The first, from the triumph in July 1979 through the end of 1980, was generally a time of planning and reorganization and of response to the immediate problems and damage created by the war. The second, 1981 and 1982, were years of policy modification and adjustment and of rapid and relatively unimpeded program expansion. The third, 1983 through 1987, saw the full development of the Reagan administration's policy of low-intensity conflict, effectively bringing all social programs under siege and causing a policy shift toward program reinforcement and defense. The fourth, from 1988 until the change of government in 1990, was a struggle for survival. In spite of the promise of peace, economic and military aggression continued. In the face of rising demand, financial and personnel shortages made it difficult to restore and improve programs and services.

Reorganization and Recovery: 1979-1980

On coming to power in July 1979, the new government confronted serious problems. The economy was in shambles. To address the social and economic needs of the people and to promote the revolutionary process, new programs had to be designed and implemented. In their urgency to satisfy immediate needs with limited resources, planners and policymakers put together a patchwork of programs, borrowing heavily from a wide range of other countries and their own past experiences. During this period interministerial coordination was limited, which led to some inconsistencies and even contradictions.

In the social sector, problems were particularly serious. The promised programs were either new or considerably larger than those that had existed under Somoza, but because social programs are not revenue producing, extreme care had to be exercised to avoid the misallocation of resources. Such misallocation had been experienced in other developing countries.[17] From the very beginning, the role of the mass organizations in generating popular support and participation was a key factor in the success of social-sector programs.[18]

Health

The health-care-delivery system under Somoza was disorganized, inefficient, and greatly biased toward providing curative care for the small minority of urban elites.[19] The major commitments of the Ministry of Health (MINSA) during the first period were to work toward the unification of the health system and to restore prewar health facilities. The creation of a National Unified Health System brought together several previously separate health groups: the social security system, the Ministry of Health (which provided preventive care through health posts), the military hospital, and the various national and local social assistance boards (which maintained public clinics and hospitals for the indigent). The National Unified Health System did not include private facilities, although it did develop a cooperative working agreement with some of the private, nonprofit providers. MINSA also took over the training of health personnel, increasing significantly the number of people prepared at all levels, and provided training, materials, and health personnel for the efforts of several other government programs.

The most significant policy innovation for health was to make government health care open to all. Where facilities already existed, this increased utilization by the masses significantly and led to greatly increased expectations in previously underserved areas. In this early period, emphasis was on curative care because of both the traditional system and the influence of the more highly trained professionals.[20]

Education

As with health, the prerevolutionary situation in education was poor. The illiteracy rate (50 percent) and the yearly dropout rate (50 percent) were among the highest in Latin America, and schools were concentrated in the urban areas. The better schools were private and charged tuitions that excluded all but the children of the most wealthy.

The process of reorganization for the Ministry of Education (MED) was not difficult, given the relatively centralized organization that had existed under Somoza. Most of the effort was directed toward better integration of planning and curriculum development and expansion of programs in preschool, technical, special, and adult education. A substantial number of new schools were built, many by popular initiative. In the first two years, community projects accounted for 85 percent of the 739 schools built, most in rural areas.[21]

By far the most ambitious and well-known effort of MED, if not of the whole revolutionary process, was the Literacy Crusade of 1980. Within two weeks of the triumph, planning for a nationwide literacy project began. The process followed a pattern that was to be repeated in similar programs over the years. A core group of Nicaraguans, working with the support of international volunteers, reviewed theoretical and practical examples. The basic model selected was the one developed by Paulo Freire, which emphasized the active participation of the learners in the process.[22] There were modifications to fit the unique Nicaraguan circumstances and accommodations for the non-Spanish-speaking peoples of the Atlantic Coast, introducing variants of the model adapted to their languages. The program was also modified to reflect the fact that the empowering process of the model was supported and encouraged by the government.

A total of 88,000 volunteers, primarily young, urban, high school and college students, were recruited and trained in the basic methods of teaching. From March until August 1980, these volunteers lived and worked with their adult students across the country. Each was assigned to a small group of students, usually holding classes for two hours every weekday. During the day the volunteers learned from their students, as they worked with members of their host family or on programs for community improvement. They received technical support from a network of coordinators and weekend workshops and a daily radio program. Members of the community, usually working through the mass organizations, provided transportation, food, and shelter. Encouraged by the participatory nature of the model, volunteers and students learned together. They examined and challenged their perceptions of themselves and of each other, the system that had existed under Somoza, and the meaning of the revolutionary process.

By the end of the five-month crusade, more than 400,000 adults had completed the course and passed the basic literacy examination. It was estimated that the adult illiteracy rate was lowered from 50 percent to 13 percent.[23] In terms of effectively reducing illiteracy, the crusade was a tremendous success, acknowledged by UNESCO when it awarded Nicaragua the Literacy Prize in 1980. But the long-term impact was even more significant. The crusade itself was merely the beginning of a process for transforming education and defining the nature of the revolutionary process. Although there were those who criticized both the method and the goals of the literacy crusade, most of the population viewed the results as a confirmation of the commitment of both the JGRN and the FSLN to promote social justice.

Social Security and Welfare

Social security and welfare were separate programatic areas under Somoza and remained separate during the first period. The prerevolutionary Institute of Social Security covered only about 10 percent of the population. Although the system provided disability and retirement payments, its primary function was to provide medical care for its subscribers. With the reorganization of the government health system and the incorporation of the social security health facilities into the National Unified Health System, the Institute of Social Security devoted itself to incorporating a larger portion of the population into the social security program.

The problems of organization for the Ministry of Social Welfare (MBS) immediately following the triumph were great, primarily because such a ministry had not existed under Somoza. As in many other Latin American countries, most of the functions of social welfare were carried out by religious and private charitable agencies. The new MBS set for itself the goal of organizing under its supervision the diverse programs directed toward the resolution of social problems. These programs included homes for the elderly and for orphans; training and rehabilitation for drug and alcohol abusers, for juvenile delinquents, and for the disabled; and emergency relief for refugees and families in need. During this first period, the MBS not only developed a national coordination of the existing services but also created new programs. To the single child-care center that existed under Somoza were added 17 new urban centers and 14 rural infant centers. Among other new programs were 3 rehabilitation centers for the disabled, 3 centers for abused or abandoned children, 3 new homes for the elderly, and nutrition programs, which served more than 250,000 children and pregnant or nursing women.[24]

Housing

The war contributed to the already serious housing situation that existed under Somoza. The Somoza regime never fully recovered from the effects of the 1972 earthquake, and most of the housing built in the recovery effort was designed for middle- and upper-income families.[25]

Efforts of the new Ministry of Housing and Human Settlements (MINVAH) during this first period focused on reorganization, planning, and the development of legislation. New laws introduced rent control and restructured mortgages. The law with the broadest impact mandated the consolidation of illegal subdivisions, cleared the way for nearly half the urban householders to acquire title to their land, and outlined policies for the provision of supportive infrastructure. By way of satisfying immediate needs, some 1,146 new houses were constructed and repairs were made to 4,676 houses damaged by the war.[26]

Adjustment and Expansion: 1981-1982

The period from 1981 through 1982 was described to me be a vice-minister of education as one of "relative bonanza." Most of the reconstruction work had been completed, and many of the problems of organization within the various ministries had been overcome. A clearer and more widely accepted view of the revolutionary goals was developed.[27]

Local and regional organization was strengthened, and a new system of reorganization was enacted to decentralize government programs and make their administration more efficient.[28]

With the economy regaining strength, Nicaragua had the highest rate of economic growth in Central America during this period. The agrarian reform program sailed along, and agricultural production began to incrase toward prewar levels.[29] Although military expenditures were high and climbing, they were still exceeded by public spending in the social sector. Public spending in health and education, which under Somoza had been the lowest in the region, surpassed that of El Salvador, Guatemala, and Honduras and nearly equaled that of Costa Rica.[30]

Popular participation continued at a high rate, and organizational effectiveness was increased. Nearly two-thirds of the adult population belonged to one or more of the mass organizations, and many others participated occasionally through special mobilizations. Participation was not limited merely to providing physical labor for government projects. The mass organizations were involved more and more in planning, organizing, administering, and evaluating a wide range of public progams.[31]

But although internal development and international support increased during this period, so did aggression against Nicaragua. The Reagan administration canceled loans and PL 480 food credits and began to use its influence to block international loans.[32] The counterrevolutionaries began to step up their military operations against government targets. War damage to the economy during this period was estimated to be $40 million:[33] small by comparison to later years, but still equal to one-third of the 1982 public expenditure for health. Increasingly, social programs and participants became the targets of the counterrevolutionaries.

Health

MINSA received top priority among the social-sector ministries during the second period. The government budget for health was greater than for education, a rarity in Latin American countries.[34] All types of programs improved. Construction of four new regional hospitals began, and many new health posts were established. With a significant increase in the number of medical personnel at all levels, the number of medical consultations increased by over 20 percent.[35]

During this time there was a noticeable shift from a concentration of resources and services in urban areas to a dispersion toward underserved (primarily rural) areas. Dramatic increases in accessability and utilization were seen in poor urban neighborhoods, in the interior, and on the Atlantic Coast. There was an even more noticeable shift from curative health to preventive health. The oral rehydration program, greatly expanded with the opening of more than 300 centers, was credited as the key in the significant reduction of infant mortality.[36]

Major efforts in environmental sanitation included community programs for garbage removal and latrine construction.[37]

The programs that drew the most attention, including the recognition of the World Health Organization and UNICEF, were the campaigns carried out by the health brigades during the Popular Health Workdays. Using as a model the successful Literacy Crusade, MINSA organized and trained community volunteers for a series of national inoculation campaigns. Popular participation and cooperation were widespread, and the results were dramatic: Polio and diphtheria were effectively eliminated, and measles, tetanus, tuberculosis, and whooping cough were greatly reduced.[38]

But as the health programs became more widespread and more successful, they came to be seen as appropriate targets by the counterrevolutionaries, who killed three health workers during this period.[39] There were incidences of sabotage of expensive medical equipment,[40] and several health facilities were damaged or destroyed. The most notable was the destruction of the hospital in the Atlantic Coast community of Bilwaskarma.[41]

Education

In this second period, MED continued to expand both the enrollment of students and the construction of schools, completing more than three times the number of schools that it had built in the previous period. Special attention was given to underserved rural areas and to the construction of secondary schools in underserved areas of the interior. Enrollment neared 900,000 students, with primary and preschool totals showing the greatest increases.[42] Planning and curriculum development were expanded, and MED began to publish new textbooks. The regionalization and reorganization of MED was formalized in 1982, and the Vice Ministry of Adult Education was established.[43]

The most significant growth took place in adult education. Following the Literacy Crusade, Basic Popular Education Centers were set up to reinforce and extend the gains made.[44] More than 150,000 adults continued in these programs. The total number of teachers grew from 12,975 under Somoza to more than 40,000. Of these, 20,000 were teachers—who had little formal training but who had learned through experience—working in the Basic Popular Education Centers.[45] Both teachers and students participated at some risk, for they also became prime targets for the counterrevolutionaries. In 1982 four adult education teachers and assistants were killed, and others were kidnapped or threatened because of their activities.[46]

The active participation of the population was vigorously promoted by MED. In his *Theology of Liberation*, Gutiérrez defined liberation as the means "to seek the building of a *new man*."[47] In January and

February 1981, in community meetings across the country, more than 50,000 people discussed a set of fifty-five questions. The point was to define the qualities of this "new man" and to describe the educational system that would produce and nurture such qualities.[48] This was part of a conscious strategy to reinforce the principle that "the people are active participants in the great tasks of education, thus assuring that education in the new Nicaragua is a manifestation of the popular will."[49]

The results of the community discussions were forwarded to MED. They were analyzed by the directorate of the FSLN and the National Council of Education and were eventually synthesized into a document, *Goals, Objectives, and Principles of the New Education*. This was approved in March 1983 and became the principle planning document for MED. Reflecting the influence of Gutiérrez and Freire (among others), it defined the goal of education as follows: "To completely and wholly form the personality of the New Nicaraguan Man, by developing his intellectual, moral, esthetic, and spiritual capabilities, which will constitute him as a man and as an active subject in the process of transformation that is building the new society day by day."[50] In several places the role of active popular participation was emphasized. It declared that "the student must be *an important agent of his own formation*"[51] and that the educational process must develop "the conviction that the *organized participation of the people* in the social process and in the tasks of the Revolution is *the practice of popular democracy*."[52]

Social Security and Welfare

The major change during the second period for these programs was the combination of the Ministry of Social Welfare with the Nicaraguan Social Security Institute to form a new ministry-level agency, the Nicaraguan Institute of Social Security and Social Welfare (INSSBI). INSSBI continued to incorporate new workers into the Social Security program and by the end of 1982 had nearly doubled the number of subscribers.[53] Pension and disability benefits were granted to a number of special groups such as neighborhood watch members and circus workers. In 1982 for the first time, more than half the benefits paid were generated by deaths and injuries caused by counterrevolutionary aggression.[54]

The social welfare programs during this period began to show the effects of a reduced budget. Few new child-care centers were opened, and several pilot programs had to be curtailed. Increased emphasis was given to integrating the community and the mass organizations into the provision of services. Case workers facilitated the development of community support to help their clients deal with physical and mental disabilities, drug and alcohol problems, and physical abuse and abandonment.[55]

Housing

In both 1981 and 1982 MINVAH increased the number of housing units that it built, completing a total of 5,762 in this period, more than five times the number for the previous period. Although more than half these units were in Managua, a shift began toward the underserved areas of the interior.

There was also a shift toward facilitating housing for the very poor. MINVAH realized that its funds were too limited to build even low-cost housing for all that needed it. Therefore, two new progams were initiated: the Materials Bank and the Progressive Urbanizations. The former was a program for the production and distribution of housing materials that could be purchased at low cost and with low-interest financing. The latter was a sites-and-services program to provide low-cost, controlled residential development in the urban centers. During this period 551 units were completed under the Materials Bank program, and nearly 10,000 parcels were distributed under the Progressive Urbanizations.[56]

Reinforcement and Defense: 1983–1987

In the period 1983-1987 there was a marked hardening of the position of the Reagan administration toward Nicaragua. While expressing verbal support for a negotiated settlement of differences, the Reagan administration seemed to be following the recommendations of the Rand Corporation's 1984 report: rejection of accommodation as untenable, emphasis on "diplomatic efforts to isolate the regime, raise the regime's costs, reduce the support it receives from Latin America and Europe,"[57] and a strengthening of "the rebel forces to concentrate their attacks on economic targets."[58] This was part of a conscious shift to a new type of military strategy, "low-intensity conflict."[59]

During this period the Reagan administration continued its diplomatic and economic campaign against the Nicaraguan government, eliminating the sugar quota, closing the Nicaraguan consulates in the United States, continuing to block international loans and grants and eventually, in May 1985, declaring a complete trade embargo. "Military intimidation increased. The goal was . . . to squeeze the economy by forcing a massive diversion of resources into defense. The strategy aimed to exacerbate social problems and tensions, eroding popular support for the revolution by making it ineffective in people's lives"[60] and to produce a heavy psychological impact on the civilian population.[61]

As the U.S. Congress moved from prohibiting covert aid to approving overt aid, the counterrevolutionary forces stepped up their attacks,[62] and the estimated number of men under arms rose from some 5,000 to over 15,000. The counterrevolutionaries increased their campaigns against civilian as well as military targets.

Overall, there is a conscious effort to reduce the presence of the civilian government, to remove successful social programs and the ideological influence which comes with them. The strategy aims to create the impression of government weakness and contra strength. In practice, this means the targeted torture and assassination of teachers, health workers, agricultural technicians and their collaborators in the community. This is not, as many critics charge, "indiscriminate violence against civilians." Nor are the killings random acts of terror by incorrigibly brutal ex-National Guardsmen. Rather, the violence is part of a logical and systematic policy, and reflects the changing pattern of the war.[63]

The effects of the aggression of the Reagan administration and the counterrevolutionaries during this period were serious but not fatal. The total cost of the war was great, and estimates varied widely. The Nicaraguan government in its case before the World Court in 1985 calculated the amount at more than $1.6 billion in direct and indirect damages. This was approximately equal to Nicaragua's total export earnings for four years.[64] The proportion of the national budget that went for defense rose to 37 percent in 1983, passing health and education expenditures under the FSLN for the first time.[65] After 1985, defense expenditures accounted for more than half the national budget.

Although war and economic problems had a serious negative impact on social program development, many did not see them as the key factors impeding progress. As one MED official acknowledged, "We can't fall into blaming the war for all our problems in education: that's a cop out. The difficulties are in our methods, our work and the conceptions we hold. The war is a fundamental element we need to take into account, but it's not the cause of all our problems."[66]

Among the many social and political problems that created obstacles to the development of social programs and reduced the scope and effectiveness of popular participation, the most serious was bureaucratization. There were complaints of inefficiency and insensitivity of the program directors. The mass organizations were frequently viewed more as a source of labor for the accomplishment of government programs than as participants in the process of decision making: "At times the participation of the mass organizations is merely formal, reduced to validating with their political prestige and moral authority the policies pushed by the administration."[67]

Freire had warned against this tendency when he wrote, "The moment the new regime hardens into a dominating 'bureaucracy' the humanist dimension of the struggle is lost and it is no longer possible to speak of liberation."[68] This was the issue that Vilas was addressing when he made the distinction between two different aspects of bureaucracy: "the slowness of procedures, paperwork and unjustified delays [and] the separation of the state apparatus from their social bases. The former is an administrative issue; the latter is a political problem."[69]

Social-sector programs suffered in this period. There was a freeze put on the extension of services for the urban areas, and investment in the social sector was reduced severely.[70] The FSLN tried to maintain the support of mass organizations, responding to their complaints and concerns,[71] and developing programs in their support. The priority programs of health, adult education, and agrarian reform were reinforced and expanded, particularly in the rural areas, offsetting the traditional preference for the more visible but less productive urban masses.

Health

Throughout the third period MINSA remained an FSLN priority. Although investment in new facilities was severely curtailed after 1982, programs in preventive health and early treatment in rural areas were maintained. In spite of the fact that nearly 100 health facilities were destroyed or closed due to hostilities, those in service remained above the 1982 total.[72] More impressive was the fact that the numbers of medical consultations, traditionally concentrated in Managua and León, were proportionate to each region's population for the first time in history.[73] Although the U.S. embargo seriously affected the importation of medications and spare parts for repairing medical equipment,[74] it also stimulated innovative responses in equipment repair and herbal medicine substitutes.[75] Polio and diphtheria appeared to be things of the past for Nicaragua, but earlier advances against measles and malaria were being slowly eroded.[76] Difficulties in serving the more isolated areas in some cases served to reinforce popular participation through the mass organizations and local health committees.[77]

But the negative effects were great. In this period an estimated 11,000 persons were killed and 5,000 were wounded as a result of the aggression,[78] among them 35 health providers killed, 11 wounded, and 28 kidnapped.[79] More than 5,000 health workers were mobilized for defense, representing a serious drain of resources from the civilian population. Nearly 100 health facilities were destroyed, including 3 belonging to the Nicaraguan Baptist Convention.[80]

Education

During the 1983–1987 period MED was severely strained to maintain the gains made in the first years. Innovative programs, such as bilingual education for the Atlantic Coast area and rural work-study schools, were reduced or put on hold.[81] Enrollment at all program levels, having reached a high of 939,793 in 1983, declined nearly 10 percent over the next two years, then began to recover in 1986.[82] Investment in new facilities nearly came to a halt, and expansion was limited to resettlement projects as part of the policy to give priority to the productive sector. Major efforts were directed toward curriculum revision, improving academic quality and performance, stimulating creative alternatives to resolve material shortages, and reinforcing the popular support of education at all levels.

As MED was extended into the most remote areas of the country in both regular programs and special adult education programs, MED personnel and facilities were particularly susceptible to attack by the counterrevolutionaries. In this period MED suffered extensive losses. More than 200 teachers and students were killed, and many were kidnapped. More than 50 schools were destroyed or severely damaged, and more than 500 had to be abandoned due to the hostilities.[83]

Even though Nicaragua continued to receive international support, the Reagan administration's efforts to discredit the Nicaraguan government caused a reduction in support from educational programs such as the Latin American Scholarship Program of American Universities (LASPAU), which had provided professors to Nicaragua. Threats of U.S. military intervention were said to have led to the withdrawal of 1,000 Cuban teachers.[84]

Social Security and Welfare

INSSBI made its greatest gains in social security coverage during the period 1983–1987. The number of subscribers rose to more than 355,000. Most of this increase was accomplished by extending coverage to people in the interior of the country, particularly agricultural workers.

The number of child protection centers was greatly expanded during this period, particularly in the rural areas and in conjunction with the development of agricultural cooperatives and new settlements. The School of Social Work, which had been closed for reorganization since 1980, was reopened in 1984 and began training much-needed professionals.[85]

During this period, INSSBI experienced an accelerating demand for its services because of the aggression of the counterrevolutionaries. More than 250,000 people had been displaced by the war. The costs of INSSBI programs—which managed to provide material assistance to fewer than half of these refugees—exceeded $15 million.[86] Pensions for other war-caused deaths and disabilities constituted an increasing proportion of all social security payments.[87] Although international aid continued to support INSSBI programs (particularly through food and other gifts-in-kind), cash donations, which had reached a record high in 1983, decreased about 50 percent by 1985.[88]

Housing

The activities of MINVAH during the third period continued at an accelerated pace. The number of housing units completed was higher than in previous periods. The most noticeable policy change was the shift of activity from Managua and other urban centers to the rural areas of the interior. For example, MINVAH completed a record high of 4,513 units in 1983. But only 25 percent were in Managua, as compared to over 60 percent before 1983.[89] Although the resettlement efforts had been under way for some time, a major increase in activity took place in this period. Housing provided by MINVAH in the new settlements ranged from conditioned sites with a minimal roofed structure, to sites with completed, prefabricated units.

Unfortunately, this did little immediately to deter the flow of migrants to the cities, and the limited funds available to MINVAH were not used for urban development in this period. Nevertheless, the granting of property titles continued as fast as technical limitations would allow, and there was a considerable amount of owner-built housing. In the rural areas, the Materials Bank program increased its activities. Alternative construction materials were developed to replace previously imported materials and to make up for the decrease in lumber harvesting caused by counterrevolutionary activities in the forested regions of the country.

Struggle for Survival: 1988–1990

Through extraordinary effort and at great cost, by 1988 Nicaragua had accomplished the strategic defeat of the counterrevolutionary armed forces. The signing of the first of the Central American peace accords at Esquipulas in August 1987 brought the promise of peace at long last. Subsequent agreements over the next two years consolidated the process. But a final peace agreement and the disarming of the counterrevolutionary forces continued to be elusive. The hard-line elements within the counterrevolutionary leadership, encouraged by reactionary elements in Nicaragua and supported by allies in the U.S. and in Central America, maintained their intransigence. Both the people and the government of Nicaragua were hard hit economically, and the U.S. Congress chose to make their situation more difficult by authorizing euphemistically designated "humanitarian aid" for the counterrevolutionary forces.

While military activity was reduced during this period, Nicaragua experienced extreme economic difficulties. Foreign aid dropped to less than one-half of its 1984 total. Inflation, which had passed 1,000 percent in 1987, topped 30,000 percent in 1988, before coming back to 1,300 percent in 1989. Economic activity continued to decline. Exports, which had dropped for several years, showed a modest increase in 1989, resulting in a significant reduction of the trade deficit.[90]

The FSLN struggled to attain economic and political stability. Even without continued subversion and economic aggression promoted by the United States, this would not have been an easy task. With it, the obstacles seemed almost insurmountable. And as if these problems were not enough, Hurricane Joan swept across the country in October 1988.

Although a strong Civil Defense response kept loss of life remarkably low, the economic damage was staggering. Total damages were calculated by the Economic Commission of Latin America to be $840 million, including capital damages of over $540 million. This included the loss of more than 300 schools (the replacement cost for which was estimated to be $5 million), and more than 40,000 houses—more than the government had been able to provide in its first nine years.[91]

The FSLN responded to diminishing revenues and hyperinflation, and the civil discontent that these encouraged, while preserving the basic promises of political and economic pluralism. The result was a patchwork of measures, many of which resembled the conservative recommendations of the World Bank: currency devaluations, severe reductions in government subsidies and employment, and an increased reliance on market factors in economic decisions. In an effort to reduce bureaucracy and the deficit, in early 1988 the government initiated a process of "compaction." Through this process a number of ministries and agencies were combined or eliminated, their functions and personnel discontinued or transferred to other units. Although these measures seemed to have a positive economic effect, the political and social costs were great. The minor increases in budget for social-sector programs were hardly sufficient to maintain current programs, and many were reduced. The combination of economic hardships and psychological stress took its toll on the supporters of the revolutionary process, making it ever more difficult to maintain popular participation. "The sheer fatigue of living under constant threat of attack has worn people down, sapping their willingness to look out for anyone but themselves."[92]

Somewhat belatedly, the FSLN took seriously the erosion of participation within the mass organizations. Particularly within the CDS, participation had been perceived as partisan. Many families maintained their affiliation marginally and only to the extent that they felt they had to in order to receive subsidized food and other benefits.[93] Omar Cabezas, an FSLN hero and very popular among the poor, was appointed national director of the CDS. His efforts to depoliticize the CDS (including changing their name to Community Development Committees) revitalized and broadened participation.[94] Similar efforts to encourage true democratic participation were undertaken in social-sector programs.

Through the campaign for the elections of 1990, the FSLN continued to promote its social-sector programs as one of its strongest attributes. The opposition parties seemed to recognize the popularity of these programs. Their campaign platforms suggested few and generally minor changes, most designed to improve rather than alter the provision of services. The only significant change, proposed by UNO, called for the elimination of the National Unified Health System and support for private health care.[95]

Health

As armed attacks dropped off in this period, activities in health care increased toward earlier levels. Overall services in most areas were below the highs reached in the first few years, although they were far ahead of the prerevolutionary period. Comparing yearly activity in 1989 to that of 1979, medical consultations increased threefold to 6.3 million, vaccinations increased fivefold to 5.1 million, and maternal/infant examinations increased more than twentyfold to 1.8 million. Over the ten-year period from 1979 to 1989 there were more than 30 popular health campaigns. Health-care capacity was increased by 50 percent with the construction of 205 new health facilities.[96]

Two health problems became more serious, and a new problem emerged. The increased use of antipersonnel mines by the counterrevolutionaries led to an increase in the number of amputations performed. The incidence of abortions (still illegal in Nicaragua) was high. In 1988 more than 4,000 women reported for medical treatment after undergoing unsuccessful attempts, and the death rate for these was six times that for traffic accidents. And in 1988 the first cases of AIDS were reported, including two deaths. Although the incidence of AIDS was lower than other Central American countries, the threat to the Nicaraguan health system was serious, given its limitations and its dependence on a high level of blood transfusions due to war-related trauma.[97]

The training of health-care professionals continued, but there were many problems. There continued to be friction between the advocates of a high-level professional training and those who favored broad-based paraprofessional training. The political dominance of the latter group discouraged many physicians and health technicians. Poor working conditions and low wages for physicians in the public sector[98] encouraged many to move to private practice or to emigrate. The process of "compaction" hit MINSA hard: The national payroll was reduced 70 percent.[99] Three-quarters of the physicians were hospital based, primarily in Managua and León, reinforcing the tendency of patients to avoid health centers and health posts in favor of going directly to the nearest hospital for treatment. The training and use of health-brigade workers was diminished by the drop in support of the popular organizations and the competition for the time of volunteers.[100]

MINSA responded to these difficulties in several ways. On an organizational level, decentralization was accelerated. More responsibility for planning and for action was delegated to regional and local groups through the new Territorial Health Systems policy. An increased effort was made to reenergize popular participation through the mass organizations and the Popular Health Councils. A comprehensive program, the Campaign for the Defense of the Lives of Children, was initiated with interministerial coordination.[101]

Efforts were made to increase the rational training and utilization of health personnel. Specialty hospitals were discontinued, and more physicians were to be trained in family practice.[102] And the problems of high costs and the lack of sufficient financial resources were addressed through better management and experimentation with fees for certain services and medications for those who were deemed able to pay.[103]

Education

During the fourth period MED experienced continued problems with financing, recovering somewhat with the "peace dividend" that was a result of reduced military spending in 1989. A major effort was directed toward replacing and repairing the schools hit by Hurricane Joan.

More than the other social-sector ministries, MED continued to work toward developing the support of and encouraging the participation of the masses. The constitution of Nicaragua, carefully crafted by the members of the National Assembly elected in 1984 and officially adopted on January 6, 1987, emphasized the role of popular participation in education. "The state promotes participation of the family, community and individuals in education," which is "a single, democratic, creative and participatory process."[104] Adult education merited its own special article: "Adults shall be offered educational opportunities and training programs. The state shall continue its programs to eradicate illiteracy."[105] Although MED experienced a decline in popular support, it redoubled its efforts, primarily through the decentralization of planning and through adult education. MED was more effective than most other ministries in generating local input in the planning of its programs.[106]

Adult education continued to be a key element in MED's efforts. Through the Popular Education Collectives many adults who had become literate during the national Literacy Crusade continued their education. These were small groups led by volunteer teachers (most without formal training), who received support and guidance from MED. The collectives were generally informal, and their curriculum tended to follow the interests of the participants. A more formal education was provided through Adult Education Centers. These had a more formal and fixed curriculum and employed salaried teachers. The MED depended on both of these forms to maintain a two-way dialogue with the people.[107]

As with personnel in the health sector, it was extremely difficult to train and retain teachers. Although the number of teachers increased from 13,900 in 1979 to more than 35,000 in 1989, 60 percent of them had no formal training.[108] Moreover, wages for teachers were much less than for health professionals. In spite of efforts of the government to control inflation by holding wages down, even MED supported the teachers' union strike for higher wages in 1989.[109] In 1990 it was estimated that 25 percent of the teachers had quit because of low wages (in addition, 300 had been killed by the counterrevolutionaries).[110]

Social Security and Welfare

During the 1988–1990 period, the social security program maintained the increase in subscribers, and the number of beneficiaries rose sharply. From 1979 to 1989 the number of subscribers increased from 122,597 to 286,945, and the number of people receiving pensions rose from 7,918 to 67,352. The most dramatic increase was for war-related pensions, which increased nearly 20 percent between 1987 and 1989. In spite of the great increase in pensions, the fund had a positive balance when the new government took office in 1990.

During this period INSSBI maintained its level of social services in most areas and increased it in a few. The number of centers providing services rose by 5 percent, and the number of persons receiving services, by about 20 percent. The total number of centers attending to children in 1989 was 275, of which 75 percent were located in rural areas. Of these, 60 had been started by popular initiative and continued to be run by the local communities. In all, they served more than 40,000 children in 1989.[111]

The greatest increases in demand came from war-related causes and from the effects of Hurricane Joan. As part of the government move to integrate programs and planning, INSSBI was given the role of coordinating the national and international recovery assistance following that disaster. This coincided with INSSBI's responsibility for the repatriation and resettlement of refugees returning from Costa Rica and Honduras. During this period INSSBI processed 32,000 civilians who returned voluntarily.[112]

The war activity, although diminishing, still increased the count of disabled persons and orphans. By 1989 there were more than 16,000 war orphans, and the number of combat disabilities exceeded 3,500. Nearly 700 of the disabled had had one or both legs amputated, primarily as a result of antipersonnel mines. In addition to providing pensions, INSSBI was responsible for the rehabilitation programs, including physical and occupational therapy.[113]

INSSBI continued its efforts to decentralize and to reach unserved populations. Social workers were assigned to neighborhood centers and were encouraged to work with community groups to resolve local problems. They were especially effective in dealing with child abuse and neglect. During this period nearly 4,000 cases of child neglect were processed, and local programs were initiated to generate community support for prevention and treatment. An especially positive program was begun in Managua, where social workers and merchants in the

Mercado Oriental cooperated to provide child care and recreation facilities for unsupervised children in the area.

Housing

MINVAH was the most severely affected social-sector ministry during this period. In 1988, MINVAH was phased out in the "compaction" process, and most of its functions were turned over to the regional and municipal governments, while some of the construction projects were continued under the direction of other ministries.[114] From 1979 to 1988, MINVAH had supported the construction of more than 15,000 houses in Managua and had distributed approximately 40,000 lots.[115] In the rural areas MINVAH supported the settlement of more than 300 new communities. In these communities 10,017 houses were provided by MINVAH and an additional 3,419 by other state agencies.[116] Rural agricultural and industrial workers received more than 5,000 houses.[117] But overall housing activity diminished during the period 1988–1990. The phasing out of MINVAH confirmed the observation that the state could not afford to provide public housing on a large scale. In 1987 MINVAH completed only 370 units.

In Managua the struggle to satisfy housing demand, most of which was caused by internal growth, continued.[118] The city had already exceeded its capacity to provide for the population's needs: Water was rationed and sewerage was deficient. Although the growth of squatter settlements had slowed somewhat since 1985, there were still several new ones each year. In most cases the vast majority of the occupants had illegal connections to water and electricity supplies.[119] In 1989 the mayor of Managua estimated that the housing deficit for the city was 80,000 units and increasing by 12,000 per year.[120] In that year his office distributed approximately 2,000 lots and conferred 6,534 property titles.[121]

The most active area for housing construction during 1989 was in the Atlantic Coast area. In Bluefields alone, more than 4,600 homes were destroyed by Hurricane Joan. International agencies were committed to build nearly 3,000 units, with the Cuban government pledging to build 1,000 units and infrastructure.[122] Yet these efforts were not sufficient even to replace the losses, let alone to respond to increased demand.

Conclusion

For more than ten years following the overthrow of Somoza, the Nicaraguan people, led by the FSLN, strove to establish social justice through the revolutionary process, giving a preferential option to the poor. Key policies and programs were developed and implemented through the ministries of the social sector, especially the Ministries of Health, Education, Social Welfare, and Housing. The policies of the FSLN stressed an active participation of the masses in the planning and realization of these programs.

Even the most vocal detractors of FSLN policy have acknowledged the success of many of the social programs, especially the Literacy Crusade and the many health projects. In all the social sectors, programs have been successful in reaching many people previously unserved: the urban poor, rural peasants, isolated indigenous groups, women, children, elderly, and disabled. But the question remains: How could the FSLN have improved its record? Several answers have been proposed.

First and foremost, the true test of the FSLN policies could have been realized only if they had not been vigorously opposed by the policies of foreign governments. The direct and indirect aggression sponsored by the United States severely limited the ability of the Nicaraguan people to achieve their social program goals.

Second, the FSLN tried to accomplish too much, too soon. Many have argued that a slower pace, extending services gradually as resources were increased, would have allowed a more rational development. Although this might have meant that some deserving citizens would have been left out (in the short run), at least unrealistic expectations would not have been created.

Third, the FSLN tried to please too many different factions. Some have argued that it is not possible to placate the private sector in the hope that it will cooperate with what is essentially a socialist program. Whether a more hostile attitude toward the private sector (especially the reactionary and counterrevolutionary groups) would have made matters better or worse is difficult to judge.

Fourth, the FSLN did not take seriously enough the need to promote the democratic and participatory role of the masses in the revolutionary process. Too often the mass organizations became the means to carry out the policies of the government, rather than the generating force for their formulation.

Of these possible answers, the first and fourth seem to have the most support. Perhaps without the external threat and aggression, the FSLN would have had the patience to promote a more thoroughly participatory process. There is strong evidence provided by many of the government's policies that the validity of such a strategy was clear to many of the leaders. The policies of the Ministry of Education and the Institute of Social Security and Social Welfare are particularly good examples.

With the election of a new government, the FSLN policies, partially institutionalized in the constitution and in the agencies of the government, face the test of politics and the popular will. Whether and how they might survive would be of interest not only to the people of Nicaragua, but to all who have an interest in promoting social justice.

Notes

1. Edward Weisband, ed., *Poverty Amidst Plenty* (Boulder, Colo.: Westview Press, 1989), pp. 10ff.

2. John Arthur and William H. Shaw, "What Is Justice?" in ibid., p. 26 (emphasis in the original).

3. Paul Streeten, *First Things First: Meeting Basic Human Needs in the Developing Countries* (New York: Oxford University Press, 1981), p. 34.

4. Gustavo Gutiérrez, *A Theology of Liberation* (Maryknoll, N.Y.: Orbis Books, 1973), pp. 24–25 (emphasis in the original).

5. Gobierno de Reconstrucción Nacional, *Primera Proclama del Gobierno de Reconstrucción Nacional* (Managua: Difusión y Prensa, 1979).

6. Gobierno de Reconstrucción Nacional, *The Philosophy and Politics of the Government of Nicaragua* (Managua: Dirección de Divulgación y Prensa, 1982), p. 13.

7. Sheldon Annis and Peter Hakim, eds., *Direct to the Poor: Grassroots Development in Latin America* (Boulder, Colo.: Lynne Rienner Publishers, 1988), p. 1.

8. Gita Sen and Caren Grown, *Development, Crises, and Alternate Visions* (New York: Monthly Review Press, 1987).

9. Michael Bamberger, *The Role of Community Participation in Development Planning and Project Management*, EDI Policy Report No. 13 (Washington, D.C.: World Bank, 1988), p. vii (emphasis in the original).

10. Paulo Freire, *Pedagogy of the Oppressed* (New York: Seabury Press, 1968), p. 167.

11. Ibid., p. 56.

12. Gutiérrez, *A Theology of Liberation*, p. 91.

13. Gobierno de Reconstrucción, *Philosophy and Politics*, p. 13.

14. Sen and Grown, *Development*, p. 40.

15. Freire, *Pedagogy of the Oppressed*, p. 178 (emphasis in the original).

16. Ibid., p. 167.

17. Emmanuel Jimenez, "The Public Subsidization of Education and Health in Developing Countries: A Review of Equity and Efficiency," *World Bank Research Observer* 1, no. 1 (January 1986), pp. 111–129.

18. For more extensive treatment of the Sandinista mass organizations, see Gary Ruchwarger, "The Sandinista Mass Organizations and the Revolutionary Process," in Richard Harris and Carlos Vilas, eds., *Nicaragua: A Revolution Under Siege* (London: Zed Books, 1985), pp. 88–119, and Luis Serra, "The Grass-Roots Organizations," in Thomas W. Walker, ed., *Nicaragua: The First Five Years* (New York: Praeger Publishers, 1985), pp. 95–114.

19. For more information concerning the prerevolutionary period, see Thomas John Bossert, "Health Care in Revolutionary Nicaragua," in Thomas W. Walker, ed., *Nicaragua in Revolution* (New York: Praeger Publishers, 1982), pp. 259–272; and Harvey Williams, "Organization and Delivery of Health Care: A Study of Change in Nicaragua," in John H. Morgan, ed., *Third World Medicine and Social Change* (Lanham, Md.: University Press of America, 1983), pp. 285–298.

20. Bossert, "Health Care."

21. Ministerio de Educación (MED), *La Educación en Tres Años de Revolución* (Managua: MED, 1982).

22. Freire, *Pedagogy of the Oppressed*. For greater detail on the Literacy Crusade, see Sheryl Hirshon, *And Also Teach Them to Read* (Westport, Conn.: Lawrence Hill, 1983); Valerie Miller, *Between Struggle and Hope: The Nicaraguan Literacy Crusade* (Boulder, Colo.: Westview Press, 1985); and Colin Lankshear, *Literacy, Schooling and Revolution* (London: Falmer Press, 1989).

23. Landshear, *Literacy, Schooling and Revolution*, p. 191.

24. Reinaldo Antonio Téfel, Humberto Mendoza López, and Jorge Flores Castillo, "Social Welfare," in Walker, *Nicaragua: The First Five Years*, pp. 365–382; Ministerio de Bienestar Social (MBS), *Informe de Actividades: 1979–1981* (Managua: MBS, 1981).

25. For more information concerning the prerevolutionary period, see Harvey Williams, "Housing Policy in Revolutionary Nicaragua," in Walker, *Nicaragua in Revolution*, pp. 273–290.

26. Ibid., pp. 279–284.

27. Gobierno de Reconstrucción Nacional, *Philosophy and Politics*.

28. Charles Downs, "Local and Regional Government," in Walker, *Nicaragua: The First Five Years*, pp. 45–63.

29. Jaime Wheelock Román, *Entre la Crisis y la Agresión: La Reforma Agraria Sandinista* (Managua: Editorial Nueva Nicaragua, 1985).

30. Ruth Leger Sivard, *World Military and Social Expenditures 1985* (Washington, D.C.: World Priorities, 1985).

31. Ruchwarger, "Sandinista Mass Organizations."

32. Michael E. Conroy, "External Dependence, External Assistance, and Economic Aggression against Nicaragua," *Latin American Perspectives* 12, no. 2 (Spring 1985), p. 52.

33. Nicaraguan Interfaith Committee for Action (NICA), *Nicaragua Update* 7, no. 5 (September/October 1985), p. 6.

34. Sivard, *World Expenditures*, p. 35.

35. Ministerio de Salud (MINSA), *El Sistema Nacional Unico de Salud: Tres Años de Revolución* (Managua: MINSA, 1982).

36. Thomas John Bossert, "Health Policy: The Dilemma of Success," in Walker, *Nicaragua: The First Five Years*, pp. 347–363; and Williams, "Organization and Delivery of Health Care."

37. Bossert, "Health Policy."

38. MINSA, *El Sistema Nacional*.

39. Committee for Health Rights in Central America (CHRICA), *Health Consequences of War in Nicaragua* (San Francisco: CHRICA, 1986).

40. "The Health Situation in Revolutionary Nicaragua," *Envío*, no. 23 (May 1983), p. 7c.

41. "Black Scholar Interviews: Mirna Cunningham," *Black Scholar* 14, no. 2 (March/April 1983), pp. 17–27.

42. MED, *La Educación en Tres Años*.

43. Rosa María Torres, *La Post-Alfabetización en Nicaragua* (Managua: INIES, 1983).

44. MED, *La Educación en Cuatro Años de Revolución* (Managua: MED, 1983).

45. Ibid., p. 9.

46. "Sequel to the Literacy Campaign: Adult Education in Nicaragua," *Envío*, no. 17 (November 15, 1982), pp. 14–21.

47. Gutiérrez, A Theology of Liberation, p. 91 (emphasis in the original).

48. Deborah Barndt, "Popular Education," in Walker, Nicaragua: The First Five Years, p. 329.

49. Sergio Ramírez Mercado, The Political-Educational Plan of the Sandinista Popular Revolution (Boston: Central American Affinity Groups of the Western Suburbs of Boston, 1988), p. 10.

50. Ibid., p. 11.

51. Ibid. (emphasis in the original).

52. Ibid. (emphasis in the original).

53. Instituto Nicaragüense de Seguridad Social y Bienestar (INSSBI), Memoria 1982 (Managua: INSSBI, 1983).

54. Ibid., Table 17.

55. Centro Latinoamericano de Trabajo Social (CELATS), Política Social y Trabajo Social: I Seminario de Trabajo Social en Nicaragua (Lima: CELATS, 1982).

56. Harvey Williams, "Housing Policy," in Walker, Nicaragua: The First Five Years, pp. 383-397.

57. Edward Gonzalez, Brian Michael Jenkins, David Ronfeldt, and Caesar Sereseres, U.S. Policy for Central America: A Briefing (Santa Monica, Calif.: Rand Corporation, 1984), p. 21.

58. Ibid.

59. Sara Miles, "The Real War: Low Intensity Conflict in Central America," NACLA Report on the Americas 20, no. 2 (April/May 1986), pp. 17-48.

60. Ibid., p. 30.

61. Ibid., p. 32. Other acts of psychological harassment included the frequent overflights of low-flying supersonic reconnaissance aircraft, which created sonic booms, causing the population to believe they were being bombarded.

62. Average battles per day rose to 1.35 in 1983 and to 4.10 in 1984. Attacks against civilian and economic targets increased to 115 in 1983 and to 165 in 1984. Juan Arrien, La Educación en el Contexto de la Agresión Militar (1983-1985) (Managua: MED, 1986), p. 4.

63. Miles, "The Real War," p. 34.

64. "A Survival Economy," Envío 4, no. 52 (October 1985), p. 2b.

65. Wheelock, Entre la Crisis y la Agresión, p. 84.

66. Eduardo Baez, quoted in Heather Chetwynd, An Enormous School Without Walls: Nicaraguans Educating for a New Society (Toronto: Participatory Research Group, 1989), p. 42.

67. Carlos M. Vilas, The Sandinista Revolution (New York: Monthly Review Press, 1986), p. 228.

68. Freire, Pedagogy of the Oppressed, p. 43.

69. Vilas, The Sandinista Revolution, pp. 228-229.

70. Women's International Resource Exchange (WIRE), "Nicaragua 1984: Human and Material Costs of War," in WIRE, Nicaraguan Women (New York: WIRE, 1984), p. 33.

71. "A Revolution That Is Self-Critical," Envío, no. 17 (November 1982), pp. 9-13.

72. MINSA, "Sobre los Efectos de la Agresión en el Sector Salud," Managua, 1986, mimeo., Table 8.

73. Ibid., Table 3.1.

74. NICA, "The Embargo Affects Health Care," *Nicaraguan Update* 7, no. 6 (November/December 1985).

75. Barron Lerner, "Herbal Medicine Program Underway," *Links: Central American Health Rights Network* 2, no. 4 (1985), p. 9.

76. Pan American Health Organization (PAHO), *EPI Newsletter* 7, no. 6 (December 1985), p. 7; PAHO, "Status of the Malaria Programs in the Americas," *Epidemiological Bulletin* 7, no. 1 (1986), pp. 1–5.

77. Richard Garfield, "Revolution and the Nicaraguan Health System," *Medical Anthropology Quarterly* 15, no. 3 (May 1984), pp. 69–70.

78. MINSA, *Sobre los Efectos*, p. 5.

79. Ibid., p. 7.

80. NICA, "The Baptist Church in Nicaragua," *Nicaragua Update* 7, no. 5 (September/October 1985).

81. Katherine Yih and Alice Slate, "Bilingualism on the Atlantic Coast: Where Did It Come From and Where Is It Going?" *Wani: Revista Sobre la Costa Atlántica*, no. 2-3 (December-May 1985), pp. 23–56; "A New Challenge: A People's Education in the Midst of Poverty," *Envío* 4, no. 48 (June 1985), pp. 1c–8c.

82. Central American Historical Institute (CAHI), "Education in Nicaragua: More Students, But What Are They Learning?" *Update* 5, no. 21 (May 23, 1986), pp. 1–4.

83. Arrien, "La Educación," pp. 5–6.

84. Charles Stansifer, "Observations on Salvadoran and Nicaraguan Education," *LASA Forum* 15, no. 1 (Spring 1984), p. 29; Marc Edelman, "Lifelines: Nicaragua and the Socialist Countries," *NACLA Report on the Americas* 19, no. 3 (May/June 1985), p. 48.

85. "Reapertura de la Carrera y Situación Actual," *Revista de Trabajo Social*, no. 1 (November 1985), pp. 1–2.

86. INSSBI, *Logros 85* (Managua: INSSBI, 1986), p. 10.

87. INSSBI, *Seis Años de Revolución en el INSSBI* (Managua: INSSBI, 1985), p. 3.

88. Ibid., p. 29.

89. Ministerio de Vivienda y Asentamientos Humanos (MINVAH), "Los Asentamientos Humanos de Centro América y Panamá: Nicaragua," Paper presented at the 11th meeting of the Permanent Central American Conference of Housing and Urban Development, Managua, August 19-25, 1984.

90. "Nicaragua: Low Intensity War and Revolutionary Maneuvering," *Envío* 9, no. 105-106 (May 1990), pp. 28–33.

91. "Blown Away: Hurricane Joan Puts Nicaragua at Risk," *Envío* 7, no. 88 (November 1988), pp. 9–18; "Toll Rises from Hurricane Joan," *Envío* 8, no. 90 (January 1989), pp. 28–35.

92. Antonio Dajer, "Revolutionary Evolution," *Links Health and Development Report* 6, no. 4 (Winter 1989-90), p. 6. For an excellent in-depth description of the long-term effects on a typical Nicaraguan family, see Diane Walta Hart, *Thanks to God and the Revolution: The Oral History of a Nicaraguan Family* (Madison: University of Wisconsin Press, 1990).

93. Stener Ekern, *Street Power: Culture and Politics in a Nicaraguan Neighbourhood*, Bergen Studies in Social Anthropology, No. 40 (Bergen, Norway: Department of Social Anthropology, University of Bergen, 1987).

94. Omar Cabezas, "A Organizarnos por la Comunidad," *Cuadernos de Sociología*, no. 7-8 (May-December 1988), pp. 94-100; "CDS: Revolution in the Barrio," *Envío* 8, no. 98 (September 1989), pp. 26-37.

95. "Ideologies in Conflict: Platforms of Four Nicaraguan Political Parties," *Envío* 8, no. 101 (December 1989), pp. 22-39.

96. *Barricada Internacional* 10, no. 316 (May 19, 1990), p. 17.

97. "Health: Taking AIDS Seriously," *Envío* 8, no. 92 (March 1989), pp. 15-18.

98. The monthly wage for a public-sector physician is roughly the equivalent of the price of 32 pounds of good beef: "Revolutionizing Health: a Study of Complexity," *Envío* 7, no. 80 (February-March 1988), pp. 23-38.

99. Dajer, "Revolutionary Evolution."

100. R. Giuseppi Slater, "Reflections on Curative Health Care in Nicaragua," *American Journal of Public Health* 79, no. 5 (May 1989), pp. 646-651.

101. John M. Donahue, "International Organizations, Health Services, and Nation Building in Nicaragua," *Medical Anthropology Quarterly* 3, no. 3 (September 1989), pp. 258-269.

102. Slater, "Reflections."

103. Susan Apstein, "Public Hospitals in Nicaragua Open Private Wards for Paying Patients," *Militant* 54, no. 9 (March 2, 1990), p. 15.

104. National Assembly of Nicaragua, *The Constitution of the Republic of Nicaragua* (Managua: Government of Nicaragua, 1986), Articles 118 and 117.

105. Ibid., Article 122.

106. Juan B. Arrien and Róger Matus Lazo, *La Planificación Participativa de la Educación* (San José, Costa Rica: Industrias Herrera S.A., 1988); Chetwynd, *An Enormous School Without Walls*.

107. Heather Chetwynd, *Nicaragua: The First Steps: Adult Popular Education in Nicaragua* (Toronto: Participatory Research Group, 1988), p. 15.

108. *Barricada Internacional* 10, no. 314 (April 21, 1990), p. 9; *Barricada Internacional* 10, no. 316 (May 19, 1990), p. 16.

109. Seth Galinsky, "Nicaragua: Gains for Teachers Announced," *Militant*, June 23, 1989, p. 8.

110. *NICCA Bulletin*, March-April 1990, p. 3.

111. Ricardo Chavarría, vice-minister of INSSBI: personal communication.

112. Ibid.

113. "Nicaraguans, Disabled by the War: Reintegrated, Not Forgotten," *Envío* 7, no. 84 (August 1988), pp. 9-23.

114. "Housing: Building a Policy from the Ground Up," *Envío* 7, no. 84 (July 1988), pp. 16-23.

115. *Barricada Internacional* 10, no. 312 (March 24, 1990), p. 11.

116. Kosta Mathéy, *Housing and Settlement Policies in Nicaragua* (Munich: Trialog, 1989).

117. *Barricada Internacional* 10, no. 312 (March 24, 1990), p. 11.

118. Ninette Morales, Rubén Ardaya, and Bolívar Espinoza, "Asentamientos Espontáneos no son Causa de la Crisis Urbana," *Boletín Socio-Económico*, no. 2 (April 1987), pp. 10-14.

119. Ibid.

120. Judy White, "Nicaraguan Assembly Bans Evictions During Election Time," *Militant* 53, no. 50 (December 15, 1989), p. 10.

121. *Barricada Internacional* 10, no. 312 (March 24, 1990), p. 11.

122. Susan Dobkins, "Bluefields: One Year After the Hurricane," *Witness for Peace Newsletter* 6, no. 4 (August/September 1989), pp. 12–13.

TEN

Traditional Medicine
in Revolutionary Health Care

KIRSI VIISAINEN

At the time of the 1979 triumph, a primary goal of the Sandinista government was to improve the health status of the population by organizing the chaotic health-care system inherited from the Somoza regime into the National Unified Health System (SNUS). The shift to planned health care, which involved much popular participation, also brought a change in the official attitude toward traditional medicine[1] and a change in its status. In particular, traditional midwives, who had been ignored, became a potential resource of primary health care.

The plans of the revolutionary government to integrate traditional medicine into the health-care system, rather than unique, were in line with a position strongly promoted by international health agencies to health planners in Third World countries as a way of extending access to primary health care despite scarce resources.[2] Similar integration programs were designed and implemented in several Third World countries; most of these programs concentrated on the training of traditional birth attendants because their work was assumed to fit more easily than that of other traditional agents into primary health care. In the case of Nicaragua, the shift toward integrating traditional practices into the health-care system was gradual, part of the trend toward encouraging popular participation in health that was one of the principles of the postrevolutionary Nicaraguan health policies.

Mesoamerican Traditional Medicine

Nicaragua in the 1970s and 1980s, like most societies in the world, was a medically pluralistic society. Along with the biomedical tradition, which had the dominant position within the official health-care system, there was a rich parallel tradition of folk medicine, which had evolved from the pre-Columbian indigenous and the colonial Spanish healing practices. Since Nicaraguan traditional medicine was not an organized medical system based on a literate tradition, there was no uniform body of knowledge for referral. Its practitioners, *curanderos* (healers), *sobadores* (masseuses and bone setters), *conocieras* (experts in use of medicinal plants), and *parteras* (midwives), based their practice either on an ancestral knowledge, which they had learned through an apprenticeship, or on their own empirical experience.[3] The tradition, which was transmitted from generation to generation orally, had its origin in Mesoamerican humoral medicine, according to which good health results from a balance between hot and cold elements in the body and in its environment.[4] Although this belief was widely spread within Mesoamerican indigenous and mestizo cultures, the way in which traditional medicine was practiced was not uniform throughout the region. Its practices had been greatly influenced by Spanish popular medicine in colonial times and by biomedicine in the twentieth century.

Traditional Medicine Under the Somozas: Medicine of the Poor

The official health system during the Somoza regime was poorly integrated, disorganized, elitist, and served only a fraction of the population. Since there were no specific studies done in Somoza's Nicaragua about the use of traditional medicine among the population, it is not known whether people with better economic resources resorted to it. They had certainly more choices of medical practices than the poor had, as the existing network of biomedical health services was for the most part private and concentrated in urban areas. For the vast majority of the population, especially in the rural areas, traditional medicine was their primary (and often only) source of health care. In urban poor neighborhoods, too, people relied more on popular practitioners than on official health services.[5]

The Ministry of Public Health under the Somozas had no organized policy toward traditional medicine other than declaring it illegal. There was mutual mistrust between it and the dominant biomedical tradition; traditional medicine was largely ignored by the official sector.[6] Its practitioners, however, faced a threat of prosecution if their actions drew the attention of health authorities. The motive to persecute traditional practitioners was a result of the commercial nature of the dominant biomedical practice at the time: Doctors saw traditional healers and midwives as rivals to their private practice.[7]

For the government the protection of doctors' income was probably not so important as was suppression of the political associations imputed to traditional practitioners as representatives of the health care of the poor. Thus, during relatively peaceful times, they were merely ignored. In the period of the popular revolutionary movement, however, they were openly persecuted, as they were associated with the subversive forces. Suspected of helping the guerrillas elude the National Guard, several traditional midwives were arrested and assassinated while on their way to assist in births during the insurrection.[8]

In the late 1970s, however, international health agencies began paying more attention to the promotion of the role of traditional agents in the delivery of primary health care.[9] Though Somoza's Ministry of Public Health did not make any serious efforts to integrate traditional medicine or its practitioners into the health-care system as such, a midwife-training project was carried out in Nicaragua in 1976–1978 with the funds and assistance from United States Agency for International Development (USAID) and Pan American Health Organization (PAHO).

This program was an attempt not only to upgrade the working methods of traditional midwives in assisting births but also to introduce a family-planning program. Traditional midwives were taught about hygiene in birth assistance and about contraceptive methods. At the end of a five-day course, they were provided with a kit of simple instruments, a supply of drugs to be distributed, and a license to practice. During the short time that elapsed between the introduction of this program and the Sandinista revolution, there was no organized follow-up study on the effect of the training on the birth-assisting practices of the midwives. Nor was there organized supervision of the *parteras*. Health officials did monitor drug distribution to the midwives, and it was reported that after two years 64 percent of the trained midwives had returned to refill their supply of medicine at the health establishments.[10] The objective of the program, according to USAID, was to provide "low-cost health delivery," but it also had political implications: This low-cost social reform was meant to calm and control political unrest, as it was strategically implemented in areas where guerrilla activity was most intensive.[11]

Traditional Medicine
in the Revolutionary Health-Care System

The Sandinista revolution was the starting point for a profound transformation in the way in which the official health-care system was organized in Nicaragua. It also led to the redefinition of the relationship between the health-care system and traditional medicine. A gradual integration of some parts of the parallel medical tradition into the official system began during the decade of Sandinista rule.

Though the Ministry of Health (MINSA) never explicitly declared a favorable position on traditional medicine, it implemented very cautious changes toward the integration of those elements of this tradition that would least conflict with biomedicine. These included training *parteras* to work as primary-health-care workers and investigating possibilities for using some traditional medicinal plants within primary health care. The limited economic possibilities that the government had for providing Western allopathic medical services for the population, especially at the time of the contra war, spurred the interest in use of popular health-care resources. But this interest was inhibited by the strong influence that the biomedical tradition had on the thinking of health planners and medical practitioners.

In the first post-Somoza years the main focus of health planning was on creating a health-care system that would provide equal access to biomedical care for the population; it was thought that equal access would lead to the withering of the presumably unnecessary traditional practices in the country. The attitude of health planners toward traditional practitioners was one of tolerance. Although they were no longer persecuted, no special measures were taken to promote their position. MINSA was headed by medical professionals, and in the first years the focus of planning tended to be in curative Western medical care. The difficulties of directing the health resources toward primary and preventive care have been well documented.[12] Traditional medicine as a health-care resource initially received even less serious attention from the biomedically trained decision makers than did preventive medicine.

Before long, however, it became clear that professional and institutional biomedical care for the whole population was impossible, given the country's manpower problems.[13] At this point MINSA started training volunteer health workers (brigadistas) to participate in popular-health campaigns, and traditional practitioners, specifically midwives, were recognized as a possible resource in confronting problems of maternal and infant health care. This did not represent a major organizational change in the way that childbirth was taking place in the country. Rather, it was an acceptance of the situation as it was—traditional midwives were assisting most of the births in the country. Since they were already practicing, the task was to get them to work within the health-care system rather than outside it.

MINSA's approach toward traditional medicine was cautious for political reasons, as health care was vital for establishing the legitimacy of the revolutionary government. The policy of providing health care for all was embedded in the ideology that Western medical care, which before had only been available to the rich and upper classes, was to be equally available for all. Moreover, the people were to be educated about the principles of biomedicine in popular-education programs and health campaigns. The aims of the new health policy were not only to give people access to biomedical care but also to educate them to think about their health and illness in biomedical terms. As a regional director of MINSA commented: "We cannot politically change our course to recommending traditional practices. That would be contradictory, as we have just taught the population that they have a right to Western medicine."[14] His statement typified the underlying tone of the statements of several medical practitioners regarding traditional medicine and its practices.

Nevertheless, the government had a strong commitment to popular participation, and including traditional practitioners in official health care was seen as a part of that commitment. MINSA recognized the political importance of respecting popular traditions and customs in connection with health. However, the recognition of traditional medicine as a resource for health care was based more on economic reasons and on a need to recognize the popular cultural values than on any deeply felt belief in the effectiveness of traditional practices.

Midwife-Training Program

MINSA's first maternal and infant health-care plans included the goal of directing all births to hospitals or health centers provided with beds. The increased accessibility of hospital care, as well as the rising birthrate, did cause an increase in the number of hospital births, but it was soon realized that it would be impossible to extend to all pregnant women in the country the possibility of giving birth in a hospital. There were simply not enough hospital beds for those eligible and not enough money to build new ones. Moreover, although in Managua the only hospital providing obstetrical care was flooded with patients, in the countryside most *campesina* women preferred giving birth in their homes with traditional midwives even when institutionalized care was available. New health centers with beds were built in remote areas of the country, but these facilities were used for only approximately 30 percent of the births.[15] From 1977 to 1983, the portion of births occurring in hospitals increased only slightly, from 37 to 43 percent, despite MINSA's efforts to increase hospital births.[16] A countrywide study covering more than 2,000 births in 1985 indicated that 72 percent of all home births were attended by traditional midwives.[17]

When it was clear that births could not be brought to institutions, MINSA decided to organize and control home births by training the traditional midwives and involving them in the primary-health-care program. Rather than training new forces and creating a new network of health-care workers, the policy was to recruit the existing, established, and practicing midwives and invite them to take part in training courses and thus become a part of SNUS. In the light of experiences in other countries where midwife-training programs had been established for years, this probably was a wise decision. Programs that introduce newly trained birth attendants into communities that have used traditional midwives have tended to fail because of low rate of popular acceptance.[18]

A nationwide training program for traditional midwives began in 1982. In the plans of the Maternal and Infant Care Division of MINSA, the primary objective of this training was the reduction of infant mortality attributed to neonatal causes by changing the working methods of the midwives. The other main goal was expressed in the first *Handbook of Traditional Midwives*: "In bringing the traditional midwife into the heart of the United National Health System . . . we are making her part of the health team of the area."[19]

The handbook listed the tasks that the trained *partera* would perform for MINSA. She was to be involved in practically all the programs of maternal and infant care, working side by side with the *brigadistras* and the health post nurses. Most important, she was to educate people about the use of health-care services, urging women to go to their prenatal checkups and urging them to take the children to the growth-and-development checkups. She also was to report all her activities to MINSA. This meant integrating the *partera* into the health-care system not only as birth attendants but also as popular health-care workers.

The handbook also reflected the political role that the midwives were to have as representatives of the revolutionary health-care system. Midwives were seen as naturally influential people in their communities who could easily become trusted popular leaders in health and could then work as links between the population and the official health-care system. MINSA's expectations were high. Indeed, a MINSA representative said at the end of a course to the newly graduated *parteras*, "You are the Ministry of Health in miniature."

The Nicaraguan *partera* attending the training courses was typically an illiterate middle-aged woman who had been attending births for an average of twenty years. She had learned her skills from her mother or another knowledgeable woman in her family or just from the experience of the births of her own numerous children. She was known and respected in her community and was usually remunerated on a voluntary basis by the family of the newborn. When the program started, most midwives were suspicious of it and had to be persuaded to participate, as the memories of earlier persecution were too fresh. "When the nurses first came looking for us *parteras* in the villages, I hid, as I thought they were coming to arrest me. When they said that they wanted to train me I declined as I thought it would be too difficult because I was too old and could not read and write. But they insisted that it was not necessary, so I went." This is how a seventy-year-old midwife from Region I described her first involvement in the program.[20]

The training employed culturally relevant information about the traditional working methods of the midwives. Special methods, such as sociodramas, demonstrations, and pantomimes, suitable for an illiterate older audience were designed.[21] But even with the most sensitive approach, how much could be altered in five days, when the participants had an average of twenty years of experience, working the traditional way? The educators in charge of the training were quite realistic about the possibility of changing ancient traditions with a short course; they saw as their most important goal winning the confidence of the *parteras* so that these women would keep coming back to the meetings and would also start referring patients to the health institutions. Thus in practice, the program presented in MINSA's handbook in 1982 was seen more as an ideal than a realistic goal for midwife training by the trainers themselves, and the handbook was considered far too complicated and biomedically oriented to be useful for the day-to-day practice of the midwives.[22] Paradoxically, however, in practice the initial training course was often the only contact most midwives had with the official health-care system, as most health areas were not able to organize follow-up training for the midwives effectively.

More than 3,000 midwives had participated in the five-day courses by 1984. Since the training program was part of maternal and infant care, it was initially a priority at MINSA. However, as the war required increasing attention of the health planners and consumed most of the resources, midwife training, like many other primary-health-care programs, had to be cut back during the years of the strongest military activity, and it was only starting to revive in the last years of the decade. The health plan of 1988–1990 no longer presented an increase in hospital births as a goal, proposing, rather, to maintain the existing ratio. In 1989 maternal-health-care planners asserted that the use of traditional resources within the health policy would be a temporary step and that in the future, in a better economic situation, there would be a supply of biomedically trained health workers who could take over the work of the midwives. MINSA had already started training obstetrical nurses and was investing in the training of health post auxiliary nurses to become birth attendants as well.[23]

After seven years of experience in training the midwives, what had been accomplished by the program supporters? As most of the midwives were not regularly reporting to the health centers, the records kept by health authorities would not show to what extent they actually worked within their popular-health-worker role or the outcome of their work. The only indicator monitored by MINSA was the ratio between home and hospital births. The rate of home births remained between 55 and 58 percent of registered births. In 1985 a nationwide comparative study of home and hospital births indicated that the perinatal death rate was higher in hospital births than in home births, but that more children died during the birth process in home births. Unfortunately this study did not distinguish perinatal mortality rates of trained midwives and attendants with no training. The great majority (72 percent) of home births were attended by midwives, the rest by family members and nurses (24 percent and 3 percent respectively). Overall, the study drew attention to the rising perinatal mortality rate of the overcrowded hospitals and presented the reasons for including midwives in primary care as cultural and economic: "The assistance of births at home [by midwives] relates to folkways that are difficult to modify, to geographical problems of accessibility, and to the limited capacity and resources of the [official] sector. These factors make necessary the redefinition of [assistance by midwives], at least for now, as the primary level of health care."[24]

Case Study: Midwives in Region I

Region I, situated in the northern part of the country at the border of Honduras, was one of the areas where the midwife-training program was well established by 1989. A regional training center was founded in 1985 in Estelí, the regional capital. By July 1989, 432 midwives had been trained in the region, and around the city of Estelí alone 65 practicing midwives were officially registered. About 30 midwives came regularly to the monthly meetings at the center, where they heard lectures from health educators and medical doctors and had a chance to exchange experiences. In other areas of the region the local health centers were in charge of the follow-up training of the parteras, although this in practice meant that the parteras could come to the center to restock their kits, rather than be offered additional organized training. In fact, very few of the trained midwives outside of the city of Estelí actually were in regular contact with the health-care system, especially since the stock of supplies in the health centers was often empty.[25]

Based on my interviews with several trained midwives in Region I in 1989, it can be concluded that most of them had actually changed their way of attending births very little. They adapted to the use of scissors instead of a heated machete for cutting the umbilical cord, and some of them had started doing vaginal examinations. The biggest change was that those midwives who were regularly attending the meetings felt comfortable sending problematic births to the hospital, rather than attending them themselves. The vast majority of them, however, felt that they could not take patients to the hospital themselves. The hospital staff would not allow midwives to enter with a patient and would not treat her as a health worker who could give some useful information about her patient. Instead she would be treated like any person accompanying a patient and often rudely shooed away. The hospital did not record whether their patients had been referred by traditional midwives. Thus, an early diagnosis of a problematic birth correctly done by a midwife would go unnoticed by the hospital staff, but they would certainly notice the cases where a home delivery had led to complications and the attempts of a midwife to treat them had been unsuccessful.

The doctors' opinion about midwife practice was thus grounded in their (limited) empirical evidence of it: "Any woman who has been touched by a midwife can be considered a high risk case [in obstetric care]."[26]

Few midwives actually took up the role of a village health worker, but most of them participated in regular vaccination campaigns along with the health *brigadistas*. Active promoting was not part of a traditional *partera's* way of working: "I do not go from house to house looking for pregnant women. If they need me, they come to me."[27] The extent to which the midwives actually fulfilled their roles as "MINSA in miniature" seemed to depend greatly on the relationship they had with the local health workers. The health post nurses were officially in charge of the training follow-up and the supervision of the midwives in their area. This task was, however, impeded by several factors. The nurses had no training in childbirth practices, let alone in methodology of midwife training; thus they did not feel prepared to take over the supervision of the midwives other than administering their reports of activities and distributing materials. Also, the health post nurses were often young and recently graduated and were not seen by the midwives as being in a position of authority. The midwives would go to the health post to collect more materials, but as supplies were unreliable, most midwives would not bother to go just for the sake of reporting. The contact between the traditional *parteras* and the official health-care system that had been established by the training courses was thus not followed up by the primary-health-care system or by the hospitals. The health workers on different levels of the system were not prepared to accept trained *parteras* as "a part of the team," as stated in the MINSA handbook. The majority of the midwives continued working on their own, carrying their UNICEF kits and diplomas as a token of symbolic rather than actual recognition by the official health-care system.

Medicinal Plants in Primary Health Care

Nicaraguan traditional health practitioners, *curanderos* and *parteras*, used a wide arsenal of herbal medicine, most of which was based on the teachings of Mesoamerican humoral medicine. However, the use of herbs was also part of popular and common knowledge, as herbal medications were widely employed in peasant households even without first consulting traditional practitioners. Herbal medicine received no special attention by health planners during the first years of postrevolutionary health care. At that time, the main focus of the system was to assure the distribution of Western pharmaceutical products throughout the country through a network of popular and private pharmacies.[28]

As in most Third World countries, pharmaceutical products in prerevolutionary Nicaragua were widely advertised and available over the counter in pharmacies and also in markets and stores. The rate of self-medication, including use of antibiotics and other prescription drugs, was high. Nicaraguan physicians used to prescribe medicine quite freely, and the visiting salesmen of international drug companies made sure that the latest products were available and known about by the doctors and the public.[29] In the first years of the National Unified Health System, all drugs were given for free in the state pharmacies and hospitals, and the consumption increased dramatically. The national production of drugs in Nicaragua was very limited. Until 1984, 80 percent of all the medicaments consumed in the country were imported from the United States. The economic crisis brought by the contra war made the drug-supply situation very difficult and forced Nicaraguans to look for drugs wherever they could get them at the least expense. MINSA formed its first list of 667 basic drugs according to the epidemiological characteristics of the country. Year by year, as the budget restrictions became tighter, the basic list got shorter, and by 1987 it consisted of 350 drugs, only 100 of which could be produced in local laboratories. Most of the raw materials had to be imported, and more than 60 percent of all drugs consumed were still foreign imports.[30]

The economic reality and dependency on the international drug market led MINSA to look for national alternatives to overcome the severe drug shortage caused by the blockade. The abundance of medicinal plants in Nicaragua and their use and acceptance by the population were seen as an opportunity to solve at least a part of the shortage of medication that existed in the country. The promotion of medicinal plants was problematic, however, because the popular knowledge about the treatments was fragmented and the practice of traditional healers varied. Though MINSA did not formulate any norms regarding the use of herbal medicine, it launched a long-term project to investigate the pharmacological properties of the plants most widely used in Nicaragua.

The research on the usefulness of medicinal herbs started in 1985 as a pilot project conducted by the MINSA headquarters in Region I, in the north of Nicaragua. In the first phase, data on the use of medicinal herbs were collected. For the project, 845 secondary-school students and 61 science teachers interviewed more than 3,000 people who were known to have special knowledge about herbs and their use. Data and samples of more than 300 medicinal plants were collected, and at the same time, local radio stations asked people to call in their household recipes on how to prepare and use herbs for everyday ailments. A total of 775 herbal prescriptions were recorded, and a regional research center with access to international data banks was founded to investigate the pharmacological properties of the plants most often used. Even in this aspect the U.S. economic blockade was effective: All North American data banks were out of reach for the Nicaraguan researchers.[31] Pilot projects to cultivate and process dried herbs for retail sales through a botanical pharmacy were also started.

This large-scale project was initiated by local interests in a region that was severely affected by the war and had difficulties in distributing medications to the remote health posts, and as such it is an example of influence going up from the local level to central planning. Only after the results of this first project for the "rescue of popular medicine" were at hand and the first card catalogues of information about traditional herbs had been distributed to all health posts and centers of the region did the national MINSA express interest in these activities. With national-level ministry involvement, the project started expanding to other regions of the country in 1986.[32]

With a ministerial resolution in April 1989 the status of the research center in Estelí was changed to that of a national entity, the National Center of People's Traditional Medicine (CNMPT). Under direct supervision of the national MINSA office, this center was put in charge of research activities in all the regions. In the founding resolution the minister of health stated that the center was created to find substitutes for imported medicaments in order to increase the economic independence of the country.[33] The center was in charge not only of investigating, producing, and distributing medicinal plants but also of educating health workers and the public about the *proper* use of medicinal plants, that is, the use that had been proven efficacious by clinical tests and laboratory analysis. By educating the public with specially edited radio programs, broadcast daily by Radio Liberación in Estelí, the health planners hoped that the self-medication with commercial products would diminish because people in urban areas would learn the traditional way of utilizing herbal medicaments for the common ailments.[34]

Although in 1989 the CNMPT was collecting data on medicinal plants on a national level, its other activities were restricted to Region I. Educational programs for health-care workers concerning the use of herbal medicine had not yet been implemented, and there were no regular contacts between the center and the educational coordinators of MINSA at the regional level. However, health workers, both nurses and doctors, in health posts and centers were prescribing herbal medicine without official guidelines to do so. In Region I, heavily affected by contra aggression, herbal medicine had become a part of medical practice during the time of war and drug shortages. The auxiliary nurses in the health posts and the general practitioners in health centers in the rural areas of the country had to make use of their common knowledge about the use of the plants.

In August 1989 the regional MINSA office surveyed 70 physicians and 265 auxiliary and registered nurses on their knowledge about and rate of using medicinal plants. The vast majority of the respondents had a positive opinion about using herbal medicine in their work. Eighty percent of the doctors had at least sometimes prescribed herbal medicine to their patients and 13 percent used it regularly; for auxiliary nurses the figures were 89 and 15 percent respectively. The nurses prescribed herbs most commonly for respiratory infections and diarrhea and had acquired their knowledge about medicinal plants from the popular media as well as from family and friends.

Most of the respondents saw the usefulness of herbs in economic terms, as affordable substitutes for biomedical drugs. A young doctor expressed her reasons for prescribing medicinal plants as follows: "The medicinal plants, on top of being effective for certain ailments, carry much less of a risk of adverse effects, are more economic, and easier for the patients to obtain."[35] There seemed to be a consensus among the practitioners and health planners that the use of herbal medicine was an emergency measure to deal with the acute economic crisis and drug shortage, and it was too early to tell whether this would give herbal preparations a permanent position within official health care. In traditional practice, however, the role of medicinal herbs was much more important than that described by health workers. Herbs were a component of a healing process that often responded also to cultural, social, and psychological aspects of the illness experience.[36]

Conclusion: Problematic Pluralism

The two programs described above highlight the cautious and somewhat ambiguous steps toward official pluralism within the Sandinista health-care system. The integration policies did not ascribe an official status to traditional medicine within SNUS for two reasons. First, these policies were driven by economic necessities and by a political commitment to popular participation in health, whereas MINSA wanted to keep the basis of the health-care system biomedical. The incorporation of traditional midwives into SNUS and the use of traditional medicaments were seen as a transitional phase in the development of the health-care system. Among health planners and health practitioners, it was assumed that traditional medicine would not be needed once economic development reached such a level that biomedicine could be established as a primary source of health care for all.

Second, the premise of the two programs was to change some traditional practices to make them fit into the biomedical model of health care, but hardly any efforts were made to change the health-care system to accommodate traditional medicine. The program to integrate herbal medicine into the official health-care system attempted to change the character of that medicine to a scientifically proven practice. Although, in 1989, experiences of using herbal medicine in the health-care system were limited, they were apparently quite readily accepted by the primary-health-care practitioners. However, their approval was based on empirical experience, on clinical impressions, rather than on scientific evidence of efficacy. Also, there was little evidence of the health-care institution consciously adapting and modifying its own principles to incorporate the traditional practitioners into it. Traditional midwives were recognized as legitimate practitioners, but the official health-care system was not ready to accept the traditional premise of their practice. MINSA wanted to incorporate them as trained health workers, not as traditional midwives, and their place was defined to be on the lowest level of the hierarchical system. Hospital staff seemed to have a hard time accepting *parteras* into the system, and MINSA did not use its scarce resources to train them to think otherwise. As a result, most of the midwives had very limited contact with the official system after their training and they continued working within the traditional framework, although with a recognition of the ministry.

Yet independent of the ambiguous official policies, the medical culture of Nicaragua remained pluralistic. Traditional medicine continued to be an alternative to the official health-care system in spite of the legitimization of parts of it. Pluralism in medical culture lived through the revolutionary changes in society and health care because it offered a variety of approaches to alleviate suffering. People sought traditional healers and midwives, whether they were part of the system or not, because traditional practitioners could provide care that was congruent with the cultural and psychological needs of the people. For rural women, the choice of a form of childbirth was not based on the level of scientific knowledge of the practitioners or solely on the women's economic resources but also on the meaning that childbirth had in their lives. They saw childbirth as a normal life event, which was best dealt with by another woman with a similar experience, and the midwives' conceptualization of childbirth was congruent with the folk model. For rural women, giving birth at home with a midwife was a self-evident choice, preferable to going to a hospital.

Very little is known about how effective traditional medical systems were in dealing with pathophysiological processes, but even if the rate of "cure" was not very high, it can be stated that the very existence of alternative medical systems is necessary to the psychological well-being of people, and alternatives exist because of people's needs. The efficacy of the traditional methods was based on their potential to heal: to deal with patient's perceptions and experience of illness, rather than pathophysiological processes. People had a practical concern about health care: They were more interested in its effects on their well-being than in whether it was scientific or nonscientific. Although for MINSA the recognition of traditional medicine was problematic, people in general saw nothing problematic about using both traditional and biomedical practices. In their experience, traditional and modern medicine were complimentary rather than conflicting options for health care.

Notes

The research for this study was made possible by a grant from the Social Sciences Research Grants Committee at McGill University. I am indebted to many people in Nicaragua for their cooperation and assistance during my fieldwork in 1989: to the officials of MINSA in Region I, to the staff of CNMTP, and especially to the educators and midwives in the training center in Estelí. I would like to thank Allan Young, Gabriela Vargas Cetina, and Thomas W. Walker for valuable suggestions for revision on earlier drafts of this chapter.

1. By traditional medicine I mean the wide range of medical beliefs and practices that are also referred to as indigenous, folk, popular, informal, or alternative medicine. Biomedicine refers to the Western medical tradition, for which the terms *allopathic* and *cosmopolitan medicine* are also used.

2. WHO/UNICEF, *Alma-Ata: Primary Health Care. Report of the International Conference on Primary Health Care* (Geneva: WHO, 1978).

3. Alejandro Dávila Bolaños, *Medicina Indígena Pre-Colombina de Nicaragua* (Estelí: Editorial Imprenta, 1974).

4. There is a debate among scholars whether the Mesoamerican humoral medicine originated in pre-Columbian or in colonial Spanish medicine. George Foster argued for the introduction of humoral medicine by the Spaniards; Alfredo López Austin argued that an "indigenous dual cosmovision" existed in Mesoamerica before colonization and that it merely incorporated elements of Hispanic humoral medicine into it. See George Foster, "Relationships between Spanish and Spanish-American Folk Medicine," *Journal of American Folklore* 66 (1953): 201–217; and Alfredo López Austin, *Textos de Medicina Náhuatl* (Mexico: UNAM, 1984), pp. 16–31, and *Cuerpo Humano e Ideología* (Mexico: UNAM, 1980), pp. 303–318.

5. Harvey Williams, "Organization and Delivery of Health Care: A Study of Change in Nicaragua," in John H. Morgan, ed., *Third World Medicine and Social Change* (Washington, D.C.: University Press of America, 1983), pp. 288–290.

6. Viviane Luisier, *Te Voy a Ayudar Nada Más . . . Apuntes sobre las Parteras Empíricas en Nicaragua* (Managua: Copiaco, 1985).

7. Ibid.

8. This point was brought up in several of the author's interviews with thirty-eight traditional midwives in Region I, June–August 1989.

9. WHO/UNICEF, *Alma-Ata: Primary Health Care*; WHO, *The Promotion and Development of Traditional Medicine*, Technical Report Series 622 (Geneva: WHO, 1978).

10. James Heiby, "Low-Cost Health Delivery Systems: Lessons from Nicaragua," *American Journal of Public Health* 71 (1981): 514–519.

11. Luisier, *Te Voy a Ayudar Nada Más*, pp. 26–34.

12. See Thomas Bossert, "Health Policy: The Dilemma of Success," in Thomas W. Walker, ed., *Nicaragua: The First Five Years* (New York: Praeger Publishers, 1985), pp. 347–350; and John Donahue, "Planning for Primary Health Care in Nicaragua: A Study in Revolutionary Process," *Social Science and Medicine* 23 (1986): 149–157.

13. Thomas J. Bossert, "Health Policy Making in a Revolutionary Context: Nicaragua, 1979–1981," *Social Science and Medicine* 15 (1981): 225–231.

14. Author's interview, August 1989.

15. Author's interview with Vilma Jímenez, in the Maternal and Infant Care Division of MINSA, in Managua, September 1989.

16. *Plan de Salud 1983* (Managua: MINSA, 1983).

17. *Enfoque de Riesgo en la Atención Materno-Infantil*, Taller Internacional, Managua, December 9–10, 1986 (Managua: MINSA, 1986).

18. For examples of other training programs see A. Mangay-Maglacas and H. Pizurki, eds., *The Traditional Birth Attendant in Seven Countries: Case Studies in Utilization and Training* (Geneva: WHO, 1981).

19. *Manual de Parteras* (Managua: MINSA, 1982), as quoted in Yeshi Neumann, "Birth and Tradition, Lay Midwives in Nicaragua's National Health System," *Nicaraguan Perspectives*, no. 12 (1986): 38.

20. Author's interview with a midwife attending the training course in Ocotal, May 1989.

21. Luisier, *Te Voy a Ayudar Nada Más*, and Neumann, "Birth and Tradition," pp. 37–40.

22. Author's interviews with the educators at the Casa de la Preparación del Parto Natural in Estelí, June 1989.

23. Author's interview with Vilma Jímenez.

24. *Enfoque de Riesgo*, p. 87.

25. This paragraph is based on author's interviews and discussions with MINSA administrators, health workers, and midwives in Region I, May–September 1989.

26. Author's interviews with the hospital staff of the obstetric ward in the Hospital Alejandro Dávila Bolaños in Estelí, June 1989.

27. Author's interview with a middle-aged rural midwife in Region I.

28. "Revolutionizing Health: A Study in Complexity," *Envío* 7, no. 80 (February 1988): 22–39.

29. An account of a traveling drug salesman's work can be found in Tomás Borge's autobiographical work, *La Paciente Impaciencia* (Managua: Editorial Vanguardia, 1989).

30. "Revolutionizing Health," pp. 34–35.

31. Author's interview with Uriel Sotomayor, director of the National Center of People's Traditional Medicine (CNMPT), in Estelí, September 1989.

32. CNMTP, *The Rescue of the People's Traditional Medicine and Its Integration into the Local Health Systems of Central America* (Estelí: MINSA, 1988).

33. Resolución Ministerial No. 74, April 24 (Managua: MINSA, 1989).

34. Author's interview with Juanita Brüssel, director of research, CNMPT, in Estelí, September 1989.

35. The results are preliminary data from *Encuesta Sobre el Conocimiento de la Práctica de la Medicina Tradicional*, MINSA Region I, Estelí, September 1989.

36. Arthur Kleinman and Lilias H. Sung, "Why Do Indigenous Practitioners Successfully Heal?" *Social Science and Medicine* 13B (1979): 7–26.

ELEVEN

Agrarian Reform

EDUARDO BAUMEISTER

The Context of Agrarian Reform

One of the most important aspects of social and economic change during the Nicaraguan revolution was agrarian reform.[1] To understand the reform's most salient features, it is necessary to recall two determining factors: the peculiarities of the agrarian structure that the revolution inherited and the dynamic in which the political process was developed, specifically the politics of internal alliances and of confrontation with the counterrevolution organized by the United States. Although all Nicaraguan society was affected by the contra war, the war's impact was most evident in the rural areas, where the bulk of the armed confrontations and most of the recruitment of the combatants of both factions took place.

The Inherited Structure

The nature of Nicaraguan agriculture, in terms of prevailing units of production as well as the resulting social composition, was different from that predominant in Central America and the Caribbean. Nicaraguan agriculture was typified neither by large haciendas and a peasantry subordinated by rent nor by great plantations controlled by foreign capital, which might have generated a concentrated and militant agrarian proletariat. Nor did a peasant class with strong indigenous traditions form part of the picture. In fact, Nicaraguan farming had nothing like the big coffee plantations of El Salvador or Guatemala; or the great plantations of Honduras, Costa Rica, or Cuba; or the peasant communities of the Guatemalan high plateau.

In Nicaraguan farming there were simply not enough precapitalist features to direct an agrarian reform that would destroy semifeudal patterns and develop capitalism in the countryside. Nor were capitalist practices sufficiently consolidated, as in Cuba, to open the way to a rapid and massive transition to state-run or collective methods of production.

The best-known characteristic of the old agrarian structure was the presence of an important nucleus of small- and medium-sized producers, distinct from a typical peasant class and from agrarian capitalism. That is to say, there was a group of peasants with medium-sized holdings and a small, extended middle class. These producers had a significant influence on the production of coffee, livestock, cotton, and, of course, on such traditional staple grains (*granos básicos*) as beans and corn. In the late 1970s, while the producers of more than 100,000 pounds of coffee accounted for 30 percent of the national production in Nicaragua, large-scale coffee growers in El Salvador or Guatemala controlled more than two-thirds of the total production. Likewise, in the early 1970s, while cotton production in Guatemala was in the hands of 161 producers, with an average area of 463 hectares,[2] in Nicaragua at the same time there were 2,671 producers, with an average area of 26 hectares. Whereas the big cotton growers in Guatemala controlled more than three-quarters of national production, their counterparts in Nicaragua contributed only a little more than 40 percent.

This peculiar agrarian configuration is explained by three factors. First, Nicaragua had the lowest population density in Central America. It had in addition a unique advantage that would continue to be exploited throughout the Sandinista revolution: an ample as-yet-uncultivated agricultural frontier in its central-eastern section. This facilitated the opening of large new zones to commercial production when main highways were laid out after World War II. In that expansion, nuclei of peasants and small and medium producers would play a part in strengthening the growth of coffee, livestock, and staple grains.

Second, for structural and political reasons, a class of great national or foreign owners such as might have monopolized agro-export production with the intensity seen in other Central American and Caribbean countries never came into being in Nicaragua. Frequent and long civil wars between factions of the propertied classes drained their financial resources. At the same time, the intra-elite struggle for hegemony made it difficult in the late nineteenth and early twentieth centuries to build a fully unified labor market with an abundant salaried labor force or with mechanisms of forced labor such as existed in other agro-export expansions during the period. For its part, Sandino's guerrilla war of the 1920s also hurt the few North American enclaves.

Third, and in concordance with the first two factors, there was a growing differentiation in the twentieth century, especially after World War II, between big landowning factions involved in highly commercial activities such as banking and agro-industry and those small, medium, and large producers concerned mainly with the production of primary products for domestic consumption, which involved little external input or financing. A study conducted in the early 1970s disclosed that the capital interests controlling the three great financial groups—the Somoza family; the Bank of America, associated with the Pellas family; and the Nicaraguan Bank—accounted for 22 percent of agricultural production.[3]

As a consequence, the structural situation in which agrarian reform would take place in post-Somoza Nicaragua had some distinctive elements. It featured a base of very heterogeneous producers, including the strong presence of small- and medium-sized factions, which, in the three decades prior to the revolutionary triumph, had given rise to new layers in the propertied classes: cotton growers in the Pacific region and many new coffee producers in the central region. These, in turn, had partially proletarianized an ample segment of the peasant nuclei through the expansion of territory used for cotton growing and cattle raising. For its part, the Somoza family, high officers of Somoza's National Guard, and politicians of Somoza's Liberal Nationalist party (PLN) monopolized nearly 16 percent of the land in farms that included modern sectors— sugar, irrigated rice, and export tobacco—and large areas dedicated to cattle raising.

These characteristics show that, from the structural point of view, Nicaraguan agriculture was quite different from its counterparts in those Latin American countries where deep agrarian reform programs have taken place. There was no strong set of semifeudal relationships that might have given way to confrontations between vast peasant masses and absentee landowners; no great plantations controlled by foreign capital that might have stimulated nationalism; and no traditional indigenous peasant community capable of demanding a return to a pre-Hispanic, communal past.

Neither had there been an agrarian stagnation, as was common in some countries where agrarian reform emerged in this century. Rather, the height of the revolution at the end of the 1970s and its bases in farming (technicians, small and medium producers of the central-interior region, salaried workers of the North Pacific, and groups of modern bourgeoisie linked to cotton and sugarcane) were the product of a rapid growth of farming. With the exception of the poor who were proletarianized by the first extensive cultivation of cotton, the rest had benefited economically from the strong agricultural development following World War II. The weakness of the Somoza scheme of domination in farming, rather than being based strictly in structural matters, is better understood in sociopolitical terms: The Somoza system simply failed to incorporate into the political system, in a legitimate manner, the social forces that emerged in the three decades prior to the Sandinista victory. These forces included modern sectors such as the bourgeoisie, small and medium dirt farmers (*chapiollos*) in the central interior, and salaried workers. However, at its heart, the Somoza system relied on co-optation and coercion rather than legitimizing incorporation. Anastasio

Somoza García himself described it as the "principle of the three Ps": *plata* (money) for friends, the *palos* (clubs) for vacillators, and *plomo* (lead bullets) for enemies.

For the most part, the behavior of the modern or traditional middle sector that joined the Sandinista initiative can be explained by the lack of representation and incorporation into the political system. In effect, these new social forces were long inhibited in forming their own corporate organizational entities. They finally did so only at the end of the 1970s.

The Association of Cotton Growers of León (ADAL) was founded only in mid-1978. Although it had forerunners, it managed to reestablish itself through the initiative of young cotton growers linked with the Sandinista National Liberation Front (FSLN). Many members of ADAL became important figures in the revolutionary government. Most small and medium producers—in whom traits of peasants and small capitalists mingle—had little organizational expression. Those forerunners that did exist in the 1970s were weak and ephemeral. It is not surprising, therefore, that the nuclei of peasants and medium producers that aligned themselves with Sandinista guerrillas in the 1970s would become vital to the establishment of the National Union of Farmers and Ranchers (UNAG) in April 1981.

Something similar occurred when the Rural Workers' Association (ATC) was founded in early 1978 on the initiative of one of the three FSLN factions. Though the ATC succeeded in incorporating the semi-proletarian agrarian sectors of the north and central Pacific, it would not have a full constitution until after July 1979.

The Political Determinants
of the Agrarian Reform Process

The program of the Governing Junta of National Reconstruction, which replaced the Somoza government in July 1979 and which was supported by all the sectors that had opposed Somoza, included three very explicit elements relating to the agrarian question: (1) the nationalization of the banking system, (2) state control of the purchase and exportation of principal agricultural products, and (3) the implementation of an agrarian reform program utilizing properties confiscated from the Somocistas, from debtors delinquent to the banking system, and from the large idle estates. These ideas contained the seeds of conflict. They were acceptable to the large anti-Somocista coalition, which supported the nationalization of properties of the Somozas and their accomplices for use in agrarian reform; but they would cause confrontation with other important elements of the Nicaraguan elite (private banks, commercial exporters, and big landowners that leased their lands to different strata of cotton producers). They would inevitably also involve hurting even the less-modern sector of the proprietary classes.

These facts were connected to the grass-roots nature of the popular insurrection as well as to the differences within the propertied classes, in particular among the medium- and even large-scale producers not associated with the three hegemonic banking and commercial groups mentioned above. These differences produced tense relations with strong non-Somocista sectors.

It is interesting to observe that the political oversimplification with which Nicaraguan matters, both before and after the triumph, are habitually interpreted tends to impede an understanding of structural tensions that existed in Nicaraguan society in the late 1970s. Throughout the course of the 1980s, various significant changes would take place in the social bases of the Sandinista coalition in power. On the one hand, from the moment of the creation of UNAG in April 1981, the peasants (as noted in Chapter 3), would truly enter the national political scene. Of course, created under the aegis of the Sandinista Front, UNAG's organizational cohesion was still somewhat primitive even at the end of the first decade. Nevertheless, for the first time in the history of their country, the peasants had an organization to represent their interests. During the same period, however, a good part of the bourgeoisie that originally had joined the revolutionary coalition had become estranged from the Sandinista "process," first withdrawing political support and then becoming uncooperative in the economic realm.

But the fundamental change in the relationship among political forces would be propelled by the upsurge of counterrevolutionary activity late in 1981. Though very small, isolated counterrevolutionary bands had begun to operate within the first year of the revolution, they were abruptly fortified, if not eclipsed, at the beginning of the Reagan administration by the massive entrance into their ranks of ex–National Guardsmen backed by the U.S. administration, which became the godfather of the entire movement.

Contra activity would be mounted in various pivotal areas and would succeed in influencing substantial groups of the peasantry both in the border zones shared with Honduras and Costa Rica and along the wide farming frontier that separates the central and Atlantic regions of Nicaragua. The contras' first point of support in rural society would be medium and large coffee growers and other producers affected by their connection with Somocism. With their support, the contra movement would succeed in gaining the loyalty of peasants subordinate to these producers, including salaried workers.

Various elements would fall prey to social penetration by the contras. Many rural folk were frightened by the language of revolutionary activists, especially at the intermediate and local levels, who seemed to

Table 11.1   Evolution of State Control of the Corn Market in Peasant Regions (thousands of hundredweights)

| | Region | | | |
	I	V	VI	National Total
1980	42.66	8.58	38.53	484.79
1981	86.66	50.94	51.38	827.43
1982	72.73	25.48	45.92	730.84
1983	154.92	76.47	163.25	905.13
1984	306.50	30.50	176.90	1271.50
1985	234.70	1.40	87.70	1202.80
1986	153.22	25.00	131.04	1699.73
1987	163.25	30.00	71.50	1035.15
1988	88.50	8.20	63.70	720.10

Source: Center for the Investigation and Study of Agrarian Reform (CIERA), La Reforma Agraria en Nicaragua, 1979–1989, vol. 9 (Managua: CIERA, 1989), p. 383.

associate revolution with collectivization of the land and state control of marketing. And the state was, in fact, coming to play an ever-expanding role in marketing (see Table 11.1). Accordingly, through the mid-1980s, there was a growing split between the state and some segments of the peasantry. For some, therefore, involvement in or support for the contras seemed a logical way of protecting their private property or enterprise against real or imagined threats from the revolution.

Between 1980 and 1985, the state attempted to obtain a virtual monopoly on the commercialization of staple grains, even though according to the laws in force, the producers could, if they wished, trade freely. In practice, farmers were urged to sell to the state marketing enterprise. In 1986, a new policy was begun, freeing the sale of products in the internal market.

According to Table 11.1, the state was able to maintain its national inventories of corn at an almost constant level between 1984 and 1985, but there was a marked slump between those two years in the amounts of corn it could purchase in typically peasant regions (Regions I, V, and VI). In 1986, even with the freeing of the markets and some inventory recovery in these regions, 1984 levels had not yet been regained.

The war and the economic crisis produced a set of "transactions" between the state and the peasantry. By the mid-1980s, the peasantry was the most important base of social support for the revolutionary process as well as for the contras. The war accelerated the economic crisis that Nicaragua had been experiencing practically since the July victory. This and a certain urban bias to its initial policies—explained in part by the principal urban bases of the 1979 triumph—had a bearing on the strong deterioration of the terms of rural-urban exchange and a marked decrease in basic goods available in the countryside. As we have seen, the peasant response had been quite classic: a reduction in production, particularly that of products marketed by the state.

Eventually, in the period between 1984 and 1986, the state and party got the message. Agrarian reform was accelerated and the state showed flexibility in accepting a greater variety of ways in which the newly affected lands could be worked. These would include collective, semi-collective, and individual private modes of production. The marketing of products was freed. UNAG was strengthened and, through its creation of a chain of Peasant Stores, came to play an important role in supplying badly needed goods to the countryside. These changes came in the years of greatest confrontation with counterrevolutionary forces, beginning in 1984, when the contra military presence was at its peak. They also coincided with the beginning of the so-called strategic defeat of the contras in 1985 and 1986. The latter was accomplished through a massive offensive by the Sandinista People's Army (EPS). The army, fortified by a sweeping military draft, was even able to make rapid, but effective, "hot pursuit" incursions into contra bases in Honduran territory.

The most significant element of this Sandinista equation is the break with a principal tradition of previous revolutionary processes: the association between increments of war against counterrevolutionary forces and "Jacobinization" (radicalization), as seen in a majority of revolutions over the past two centuries. In Nicaragua, though the war became very costly in human and material resources, the opposite of Jacobinization took place. Late in 1984, at the height of the contra offensive, nationwide elections were held, and the following year a very open process of constitution making began. At the same time, a policy of shifting benefits toward the countryside also was instituted.

This shift, which Sandinista militants would subsume under the word *flexibilization*, involved not only a stepped-up process of agrarian reform, greater tolerance for new forms of land tenure, and the freeing of the marketing of staple products but also the deeding of lands occupied by squatters and the breakup and deeding of some state farms. In the end, the state would cede a substantial part of its lands. State ownership of land, which had risen from 1.3 to 1.5 million manzanas[4] between 1980 and 1983, was reduced to 948,000 manzanas by 1988.

Thus, war and economic crisis altered the social profile of Nicaraguan agriculture. It did not, however, cause the demise of the entire traditional private sector. Just as peasants and some progressive medium and large landholders were organized through UNAG, the traditional landholders expressed themselves corporately through the Superior Council of Private Enterprise (COSEP). In the beginning, because of its important role in political matters, there had been a tendency to overestimate COSEP's economic importance.[5] Yet even in the early 1980s, its members contributed less than one-fourth of total national farm production. By the end of the decade they were down to less than one-fifth. Agrarian reform, flight into exile, elite reluctance to reinvest, and the general constraints that the country was experiencing all contributed to that reduction.

Nonetheless, it is necessary to bear in mind that the whole economy had contracted significantly during the first decade and particularly from 1984 on, after the full impact of the war began to be felt. Farm exports in the late 1980s were less than half those attained in the late 1970s. Keeping this in mind, one can better view the potential of the different sectors of ownership (state, private traditional, small and medium production, and the cooperative sector). In this light it is clear that although the traditional private sector had continued to play a role in Sandinista agriculture, its future productive potential would be determined by the political path of the country. The same could be said of the state sector. Of the rest, that is to say, most of the producers and the bulk of land in farms, one can say that their behavior and expansion would be less determined by the future of politics, except, of course, by the consolidation of a lasting peace.

The Impact of Agrarian Reform

Ten years of agrarian reform profoundly modified the profile of the agrarian structure of the country. The reform had affected 28 percent of the land under cultivation; and 43 percent of all peasant families had received land. If one includes those who received titles to the national land on which they had been squatters in the central and frontier agricultural regions, the social weight of the reform tips in at around 60 percent of all peasant families.[6] Meanwhile, large landholdings were reduced from 36.2 to 13.5 percent of the land in the decade from 1978 to 1988 (see Table 11.2).[7]

What is most important about the resulting agricultural structure is the central role that the small and medium producers came to play alongside the cooperative sector. In effect, the big producers, generally closer to COSEP (who in the late 1980s totaled about 700 individuals), and the state sector together held only 25 percent of the land in 1988, whereas after the downfall of Somocism, they had controlled almost 40 percent of the agricultural land.

With almost 30 percent of the land surface in the reformed sector, Nicaragua clearly falls into the category of countries that have experienced profound agrarian reform. Nicaragua's agrarian reform was not a cosmetic one, the type that generally occurred in Latin American countries as part of the Alliance for Progress in the 1960s. Rather, judged by the amount of land affected, it ranks with such agrarian reform programs

Table 11.2   Structure of Land Tenure: Holdings of Various Sectors

	1978	1988	
	Percent	Total Area	Percent
Private sector (manzanas)			
500+	36.2	1,087,149	13.5
200–500	16.2	1,033,586	12.8
50–200	30.1	2,293,293	28.4
10–50	15.4	1,218,261	15.1
Less than 10	2.1	167,726	2.1
Reformed sector (manzanas)			
State-owned area		948,230	11.7
Production cooperatives		921,491	11.4
Credit and service cooperatives		133,620	1.7
Work collectives		23,509	0.3
"Dead furrow" cooperatives[a]		37,060	0.5
Individual assignations		209,974	2.6
Total	100.0	8,073,899	100.1

[a] In "dead furrow" cooperatives the land was owned collectively but farmed each year in individual plots. The land was first plowed and then plots were separated by unplanted furrows, which marked the temporary boundaries.

Source: Center for the Investigation and Study of Agrarian Reform (CIERA), La Reforma Agraria en Nicaragua, 1979–1989, vol. 9 (Managua: CIERA, 1989), p. 39.

as those undertaken in Peru under the government of Juan Velasco Alvarado, in Chile before the military coup of Augusto Pinochet, or that developed by the government of Colonel Jacobo Arbenz in Guatemala at the beginning of the 1950s (a reform that was reversed after the CIA-sponsored counterrevolution in 1954).[8]

Phases of the Agrarian Reform

The process by which 28 percent of Nicaragua's land was affected by the agrarian reform in the first decade was punctuated by various initiatives and phases. Immediately after the triumph of July 1979, direct confiscation from the Somocistas and officers of the old National Guard was responsible for 56 percent of the reformed land area. Subsequently, in 1981 and 1986, agrarian reform laws were enacted, accounting for the rest of the land incorporated into the reformed sector. These two laws were similar in that, unlike agrarian reform laws in other parts of Latin America, they did not penalize the landowner for the size of her/his land; rather, they confiscated land that was inadequately or not used. In this way the reform did not destroy the modern productive largeholder sector. But the laws differed from each other in that, whereas the 1981 law did not include farms of less than 500 manzanas in the region of the Pacific or 1,000 manzanas in the rest of the country (except

Table 11.3   Indicators of the Evolution of Agrarian Reform (in thousands of manzanas)

	Area Given to the Peasantry per Year	Area Taken by the Agrarian Reform from the Private Sector per Year	Area Owned by the State at the End of Each Year
1981–1982	133	245	1,278
1983	294	251	1,390
1984	241	106	1,226
1985	108	239	1,211
1986	315	449	1,088
1987	178	142	965
1988	57	30	948

Source: Center for the Investigation and Study of Agrarian Reform (CIERA), La Reforma Agraria en Nicaragua, 1979–1989, vol. 9 (Managua: CIERA, 1989), pp. 39, 40, 41.

Table 11.4   The Impact of the Three Reforms: Percent and Average Size of Confiscated Property

	Percent of Total Area	Average Size of Properties (Manzanas)
Confiscation of the Somocistas	57	1,083
1981 law	27	674
1986 law	16	595

Source: Center for the Investigation and Study of Agrarian Reform (CIERA), La Reforma Agraria en Nicaragua, 1979–1989, vol. 9 (Managua: CIERA), pp. 39, 40.

those that had been abandoned), the second law eliminated the lower exemptions.

In the first years, the bulk of the affected lands went into forming state enterprises, whose holdings in 1983 extended over approximately 1.4 million manzanas (see Table 11.3). The nonstate segment of the reformed sector amounted to relatively little territory.

Whereas immediate posttriumph confiscation of properties of the Somozas and their cronies affected mainly modern farms (sugar, cotton, and coffee) in the Pacific region, the 1981 and 1986 laws had a major impact on the interior. The policy was based on two factors: the need to hit nonproductive or underproductive holdings and the desire to benefit the bulk of the peasantry, especially in areas badly hit by the contra war. Tables 11.4 and 11.5 show the impact of the three reforms.

It is interesting to observe that the even more radical 1986 law—which eliminated the exemption on holdings of less than 500 manzanas in the Pacific and 1,000 manzanas in the rest of the country—did not cause a major setback for farms of less than 500 manzanas. The average size of the farms confiscated from the Somocistas was 1,083 manzanas

Table 11.5   The Geographic Impact of the Three Phases of the Reform (in percentages)

	Pacific	Rest of the Country
Confiscation of the Somocistas	52	48
1981 law	50	50
1986 law	24	76
Total beneficiaries[a]	28	72

[a] Includes the beneficiaries of national land entitlement.

Source: Center for the Investigation and Study of Agrarian Reform (CIERA), *La Reforma Agraria en Nicaragua, 1979–1989*, vol. 9 (Managua: CIERA, 1989), pp. 40, 42, 45, 55.

(774 hectares), a blow concentrated on large properties. The 1981 law (applied between October 1981 and the end of 1985) affected farms with a medium size of 674 manzanas. However, the farms affected by the 1986 law were not significantly smaller on the average, having an average size of 595 manzanas. In addition, confiscations under the 1986 law account for only 16 percent of the total for the whole decade, another indication that the "radical" language of the text did not translate fully into practice.

Beginning in 1986, the nonstate sector—consisting of the Sandinista Agricultural Cooperatives (CAS), peasants that had received land from the agrarian reform and were organized under credit and service cooperatives (CCS), and individual producer beneficiaries—was larger in area than the state sector. In actuality, the state sector represented 38 percent of the reformed sector, while the remaining 62 percent included various forms of peasant production and cooperatives having direct support from the agrarian reform.

Another central characteristic of the second phase of agrarian reform, especially after 1984–1985, was that the property being distributed was taken primarily from the state sector rather than from large private landholders. The total area affected by the reforms (2.3 million manzanas) had remained practically unaltered since 1985. The post-1985 changes were made possible, in fact, only by the willingness of the state to give up more than one-third of the land that it had acquired from 1979 through 1984.

Social Beneficiaries of Agricultural Reform

The most important effect of state policy on agriculture in the ten years of revolution was the strengthening of the role of the small and medium farmers as agents of production. In contrast to their counterparts in countries such as Guatemala, El Salvador, or Cuba before 1959, these groups were already important before 1979 in agro-export, cattle raising, and the production of staple grains. But the groups' economic and political importance, as noted earlier, increased in the latter part of the second phase of agrarian reform, after 1984–1985.

Whether through the distribution of confiscated lands to peasants, the titling of squatter-held lands on the agrarian frontier, and the expansion of credit or through the strengthening of UNAG, the broad and heterogeneous sector composed of small and medium producers became the central actor in Nicaraguan agriculture. As of 1989, it was estimated that small producers (poor and medium-sized peasants), production cooperatives, and credit and service cooperatives constituted approximately 47 percent of the national farm production. Medium producers, that is, the prosperous peasantry and the fringe of the agrarian bourgeoisie, accounted for another 14 percent. Large private producers did not exceed 17 percent. And the state sector weighed in at 22 percent of the gross production.

The state, in the years prior to the economic reform of 1988–1989, put great emphasis on investments in state enterprises and new agro-industrial projects (see Chapter 12). The cumulative effects of aggression and a sharp decline in external resources available for these big projects brought this process of capital formation in farming to a halt. However, in the period after 1985–1986, when the agrarian reform veered toward free commercialization of basic staples, there was a strong burst of activity by small and medium dirt farmers (chapiollos), who were much more disposed to produce in the difficult national economic situation than were many state administrators and wealthy bourgeoisie.

It is significant to point out that between 1985—the year in which land under production was most reduced as an effect of the war—and 1988–1989, the small producers and the cooperatives added more than 100,000 harvested manzanas, while the big producers and the state maintained the same levels or reduced their total area under cultivation. This push from the peasantry was centered on staples. The great challenges of the 1990s would be to transfer some of this burst in peasant productivity into the production of export products such as coffee, sesame seed, and cattle and to find a viable path of development for Nicaraguan agriculture within the framework of strong external restrictions.

The Debate over Agrarian Reform

The 1980s produced a constant debate, on the one hand, over who should be the principal beneficiaries of the recuperation and development of farming, and on the other, over the best technologies and the types of investment to increase the proven capacity of the sector. This debate was implicitly linked to a discussion of the material and social bases of the desired agrarian structure.

The principal beneficiaries of public policy on agriculture were the state enterprises, the production cooperatives, and the individual small and medium producers. The question of the methods of expansion of agriculture concerned the relative strength of intensive and extensive forms of production. More concretely, it focused on whether the emphasis should be on the expansion of the proven capacity through new investments or the emphasis should be on a more intensive utilization of the land and the available agrarian work force.

At root, differing concepts of economic as well as sociopolitical development were being debated. At the level of public policy, practice and conceptual discussion focused on: (1) the quantity and fate of the lands affected by agrarian reform; (2) the distribution of farm credit among the different actions; and (3) the characteristics and beneficiaries of the investment process.

The evolution of Nicaragua's agrarian reform was discussed above. One can observe an overall increase in institutional credit for all productive sectors. In connection with this, it is worth remembering that whereas in the Somoza years only one-third of the agricultural area was financed by banks, 75 percent received such support during the first decade of the revolution. Only after June 1988, with the modifications in credit policies that came about as part of the new austerity, was the bank financing of agriculture brought into question.

The issue of increasing capital investment in machinery, irrigation, agro-industrial construction, and other areas related to the development of the material infrastructure of production caused the most debate. If we look at the entire first ten years, we observe a formidable increase in capital formation in agriculture. Whereas the rate of accumulation in the 1970s had not exceeded 7 percent annually, halfway through the 1980s it reached 30 percent of new investments in fixed capital and agricultural gross domestic product. The Program of Public Investments (PIP) alone came to represent almost 25 percent of the agricultural product (see Table 11.6). This was the result of a concept of capital intensive development that made the state sector, followed by a nucleus of production cooperatives, the principal recipients of that investment.

The growing economic problems and the resultant austerity policies initiated in February 1988 abruptly halted this process of large-scale investment. As Nicaragua entered the 1990s, the problem of selecting the most adequate method for the formation of agrarian capital within the severe economic and sociopolitical constraints the country was sure to face remained unsolved.

From Table 11.6 one can also see that the moments of maximum intensification of the state investment corresponded also with the so-called switch (*viraje*) in the direction of agrarian reform. In this sense, the situation was similar to other agrarian transformations—especially

Table 11.6   The Program of Public Investment in Agriculture (in millions of 1980 cordobas and percentages)

	Public Investment (PIP)	PIP/Agricultural GDP
1980	592	12.9
1981	496	9.8
1982	544	10.3
1983	640	11.5
1984	1,120	21.3
1985	1,182	23.5
1986	1,130	24.6
1987	1,053	23.8
1988	542	12.3

Source: Center for the Investigation and Study of Agrarian Reform (CIERA), La Reforma Agraria en Nicaragua, 1979–1989, vol. 9 (Managua: CIERA, 1989), Table 300, p. 366.

that of Mexico—in that there was a connection between handing over lands to the peasantry and huge investments of capital (in the Mexican case, for the benefit of private sectors; in the case of Nicaragua, of state enterprises and a reduced nucleus of production cooperatives).

Conclusions and Tentative Prognostication

During the Sandinista revolution there were substantial advances in agrarian reform as well as a significant process of new investments, a broadening of credit, and, in general, an attempt to modernize agriculture. The modernization effort included a growth in mechanization, the use of agro-chemicals, and large state agro-industrial projects. Here one notes the ideological imprint of both the socialist camp and Latin American developmentalism. But it is also true that the Sandinistas placed engineers and technicians from traditional families of the Pacific in important positions in the farming sector throughout the 1980s in an attempt to attain national unity. That was one way of incorporating elements of the middle sectors and traditional families in the revolutionary project.

An important unanswered question of the decade of the 1980s concerns the impact, in both political and production terms, that the large state projects might have made, had it not been for the devastating effects of the war of aggression. Even though the war bears the main responsibility for the country's serious economic problems, it is also evident that this strategy of development under any circumstances would have brought at least some negative consequences. On the one hand, as we noted above, it absorbed a great mass of resources. Nicaragua went from a rate of capital accumulation in agriculture of about 7 percent annually before the revolution to about 30 percent during the investment furor of the 1980s. Second, the developmentalist bias, with its capital intensive projects, had little positive impact on territories and human populations.

And third, this massive injection of resources—without a doubt the highest in Central America in the 1980s—was not primarily directed toward recovering former levels of production. Its implicit purpose was the "refounding" of Nicaraguan agriculture on new material bases.

Had the FSLN won the 1990 election, the challenge of the 1990s would have been to shape an agricultural development strategy that would realistically recognize and accept existing agrarian structures and the strong limitations facing the Nicaraguan economy while, at the same time, pursuing a sociopolitical project aimed at strengthening grass-roots civil society and creating the conditions of growth and greater social justice. In the 1980s, the *chapiolla* factions (small and medium individual producers and the cooperative sector) and those large farmers who used relatively little capital and few external resources had not been as completely involved as they might, as subjects of development in public policy.

As this was being written, the probable future impact of UNO policy on agrarian reform was unclear. The FSLN electoral defeat was greater in the rural, interior parts of the country than in the urban areas—a reflection, in part, of the profound economic hardship caused by the contra war in the countryside. At the same time, agrarian policy that was excessively centered on state farms, state control of commerce, and the authoritarian methods of government technocrats had embittered relations between a segment of the peasantry and the revolution.

However, it appeared unlikely that policies of the UNO government would be more congenial to the rural population than those of its predecessor. Upon assuming office, the Chamorro administration placed members of the old agro-export bourgeoisie in charge of the agrarian public sector. Those people were determined to reprivatize much of the land that had been nationalized in the agrarian reform and to denationalize foreign trade and the banking system. State farms were deliberately underfinanced in an apparent effort to drive them into bankruptcy. And dispossessed owners were given the opportunity to rent "unutilized" parts of their former holdings. However, state farm workers, organized by Sandinista unions, staged strikes and demonstrations to block this obvious effort to undo the revolution, and after the massive strikes of July 1990, the Chamorro government was forced to reverse itself, at least temporarily. Thus, as of the beginning of 1991, it was difficult to predict the degree to which the attempt to return to the past would succeed. Probably part of the land in state hands would revert to its former owners. If so, the old agro-export bourgeoisie would recover some of its former strength, perhaps reentering the North American market with non-traditional products. Nevertheless, the alliance that had been forged between Sandinism and important nonoligarchic land-owners and rural groups was likely to make a complete return to the prerevolutionary period difficult. The most likely scenario would be a long period of hegemonic crisis in the countryside with the oligarchic "project" being unable to come to full fruition.

Notes

1. For an earlier general overview of Nicaragua's agrarian reform see Joseph R. Thome and David Kaimowitz, "Agrarian Reform," in *Nicaragua: The First Five Years*, Thomas W. Walker, ed. (New York: Praeger, 1985), pp. 299–315.

2. One hectare equals 2.471 acres.

3. From Harry Wallace Strachan, "The Role of Business Groups in Economic Development: The Case of Nicaragua," D.B.A. Dissertation, Harvard University, 1972, p. 81.

4. In Central America, 1 manzana equals 1.73 acres.

5. The overestimation of the importance of big landholdings began with an exaggeration of Somoza holdings. Sources with widely different political perspectives at first supposed that the Somozas controlled at least 50 percent of national farm production. On the politically conservative end of the spectrum, see Ralph Lee Woodward, *Central America: A Nation Divided* (New York: Oxford University Press, 1976), p. 122: "It has been estimated that by 1970 they [the Somoza family] owned more than half of the agricultural production of the republic." Toward the other end of the political spectrum, see Jaime Wheelock Román, "La Reforma Agraria en marcha: El programa sandinista para los campesinos de Nicaragua," *Perspectiva Mundial* 3 (16), September 1979, p. 20: "Practically 40–60 percent of these arable lands were controlled by the Somoza family. And, if we add the Somocistas in general, that number can be raised to some 70 percent."

6. Center for the Investigation and Study of Agrarian Reform (CIERA), *La Reforma Agraria en Nicaragua: 1979–1989*, vol. 9 (Managua: CIERA, 1989), p. 56. Given the absence of census material on farm populations, it is possible only to estimate roughly that peasants (excluding landless, salaried workers) consist of 130,000 to 160,000 families. The total that had received land (excluding those who received titles for land upon which they were already squatting) by December 1988 reached 77,430 families.

7. My interpretation of the data in CIERA, *La Reforma Agraria en Nicaragua, 1979–1989*, vol. 9, is different from CIERA's, and my results varied substantially from those in CIERA's Table 1, p. 39. The differences are the following: (1) I define "the reformed sector" as the lands that were effectively redistributed. Thus special titling goes under the private sector. This also applies to lands of indigenous communities and abandoned lands (since even though those lands belong to different sectors of ownership, including the reformed sector, there are no data to assign them proportionally). (2) I estimate the distribution of the reformed area according to the nature of the farms from which the affected lands come. For this purpose I use an estimate of the General Direction of Agrarian Reform for November 1986, that encompasses an area equivalent to 80 percent of that attained by the end of 1988. The data are found in Ministry of Agricultural Development and Agrarian Reform (MIDINRA), "Consolidado de propiedades adquiridas por el MIDINRA por diferentes decretos," unpublished

document, 1986. It shows that 80.6 percent of the affected area had been in farms of more than 500 manzanas, 12.2 percent in farms of 200 to 500 manzanas, 6.1 percent in farms of 50 to 200 manzanas, 1.0 percent in farms of 10 to 50 manzanas, and 0.1 percent in farms of less than 10 manzanas. (3) Owing to the rounding of numbers, I get 899 manzanas more than the estimate of the farm surface area presented by MIDINRA.

8. The most important agrarian reform programs in Latin America were as follows (countries and percentages of agricultural land affected): Chile (1965–1973), 40 percent; Peru (1968–1975), 42 percent; Guatemala (1952–1954), 33 percent. *Source: Alain de Janvry, The Agrarian Question* (Washington, D.C.: Johns Hopkins University Press, 1981), p. 206.

TWELVE

Economic Policy

JOSEPH RICCIARDI

The tenth anniversary of the Nicaraguan revolution celebrated a dual victory of the Nicaraguan people in the military arena: victory over the Somoza dynasty and victory over foreign intervention by the U.S.-backed contra. The mere survival of the Sandinista state after relentless foreign military and economic aggression, in addition to nature's own unkindness of flood in 1982 and hurricane in 1988, testified to the strength and popular character of the revolution. Yet, after ten years, there was little cause for celebration as popular support succumbed to defeat on the economic battle front: There were no resources to reactivate and restructure Nicaragua's ailing economy. During the first decade, Sandinista economic policy moved in stages from revolutionary economic planning to the harsh reality of stabilization. This trajectory from revolution to stabilization was not solely the consequence of foreign aggression but also the result of political and economic tensions that derived from the government's "mixed economy" strategy for economic development. The financial distortions that fueled the 1988–1989 hyperinflation and ultimately forced the implementation of stringent stabilization policies cannot be understood simply as a consequence of the impact of foreign aggression and the adversity of the international economy. They must be viewed, as well, as the result of costly policy compromises stemming from efforts to preserve the cooperation of the private sector. The internal tensions of managing a mixed economy played an important role in spawning the inflation-generating deficits that set the economy back to a survival footing at the end of the 1980s and ultimately forced the Sandinistas to relinquish political control of the state in 1990.

An Overview
of the 1988–1989 Economic Crisis

In 1988 and 1989, Nicaragua experienced its deepest economic crisis since the insurrection, confronting simultaneously three major problems:

(1) unprecedented peacetime levels of negative real growth, (2) hyperinflation, and (3) severe external imbalance. First, in lost production, the country's crippled productive apparatus suffered a secular decline in real output from 1983 to 1989. Only three out of the ten years of the revolution generated positive real economic growth: 1980, 1981, and 1983. In 1988 real gross domestic product (GDP) fell 8 percent, with sustained losses projected for 1989, bringing GDP per capita to one-half of its prerevolutionary (1976-1977) levels (despite extensive out-migration). Private per capita consumption (compensated in part by increased social spending prior to 1985) dropped over 70 percent during the same period.[1]

This production crisis strained Nicaragua's development project. The roots of the crisis were severe supply constraints: the destruction and diversion of economic resources associated with the contra war, infrastructural decay and natural disaster, declining productivity associated with eroded real earnings, and an acute shortage of liquid foreign exchange. The economy's diminished capacity to satisfy long-standing unrealized demand generated tensions in the state's declared multiclass project for development with national unity as rival social groups struggled over relative shares of a diminished social pie. The regional peace accords only highlighted this economic disfunctioning when latent demand emerged at the end of hostilities.

Second, in 1988, hyperinflation accompanied the production tailspin—a delayed consequence of accumulated years of disproportionately high levels of state deficit spending financed by money emission. Although production declines were not uncharacteristic for the Central American region, Nicaragua's hyperinflation assumed historic dimensions: It outstripped the Bolivian experience of 1984-1985[2] and was fully comparable to the classic German hyperinflation of the 1920s. Between November 1988 and January 1989—following a summer burst in hurricane relief spending—consumer prices doubled on a monthly basis, pushing the consumer price index (CPI) to a peak 127 percent monthly rate.[3] Hyperinflations are notoriously cruel in eroding the real earnings of the poorest social classes. They unravel the payments mechanism, provoke financial collapse, and undermine political support for the state. Ironically, stabilization became a condition of existence for the Sandinistas—one necessitating a policy matrix of austerity antithetical to the original social welfare goals of the revolution.

Third, the deepening imbalances of the external sector reaffirmed the dependent character of Nicaraguan accumulation. In 1988, the country's characteristically negative trade balance reached almost one-third of GDP, with the value of imports ($802 million) outstripping exports ($223 million) by almost four to one. On the one hand, import pressures were elevated because of the highly import-intensive structure of production derived from the heritage of Nicaragua's integration into the Central American Common Market (CACM).[4] Imports of industrial inputs alone exceeded total manufacturing exports, making industry a net consumer of foreign exchange, dependent on primary product exports and external financing to maintain operations. Capital and intermediate productive inputs constituted 75 percent of the nation's total import bill. On the other hand, export earnings were severely depressed by the country's dependence on a narrow base of agricultural exports fetching declining prices in international markets, as well as war-related reductions in the volume of export production, which was particularly acute beginning in 1985. Compounding the problem of Nicaragua's external balance was the enormous growth of external debt needed to finance its trade and government budget deficits. In spite of the U.S. blockage of multilateral assistance, Nicaragua's external debt swelled from $1.3 billion in 1979 to $6 billion by 1986. Much of this debt was in the form of tied suppliers credits leading to mismatched technologies in the productive sphere and contributed little in the way of alleviating the scarcity of liquid foreign exchange.

Macroeconomic Policy Phases

The Somoza Prerevolutionary Period

Nicaragua has a long history as a small, dependent, open, food- and foreign exchange–constrained agricultural economy. During the prerevolutionary years under Somoza, macroeconomic activity was robust and stable, though distributionally skewed against the poor. Real GDP growth during the 1960s was nearly 7 percent (10 percent during the cotton boom of 1961–1965), fueled by the growth in international demand, the regional impulse of the CACM, high rates of internal investment on the order of 12–18 percent of GDP, and severe wage repression. Internal prices were remarkably stable and closely correlated with price movements in the United States—within a range of 5–15 percent annual inflation—which facilitated the country's long-standing record of real exchange rate stability until the mid-1970s. The earthquake that leveled Managua in 1972 aggravated class tensions and inflation; the latter, in conjunction with Somoza's corrupt handling of relief funds and recycled petrodollar inflows, produced an overvaluation of the cordoba from 1974 to 1979. This facilitated the immense decapitalization of the economy on the eve of the insurrection and provoked a major devaluation in 1979.

Somoza ran a classically liberal regime with no room for activist monetary or fiscal stabilization policy.[5] Monetary policy was entirely passive. Stimulative money growth with a convertible currency and inelastically supplied nontradable goods could only result in dollar conversion and capital flight—not increased output. Adjustments to external imbalances were achieved at the expense of the poor. For example, adjustment to growing trade deficits provoked by falling export prices was achieved through fiscally induced recession, which attacked output, reduced imports, and forced the swelling ranks of newly unemployed workers back into subsistence agriculture. Somoza's reliance on market forces was accompanied by a notoriously repressive state apparatus that crushed popular demands for basic needs and for a more equitable redistribution of income. The Somoza agroexport dynasty consumed the nation's resources, while poverty and malnutrition in the countryside fueled the flames that led to the 1979 Sandinista revolution.

1979–1981: Revolution,
Economic Reactivation, and Expansion

The euphoria of the Sandinista victory translated into an aggressive plan for state-led reconstruction and expansion of the economy in conjunction with an ambitious array of social welfare projects involving significant redistributions of property and income.[6] The first economic plan, Plan 1980, brought out in May 1980 by the newly formed Ministry of Planning (MIPLAN), had one long-term objective, initiating the process of a transition to socialism, and four key short-term objectives: (1) to reactivate and alter the composition of production to meet the basic needs of the poor, (2) to build national unity across social classes, (3) to construct and defend a new Sandinista state, and (4) to achieve internal and external macroeconomic balance.[7] To implement such a program it was necessary to reconcile both the social welfare goals of the revolution and the new role of the state with the country's crippled, dependent, capitalist productive apparatus, whose control remained predominantly in private hands.

The first two years of the revolution were deceptive: Foreign assistance was liberally available,[8] relaxing constraints on the state's ability to meet the newly unleashed popular consumption demand as well as to launch formidable advances in health and education services and make commitments for large state-owned productive investment projects. Nationalization of Somoza's enormous holdings, which included 21 percent of the country's agricultural land, facilitated a dramatic expansion of the state directly into the productive arena. This enabled the Sandinistas to implement a broad-based land reform project without encroaching on the private holdings of the large and medium agroexport bourgeoisie, who also welcomed Somoza's defeat but did so as an opportunity to expand their own agenda of private economic activities.

In such an environment, national unity did not involve immediate tangible economic sacrifices, nor were the financial limits to the state's social welfare goals apparent. This obscured the underlying tensions associated with the uneasy class relations that formed the basis of the "mixed economy" program for development. Such class tensions later revealed serious incompatibilities among the stated development objectives and proved enormously costly in terms of expensive policies aimed at appeasing the interests of the private sector.[9] For example, the agro-export bourgeoisie viewed direct control over the state apparatus as a necessary condition for investment, whereas the Sandinistas sought to preserve popular control of the state and extend the Area of People's Property (APP) state farms as a condition for economic reactivation. These contradictory views made it unlikely that national unity could be maintained. Similarly, it was unlikely that internal and external macroeconomic balance could be maintained by relying on extensive foreign assistance while the state was committed to large social spending projects and investments in large state enterprises.[10]

The early gains of the revolution were impressive compared to the early years of other transitional economies, such as those in Cuba and Chile, especially given the far greater extent of economic damage inflicted during the Nicaraguan insurrection, comparable to the destruction of productive wealth experienced in the Russian and Mexican revolutions.[11] The World Bank estimated that lost output from 1978-1980 was $2 billion (equal to an entire year of current GDP), with $0.5 billion in capital flight from 1977 to 1979 and the destruction of 10 percent of industrial capacity.[12] In this context, the initial demand-led fiscal stimulus of state spending helped produce a healthy 5 percent average annual real GDP growth rate for 1980-1981, as well as major advances in the provision of employment, housing, education, and health care. From 1979 to 1983 both the urban and rural poor benefited from expanded public employment, growth in health-care services, quadrupling of educational opportunities, and the provision of subsidized basic commodities.[13]

Nicaragua was also fortunate in significantly increasing rural living standards and sustaining levels of agricultural output while implementing an extensive land reform program.[14] In part, this was the result of the relatively nonconflictive and extensive expropriation of Somoza's holdings. Increased utilization of agricultural lands contributed to direct increases in food production, with a shift in the composition of output toward domestic consumption crops and away from agroexport cash crops.[15] Although serious questions remained regarding the new forms of land tenure—whether to collectivize land or services or issue individual titles to redistributed lands—it is clear that the improved living standards initially won the Sandinistas considerable political support among farmers.

It should be noted, however, that state prices for agricultural output biased the internal terms of trade against the peasantry, promoting a cheap food policy that favored urban consumers. Moreover, as the foreign exchange constraint became binding, campesinos found that manufactured goods that could be obtained in exchange for their produce were less and less available. This prompted rural organizing efforts, which in conjunction with later political and military considerations, forced a significant reversal of the rural-urban terms of trade around 1986. Such tensions between stabilizing food prices to support urban popular consumption and increasing agricultural producer prices to augment production and improve rural living standards constituted a persistent policy challenge of the mixed economy.[16]

By the end of 1981 several economic imbalances emerged, posing an ongoing challenge to development. The focus of Plan 1981 shifted to "austerity and efficiency," targeting the external sector, productivity, consumption, and surpluses as problem areas. Internally, domestic consumption had risen sharply with unleashed demand seeking to realize the gains of the revolution in conjunction with the "spilling of credit" into the countryside.[17] This placed upward pressure on imports. State spending for social welfare projects and the maintenance of an aggressive investment program nearing 20 percent of GDP (to compensate for the nonexistent investment of the private sector) proved to be far out of line with the state's tax base and thus accelerated increases in the fiscal deficit. Financing both increased consumption and the growing fiscal deficit required dramatic increases in internal credit and foreign indebtedness. Foreign credits to Nicaragua nearly doubled from 1979 to 1980 (13 percent of these were U.S. bilateral assistance), reaching nearly $730 million of new credits in 1981—feeding the illusion that such spending could persist. Given the availability of external finance, inflation was moderate—around 40 percent annually—as recourse to money emission was at that point limited.

As aggregate spending pressed against inelastic supply, however, inflationary pressures accumulated. Poor supply response was aggravated by falling productivity on the APP farms when labor took its well-deserved "historic vacation," though with less than desirable macroeconomic consequences. The resulting inflation marked the beginning of a prolonged period of overvaluation as the official cordoba rate was maintained fixed in the face of growing internal inflation. The overvalued cordoba lowered the domestic currency costs of imports and tended to dampen inflation; however, it also damaged the country's trade balance by making imports artificially cheap. This, in conjunction with the regional deterioration of the CACM and falling terms of trade for primary product exports, swelled the trade deficit and depleted foreign exchange.

The crisis deepened as a major segment of the national bourgeoisie began moving toward counterrevolution and appealed to the United

States—as was the custom historically—for resolution of their domestic predicament. There could have been no better champion of their cause than the newly elected Reagan-Bush administration, which set out to defeat the Sandinistas via a three-pronged strategy of financial, trade, and military aggression. By 1982 the U.S. government was directly responsible for blocking over $164 million in bilateral and multilateral credits to Nicaragua.[18] Overall, new foreign credits to Nicaragua in 1982 dropped nearly $230 million from 1981 levels, while export performance continued to sour by $100 million, and the fiscal deficit as a share of GDP climbed from 8.9 percent (1981) to 12.4 percent (1982).[19] The addiction to external savings resulted in a near trebling of external debt from $1.1 billion in 1979 to $3 billion in 1982, with debt service consuming nearly 40 percent of declining export earnings.

The absence of private investment and increased recourse to external debt forced the issue of the role of the state in reactivating economic activity. In the context of the social relations of Nicaragua's mixed economy, what emerged was the notion of the "state as center of accumulation." Without full nationalization of productive property, the state was to serve as planner through the centralization of economic surpluses, which were to be controlled and redirected through state investment.[20]

Socialization of the Nicaraguan economy was limited to the spheres of commerce and finance. The productive apparatus of the country as a whole remained predominantly capitalist, with nationalized productive assets limited primarily to Somoza's holdings. The banking system was nationalized in an effort to stem capital flight and to provide a more formidable arm for indicative planning through state control over credit. Agricultural commerce was nationalized so as to command the vital flow of foreign exchange associated with international transactions, as well as to attempt to regulate the internal terms of trade between the rural-agricultural and urban-industrial sectors and to provide a food safety net for the poor.

The state's ability to act as the center of accumulation depended on a number of factors: the available surpluses generated by the APP, the ability to set prices and maintain agricultural production in both the state and nonstate sectors, the ability to realize surpluses on current account, and the ability to manage credit without losing control to inflation. Such an approach was vulnerable externally to deteriorating terms of trade and foreign aggression and internally to the ongoing tensions in class relations. For example, efforts to expand the social surplus via real wage reductions and increased taxes on profits generated conflicts that weakened production, as did the generalized unwillingness of the private sector to invest.

1982–1983: Transition to War Economy
and Limited Adjustment

Rising expenditures, flagging supply, heightened polarization over control of the state, a private-sector investment strike, and growing external imbalance, all portended a deepening crisis in the revolution's third year. Added to this was the specter of military conflict: Contra operations escalated during this period; both the disaffected bourgeoisie who left the National Assembly and the ex–Somocista National Guard received their first disbursement of $24 million from the United States in November 1983. Mounting Sandinista expenditures for defense deepened the fiscal deficit. Military conflict, continued reductions in untied capital inflows, and damages from the 100-year-record floods of 1982 broke the momentum of recuperation recorded during the first three years, registering a negative 0.8 percent GDP growth in 1982.

In an effort to correct major balance-of-payments problems, the Sandinistas adopted a program to stimulate exports and discourage imports. To curtail imports the Sandinistas implemented a "public debt tax" of five cordobas on every dollar sold for the purchase of luxury goods imports. This gave rise to an array of implicit exchange rate differentials across imports that varied according to the degree of necessity of the good.

A proposed May 1982 plan to correct overvaluation and promote exports by means of a maxidevaluation was abandoned for fear of accelerating inflation and provoking recession by raising the cordoba costs of imported goods. Policymakers opted instead for selective devaluation, employing a system of multiple exchange rates in conjunction with a schedule of guaranteed producer prices to target subsidies to capitalists by sector. This system generated significant exchange rate benefits for agroexport producers and was intended to promote new sources of private investment in export production to earn desperately needed foreign exchange. Private investment was not forthcoming, however, and the program would prove to be a major source of the financial distortions underlying Nicaragua's hyperinflationary crisis.

Under the multiple exchange rate regime, agroexport producers received a preferential exchange rate via state allocation of dollars through "certificates of exchange availability" (CDDs) and a system of guaranteed prices—a government commitment to purchase output at a price determined at the beginning of each agricultural cycle.[21] The guaranteed prices, which were typically higher than world market prices at the official exchange rate, implied that the state assumed the terms-of-trade risk associated with declining export prices for the private sector. The state subsidized agroexport producers by virtue of the fact that the implicit exchange rate paid to exporters (determined by the ratio of the guaranteed price to the world market price) was higher than the official exchange rate, resulting in increased cordoba profits. The various export commodities each had its corresponding implicit exchange rate, affording agro-exporters varying degrees of compensation. The subsidies accrued at the expense of the Central Bank, which incurred exchange rate losses from printing the additional cordobas necessary to make up the exchange rate differential.

In addition, agroexport producers gained by virtue of an overvalued cordoba, which reduced the domestic costs of imported productive inputs (e.g., fertilizer, pesticides, and farm equipment) purchased from the state at the official exchange rate. This bonanza had the macroeconomic disadvantage of creating an even greater dependence on imports by making it cheaper for producers to import *new* capital goods (such as tractors) than to undertake normal maintenance on the existing capital stock. Over time this distortion in relative prices produced a dramatic misallocation of capital: Producers adopted overly capital-intensive imported production techniques, exhausting foreign exchange.

The appropriateness of the multiple exchange rate scheme is open to question. In the short run, the Sandinistas sought to protect the public from a devaluation-induced inflation and something had to be done to promote exports to restore external balance. Moreover, it was clear that foreign exchange controls were necessary to discourage capital flight. Debates continue regarding the extent to which the nominal devaluation produced by the system of implicit exchange rates in fact compensated exporters for the market damage caused by the overvalued cordoba. From the standpoint of the overall transaction, however, it is apparent that the state was bearing an enormous cost to guarantee a substantial profit margin for many of the large and medium agroexport producers. The official exchange rate reduced imported input costs, while the implicit exchange rate subsidy increased the cordoba yield from foreign sales. Indeed, many of the large agroexport producers boasted that business was better under the Sandinistas than it had been under Somoza.

The long-term problem was that gains to the export sector were not won out of increased exports but were subsidized out of the exchange rate losses to the Central Bank. In the final analysis, the gains of the agro-exporters would be borne on the backs of the urban and rural poor, who were unable to defend their earnings from the erosion of inflation that inevitably arose as the Central Bank was forced to make up the exchange rate differential by printing money. The financial losses to the Central Bank were compounded by interest rate losses that resulted from efforts to preserve fixed and subsidized nominal interest rates in the midst of an ongoing inflation. In effect, the banking system was "giving away" credit at negative real rates of interest—the chief beneficiaries being the APP and the large private agroexport producers.

One hundred percent financing of new investment projects was the standard.

Thus, by the end of 1983, policies were in place that attempted to address the foreign exchange stranglehold resulting from the loss in external assistance and the deteriorated trade position. State spending continued to grow, but without any fiscal basis. Export production had to be revitalized, but the state's control was restricted to the arena of price and credit policy in its efforts to induce new investment from the private sector, where much of the control over production lay. The resulting exchange rate and credit policies protected profits while promoting inefficient production techniques, swelling the deficits to the financial system that later fueled hyperinflation. Efforts were made to preserve the social wage, and in spite of the growing financial disequilibrium the state forged ahead with its large and costly investment projects, many of which would never see operation.

1983–1984: War Economy, Macrodisequilibrium, and Policy Indecision

The 1983–1984 period witnessed the intensification of the contra war and U.S. economic aggression. The 90 percent reduction in Nicaragua's sugar quota for exports to the United States cost the country more than 5 percent of total exports for 1983. At the same time the state was mobilizing its largest development initiative ever. By 1983 construction was under way on a series of large state investment projects: the Tipitapa-Malcatoya (TIMAL) sugar plant; the Chiltepe dairy; the port at El Bluff; the African palm and tobacco projects; and the Sebaco valley fruit, vegetable, and canning project—to name a few.[22] These projects were conceived at a time when foreign funding was readily available, but executed at a time of severe external drain.

Debates abound regarding the highly centralized, overly capital-intensive, and urban bias of these projects.[23] There was no question, however, that the projects created a monumental fiscal burden and that it would soon become untenable for the Sandinistas to finance both the state investments and the war against the U.S.-backed contras.[24] The large state projects provoked increased indebtedness and foreign exchange dependence without contributing to productive capacity in the short run. Failure to heed the foreign exchange constraint inevitably forced investment rationing, and by 1987, many projects had to be scrapped.

Growing macroeconomic disequilibria produced a crisis in which the necessity for stabilization could no longer be ignored. In 1984 the fiscal deficit of the central government *alone* swelled to 24 percent of GDP—double the 12 percent figure that is customarily associated with triggering hyperinflation.[25] The lion's share of this deficit was attributable to defense expenditures. Curiously, inflation maintained a moderate 50 percent annual rate. This contributed to the continued overvaluation of the cordoba, which helped boost imports an additional $21.5 million, deepening the trade deficit.[26] The foreign exchange subsidy to agroexport producers continued to grow while Nicaragua's international terms of trade deteriorated and the dollar shortage intensified. These foreign exchange losses of the Central Bank augmented the deficit pressures on the economy by an additional 5.5 percent of GDP.

Interest rate losses to the banking system were also on the rise, affected, in part, by the Sandinista decision to pardon (saneamiento) a share of the agricultural debt on the fourth anniversary of the revolution. The pardon provided a much-needed break for small producers.[27] In 1984 the combined interest rate and foreign exchange losses had pushed the consolidated budget deficit—to be financed out of domestic money emission—to well over 30 percent of GDP. This was clearly an unsustainable financial position. Some relief arrived from the Socialist Bloc countries, which nearly doubled their credits to Nicaragua with $597 million in loan and grant aid for 1984.

The November 1984 elections caused policy delays and indecision in responding to growing macroeconomic imbalances. But the revolution could no longer postpone the economic consequences of its efforts to reconcile growing expenditure along four fronts: (1) war finance, (2) continued investment in large foreign exchange–consuming investment projects, (3) expanded popular consumption, and (4) exchange rate subsidies to agro-export producers to preserve national unity. Military expenditure to defeat the contras claimed first priority on domestic resources. A draft was implemented, but the war effort could not be sustained without keeping economic activity alive. In a mixed economy this involved the difficult matter of mobilizing private-sector investment or at least discouraging agroexport producers from supporting the contras. The latter was achieved through subsidies and guaranteed profits for maintaining production.

The combination of the financial distortions associated with printing money to cover burgeoning state spending and the system of price and exchange rate controls designed to meet the redistributive planning objectives of the state proved to be an explosive mix. Black markets in goods and foreign exchange appeared alongside controlled markets, promoting a growing class of speculators who pursued windfall profits by arbitraging across the widening price differentials between these markets. In the foreign exchange market, the official exchange rate of 10 cordobas to the dollar could not be enforced while cordobas were being printed for deficit finance. This led to a black market rate of 600 to 1 in December 1984. In January 1988, just prior to the February monetary reform, the black market rate hovered at 60,000 to 1, against an official rate of 70 to 1.

An important force behind this widening differential was the vicious circle of monetization induced by the permanent exchange rate gap between imports and exports, designed to subsidize agro-exporters. Losses to the Central Bank implied new money creation, which placed continued upward pressure on the black market rate. This boosted the profits of black market operators, drawing foreign exchange out of the state sector. For those with access to commercial credit, the bonanza was even greater as inflation outpaced fixed nominal rates on loans. During the 1980–1984 period, foreign exchange speculators working with borrowed funds turned "real profit[s] of around 80 percent—far in excess of profit rates in agricultural production."[28] The growing mercantile mentality of the *hombre bisnero* (informal-sector merchant) fostered increased speculation at the expense of production.

In commodity markets by 1985, 4,000 *buhoneros* (petty traders) cashed in on speculative profit margins available on import and export arbitrage and from fencing state-subsidized goods across borders.[29] The *buhoneros* were among the growing ranks of informal-sector merchants who received as much as 360 times the average salary of waged workers in the state sector. The combination of low state-sector wages and the large distortions in relative prices associated with inflation finance "reinforced a speculative reconcentration of income and a 'deproletarianization' of the labor force" as workers left low-waged employment for the gains of petty trade.[30]

The policy matrix that targeted social spending and progressive redistribution had the unintended effect of inverting the very objectives of the revolution. Wage goods subsidies and price controls aimed at protecting the incomes of workers and the urban poor served, instead, the profit motive of merchant intermediaries while hurting domestic foodstuff producers. The artificially lowered prices of imported spare parts and productive inputs, instead of promoting increased production, served to enrich black market operators and speculators who diverted resources into contraband trade. Hope of socializing productive relations by means of a growth in public-sector employment was diminished by the flight of skilled labor from formal-sector state employment into petty commodity and mercantile enterprises that fed off the growing arena of profit opportunities associated with the macropolicy price distortions. The speculators, in this instance, were not the cause but the symptom and propagators of the crisis.

The emerging composition of production undermined the state's efforts at planning economic activity. Price controls unraveled with the juxtaposition of controlled and uncontrolled markets. Labor continued its migration to the informal sector—outside the purview of state planning. Estimates for the late 1980s indicate that over 60 percent of the economically active population were engaged in informal-sector activities, much of which consisted of speculative petty commerce. It is estimated that nearly one-fourth of the official GDP circulated through informal channels during 1983 and 1984.[31] With the growing distortions in relative prices, planners were paralyzed: Input prices bore no relation to resource scarcities, and overvalued exchange rates distorted beyond calculation the relation between imported and domestic resource costs.

1985–1987: Stabilization Mach I— Efforts to Correct Distortions and Stimulate Production

After the first five years of a populist economic agenda, stabilization dominated the policy arena for the remainder of the decade. In February 1985 the Sandinistas implemented a restrictive economic package that included a devaluation of the official exchange rate from 10 to 28 cordobas to the dollar, the elimination of subsidies for basic consumer goods, a rationalization of state investments, a government-spending freeze, and increased taxes. The new austerity was designed to stimulate production and neutralize distortions while heightening national defense in the face of an intensified war effort.

In the external sector, U.S. efforts to cripple the economy escalated with the mining of the harbors in 1984 and the imposition of the trade embargo in March 1985. The low-intensity-warfare strategy aimed at strangling production and foreign exchange. Mexican assistance was cut off by the International Monetary Fund (IMF), which threatened to suspend Mexican loans if the country continued oil shipments to Nicaragua. Those shipments on favorable credit terms had constituted 7 percent of Nicaragua's total external support.

Nicaragua was able to minimize the brunt of this aggression by restructuring external trade and financial flows. Lost trade shares from the United States due to the embargo were recaptured out of increased export shares to Japan (from 10.9 percent of total 1977 exports to 22.3 percent in 1985), the European Economic Community (EEC) (from 27.2 percent to 52.7 percent), and other Third World nations (from 3.2 percent to 8.2 percent)—with no substantial increase in exports to the Socialist Bloc.[32] Lost financial flows were more than offset by the substitution of Socialist Bloc credits, which reached their peak in 1985.[33] Nicaragua's deteriorated foreign exchange position effectively signaled the end of its ability to service its external debt, forcing a strategy of making payments only to creditors that offered new net lending. Socialist Bloc aid filled in for a while but had become notably absent by 1987, shifting the financial burden of domestic spending to the Central Bank, which exacerbated inflationary pressures. Figure 12.1 depicts the evolution of the composition of foreign assistance to Nicaragua. Note that aid from the Socialist Bloc eclipsed Western aid in 1982 and then declined sharply after 1985—the result of U.S.-Soviet negotiations that left Nicaragua starved for foreign assistance.

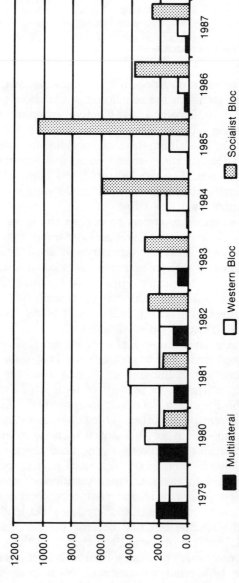

Figure 12.1   International assistance to Nicaragua by source (millions of U.S. dollars). *Source:* Data from Ministerio de Comercio Exterior.

Domestically, inflation began its trajectory from structural inflation to hyperinflation during this period. Prices jumped from an annual rate of 334 percent in 1985, to 747 percent in 1986, and 1,347 percent by 1987. By the end of 1987 inflation asserted its own autonomy, with highly variable price increases closely correlated to the black market exchange rate, no longer a function of traditional factors such as money growth, lagged prices, and production costs.[34] Domestic prices outpaced world prices, resulting in severe overvaluation of the exchange rate. This forced a renewed devaluation of the official exchange rate from 28 to 70 cordobas to the dollar in March 1986. Given the intensity of the inflation, however, most observers argued that this effort to unify the exchange rates was simply too little, too late.[35]

Nominal devaluations lagged consistently behind inflation, exaggerating existing price distortions. The classic case was that of imported gasoline, which was much cheaper by the gallon than a slice of domestically grown watermelon. With inflation at over 1,000 percent while bank loan rates fluctuated between 4 and 45 percent, huge implicit interest rate subsidies appeared. This enormous erosion in the real value of debt generated perverse scenarios in which a new truck could be purchased on state credit and paid off entirely after a year's time by simply selling off the spare tire.[36] The real costs, again, were assumed by the Central Bank. Exchange rate losses deepened as the export exchange rate climbed to 15,000 cordobas to the dollar (35,000 on the black market), against imports at the official 70 to 1 rate by the end of 1987. Dollar incentives, which were expanded to apply not only to the cattle sector in 1985 but to other agro-exporters as well, placed an additional financial burden on the state. Estimates suggest that producers with access to subsidized dollars and 100 percent financing typically repaid only 5 percent in real terms of the total value loans after inflation and subsidies. Aimed to induce wealthy private producers to maintain production in the war zones, these concessions came at an enormous cost to the state. Nonmilitary government spending was cut drastically, reducing the deficit of the central government from 23.5 percent of GDP in 1984 to 16.5 percent in 1987, despite a decline in tax revenues. Nonetheless, as a result of massive interest and exchange rate losses, the consolidated budget deficit remained at 24 percent of GDP, leaving money growth unabated to fuel the hyperinflation of 1988. (See Figure 12.2 for an account of the evolution of the various components of the consolidated government deficit and the trajectory of inflation over the 1983–1988 period.)

Nominal wage increases were implemented to soften the blow of the stabilization measures, but the increments could not stop the 50 percent erosion of real earnings from 1984 to 1987. Efforts to expand the social wage through payments in kind failed because of supply shortages. The low real earnings contributed to low productivity, high turnover, de-

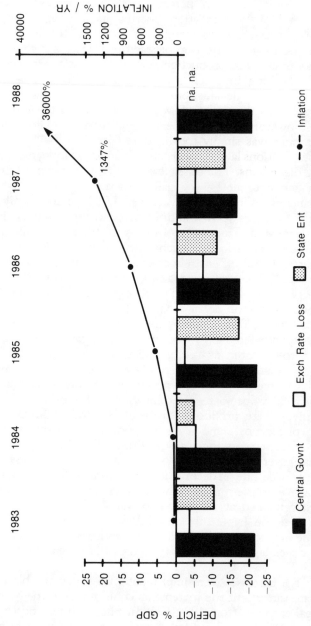

Figure 12.2 Composition of consolidated deficit and inflation in Nicaragua, 1983–1988. *Sources:* Data from BCN (Banco Central de Nicaragua) and IMF, "Nicaragua: Recent Economic Development," Washington, D.C., August 1988 (mimeo).

skilling, and the continued deproletarianization of the labor force as workers migrated to speculative commercial activities supported by the distortions in macro financial policy. The Law of Presumed Profits in conjunction with devaluation aimed to discourage this growth of intermediary operations by taxing the concentrated windfall gains.[37] The opening of the official exchange houses (casas de cambio) and the emergence of the parallel market were efforts to squeeze out the black market operators. In addition, the acceleration of land reform and the increased resource flow to the strategic rural sectors affected by the contra war also served to discourage the urban-speculative trend.

1988–1989: Stabilization Mach II—
Hyperinflation, Monetary Reform, and Orthodox Stabilization

By 1988 the vicious cycle of distortions had reached the point where the Sandinistas had effectively lost control over the economy. Debates raged between the structuralist-leaning Ministry of Agricultural Development and Agrarian Reform (MIDINRA) and the monetarist-leaning Central Bank over measures to cure the virulent hyperinflation. The issue was whether to provide incentives to promote increased supply or to enforce austerity to contain excess demand. Although elements of both approaches were necessary, the measures adopted in February and extended in June 1988 were decidedly monetarist, reflecting the short-run urgency of addressing at least the proximate cause of the crisis: excess money growth. The four major objectives of the stabilization were to: (1) realign relative prices, (2) reduce inflation by cutting the fiscal deficit (to 10 percent of GDP) and associated money emission through state shrinking, (3) relax price controls to restore investment and productivity in the formal sector, and (4) raise labor productivity through efforts to restore the deeply eroded purchasing power of formal-sector workers by dismantling the constraints of the National System of Wages and Labor (SNOTS) productivity deal system.

Key features of the February shock included a complete remonetization, introducing a new cordoba at 1,000 times the value of the old currency.[38] This measure reduced the money stock by 10 percent and dealt the contras a substantial blow, impairing their mobility within Nicaragua by destroying the value of their currency holdings.[39] Explicit and implicit exchange rates were unified into legal "official" and "parallel" rates, with a drastically devalued (3,000 percent) new cordoba at an official rate of 10 to the dollar with a subsequent maxidevaluation in June at 80 new cordobas to the dollar. This helped remedy overvaluation and reduce exchange rate losses, compressing imports and relieving financial pressure for money emission. In conjunction with government intervention in the parallel market, the profit margins of speculators and black market operators were substantially reduced, and they were confronted with heightened public scrutiny. Government budgets were cut 10 percent when forty government agencies were "compacted" into eight superministries, with a moderate increase in money wages and the loss of 8,000 public-sector jobs.

The February measures, in conjunction with a popular mobilization against speculation, produced a temporary reduction in inflation. By June, however, dwindling commodity supplies had boosted prices of basic goods by 600 percent, foreign exchange shortages forced up black market exchange rates, and the antispeculation mobilization gave way to union-led demonstrations protesting severe real earnings losses—with average wages covering as little as 7 percent of the minimum consumption basket. In June, a second round of measures included further devaluation; nearly complete elimination of price controls and subsidies; the redirection of credit flows toward private producers; credit rationing, with new ceilings at 70 percent of demonstrable financial need; and a gradual indexation of credit to establish positive real interest rates. The Central Bank pursued more-aggressive intervention in the parallel market in an attempt to recover the massive dollar drain into an overactive black market that had left the state without foreign exchange, paralyzing productive imports. Though wage increases were not part of this package, after considerable protest, token increases did appear.

The monetarist package essentially opened the economy fully to the operation of market forces, but without popular mobilization in support of the measures and without a clear indication of the long-run gains to be won from such IMF-style austerity. Carlos Vilas suggested it was the worst of both worlds, undergoing the austerity of an IMF package without the benefits of receiving the external financial assistance.[40] Liberalized prices did put basic foodstuffs back on the shelves at the supermarkets, as informal-sector production responded to the new incentives. The real question was, who could afford to pay the new higher prices? State-sector workers and the urban poor were defenseless against lost purchasing power from inflation. Those with property and merchants selling in the domestic market stood to gain until austerity wrung out all potential buyers. Those selling abroad or those transacting in dollars clearly fared the best, especially the beneficiaries of the state export promotion policy. A detailed study of income distribution in Nicaragua is still lacking, but because increased reliance on market allocation would price the poor out of the economy into subsistence production, there were fears that "two" Nicaraguas would emerge.

On the other hand, without a significant restructuring of productive relations, the planned economy option was out of the question for Nicaragua, considering that over 60 percent of the labor force was engaged in informal activities and that the lion's share of productive capacity was in private hands. Economic distortions had gone too far.

The dependent capitalist character of production, starved for capital and foreign exchange, could not be managed with grossly distorted prices and side-by-side operation of free markets and rationing systems, which only produced speculative arbitrage. Deficit-driven inflation was the inevitable outcome of war, a state-driven social welfare project that outstripped the nation's productive capacity, and a massive system of subsidies to the private sector. Those subsidies constituted the glue of a national unity program in which private capitalists were denied their traditional control over the state. As hyperinflation unhinged production and political support with the coming of peace, the Sandinistas had little choice in the short run but to adopt monetarist stabilization measures that were antithetical to the immediate development objectives of the revolution.

Of the four traditional medicines for controlling inflation, Nicaragua was stuck with the worst-case option of orthodox stabilization.[41] First, attempts to manipulate relative prices—appreciating the exchange rate or reducing real wages—could not work because overvaluation and low wages were already part of the problem. Second, liberalization of imports was untenable because Nicaragua lacked the foreign exchange needed to secure cheap imports to put downward pressure on domestic prices, nor was destroying home industry viewed as a desirable option. Third, heterodox approaches involving incomes policy and price controls had already been tried without success. What remained was fiscal consolidation—tax-raising, budget-slashing, money-contracting austerity. If there was to be any hope of avoiding the grossly regressive distributional impacts of hyperinflation and of restoring the possibility of a return to economic planning, such an emergency program would be necessary in the short run to wring out price distortions and the deficit-driven sources of money emission.

After moderate economic improvement in July, Nicaragua was devastated by Hurricane Joan in October 1988. The Sandinistas wasted no time in responding to the worst hurricane of the century, mobilizing evacuations and reconstruction efforts, which significantly reduced casualties. More than 100 people were killed and nearly one-tenth of the population was left homeless. Significant portions of the coffee and banana crops were destroyed, as well as large areas of vital rain forest. State relief efforts proved extremely costly and disrupted financial programing efforts to contain money emissions. Inflation proceeded out of control to over 125 percent *monthly* rates from November 1988 through January 1989—prices more than doubled each month, producing an annual inflation for 1988 of 36,000 percent![42]

In February 1989 yet another round of severe austerity was implemented to reduce the massive deficits that had contributed to the 11,000 percent increase in money emission during 1988. Government spending was slashed 44 percent, by about 461 billion cordobas, resulting in estimated layoffs of 35,000 public employees. With few employment opportunities in the cities, plans were to redirect the newly unemployed back to the countryside to labor in agroexport production. On the revenue side, state-owned property was sold off to the private sector and "petrocordoba" earnings were increased by raising gasoline prices.[43] Further efforts at state shrinking involved the elimination of subsidies for losses to state enterprises, as well as the state's withdrawal from direct managerial responsibilities over the firms. State enterprises were increasingly subjected to the market test and allowed to fail if necessary, while the newly formed Ministry of Economy, Industry, and Commerce (MEIC) assumed the role more of consultant than of state planning agency. To enforce these deficit reduction initiatives, the Central Bank was under orders to bring money emission to a halt.

The restructured roles of the market and the state that emerged from stabilization experiences of the late 1980s produced a form of "Nicastroika" or what some have termed an evolution toward a Scandinavian development model. This involved an increased reliance on market forces and a decentralization of political and economic institutions: The state dedicated itself to indicative planning, influencing private decisions by virtue of its control over key macro variables in the business environment. Its acceptance was rooted in a long-standing commitment to the mixed economy with the additional impulse of fresh tied assistance from the European social democracies, most notably Sweden. Future foreign assistance was linked to meeting stringent stabilization targets.

In the short run, the Sandinistas achieved considerable success in stopping the hyperinflation. This was attributable to credible, though punishing, stabilization measures and an unusual tolerance for austerity on the part of the poor. Monthly inflation rates dropped substantially in 1989: February, 45.8 percent; March, 20.1 percent; April, 12.6 percent; May, 15.5 percent; with a burst in June to 62.2 percent, followed by a continued decline in July to 8.5 percent, and August to 6.6 percent— producing the first entire quarter (July–September) of single-digit monthly inflation in two years. Improved price stability did little to reactivate production, however, particularly in the foreign exchange–producing sectors. With fresh hard currency credits not forthcoming from either the European social democracies or the crumbling East Bloc nations, deficit pressures accumulated, as the trade gap widened. In spite of concerted downsizing of the state and military budgets, it proved impossible to keep inflation in the low single digits on a sustained basis.

The new economic model introduced market forces to eliminate inefficient operations, but it was unable to promote significant new investment from a larger and more intransigent private sector, particularly given the adversity of the international terms of trade. The economy's increased dependence on private investment renewed pressures for politically targeted subsidies to quiet private-sector grumblings, rekindling financial distortions. A program of *reliquidaciones*—exchange rate compensations for private producers—was the first of such creeping distortions reintroduced in 1989. Its disbursements contributed to a substantial remonetization of the economy. The form of stabilization itself was conditioned by the tensions of the mixed economy.

1990: The End of the Revolutionary Mixed Economy

As the Sandinistas pursued economic restructuring into 1990, a number of questions remained about the future course of the revolution: Given the apparent failure of state planning efforts under existing capitalist productive relations, could the state develop the necessary managerial capacity if it were to further extend itself in the productive arena? And regarding the redistributive goals of the revolution, after the nightmare of austerity restored some semblance of price stability, what would the state offer workers and peasants in return for their many years of sacrifice for policies aimed at subsidizing private capital? Speculation on these matters was abruptly terminated by the electoral results of February 1990. The revolutionary mixed economy—in which the party of workers and peasants held state power while presiding over an otherwise crippled capitalist peripheral economy—came to an end. By April, the Sandinistas had transferred political control to Violeta Chamorro's fragmented opposition coalition, which represented primarily the interests of the Nicaraguan private sector.

Although the Sandinistas had correctly pursued the only available short-term measures to restore economic control, it was too much to expect that popular support could be maintained in the context of deepening austerity, despite the best of intentions and promises of "better days ahead." The Nicaraguan economy was simply not viable without large sustained foreign assistance flows to offset the country's acute domestic and international financial imbalances. The United States delivered the death blow to multilateral lending and even blocked South-South petroleum assistance, obstructing Venezuelan and Mexican shipments to Nicaragua. Moreover, the collapse of the Eastern European economies diverted the small hard currency credits that would have been forthcoming from the Western European social democracies (e.g., Spain and Sweden), while virtually extinguishing Socialist Bloc assistance, which had totaled over $1 billion in 1985. Given a $500 million trade deficit and a government budget deficit approaching 20 percent of GDP, the Nicaraguan economy could not survive long, even if one assumed that Socialist Bloc credits could continue at $300 million annually. It is little wonder that the Nicaraguan people, in the face of the insurmountable odds of U.S. aggression and the unraveling of the socialist economies, voted with their stomachs to trade political control of the state for a chance to eat.

Conclusions

Nicaragua ended its first revolutionary decade in economic turmoil. At the root of the 1988–1989 crisis was an accumulated excess demand for inflationary finance that was predominantly, but not solely, the consequence of deficit spending on the contra war. It was also the costly result of state efforts to manage the policy "knife edge" of the mixed economy: to advance the social welfare goals of the revolution through a state controlled by workers and peasants and simultaneously preserve the allegiance of the medium and large private agroexport producers who controlled a lion's share of vital foreign exchange–generating production and who typically refused to accept popular control of the state. Through price guarantees, exchange rate concessions, direct sub-sidies, and cheap credit, the state paid dearly to induce this powerful group of capitalists to invest their resources and stimulate production. The results were dismal.

Sandinista adoption of the mixed economy model was not conceived as a tactical end run to dodge the wrath of U.S. reprisals that would come with the establishment of full-blown socialism in its backyard. Historically, the Nicaraguan economy has been based on more than one form of production; a revolution that expropriated capitalist firms alone would not directly involve the majority of poor petty commodity producers, who would remain outside of the state sector.[44] Problems with the mixed economy arise, however, when the degree of resource extraction and redistributive backsliding necessary to preserve social peace with the private sector becomes too great.

Attempts to preserve islands of private entrepreneurs in a revolutionary economy burdened by civil war and by the expense of social reforms aimed at redressing the distributive inequities of the Somoza epoch had proven not only costly but counterproductive. The exchange rate and interest rate subsidies that enriched many agro-export producers, in conjunction with massive war expenditures, generated dramatic price distortions that crippled production and produced inflation. The real earnings of workers and peasants were hopelessly eroded by hyperin-flation. Productive inputs were misallocated, foreign exchange was wasted on artificially cheap imports, and the financial sector became a "black hole" of debt—forced to print money to paper over productive ineffi-ciencies throughout the economy. These distortions were not corrected soon enough and undermined the prospects for a socialist transition. The economy degenerated to a perverse state in which workers and peasants paid most dearly for the costs of foreign aggression and for the failed attempts to rally national capitalists to invest without political control of the state.

Stabilization became a condition of survival for the revolution. The Sandinistas made Herculean strides in damage control but, in the end, were forced to relinquish state power and to defend the revolution's gains from below. An uncertain hiatus emerged in which the UNO (National Opposition Unity coalition) was given its chance to demonstrate that submission to U.S. foreign policy interests could, perhaps, lure dollars to plug the trade gap. At the same time, however, the coalition's manifest organizational weakness and its lack of political cohesion raised serious questions regarding prospects for successful governance of Nicaragua's crippled economy. One could not rule out a reappearance of the Sandinistas—who had learned their lesson about the importance of maintaining contact with political bases among the poor. It remained to be seen whether Daniel Ortega might someday return to power and, if so, whether his return would be as conciliatory as the Jamaican Michael Manley, whose new economic program reflected the discipline of having been once thrown out of office by the forces of international capital.

Notes

I am deeply indebted to Michael Conroy, Gerardo Baltodano, and the dedicated team at the Banco Central de Nicaragua, Julio Revilla, Mike Samson, Richard Stahler-Sholk, Mario Arana, Bill Gibson, Veronica Frenkel, and Juan Abea, for their assistance with this chapter. The customary disclaimer for errors applies. I also wish to acknowledge the patience of Zoila Ramirez and the financial support of the Babson Board of Research, which made this work possible.

1. Lance Taylor et al., *Transition from Economic Chaos to Sustained Growth* (Stockholm: Swedish International Development Authority [SIDA], May 1989), report to the SPP (Secretaria de Planificación y Presupuesto) of the Government of Nicaragua. For a distorted summary presentation, see Mark Uhlig, "Nicaraguan Study Reports Economy in Drastic Decline," *New York Times*, June 26, 1989.

2. At the time, the Bolivian hyperinflation was the seventh highest in world history.

3. This most certainly satisfies Phillip Cagan's (1956) criteria for hyperinflation, which he defined as a "very rapid inflation . . . beginning in the month the rise in prices exceeds 50 percent and . . . ending in the month before the monthly rise drops below that amount and stays below for at least a year." P. Cagan, "The Monetary Dynamics of Hyperinflation," in Milton Friedman, ed., *Studies in the Quantity Theory of Money* (New York: Aldine, 1975), pp. 25–117.

4. Medal argued that Nicaragua's entry into the CACM gave rise to a relatively modern industrial sector that was superimposed upon the country's existing agro-export productive base in an entirely disarticulated fashion. See

José Luis Medal, *Nicaragua: Crisis, cambio social y politica economica* (Nicaragua: Siglo XX, 1988).

5. Bill Gibson, "A Structural Overview of the Nicaraguan Economy," in Rose Spalding, ed., *The Political Economy of Revolutionary Nicaragua* (Boston: George Allen & Unwin, 1987).

6. A number of authors (e.g., Bill Gibson, Lance Taylor, José Luis Medal) have suggested various periodizations of Sandinista economic policy. I have found most useful that set out by Richard Stahler-Sholk in "Stabilization, Destabilization, and the Popular Sector in Nicaragua, 1979–87," *Latin American Research Review* 25, no. 3, 1990.

7. For further analysis of the early stages of economic planning, see David Ruccio, "The State and Planning in Nicaragua," in Spalding, ed., *The Political Economy of Revolutionary Nicaragua.*

8. Even the United States was providing assistance until 1980.

9. For a discussion of inconsistencies among policy objectives, see Medal, *Nicaragua: Crisis, cambio social y politica economica;* and A. Benjamin, *Nicaragua: Dynamics of an Unfinished Revolution* (Walnut Publishing Co., 1989).

10. Early warnings regarding these inconsistencies were evident. For example, in 1980 an important sector of the bourgeoisie began its movement toward the contra forces when Alfonso Robelo and Violeta Chamorro resigned from the junta forcing its recomposition. Even the World Bank in its 1982 country report on Nicaragua recognized the overriding importance of the emerging standoff between the state and private sector: "Although the new leaders openly espouse a Marxist/Leninist ideology . . . the mixed economy that is emerging has left most productive and commercial enterprises in private hands, albeit under highly expanded Government influence. . . . As was to be expected, the private enterpreneurs reacted negatively to their loss of power. . . . The net result has been a deferral of much private productive investment and a sluggish economic recovery. . . . The Sandinista Government has given the private sector some economic incentives (cheap and, at times, abundant credit, low wages) but no longer-term assurances or political power."

11. John Weeks, "Private Enterpreneurship in a Revolutionary Context: A Case Study," *Journal of Development Planning* (UN), 1988.

12. World Bank, *The Challenge of Reconstruction* (Washington, D.C.: World Bank, 1981).

13. See Michael Conroy, ed., *Nicaragua: Profiles of the Revolutionary Public Sector* (Boulder, Colo.: Westview Press, 1987).

14. Ann Helwege, "Three Socialist Experiences in Latin America: A Comparative Economic Analysis," forthcoming in *Journal of Latin American Research.*

15. Helwege argued that corn and bean production increased 2–26 percent above prewar levels without a loss of export production. Rice, sorghum, and dry bean output also increased. Poultry production was four times 1975 levels.

16. See Stahler-Sholk, "Stabilization, Destabilization, and the Popular Sector in Nicaragua, 1979–87." UNAG representatives have argued that the early policy bias that frustrated the demands of the peasantry ultimately served to undermine Sandinista support by creating a social base open to the operation of the contras. As the rural terms of trade deteriorated beyond control, the state was finally forced to offer land to recapture support of the peasantry. On these debates see Marvin Ortega, "The Peasantry, Democracy and the Sandinista

Revolution: The Limits and Possibilities of Democracy in a Backward Rural Society," *Journal of Development Studies* (special issue on Rural Democracy), vol. 26, no. 4, July 1990. See also David Kaimowitz, "Nicaraguan Debates on Agrarian Structure and Their Implications for Agricultural Policy and the Rural Poor," *Journal of Peasant Studies* 14, no. 1, October 1986.

17. Basic consumption was up 23 percent, private nonbasic consumption up 34 percent, and government consumption up 30 percent over 1979 levels. Ruccio, "The State and Planning in Nicaragua."

18. Richard Stahler-Sholk, "Foreign Debt and Economic Stabilization Policies in Revolutionary Nicaragua," and E.V.K. FitzGerald, "An Evaluation of the Economic Costs to Nicaragua of US Aggression: 1980–1984," in Spalding, ed., *The Political Economy of Revolutionary Nicaragua*.

19. Note that the government deficit as share of GDP was 5 percent through 1979, then rose to 9 percent in 1980–1981, and finally 12 percent in 1982. In the early phases, this was not inconsistent with price stability, given the enormous volume of foreign credits. This situation changed abruptly as available sources of foreign funds were blocked.

20. For a theoretical discussion, see George Irvin, "Establishing the State as Centre of Accumulation," *Cambridge Journal of Economics*, no. 7, 1983.

21. The foreign exchange certificates, based on export sales, were issued in February 1982 as a form of dollar incentive that could be applied freely toward the direct purchase of imported goods. They proved ineffective in stimulating exports, however, as the government simply did not have enough foreign currency to assign to producers. See Roberto Pizarro, "The New Economic Policy: A Necessary Readjustment," in Spalding, ed., *The Political Economy of Revolutionary Nicaragua*.

22. Stahler-Sholk, "Stabilization, Destabilization, and the Popular Sector in Nicaragua, 1979–87."

23. For example, see Peter Utting, "The Peasant Question and Development Policy in Nicaragua," UNRISD (United Nations Research Institute for Social Development) discussion paper, no. 2, February 1988.

24. As Lance Taylor has pointed out, many of these investments were $100 million projects that were simply too big for a $2 billion economy.

25. Jeffery Sachs argued that countries with government deficits in excess of 12 percent of GDP typically undergo hyperinflation. This has been true for each of the recent Latin American experiences—Bolivia, Nicaragua, Peru, and Argentina.

26. The low inflation is peculiar given the enormous budget deficit and extensive recourse to monetary emission. The success of such "inflation tax" financing depends upon the public's willingness to hold the newly printed, but depreciating, money—a situation that one would not expect to persist for any long duration. However, real money balances as a share of GDP remained steady at 36 percent from 1984–1986, dropping to 28 percent in 1987, and only in 1988 did they plunge to 19 percent, triggering the hyperinflation. This willingness of the public to hold cordobas in the face of extensive inflation financing is an unusual feature of the Nicaraguan hyperinflation, accounting for its delayed eruption. See Taylor et al., *Transition from Economic Chaos to Sustained Growth*.

27. Laura Enriquez and Rose Spalding, "Banking Systems and Revolutionary Change: The Politics of Agricultural Credit in Nicaragua," in Spalding, ed., *The Political Economy of Revolutionary Nicaragua.*

28. Stahler-Sholk, "Stabilization, Destabilization, and the Popular Sector in Nicaragua, 1979–87."

29. For example, the *buhoneros* reaped substantial profits by selling subsidized Nicaraguan goods openly in Costa Rican markets and then purchasing products to be resold in Nicaragua at prices based on the black market dollar rate.

30. See Stahler-Sholk, "Stabilization, Destabilization, and the Popular Sector in Nicaragua, 1979–87," for a complete discussion of this process.

31. Carlos Vilas, "Nicaragua año cinco: Transformacion y tensiones en la economia," Managua, 1985 (working paper).

32. For a thorough analysis of the politics and composition of Nicaraguan trade relations, see Michael Conroy, "Patterns of Changing External Trade in Revolutionary Nicaragua: Voluntary and Involuntary Trade Diversification," in Spalding, ed. (trade shares data from p. 192). See also Conroy, "Economic Aggression as an Instrument of Low-Intensity Warfare," in Thomas Walker, ed., *Reagan Versus the Sandinistas* (Boulder, Colo.: Westview Press, 1987).

33. Note that these consisted predominantly of tied suppliers credits.

34. Lance Taylor has ruled out supply-side and inertial causes as key determinants of the 1988 hyperinflation, noting that the impact of wages and lagged prices was not significant. Price increases outpaced money growth but did exhibit a significant relation to the black market exchange rate.

35. Medal, *Nicaragua: Crisis, cambio social y politica economica.*

36. See E.V.K. FitzGerald, "La situación economica en Nicaragua al finales de 1987," in *El debate sobre la reforma economica* (Managua: CIERA, 1988).

37. Note the political problems associated with the informal sector—that sector was attacked as the cause of the inflation when it was merely responding to the incentives offered by misaligned macropolicy. Curiously, many of its ranks also constituted the political base of support for the Sandinistas.

38. John Miller and Joseph Ricciardi, "Nicaragua's Other War," in *Dollars and Sense*, January/February 1989. See also Michael Conroy, "Nicaragua: Structure, Dynamics, and Conditions of the Economy in 1988," conference paper, 7th Central American Congress on Sociology, Guatemala, October 1988.

39. This included large suspected holdings of counterfeit money, most likely supplied by U.S. intelligence, that was accumulated by the contras to facilitate penetration and mobility into remote rural border zones within Nicaragua.

40. Carlos Vilas, interview with Alexander Cockburn, Z *Magazine*, January 1989.

41. See Taylor et al., *Transition from Economic Chaos to Sustained Growth.* It should be noted, however, as Bill Gibson has indicated, that the nonstructural character of the Nicaraguan hyperinflation improved the chances for a more rapid cure, as occurred in the case of the Bolivian hyperinflation, which was stopped within a matter of weeks.

42. The annual 1988 estimate from the Ministry of Planning and Budget (SPP), reported in *Barricada*, July 30, 1989. Estimates vary widely. Lance Taylor computed the 1988 annual inflation at 11,500 percent.

43. "Petrocordobas" refers to state revenues generated by selling Cuban and Soviet oil shipments, which are either donated or offered on easy credit terms,

on domestic markets at near world market price equivalents. These revenues have played an important role in converting oil aid into a deficit reduction mechanism to assist in achieving fiscal balance.

44. See E.V.K. FitzGerald, "State and Economy in Nicaragua," *IDS Bulletin* (Institute of Development Studies, Sussex), 19, no. 3, 1989.

THIRTEEN

Human Rights

MICHAEL LINFIELD

During times of war, all countries restrict the civil rights and civil liberties of their citizens. International human rights treaties accept the fact that certain restrictions are legitimate during emergencies. Although countries must not resort to murder, torture, or causing disappearances, modern international law permits censorship of the press, imposition of restrictions on speech and assembly, and curtailment of normal due process rights when the security of the nation is at stake. From the standpoint of a country at war, Nicaragua's human rights record under the Sandinistas was in full compliance with the standards imposed by international human rights treaties. Its record on civil rights and civil liberties compared favorably with that of many Western European nations and even that of the United States in time of war.

Fundamental Versus Secondary Human Rights

In analyzing a country's wartime human rights record, it is necessary to divide human rights into two categories: fundamental and secondary. Fundamental human rights are those rights that are basic to the preservation of life itself. Without these rights, all other rights are meaningless. Fundamental human rights include the right to life, freedom from torture, freedom from inhumane treatment, and the right to the basic economic necessities—food, shelter, and clothing. Without these fundamental rights, life itself is jeopardized. Murder, torture, rape, and disappearances can never be justified and must be condemned against an absolute standard. These rights can never be suspended or derogated. No state of war, no threat to the nation, can ever excuse violations of these rights.

Parts of this chapter first appeared in a different form in Michael Linfield, *Freedom Under Fire: U.S. Civil Liberties in Times of War.* Used by permission of South End Press, Institute for Social and Cultural Change, 116 St. Botolph St., Boston, MA 02115.

Secondary human rights are all other rights, including most of what we term civil liberties.[1] Included among the secondary rights are freedom of speech, religion, and assembly; freedom of travel; basic due process; the right to organize collectively; and the right to participate in government.

It is necessary to remember this distinction between fundamental and secondary human rights when judging the human rights situation of a country at war. Although fundamental human rights are never derogable, secondary human rights can, are, and (some would argue) should be suspended when a country is at war. Under international law (see Table 13.1), a country may suspend all but the most fundamental human rights and civil liberty guarantees in times of war or public emergency, as long as the restrictions are proportionate to the danger facing the country.[2]

Fundamental Human Rights in Nicaragua

Although the Reagan administration consistently charged Nicaragua with wholesale human rights abuses, virtually all human rights organizations agree that the Sandinista government did not violate fundamental human rights.[3] After Somoza's overthrow, there were no verified accounts of a governmental policy of murder, torture, or disappearances in Nicaragua.[4] In fact, if we include under fundamental human rights a person's right to the necessities of life—food, shelter, health care—then the Sandinista record was better than that of almost any other Latin American or Third World country.

Although there was no *policy* of human rights abuses by the government, there were isolated *incidents* of human rights infractions. The most serious incident of this kind occurred on December 22, 1981, in Leimus, in the Atlantic Coast region. Between fourteen and seventeen civilians were killed by Sandinista soldiers.[5] The government claimed that the soldiers involved in the massacre were tried, sentenced, and imprisoned; however, information on the prosecutions has never been made public.[6] This is the only case of the Sandinista military murdering civilians that was ever documented by the OAS Inter-American Commission on Human Rights,[7] and Amnesty International stated that "no cases similar to that of Leimus have come to [Amnesty's] attention."[8]

Although the Reagan administration made continual allegations that the Nicaraguan government used torture against political prisoners, these allegations of abuse were either not credible or not verified.[9] Nonetheless, there was evidence of a policy of harsh interrogation techniques—what was commonly known throughout the United States until the mid-1960s as the "third degree." These practices included threatening the accused with indefinite detention or threatening the accused that his

Table 13.1   Derogations of Rights Under International Treaties

European Convention on Human Rights	International Covenant on Civil and Political Rights	American Convention on Human Rights
When a Nation Can Curtail Human Rights		
In time of war or public emergency that threatens life of nation	In time of war, public danger, or other emergency that threatens the independence or security of nation	In time of war, public danger, or other emergency that threatens the independence or security of nation
To extent strictly required by the exigencies	To extent and for period of time strictly required by exigencies	To extent strictly required by the emergency
Provided it is not inconsistent with other international obligations. In time of public emergency that threatens life of nation, if emergency is officially proclaimed	Provided it is not inconsistent with other international obligations and does not involve discrimination on grounds of race, color, sex, language, or social origin	Provided it is not inconsistent with other international obligations and does not involve discrimination on grounds of race, color, sex, language, or social origin
Rights That Can Never Be Suspended		
Right to life Humane treatment No slavery No ex post facto law	Right to life Humane treatment No slavery No ex post facto law	Right to life Humane treatment No slavery No ex post facto law
	Juridical personhood Freedom of thought, conscience, religion No imprisonment for non-fulfillment of contract	Juridical personhood Freedom of conscience and religion
		Rights of family Right to a name Rights of a child Right to nationality Participation in government

family members would be arrested if he did not cooperate with his interrogators.[10] However, torture (as practiced, for instance, by the French during the Algerian War) or breaking the bones of suspected terrorists (as practiced by Israel in response to the Intifada[11]) was never official Sandinista policy.

One of the centerpieces of the Reagan campaign against the Sandinistas was the accusation of Sandinista "genocide" against the Mískito Indians.

In February 1982, U.S. Secretary of State Alexander Haig exhibited a photograph showing what he claimed were Miskito bodies being burned after a "massacre" by the Sandinista government and accused the Nicaraguan government of "atrocious genocidal actions." It was later verified that the photograph had been taken four years earlier and showed Red Cross workers burning the bodies of victims massacred by Somoza during the uprising leading to the 1979 revolution.[12]

Although widely reported in the U.S. press at the time, stories of "genocide" and "massacres" were pure fabrications. The OAS Inter-American Commission on Human Rights could not substantiate the "loss of life during the relocation, with which the government had been initially accused."[13] Americas Watch reported "no evidence of widespread 'disappearances.' Miskitos interviewed at the settlements also denied any killings by the Sandinista forces."[14]

The facts of the relocation were as follows: In early January and February 1982, the government evacuated around thirty-five villages and relocated approximately 8,000 Miskito Indians from their homes. The OAS Inter-American Commission on Human Rights and Americas Watch have both said that the decision to relocate the Miskitos was justified due to the war conditions in the area at the time.[15] Nonetheless, the manner in which the relocation was carried out can be criticized, since the Miskitos were not involved in the decision to relocate and were given little, if any, prior notice of the relocation.

Other forced evacuations and resettlements of Miskito Indians from war zones and border areas also occurred. In one such evacuation in November 1982, 6,000 Miskito and Sumo Indians were evacuated from an area on the Honduran border to a resettlement camp in Wiwili, Jinotega. Other smaller evacuations have involved hundreds or thousands of people.

Unlike relocations and resettlement camps in many other countries—and unlike the U.S. government's internment of Japanese-Americans in camps during World War II—the Miskito Indians were not forced to live in the resettlement camps. Although not allowed to return to the border areas, the Miskitos could leave the resettlement camps at will and could travel or settle in any part of the country.[16] In the second half of the 1980s, as part of an autonomy program passed by the National Assembly, Miskito Indians were "repatriated" to areas of the Atlantic Coast from which they had previously been evacuated.

Freedom of Speech and of the Press

Like the First Amendment to the U.S. Constitution, Nicaragua's 1987 constitution guarantees its citizens freedom of speech and of the press. Unlike the U.S. Constitution, however, the Nicaraguan constitution states that these guarantees can be suspended "in case of war or when demanded by the security of the nation, economic conditions or a national catastrophe."[17]

Although Nicaraguans were living in a perpetual state of emergency virtually since the triumph of the revolution and the constitutional guarantees of freedom of speech and press were suspended from 1982 through 1987, Nicaragua had one of the freest presses in Central America, and its level of censorship under the Sandinistas was no greater than that imposed by the United States when it has been at war.[18]

La Prensa

La Prensa (see also Chapter 17) is the paper of the Chamorro family—one of the wealthiest and most politically influential families in Nicaragua. Violeta de Chamorro is the fifth Chamorro to serve as president of Nicaragua during the past century. When Pedro Joaquín Chamorro was assassinated by Somoza in 1978, the name *La Prensa* became associated with the struggle against tyranny. But *La Prensa* was more akin to the *National Enquirer* than to the *New York Times.* It specialized in sensationalism—at times reporting stories about a woman giving birth to chickens or about a plaster statue of the Virgin Mary sweating like a person in apparent disapproval of the Sandinista revolution.[19]

Although the U.S. government touted *La Prensa* as an independent newspaper, it was anything but. Six months after the triumph of the revolution, President Carter signed a top-secret finding that authorized the CIA to provide funds to *La Prensa.*[20] Violeta de Chamorro, owner of the newspaper, assured me in 1987 that *La Prensa* had "never received any money from the United States, not anything. We are an independent paper and are not subsidized by anyone."[21] But the following year, the *New York Times* reported that *La Prensa* had been receiving approximately $100,000 per year in U.S. governmental support.[22]

As *La Prensa* became more and more anti-Sandinista during the early 1980s, it began to publish "articles aimed at bringing down the government by any means possible."[23] Stories were published about the shortages of various basic goods—stories that caused panic buying and thus created shortages that otherwise might not have existed.

Afraid that the CIA was repeating the destabilization efforts that had been so successful in Chile—where the CIA had secretly funded the paper *El Mercurio* to create panic and hysteria as a prelude to the coup that toppled the Socialist government of President Salvador Allende[24]—the Sandinistas began to impose restrictions on *La Prensa.* Between 1979 and 1982, *La Prensa* was closed on five separate occasions for one or two days at a time for reporting news deemed damaging to national security.[25]

In 1982, as the death toll from the contra war increased, the Sandinista government declared a formal State of Emergency and imposed censorship on *La Prensa*. Many of the censored items concerned the war effort. But in addition, articles about economic shortages (real or imagined), military conscription, and seemingly innocuous digs at the government were often forbidden. In one such incident, *La Prensa* suggested that a suitable wedding gift from Nicaragua to Prince Charles and Lady Diana Spencer would be the complete works of Carlos Fonseca, the hero of the Sandinista revolution, since the books would be sure to put the newlyweds to sleep at night. This joke resulted in a suspension of the paper. Despite the restrictions, *La Prensa* was allowed to photocopy censored articles for distribution to foreign journalists and embassies in Managua. Copies of all censored articles were posted on the wall in front of the paper's building for any passerby to read.[26]

A censorship minuet between the government and *La Prensa* continued until 1986; *La Prensa* tried to print as much as possible and simultaneously wanted to provoke the censors in order to prove that freedom of the press was a Sandinista myth; the government, concerned about internal morale and an ever-escalating war, felt the need to censor anything considered sensitive, yet at the same time wished to avoid closing the paper, so the government could point to the existence of *La Prensa* as proof that freedom of the press existed in postrevolutionary Nicaragua.

For six years, the paper had carefully avoided any direct endorsement of the contras. Then, on April 3, 1986, the day before the U.S. Congress was to vote on a $100 million aid package to the contras, *La Prensa* committed journalistic suicide. On that date, Jaime Chamorro, editor of *La Prensa*, wrote an article for the *Washington Post* urging that the $100 million funding for the contras be approved—an article that in most circumstances would be considered treason. However, the House of Representatives voted down the $100 million aid package, and nothing was done to *La Prensa*. Three months later the House reconsidered the contra aid issue and voted to increase funding for the contras. The day after the House approved the appropriation, the Nicaraguan government closed *La Prensa*, claiming that the closing of the paper was in direct response to the vote in Washington.

Although *La Prensa* was closed indefinitely on July 27, 1986, the government made no attempt to take over the building or confiscate the presses of the paper. Vice President Ramírez stated that the paper could reopen as soon as it disassociated itself from the contras. President Ortega made a similar offer on August 2, 1986, in Chicago.[27]

The paper remained closed throughout 1986, with neither side budging from its previous position. With the signing of the Arias peace plan in Esquipulas on August 7, 1987, the government promised to allow the paper to reopen. On September 21, 1987, President Ortega announced a lifting of the press restrictions that had been in effect for the previous five years, and on October 1, 1987, La Prensa reopened with the agreement that there would be no further press censorship of the paper. Three months later, Violeta de Chamorro affirmed that there had been no attempt by the Sandinistas to censor the paper, nor had La Prensa engaged in any self-censorship since its reopening.[28] Within the next year, however, censorship was reimposed from time to time, although on a smaller scale than before, and the paper was closed on a few sporadic occasions. With an end to the contra war, and the signing of the Central American peace accords in Tela, Honduras, La Prensa was able to print once again without restrictions.

Journals

Besides La Prensa, only one other publication—Iglesia, a monthly published by the Catholic church—was banned. On October 12, 1985, after the first edition of Iglesia was printed but before it could be distributed, it was seized by the government. The edition was never publicly distributed, and no other edition of the paper was ever printed.

Smaller publications were printed and distributed without censorship. Each political party published its own weekly or monthly magazine without censorship. Both of the human rights organizations in Nicaragua published their own monthly reports uncensored. Newspapers, magazines, and books entering the country were not censored. Several U.S. papers, including the New York Times and the Miami Herald, as well as Time and Newsweek, were available. Foreign books were scarce, but this seems to have been due to the lack of hard currency in the Nicaraguan economy. There was no censorship of domestic or foreign books.[29]

In late July 1987, Nicaragua held its first annual international book fair. Thousands of books, published in more than forty countries, were on display and were quickly bought by Managuans. The United States was represented at the book fair by two booths: one for independent presses and an official State Department booth. At the official U.S. booth, embassy personnel handed out free copies of two anti-Sandinista books to any Nicaraguan who wanted them.[30] The books, in Spanish, were stamped "Donated by the USIS, American Embassy, Managua, Nicaragua." Hundreds of Managuans queued up to get the free books. The next morning, a four-column front-page photo in Barricada, the official Sandinista daily, showed President Daniel Ortega and Vice President Sergio Ramírez standing in front of the American eagle, viewing the books in the U.S. booth.[31]

Radio and Television

Although La Prensa was the focus of U.S. concern regarding freedom of expression, in Nicaragua as in most of the Third World, the press was not the dominant source of news for the majority of the citizens. Most people received their news from radio and TV, not from the papers. In Nicaragua, approximately half the radio stations are privately owned. In 1984, the conservative organization Freedom House found that the "radio stations are private and diverse."[32] Of the approximately thirty news programs on these stations, only one was state run. When the State of Emergency was declared in 1982, the government closed twenty-two radio news programs. After that time, there was no prior censorship of the radio, although a station was liable to postbroadcast sanctions if it overstepped the bounds of "acceptable reporting." Depending on whom one talked to, this led either to relatively free reporting or to self-censorship. Both TV stations in Nicaragua during the first decade were government owned. However, because of the small size of the country, citizens in most areas of Nicaragua could receive both television and radio broadcasts from Costa Rica, Honduras, and El Salvador.[33] The government made no attempt to jam U.S./CIA-sponsored broadcasts from these countries. In contrast to the relative freedom given most radio stations, the Catholic radio station, Radio Católica, was shut down on January 1, 1986, ostensibly for refusing to broadcast the New Year's message of President Daniel Ortega.[34] With the Esquipulas peace accords and the lifting of press censorship by the government, Radio Católica reopened uncensored on October 2, 1987. The majority of the news programs closed in 1982 were allowed to resume broadcasting in January 1988.

Media Censorship in Other Countries

Sandinista censorship of the media is not surprising, given that Nicaragua was at war practically from the beginning of the revolution. All nations—even democratic ones—censor their press when at war. In comparison with other nations—including the United States, Britain, or Israel—censorship under the Sandinistas was moderate. During the American Revolution, printers were prevented, on pain of imprisonment, from printing any Loyalist statements. Pro-Confederate papers were closed down during the Civil War. During World War I, the U.S. government established its first official censorship board, known as the Committee for Public Information. Every piece of war-related news had to be cleared before publication. At the beginning of World War II, the government closed down virtually the entire pro-Nazi press. Strict censorship guidelines were in force for the mainstream press: Not only was news about the war censored, but so was any news that might hurt home-front morale. Although there was no official censorship during the Vietnam War, the U.S. government embarked on a campaign to muzzle the opposition press: Editors were jailed, presses bombed, editorial boards infiltrated, and businesses pressured to stop advertising in the underground papers.[35]

Nor is wartime censorship confined to Nicaragua or the United States. In 1988, the British government adopted a policy making it illegal for the British media to interview members of the Irish Republican Army (IRA)[36]—a step the likes of which Nicaragua never took with *La Prensa*, which often interviewed contra leaders. Israel, in the latter half of the 1980s, was at least as restrictive. More than forty Palestinian journalists were detained during the first eighteen months of the Intifada, which began in December 1987.[37] All written material—whether imported, distributed, or in a private person's possession in the occupied territories—was subject to military inspection. All articles in Arabic-language papers had to be submitted to censors prior to publication. Numerous Arabic papers were prohibited from printing for varying lengths of time for violating censorship restrictions.[38] At least one Jewish newspaper was banned; its editors were adopted as prisoners of conscience by Amnesty International in April 1989 after being jailed by the Israeli government.[39] Palestinian (but not Jewish) residents of the Gaza Strip were forbidden to own or use "any kind of facsimile instrument for any purpose whatsoever."[40] In 1989, a noted Israeli radio broadcaster was sentenced to six months imprisonment for meeting with Yasser Arafat; a 1986 law made it illegal for any Israeli citizen to meet with members of the Palestine Liberation Organization (PLO).[41]

Public Debate

Nicaragua never required either its citizens or its public employees to take a loyalty oath. This is in contrast to U.S. wartime experience: During the American Revolution, colonists were required to swear allegiance to the revolutionary cause; those who refused were stripped of their property and legal rights. In the 1950s, a federal loyalty oath was established; more than 20,000,000 Americans were screened for "subversion" by Loyalty Boards during the Korean War era.

Despite a State of Emergency in effect for almost the entire first ten years, Nicaraguans discussed politics openly; criticizing the government seemed to be a national pastime. Observers of the 1984 elections noted wide-ranging debate, fostered by the availability of free and uncensored radio and TV air time for all opposition candidates. All parties participating in the November 4, 1984, elections "were free to be as strident as they chose in attacking the Sandinista Party and its leaders, and frequently exercised this right on television and radio time provided to them without cost [by the government]."[42] The 1990 elections were equally open and fair. Throughout the war, visitors to Managua were instantly confronted with numerous billboards for all political parties represented in the assembly, as well as graffiti and political slogans for all political persuasions on virtually every wall. On two trips to Nicaragua sponsored by the Harvard Law School Human Rights Program, I observed no inhibitions on citizens openly discussing, arguing, and criticizing, whether alone, or in the presence of soldiers, police, or government officials.[43]

Freedom of Travel

During the first decade after the revolutionary triumph, Nicaraguans were not required to carry identity cards or internal passports, nor were they normally stopped and required to identify themselves on the streets. Even at the height of the war, there was no curfew or travel restrictions, except in areas of actual armed conflict.

Denial of Passports

Despite the war, Nicaraguans could enter and leave the country at will. Exit visas were required to leave the country, but were granted pro forma. The only requirement was that the citizen did not owe back taxes and was not subject to be called up for the military draft. There was much travel (at least of upper-class Nicaraguans) to and from the United States, the country arming and supporting the contras.

This is in marked contrast with U.S. wartime policy. Throughout the Korean War era in the early 1950s, the U.S. government denied passports to any U.S. citizen whose travel would be "prejudicial to the interests of the United States." Among those denied passports were Howard Fast, Edward G. Robinson, Ring Lardner, Jr., Arthur Miller, and Carl Foreman. Linus Pauling was denied a passport for two-and-a-half years. Only after he won the Nobel Prize did the State Department finally issue him a passport; continued denial of his right of travel had become too great an embarrassment to the U.S. government.[44] At least one member of Congress, Rep. Leo Isaacson, was denied a passport when he wanted to attend a conference being held in Paris to support the Greek partisans.[45] A Federal Appeals Court judge was deprived of his passport and had to sue to get it back.[46] The government even denied a passport to a sitting U.S. Supreme Court justice, William O. Douglas, who wished to attend a conference in China.[47]

Denial of Entry Visas

Foreigners wishing to visit Nicaragua were not denied visas for political reasons. Even during the height of the contra war, Americans were free to enter Nicaragua at any time without a visa. Over 150,000 U.S. citizens entered Nicaragua during the first decade. Foreign visitors and press were everywhere; they traveled and reported without censorship or restrictions. U.S. politicians routinely visited Managua to meet with opposition leaders. They too entered without visas or restrictions. A pilgrimage to visit the editors of *La Prensa* was de rigueur for any conservative American politician visiting the region. For example, Jeane Kirkpatrick, former U.S. ambassador to the United Nations and one of the most vocal anti-Sandinista members of the Reagan administration, visited Nicaragua on October 11, 1987. Kirkpatrick was allowed to address leaders of the Sandinista opposition at the U.S. embassy in Managua and, to the applause of her audience, praised the contras.[48]

In contrast, during both war and peace, the United States has restricted the right of foreigners to enter the United States to visit or speak. It would have been unthinkable to allow Axis politicians to enter the United States during World War II to speak with sympathetic German-, Japanese-, or Italian-Americans. During the 1950s, progressives and socialists were routinely denied visas to visit or speak in the United States. Among the people excluded from the United States during the Korean War era were Maurice Chevalier, Graham Greene, Alberto Moravia, Czeslaw Milosz, Pablo Picasso, and the dean of Canterbury.[49] This policy of exclusion on ideological grounds continued. During the 1970s and 1980s, literary figures such as Graham Greene, Gabriel García Márquez, Pablo Neruda, Julio Cortazar, Dario Fo, and Simone de Beauvoir were denied visas to tour or visit the United States.

Although the Sandinistas allowed Reagan administration officials to enter Nicaragua to speak, the United States refused visas to various Sandinista officials. Both Tomás Borge, minister of the interior, and Ernesto Cardenal, minister of culture, were denied visas to visit the United States—ostensibly on "security" grounds.[50] Even Nicaraguan social scientists invited to present papers at professional conferences in the United States were routinely denied visas under both the Reagan and the Bush administrations.

Due Process

On July 19, 1979, a popular revolution, under the leadership of the Sandinista National Liberation Front (FSLN), established a new government in Nicaragua, ending fifty years of corrupt, brutal, and tyrannical rule by the Somoza dynasty. The last years of the revolution were particularly disastrous for the Nicaraguan people. From 1977 to 1979, as the FSLN gained more and more support, Somoza's troops increasingly resorted to murder, disappearances, mutilations, and torture against the civilian population.[51] Fifty thousand Nicaraguans were killed by Somoza's troops during the civil war leading up to the Sandinista victory on July 19.[52]

Two days after Somoza fled the country, the FSLN declared victory and attempted to establish civilian rule over what was left of the country and economy.[53] Despite the many years of dictatorship and the brutality of Somoza's National Guard, the new government did not accede to popular sentiment and begin mass executions of the old guard. Rather, one of the first actions taken by the new ruling junta was to abolish the death penalty.[54] Some killings of national guardsmen by civilians did take place, but the new government put a stop to such killings as soon as order was restored throughout the country and arrested many of its own supporters who were suspected of the killings.[55]

With public sentiment running strongly against the Somocistas, the new government established special tribunals for the speedy trials of former national guardsmen. Trials were public; defendants were allowed counsel. Within a few weeks, 7,000–8,000 former national guardsmen were arrested. Slightly over 6,000 were tried by the special tribunals, 1,760 were acquitted, and 4,331 received prison sentences. Prison sentences ranged up to thirty years, the longest possible sentence under postrevolutionary Nicaraguan law. No one was sentenced to death. By comparison, at the end of World War II, the French government charged 4,598 people with espionage or treason and 756 individuals were condemned to death.[56]

The procedures used by the special tribunals were criticized by many human rights organizations for relaxing the standard of proof necessary for convictions, for having lay judges, and for not providing enough time for the accused to mount an adequate defense.[57] Recognizing that abuses had occurred, the government instructed the newly created government-funded human rights organization, the National Commission for the Promotion and Protection of Human Rights (CNPPDH), to review cases tried before the special tribunals and to recommend pardons or reductions of sentences in appropriate cases.[58]

The Popular Anti-Somocista Tribunals

In 1983, as the U.S.-funded counterrevolutionary war against Nicaragua intensified, the government established special tribunals to try suspected contras. The tribunals were known as the People's Anti-Somocista Tribunals (TPAs). Between June 1983 and May 1986, 1,215 people were tried before the TPAs, and 846 were convicted. Probably the most famous of the defendants was Eugene Hasenfus, a U.S. mercenary shot down over Nicaragua on October 5, 1986. He was tried and given the maximum possible sentence, thirty years. Shortly thereafter, Hasenfus was pardoned and released by the government.

Numerous problems of due process have been noted in regard to the TPAs. A TPA conviction rate of 70–88 percent has caused some human rights organizations to express concern.[59] (But compare this with a 79.9 percent conviction rate for criminal offenses in the U.S. District Courts in 1979 and a 78.2 percent conviction rate in 1980.[60]) The fact that the judges were appointed by the executive branch and often returned to the executive after serving their term of office on the TPA put the executive in the position of prosecutor, judge, and jury, making a fair trial all the more difficult. Although each accused was guaranteed the right to a public defender at no cost to himself, the public defenders often did little good. In Nicaragua, the public defenders received no pay for representing indigent clients, they were overworked, and many did not have their heart in defending suspected contras.

The government had repeatedly stated that the TPAs were temporary measures and would be abolished as soon as aggression against the country ended.[61] On January 19, 1988, as a result of the peace discussions of Esquipulas III, President Daniel Ortega lifted the State of Emergency and abolished the TPAs.[62]

Nicaragua's use of special tribunals and lax due process procedures was similar to that adopted by Britain, Israel, or the United States during wartime. Faced with a civil war in Northern Ireland, the British government in the 1970s and 1980s suspended numerous due process guarantees. The Prevention of Terrorism Act, passed in 1973, permitted imprisonment without trial and the denial of the right to trial by jury for suspected terrorists. The temporary provisions of the act were made permanent by the Thatcher government in 1988.[63] Suspected IRA members were tried by special nonjury tribunals, known as Diplock courts. These courts later bypassed the normal due process guarantees provided other criminal defendants in the British system. In 1988, the Thatcher government proposed denying suspects the right to remain silent: Under the government's proposal, silence would be considered a sign of guilt.[64] Prime Minister Margaret Thatcher defended these actions, stating, "To beat off your enemies in a war you have to suspend some of your civil liberties for a time."[65]

Similarly, more than 5,000 Palestinians were detained without charges by the Israeli government during the first eighteen months of the Intafada. Those arrested were not allowed to meet with their lawyer until after a confession was signed. Most of the detainees were subject to six-month terms of imprisonment; many were detained repeatedly. Palestinians convicted by military court had no right to appeal, and the courts refused to hear habeas corpus petitions. Numerous Palestinians were deported.[66]

The United States also resorted to just such violations of due process when confronted by civil unrest. The U.S. version of Nicaragua's TPAs or Britain's Diplock courts was known as the Committees of Safety. During the Revolutionary War, these people's tribunals tried colonists suspected of supporting the king. Loyalists were held in prison without charges. Their property was confiscated and given to revolutionary soldiers. Hundreds of Loyalists were banished; many fled from the colonies to

Canada, becoming the first boat people in the New World. During the Civil War, President Abraham Lincoln suspended the right to habeas corpus. When Supreme Court Justice Roger Taney ruled Lincoln's actions unconstitutional, Lincoln simply ignored the Court. Between 10,000 and 30,000 civilians were arrested, tried, and imprisoned by military courts during the Civil War. Shortly after World War I, Attorney General A. Mitchell Palmer, and his assistant, J. Edgar Hoover, illegally arrested more than 4,000 American residents in what came to be known as the Palmer Raids; over 1,000 were deported without due process or trial. During World War II, 110,000 Japanese-Americans, the majority of whom were American citizens, were incarcerated in internment camps for the duration of the war. And during the Korean War, thousands of people were denied even the most minimal due process protections when they were "tried" before the House Un-American Activities Committee (HUAC) and other congressional committees.

The Regular Judicial System

Nicaragua under the Sandinistas, for the first time in the twentieth century, had an independent and honest judicial system. In 1987, of the seven Supreme Court justices, three were affiliated with the Sandinista party, and three with opposition parties. Since all justices were appointed by the National Assembly from lists submitted by President Ortega,[67] this would be akin to President Reagan or Bush nominating Democrats to half the open seats on the U.S. Supreme Court.

The main problem faced by the judiciary was lack of funding. At the height of the contra war, fully fifty percent of the national budget went for defense. In 1988, the budget for Nicaragua's entire judicial system—including all salaries, equipment, and supplies—was 7.3 billion cordobas. At the official rate of exchange, this equaled just $365,000.

Prisoners of Conscience

In the first decade of the revolution, Amnesty International adopted approximately one dozen prisoners of conscience—people arrested for the nonviolent expression of their beliefs—in Nicaragua. Eight of the prisoners of conscience were arrested in 1981: Four were Communists who were arrested for inciting strikes and saying that the government was "diverting the revolutionary process to a capitalist line." The other four were business leaders who were arrested for accusing the government of creating economic disaster by following "a Marxist-Leninist adventure." All eight were released within five months of their arrest. This compares with forty U.S. prisoners of conscience adopted by Amnesty International during the Vietnam War. The longest sentence actually served by a U.S. prisoner of conscience was twelve years.

Political Prisoners

Political prisoners in Nicaragua included former national guardsmen and contras. In general, they were not prisoners of conscience. Most were convicted of violent counterrevolutionary acts: murder, torture, the bombing of bridges, the kidnapping of health workers, and so forth. According to the International Red Cross, at the end of February 1988, there were 3,500 political prisoners in Nicaragua, mostly former national guardsmen and contras.[68] When analyzing these figures, it should be remembered that there was no bloodbath after the Sandinista victory in 1979. Former Somoza national guardsmen were not executed but were instead arrested, tried, and imprisoned. Thus, one of the reasons the number of political prisoners was initially high is precisely because the Nicaraguan government did *not* violate fundamental human rights during their revolution.

As the war wound down, the Nicaraguan government slowly began releasing political prisoners. On March 17, 1989, it released virtually all of the former members of Somoza's National Guard who had been imprisoned since the revolution. The Sandinista government granted unconditional liberty to 1,894 former guardsmen. Thirty-nine former national guardsmen who had been convicted of particularly "atrocious" crimes remained imprisoned.[69] As part of the Esquipulas peace accords, the Nicaraguan government agreed to an unconditional amnesty for the approximately 1,600 people accused of contra activity, an amnesty that was to be implemented as soon as a permanent cease-fire was established.[70] Just prior to the 1990 elections, in fulfillment of a campaign promise, President Ortega released all remaining political prisoners.

Conclusion

As we have seen (Table 13.1), according to international human rights treaties, only the most fundamental human rights are inviolable. The right to life, the right to humane treatment, and the prohibitions against slavery and ex post facto laws are the only rights recognized by all three major human rights treaties as nonderogable. Virtually all other rights—freedom of speech and assembly, freedom to travel, even the right to due process—can be suspended if the nation's independence or security is threatened. All human rights organizations and treaties agree, however, that violations of the secondary human rights and civil liberties are acceptable only "to the extent strictly required by the emergency."

Nicaragua's actions from 1979 through 1989 were consistent with its obligations under international human rights treaties. The basic non-derogable rights were respected. The Nicaraguan government did not create or tolerate death squads, establish political dungeons, or "disappear" its opponents. As the Nicaraguan ambassador to the United Nations stated shortly after the tenth anniversary of the revolution: "No reason of state—no matter how compelling—could justify the physical or moral degradation of a human being, nor . . . disrespect toward his dignity and integrity."[71] Nonetheless, for most of the time the Sandinistas were in power, various civil liberties in Nicaragua were restricted. The media were censored, special tribunals were established to try suspected contras, political opponents were sometimes harassed, and the right to travel was occasionally curtailed.

Without minimizing the violations that have occurred, it is important to note that the level of civil liberties in Nicaragua under the Sandinistas was at least as good as that maintained in the United States, in England, or in Israel when those nations were at war. Many human rights activists, myself included, would argue that many of the restrictions imposed by the Sandinistas were unnecessary and counterproductive. Nonetheless, given the devastation and havoc wreaked by the U.S.-supported contra war, the Sandinistas showed a remarkable openness, tolerance, and respect for human rights and civil liberties during their almost eleven years in power.

Notes

1. The term *secondary rights* should not be taken to mean that these rights are unimportant, only that they are not fundamental to life itself.

2. The European Convention on Human Rights states that "In times of war or other public emergency [that] threaten[s] the life of the nation," the nation "may take measures derogating from its obligations under this Convention to the extent strictly required by the exigencies of the situation" (Art. 15). Under the International Covenant on Civil and Political Rights, a country may derogate most human rights guarantees "in time of public emergency . . . [and] to the extent strictly required by the exigencies of the situation." The American Convention on Human Rights (the San José Pact), allows for derogations from human rights treaties "in time of war, public danger, or other emergency that threatens the independence or security of a State Party," but only "to the extent and for the period of time strictly required by the exigencies of the situation, provided that such measures are not inconsistent with its other obligations under international law and do not involve discrimination on the ground of race, color, sex, language, religion, or social origin" (Art. 27[1]).

3. The U.S. State Department "Reports on Nicaragua" contend that Nicaragua has a policy of blatant disregard for fundamental human rights. Human rights organizations have termed these reports "deceptive," "misleading," "irresponsible," and employing "misrepresentations" and "pervasive" misuse of data (*Human Rights in Nicaragua: Reagan, Rhetoric and Reality*, An Americas Watch Report, New York, July 1985, pp. 3, 21, 22, 26, 27). For example, the Reagan administration stated unequivocally that "in the American continent, there is no regime more barbaric and bloody, no regime that violates human rights in

a manner more constant and permanent, than the Sandinista regime" (*The Challenge to Democracy in Central America*, a joint U.S. State Department–Defense Department publication, 1986, p. 28). Americas Watch retorted, "this is nonsense" (*Human Rights in Nicaragua*, p. 140). A high-level official in the American embassy in Managua admitted to me that the State Department's characterization of the Sandinista regime was clearly false.

4. In 1981, Amnesty International stated that it had "received no convincing accounts alleging systematic ill-treatment or torture of prisoners under the [Sandinista] government" (*Amnesty International Report: 1981*, Amnesty International, London, 1982, p. 175). In 1982, Americas Watch stated that "the Nicaraguan Government does not engage in a practice of torturing, murdering or abducting its citizens" (*Human Rights in Nicaragua: November 1982 Update*, An Americas Watch Report, New York, 1982, p. 6), and in 1987, the organization reaffirmed that "the government of Nicaragua do[es] not have a policy of violating the laws of war with regard to the treatment of civilians" (*Human Rights in Nicaragua: 1986*, An Americas Watch Report, New York, April 1984, p. 13).

5. *Amnesty International Report: 1984*, Amnesty International, London, 1985, p. 182; *Nicaragua: The Human Rights Record*, Amnesty International, London, 1986, p. 26.

6. *The Miskitos in Nicaragua: 1981–1984*, An Americas Watch Report, New York, November 1984, p. 8.

7. *Human Rights in Nicaragua: Reagan, Rhetoric and Reality*, p. 22.

8. *Nicaragua: The Human Rights Record*, p. 30.

9. According to *Critique: Review of the Department of State's Country Reports on Human Rights Practices for 1984*, Americas Watch, Helsinki Watch, and Lawyers Committee for International Human Rights, New York, May 1985, the Sandinista government may use "harsh interrogation tactics, perhaps at times cruel and degrading treatment, but not the systematic and perverse infliction of bodily harm generally associated with the word torture" (p. 77).

10. *Human Rights in Nicaragua: 1986*, pp. 70–84; *Nicaragua, The Human Rights Record*, pp. 19–20.

11. See e.g., "A Costly Game of Consequences," *Manchester Guardian Weekly*, October 21, 1990, p. 12; Tom Hundley, "New Israeli Tactics to Calm Uprising," *Chicago Tribune*, July 22, 1990, p. 15.

12. See "French Rightist Paper Admits Misuse of Picture," *New York Times*, March 3, 1982, p. 5; see also *Report on the Relocation of Miskito Indians by the Nicaraguan Government in Light of International Laws and Standards*, International Justice Fund, Los Angeles, 1985, pp. 21–22; "Indian Rights Rediscovered," *New York Times*, March 5, 1982, p. 26.

13. "Report on the Situation of Human Rights of a Segment of the Nicaraguan Population of Miskito Origin," OAS Inter-American Commission on Human Rights, May 16, 1984, p. 129.

14. *The Miskitos in Nicaragua: 1981–1984*, pp. 17–18.

15. *Violations of the Laws of War by Both Sides in Nicaragua, 1981–1985*, An Americas Watch Report, New York, 1985, p. 85.

16. *Critique: Review of the Department of State's Country Reports on Human Rights Practices for 1984*, p. 80; *The Miskitos in Nicaragua: 1981–1984*, pp. 19, 22.

17. Nicaraguan Constitution, Title IV, Chapter I, Article 30, and Chapter III, Articles 66–68; Title X, Chapter I, Article 186.

18. See Michael Linfield, *Freedom Under Fire: U.S. Civil Liberties in Times of War*, South End Press, Boston, 1990.

19. See *"La Prensa*: Post-Mortem on a Suicide," *Envío* 5, no. 62, p. 34.

20. See Bob Woodward, *Veil: The Secret Wars of the CIA 1981–1987*, Pocket Books, New York, 1987, p. 111.

21. Interview with Violeta de Chamorro, Managua, Nicaragua, January 25, 1988.

22. See, e.g., "Nicaragua Bans Opposition From Getting U.S. Aid," *New York Times*, November 7, 1988, p. A11 ("In the past, American money has been openly sent to the opposition paper *La Prensa* and to a variety of other anti-Sandinista institutions"); Steven Kinzer, "La Prensa: Gadfly of the Sandinista State," *New York Times*, March 7, 1988, p. A6 (quoting Jaime Chamorro Cardenal, principal editor of *La Prensa*, who said that the newspaper has been receiving $7,000 per month from the National Endowment for Democracy, a congressionally funded organization).

23. *"La Prensa*: Post-Mortem on a Suicide," p. 33.

24. See, e.g., Shirley Christian, "Group Is Channeling U.S. Funds to Parties Opposing Pinochet" *New York Times*, June 15, 1988, p. 1.

25. *Right to Survive: Human Rights in Nicaragua*, Catholic Institute for International Relations, London, 1987, p. 82.

26. Ibid., p. 84.

27. *Human Rights in Nicaragua: 1986*, p. 116; *"La Prensa*: Post-Mortem on a Suicide," pp. 29–30.

28. Interview with Violeta de Chamorro, Managua, Nicaragua, January 25, 1988.

29. *Nicaragua*, Comment, Catholic Institute for International Relations, London, 1987, p. 27.

30. The books distributed were *Contra Toda Esperanza: 22 Años en el "Gulag de Las Americas,"* by Armando Valladares, and *Nicaragua: Revolución en la Familia*, by Shirley Christian.

31. *Barricada*, July 21, 1987, p. 1.

32. Raymond D. Gastil, *Freedom in the World: Political Rights and Civil Liberties, 1983–1984*, Greenwood Press, Westport, Conn., 1984, p. 405.

33. Howard Frederick, "Electronic Penetration," in Thomas Walker, ed., *Reagan Versus the Sandinistas: The Undeclared War on Nicaragua*, Westview Press, Boulder, Colo., 1987.

34. *Right to Survive: Human Rights in Nicaragua*, p. 88.

35. Jack A. Gottschalk, " 'Consistent with Security,' a History of American Military Press Censorship," 5 *Communications and Law* 35 (Summer 1983); Daniel C. Hallin, *"The Uncensored War"*: *The Media and Vietnam*, Oxford University Press, New York, 1986; Geoffrey Rips, *The Campaign Against the Underground Press*, PEN American Center Report, City Lights Books, San Francisco, 1981; Laurence Leamer, *The Paper Revolutionaries: The Rise of the Underground Press*, Simon & Schuster, New York, 1972; Salpukas, "Underground Papers Are Thriving On Campuses and Cities Across the Nation," *New York Times*, April 5, 1970, p. 58; Abe Peck, *Uncovering the Sixties: The Life and Times of the Underground Press*, Pantheon Books, New York, 1985. In general

see Michael Linfield, *Freedom Under Fire: U.S. Civil Liberties In Times of War*, South End Press, Boston, 1990, pp. 145–153.

36. A. S. Ross, "English Justice Falters in Face of Irish Strife," *San Francisco Examiner*, January 30, 1989, p. A-8.

37. Anthony Lewis, "How to Prevent Peace," *New York Times*, April 13, 1989, p. A19.

38. Jay Levin, "Israel: Breakdown in the Territories," *L.A. Weekly*, January 8–14, 1988, pp. 24–26.

39. Noam Chomsky, "Double Standard on Press Freedom," *Extra!* 2, no. 7/8, Summer 1989, p. 51.

40. See Alexander Cockburn, "Ashes and Diamonds," *L.A. Weekly*, November 10–16, 1989, p. 10.

41. Daniel Williams, "Israeli Activist Jailed for Meeting Arafat," *Los Angeles Times*, October 4, 1989, p. 19.

42. *Human Rights in Nicaragua: Reagan, Rhetoric and Reality*, p. 6. See also *A Political Opening in Nicaragua: Report on the Nicaraguan Elections of November 4, 1984*, Washington Office on Latin America, Washington, D.C., December 11, 1984.

43. See also *Human Rights in Nicaragua: Reagan, Rhetoric and Reality*, p. 3 ("debate on major social and political questions is robust, outspoken, even often strident").

44. See David Caute, *The Great Fear: The Anti-Communist Purge Under Truman and Eisenhower*, Simon & Schuster, New York, 1978, pp. 247–251, 507–508.

45. See Brief of Petitioner, p. 38, *Haig v. Agee*, 453 U.S. 280 (1981).

46. *Clark v. Dulles*, 129 F. Supp 950 (1955).

47. See Caute, *The Great Fear*, pp. 247–251.

48. *Human Rights in Nicaragua: August 1987 to August 1988*, An Americas Watch Report, New York, 1988, p. 31.

49. See Caute, *The Great Fear*, pp. 251–261.

50. See Robert Pear, "Nicaraguan Officials Barred from U.S. Entry by Reagan," *New York Times*, October 26, 1988, p. A14; Phillip van Niekerk, "Reagan Bars Visas for Many Nicaraguan Officials," *Boston Globe*, October 26, 1988, p. 3.

51. *Amnesty International Report: 1980*, Amnesty International, London, 1981, pp. 153–154. See also *Right to Survive: Human Rights in Nicaragua*, pp. 29–31; *Nicaragua: Revolutionary Justice, A Report on Human Rights and the Judicial System*, Lawyer's Committee for International Human Rights, New York, April 1985, p. 13.

52. *Amnesty International Report: 1980*, pp. 153–154; see also *Right to Survive: Human Rights in Nicaragua*, pp. 29–31.

53. When the Sandinistas took power, there was only $3 million dollars in the National Treasury; the rest had been looted by the fleeing Somozas.

54. Estatuto Fundamental, July 20, 1979; Estatuto Sobre Derechos y Garantias de los Nicaragüenses, August 21, 1979.

55. *Amnesty International Report: 1980*, p. 156. See also *Right to Survive: Human Rights in Nicaragua*, p. 47.

56. *Right to Survive: Human Rights in Nicaragua*, p. 48.

57. Ibid. See also *Nicaragua, Revolutionary Justice, A Report on Human Rights and the Judicial System*, pp. 33–40.

58. Ley de Gracia (Clemency Law), Decree #854 (October 24, 1981).

59. See *Human Rights in Nicaragua, 1986,* pp. 91–92; see also *Right to Survive: Human Rights in Nicaragua,* pp. 59–63.

60. *Annual Report of the Director, 1980,* Administrative Office of the United States Courts, Washington, D.C., pp. 97–98.

61. "The [Supreme Court] always pointed out that [the TPAs] had to be eliminated. We always maintained that position" (Interview with Alejandro Serrano, chief justice of the Supreme Court of Nicaragua, January 27, 1988, Managua, Nicaragua).

62. Decree 296 (January 19, 1988) suspended the functioning of the TPAs; Decree 297 (January 19, 1988) lifted the State of Emergency. See *Barricada,* January 19, 1988, p. 1.

63. A. S. Ross, "English Justice Falters in Face of Irish Strife," *San Francisco Examiner,* January 30, 1989, p. A8.

64. R. C. Longworth, "Britain to End Civil Right," *San Francisco Examiner,* October 2, 1988, p. A2.

65. As quoted in Ross, "English Justice Falters in Face of Irish Strife."

66. "Israel Criticized on Palestinian Detentions," *San Francisco Chronicle,* June 1, 1989, p. A23; Levin, "Israel: Breakdown in the Territories," p. 20.

67. Constitution of the Republic of Nicaragua, Title VIII, Chapter V, Article 163.

68. *Human Rights in Nicaragua: August 1987 to August 1988,* p. 79.

69. "Nicaragua Releases 1,894 Former National Guardsmen," *New York Times,* March 18, 1989, p. 1.

70. *Human Rights in Nicaragua: August 1987 to August 1988,* p. 11.

71. Statement by Alejandro Serrano Caldera, ambassador, permanent representative of Nicaragua to the 44th Session of the United Nations General Assembly, United Nations, New York, October 6, 1989.

FOURTEEN

Foreign Policy

HARRY E. VANDEN

To understand how Nicaraguan foreign policy evolved from 1979 to 1990, one must keep in mind that the Sandinistas came to power a decade after there were documented shifts in Latin American foreign policy away from patterns imposed by U.S. hegemony.[1] For some time before the 1979 victory, one could discern the general outline of Sandinista foreign policy. The *Historic Program of the FSLN*, brought out in 1969, contained an entire section on "Independent Foreign Policy," which began with the premise that the Sandinista revolution would establish "a patriotic foreign policy of absolute national independence." This and subsequent FSLN statements were equally clear as to Nicaraguan resolve not to have a foreign policy that was subordinate to that of any other nation (particularly the United States). However, this program also stated clearly that Nicaragua would "accept economic and technical aid from any country so long as it does not imply any political strings."[2]

This orientation was equally evident in foreign policy statements by the Government of National Reconstruction, which promised to "follow an independent and nonaligned foreign policy that relates to all nations that are respectful of self-determination and just and mutually beneficial economic relations."[3] Thus from 1979 to 1990, Nicaraguan foreign policy was designed to chart an independent course and break a long-standing dependent relationship with the United States. Painfully aware of the inherent limitations of small state actors on the world stage, the new leaders knew that such states had to avail themselves of all political, diplomatic, and legal avenues to achieve their policy objectives. Accordingly, they decided early on to use international organizations, international law, and diplomatic contacts with a wide variety of nations to protect the new political order in Managua. Such a foreign policy implied frequent recourse to the international legal system, which— unlike power politics—did not recognize the superiority of any state in or out of a region; indeed, the United Nations system was based on the concept of the sovereign equality of all states (Article 2, UN Charter), meaning that all states were equal and were to exercise their sovereignty in matters of their own politics (as long as they did not violate the rights of other states or the fundamental human rights of their own citizens). Further, regional documents like the Charter of the Organization of American States specifically prohibited one state's intervention (military or political) in the internal affairs of another.[4]

Nor was Nicaragua alone. From the 1950s on, Third World peoples increasingly had been ready to challenge attempts by European or Western states to control their states directly or indirectly. This was reflected in anticolonial movements and wars of national liberation in Africa and Asia, in increased friction between the United States and independent-minded Latin American states, and in a general interest on the part of Third World states to seek a more independent course through the Nonaligned Movement. Likewise, the use of a mass-based, highly organized, and strongly political type of guerrilla warfare (a people's war) restructured power relations in much of the Third World. Indeed, beginning with the guerrilla struggle against the U.S. Marines in Nicaragua from 1927 to 1933, popular forces were able to use variants of people's war to stalemate and often defeat well-equipped military forces from Europe or North America.

The Sandinista government that came to power in July 1979 had a very nationalistic, anti-imperialistic worldview. The new leaders believed they had been the victims of U.S. hegemony and intervention since the time the U.S. filibuster William Walker took control of Nicaragua in the 1850s. Credence was lent to this view by the frequent and often extended intervention of the U.S. Marines, the constant pressure to follow the U.S. lead in international affairs, the frequent meddling in internal affairs by U.S. diplomats and political leaders, and the continuing U.S. support for the Somozas from the 1930s until early 1979.[5]

As the name of the Sandinista movement suggests, the new Nicaraguan leadership was strongly identified with the struggle of Augusto César Sandino against the U.S. Marines. In addition, the Sandinistas were very proud of the fact Sandino had been able to wage a successful guerrilla war against the United States, force a political settlement, and thus write one of the first chapters in the history of successful people's war. Utilizing the lessons learned from Sandino in combination with those learned by the popular forces in Vietnam, Algeria, and Africa, they were able to mobilize the Nicaraguan people politically and thus defeat the U.S.-backed Somoza dictatorship. Having done so, they were resolute in their determination to exercise their sovereignty fully and defend Nicaragua's status as a nation-state that was equal to any other in the international community.

Nonalignment remained one of the key elements in Nicaraguan foreign policy. Beginning with the original 1969 FSLN program, the Sandinista leadership that came to rule Nicaragua steadfastly maintained its nonaligned orientation. In fact, after coming to power, the Sandinistas not only became active members of the Nonaligned Movement, but they also used their ties with the nonaligned to explain their policies and garner much-needed international support for their actions. In the process, they took full advantage of policy options created by the development of the Nonaligned Movement that had recently become available to Latin American nations.

However, even if conditions were changing rapidly in Africa and Asia, traditional aspects of the Inter-American system made nonalignment more difficult in the Western Hemisphere. Since the 1823 Monroe Doctrine, the United States had reserved an hegemonic position for itself. It was the first among equals and as such enjoyed rights and responsibilities that did not accrue to "lesser" states.

After Sandino was assassinated in 1934 and his army disbanded by the U.S.-organized National Guard, the resulting Somoza family dictatorship remained in power until July 1979. Its foreign policy was characterized by almost total subservience to North American policy interests. A Somoza could always deliver the Nicaraguan vote in crucial meetings of the United Nations or the Organization of American States. Nicaragua, like most of its fellow republics, remained closely allied to the United States from the 1930s through most of the 1970s. Nonetheless, new trends were developing. Led by the postrevolutionary independence in Mexican foreign policy, other Latin American states pushed to enlarge the parameters of their action in foreign affairs. However, this process was complicated by the interjection of the cold war into the hemispheric system in the 1950s. This permitted less maneuverability on the part of the Latin American nations, since it was assumed that common cultural, historic, economic, and political ties inextricably bound them to the West in the North American war with Eastern communism.

As suggested by the Cuban (1961) and Guatemalan (1954) cases, the United States tended to overreact to nationalist programs to change internal or external economic and political relationships. Deviation from Western policies was perceived as an unwarranted, active movement toward the Communist camp. But foreign policy initiatives that were fundamental to India's relations with both camps in Asia were prohibited for neighboring Latin American nations. After the 1959 revolution in Cuba, the United States reacted negatively to Cuba's changing internal and diplomatic policies, and as Cuba sought internal restructuring and new external alignments, U.S. displeasure increased and was ultimately expressed in the CIA-sponsored Bay of Pigs invasion. The economic and political realities of the 1960s, the example of Cuba, and a general increase in Third World independence and assertiveness combined to encourage other Latin American nations to reevaluate their foreign policy options. By the late 1970s, increasing numbers of Latin Americans experienced a growing affinity with the assertive Third World nationalism that emanated from the meetings of the Nonaligned Movement. In the years that followed, the movement came to include several Latin American nations: not only Cuba, Nicaragua, and Peru, but also Argentina, Colombia, Bolivia, Ecuador, and Panama. Venezuela became a member in 1989. Brazil, Costa Rica, and Mexico attended the frequent conferences as observers. The once small group of twenty-five had expanded to nearly one hundred nations by the time the FSLN defeated Somoza's forces in July 1979.

Relations with the United States

Relations between Nicaragua and the United States were difficult from the outset. The first U.S. response to Nicaragua's agenda of nonalignment developed during 1978 and 1979, when the Sandinistas were in the final phases of defeating Somoza. The Carter administration reluctantly moved to a policy of promoting what many termed "Somocismo without Somoza," which would have jettisoned the old client-dictator but would have preserved the old class relationships and political structures such as the National Guard and Somoza-controlled Liberal Nationalist party, while essentially excluding the FSLN.[6]

Even though the Carter administration had tried to stop the Sandinistas from coming to power, it finally acknowledged the inevitability of Sandinista victory. After the victory, both sides did sincerely try to get along. For their part, the Sandinistas knew that they could ill afford to be excluded from the Western economic system. The Cubans had warned them they should not unnecessarily isolate themselves from the United States, and the Soviets had let it be known that they were unwilling to underwrite the economic expense of a second Cuba in the Americas. For its part, the Carter administration, which was also aware of these facts, did not want to be party to the type of mutual overreaction that had occurred between Cuba and the United States two decades before. Rather the U.S. government hoped that by being friendly and supplying aid, it could moderate the revolutionary process and perhaps eventually defuse it, as had been done with the Bolivian revolution in the 1950s.[7]

The inauguration of Ronald Reagan, however, marked a watershed in U.S. policy. From then on, although apparent efforts at accommodation would occasionally surface, the dominant theme was confrontation. On the one hand, the Sandinistas insisted on maintaining their hard-won independence in foreign affairs. On the other, the Republican administration came to office with an inflexible mind-set on Nicaragua. It was dedicated to removing the Sandinistas from power by whatever means necessary. As Walter LaFeber noted in the introduction to *The Central*

American Crisis, "the Reagan administration used war, not negotiations, as its state policy."[8] As the policy of the new administration evolved, diplomacy was used less and less and the military option became almost the only option. If the new government in Nicaragua could not be toppled by a well-orchestrated destabilization plan, as the United States had managed in Chile in the early 1970s, then military activity by locals and the CIA would be used to topple the government, as was done in Guatemala in 1954. Nicaragua quickly became the testing ground for the newly devised doctrine of low-intensity conflict, whereby local people would be employed to wage guerrilla-style warfare against a regime the White House wanted ousted. This precluded the necessity of deploying U.S. troops or of committing large amounts of high-visibility military assistance. Finally, if all else failed, the United States still had the option of committing large numbers of U.S. troops, under the appropriate pretext, as had been done in the Dominican Republic in 1965.

Despite the hostile U.S. stance, Nicaragua was determined to maintain its autonomy. The Sandinistas also understood military force and enjoyed widespread popular support. They, too, knew what had happened to Salvador Allende in Chile in 1973, Jacobo Arbenz in Guatemala in 1954, and Juan Bosch's progressive forces in the Dominican Republic in 1965. Moreover, they also knew what had happened at the Bay of Pigs in 1961, when a CIA-organized and -backed invasionary force of Cuban exiles had been soundly defeated by the mobilized Cuban armed forces and the armed popular militia. The Sandinista leadership was dedicated to enlightened international relations and the full use of the UN system. It was, however, equally aware of the nature of real politik and the fact that even under the UN Charter, nations were clearly granted the right of self-defense (Article 51). Thus, the Sandinista leadership was careful to make sure that it had a competent military force to protect Nicaraguan sovereignty. If forced to do so, Sandinista Nicaragua would resort to arms to make sure that the gains of the revolution would not be reversed, as they had been in Guatemala and Chile (both of which reverted to brutal military dictatorships for years after their revolutions were overthrown by CIA-planned counterrevolutions).

Policymakers in the White House wanted to impose traditional U.S. hegemony. They were willing to resort to some very questionable practices to do so. In the words of Ronald Reagan, they wanted to make the Sandinistas "cry uncle."[9] The White House believed so fervently in the righteousness of its cause that it felt compelled to exceed legal, ethical, and moral norms of society to achieve its objectives.[10]

Ironically, the U.S. reversion to militaristic policies (the doctrine of low-intensity conflict specifically) came just as the traditional U.S. role in Latin America was undergoing significant change. After 1978, the

Latin American states were searching for new economic and political relationships in the international arena as U.S. hegemony declined. U.S. actions may be explained by reference to Paul Kennedy's thesis (great powers degenerate into military conquest when they no longer have economic potency) in *The Rise and Fall of the Great Powers: Economic Change and Military Conflict from 1500 to 2000.*[11] Thus as U.S. economic power declined, the resurgent conservative bloc in the United States wanted to employ military power to return to the status quo ante. "In this view, U.S. dominance over the Western Hemisphere as it was manifested [previously] was the normal . . . and desirable . . . state of things. It was this world view which, under Ronald Reagan's leadership, was to shape U.S. responses to the Nicaraguan revolution."[12]

In the case of Nicaraguan relations with the United States, diplomacy and recourse to the United Nations and to international law would continue to be necessary but not sufficient. The Sandinista leadership had to dig in its heels and responded to Reagan's challenge with "aqui no se rinde nadie" (nobody gives in here). The new Nicaraguan leaders fought off the contras and made it plain that a U.S. invasion would be difficult, costly, and protracted. But the costs involved were high. Indeed, it was precisely the deteriorating economic conditions and the fear of continuing loss of life in the contra war that combined to generate the protest vote that elected UNO's Violeta Chamorro in 1990.

Nicaragua was clearly dedicated to the maintenance of an independent foreign policy that most closely resembled that of other nonaligned states. But the increasingly confrontational and militaristic thrust of U.S. policy in the 1980s showed how difficult it would be to pursue that policy. The new Nicaraguan leadership was faced with a major challenge to the foreign policy course it had charted. By the early 1980s it had become clear that it would not be easy to maintain sovereign independence. Largely successful efforts by the Reagan administration to cut Nicaragua off from Western military suppliers and the high cost of such supplies had forced Nicaragua to rely increasingly on military goods from the socialist countries. Yet, to be forced into narrow relations with one power bloc would delimit Nicaraguan policy options consid- erably. Indeed, increasing dependence on a few Socialist states would validate the view of the ideological Right in the United States that Nicaragua was already under the wing of the Soviet Union and would indeed follow Cuba's path.

The true independence of Nicaraguan foreign policy was put to the test. Nicaragua had to pursue several foreign policy initiatives simul- taneously. While it fought off the U.S.-backed contras, it tried to negotiate with the United States (some direct conversations were held in Manzanillo, Mexico, in 1984, an election year in the United States and Nicaragua) and engaged in a very successful campaign in people-to-people diplomacy by encouraging more than 150,000 U.S. citizens to come to see the revolution. Several hundred even stayed to help the government or prorevolutionary organizations. On their return, many of these travelers became activists and most formed or joined solidarity groups. They and those they convinced upon their return helped to challenge the Reagan administration's disinformation campaign against Nicaragua. A growing number of U.S. voters also pushed for a less bellicose foreign policy toward Managua. The Nicaraguan leadership also managed occasional contact with congressional leaders, such as House Speaker Jim Wright. Thousands of young people from Western Europe were invited to sympathize with the revolution or enlist in solidarity organizations in their home countries. Aided by their support, the Nicaraguan leadership carefully cultivated good relations with all the Western European governments. Ties with socialist states were also strengthened, but not to the exclusion of extensive bilateral relations with other states. Good ties with a variety of Latin American states were maintained and utilized to rally Latin support for Nicaragua or occasionally invoke Latin censure of U.S. interventionist actions against Nicaragua. Ties were expanded with African, Asian, and Middle Eastern nations.

Furthermore, Nicaragua became very active in the Nonaligned Movement, used the United Nations extensively to cultivate friendly relations with a wide variety of nation-states, and employed UN peacekeeping mechanisms to protect itself against U.S. intervention. It also won a decisive victory against the United States in the International Court of Justice, having employed several U.S. legal experts to do so.

The new leadership was fully aware of the economic and political limitations that existed for a small independent nation like Nicaragua.[13] Thus a fundamental proposition of Nicaraguan foreign policy remained the defense of small countries against large ones.[14] Nicaragua's relations with the nonaligned continued to be one of the principal bulwarks of this policy.

Relations with the Nonaligned Movement

Less than two months after the new government established itself in Managua, the Sandinistas decided to make their country a member of the Nonaligned Movement. Nicaragua sent a delegation to the Sixth Summit of the Nonaligned Movement when it convened in Havana in early September 1979. Declaring that the Sandinistas favored the restructuring of their international relations on the basis of justice and that they desired a new international economic order, junta member Daniel Ortega explained that the Nicaraguans were joining the Nonaligned Movement because in it they saw "the broadest organization of the Third World States that play an important role and exercise increasing influence in the international arena and in the people's struggle against imperialism, colonialism, neocolonialism."[15] Nicaragua had clearly taken a different tack from the days when Somoza declared he was the best friend the United States ever had. It would seek much greater diversification in its diplomatic and economic relations. The September 1979 summit of the nonaligned countries was an ideal international forum for the declaration of the new Nicaraguan foreign policy. By appealing to the Nonaligned Movement, Nicaragua had access to support from outside the U.S.-dominated Inter-American System.

Nonalignment came to be the expression of a newfound independence. From an artificial foreign policy that had been a faithful "echo" of the position of the United States in international and regional forums like the United Nations and the OAS (Nicaragua had even endorsed the intervention in Guatemala in 1954 and permitted the use of Puerto Cabezas for the 1961 Bay of Pigs invasion of Cuba), Nicaraguan foreign policy became fiercely independent. Nicaragua would pursue a foreign policy based on defined interests. Specific goals might change, but fundamental tenets would include nonalignment, anticolonialism, and pluralism in internal politics and international relations.[16] Nonalignment seemed the most effective way to protect the newfound autonomy. Unlike the historical subservience to U.S. interests, nonalignment might well mean criticism of the North American position in Latin America and the Third World. However, this did not mean that Nicaraguan foreign policy was categorically hostile to that of the United States—only that the new regime reserved the right to judge other nations' actions according to its own criteria. Nicaraguan nonalignment must, therefore, be understood within the context of the country's revolutionary experience.[17]

Clearly there was a natural convergence in the goals of the movement itself and the historical and philosophical base upon which Nicaraguan foreign policy rested. Thus it would be unreasonable for Nicaraguan foreign policy to ignore other revolutionary struggles, whether in Central America or other regions of the Third World, in order to prove its nonalignment as defined by the United States. Because of the anticolonial and revolutionary philosophy and historical experience, the "natural" foreign policy of Nicaragua sometimes found expression in anti-imperialist positions. However, it did so as much because of how the United States defined its foreign policy as because of how the Nicaraguans conceptualized theirs. Indeed, given the historical and political context, it might have been nearly impossible for Nicaragua to define nonalignment to the satisfaction of the United States, since this would suggest the continuation of a dependent foreign policy.[18]

The Nonaligned Movement soon became an important tribunal for Nicaraguan foreign policy. In summit and ministerial meetings of the nonaligned, Nicaraguan representatives made sure Nicaraguan and Central American topics were on the agenda for discussion and that members of the movement were kept informed about hostile actions toward their state. The results were generally quite positive. For instance, in the ministerial meeting in New Delhi in February 1981, a resolution was passed that "condemned the political and economic aggression, both direct or through certain international financial organizations, which was being exercised or attempted against Nicaragua in order to interfere with the revolutionary process."[19] Nicaragua was also successful in convening an Extraordinary Meeting of the Coordinating Bureau of the Nonaligned Countries on Latin America and the Caribbean in Managua from January 10 to 14, 1983. This proved to be a major diplomatic coup for Nicaragua, as eighty-nine delegations focused their attention on an agenda that was dominated by Nicaraguan and Central American problems. More precisely, "by acting as host to the meeting . . . Nicaragua appeared to have succeeded in focusing [attention] on the growing number of attacks by Honduran-based anti-Sandinista rebels into northern Nicaragua."[20] Although the final declaration was watered down by pro-Western states, it still called for the peaceful resolution of differences between the warring groups in El Salvador and for direct negotiations between the United States and Nicaragua. This also set the stage for the continued discussion of Central America in the Seventh Summit of the Nonaligned Movement, held in New Delhi in March 1983.[21] Indeed 13 percent of the proceedings was devoted to discussion of Nicaraguan and Central American problems, with particular attention focused on U.S. actions in support of the contras.[22]

Nicaragua also had much support for its bid to host the next nonaligned summit and to serve as president of the Nonaligned Movement. It was not, however, successful in this endeavor, as some states expressed reservations about the physical capacity of a nation at war and the nature of the ties that Managua maintained with the Socialist Bloc.

Setting aside any initial disappointment about the outcome of the movement's presidential selection, Nicaragua actively continued to employ the movement and to initiate and maintain good relations with a wide variety of states. This proved to be a key element in its strategy of not allowing itself to be isolated or forced to narrow its diplomatic and commercial relations to a small group of mostly Socialist states. Thus in the 1986 Eighth Summit of the Nonaligned Movement in Harare, Zimbabwe, Nicaragua was able to make sure that 15 percent of the discussion was focused on Nicaragua, Contadora, and the Central American peace process and that there were several condemnations of U.S. intervention.[23] In the 1987 ministerial reunion in Guyana, a special Committee of the Nine was established to oversee events in Central America. Nicaragua and the Central American peace process were also prominently considered in the Ninth Summit of the Nonaligned Movement in Belgrade in September 1989. The meeting ended with a declaration that supported the Central American Peace Accords and called on governments outside the region—particularly the United States—to respect the decisions taken by the Central American heads of state.[24]

Nicaragua and the United Nations

The predominance of nonaligned nations in the United Nations (103 out of 159) in the early 1980s also helped set the stage for Nicaraguan initiatives in that organization. In October 1983 Nicaragua made a bid for a seat on the Security Council. The United States lobbied hard against Nicaragua, proposing the Dominican Republic instead. Despite the opposition, nonaligned Nicaragua was able to secure the 104 votes necessary for the required two-thirds majority. This marked a major triumph for Nicaragua (and a defeat for the United States) and gave Managua immediate access to the Security Council.

In March 1984, Nicaragua took full advantage of its new status to request that the Security Council convene to hear charges concerning threats to its security. U.S. aggression in the form of contra attacks from Honduras was denounced, and the assembled states were made aware of the nature of the illegal activities against the Central American state. This and similar meetings proved to be excellent means of calling attention to threats to Nicaraguan security and embarrassing the United States. By 1989, Nicaragua had convened the Security Council fifteen times to consider charges of external aggression. Two resolutions calling for an end to the conflict were passed, and the United States vetoed four others. Nicaragua was also able to use the powers of the General Assembly to obtain the passage of four resolutions condemning the U.S. trade embargo and of others that called on the United States to implement the decision of the International Court of Justice.[25] One such General Assembly resolution passed in October 1988 ordered the United States to end the arming and training of insurgents against Nicaragua and to pay the damages caused by military attacks. The fact that the United States and Israel were the only two states voting against the resolution was even more telling.[26] Addressing the General Assembly earlier in October, Nicaraguan Foreign Minister Miguel d'Escoto had denounced U.S. policy toward Central America and called for such a resolution. The outcome of the vote suggested not only the wide base of support this Nicaraguan initiative enjoyed but also the fact that U.S. actions and its position before the World Court had isolated it on this and related issues in the United Nations. Furthermore, it seemed a clear vindication of two fundamental orientations in Nicaragua's foreign policy: to have cordial diplomatic relations with as many states as possible and to maximize those peacekeeping mechanisms inherent in the United Nations and other international organizations and in the international legal system.[27]

Taking great care not to allow itself to be isolated, the new government, for instance, greatly expanded the number of states with which Nicaragua maintained diplomatic relations. Whereas the old Somoza dictatorship had relations with only 41 states, the new government had diplomatic ties with 117 by 1989. In Africa alone the number of states with which Managua maintained ties was increased from 26 to 52.[28] Many of these ties were assiduously cultivated in the Nonaligned Movement and the United Nations. This also helped to account for Nicaragua's election to the Security Council, to the presidency (and thus country host) of the World Parliamentary Union, and to many leadership positions in UN committees.[29]

International Court of Justice

The new government in Managua had to fight on many fronts to defend the accomplishments of the revolution. While engaging in a bitter military struggle against the contras, it was defending itself by other means in the Nonaligned Movement and the United Nations, maximizing its influence through bilateral relations, and it finally sought justice in the World Court.

Many revolutionary regimes in the Third World were loath to confide in international law or the International Court of Justice because of what they believed to be a strongly Western and capitalist bias in the international legal system. Some Third World states even warned Nicaragua that it should not expect justice from the World Court.[30] Nicaragua, nonetheless, pursued legal remedies to U.S. aggression.

In 1984 Nicaragua brought suit against the United States in the International Court of Justice (ICJ), arguing that Reagan administration actions against Nicaragua were violations of fundamental precepts of international law in regard to intervention, the mining of Nicaraguan harbors, and contra violations of the laws of war as embodied in the Geneva conventions. Pursuing their case vigorously (and with the help of the U.S. law firm Reichler and Applebaum and Abram Chayes, a professor at Harvard Law School),[31] the Nicaraguans achieved their first victory in May 1984, when the court rejected the U.S. contention that the ICJ did not have jurisdiction in the case, and further stated: "The right to sovereignty and to political independence possessed by the Republic of Nicaragua, like any other state of the region or of the world, should be fully respected and should not in any way be jeopardized by any military and paramilitary activities which are prohibited by the principles of international law."[32]

Apparently all too aware of the illegal nature of U.S. actions, the Reagan administration then did exactly what the Islamic Republic of Iran had done when the United States sued it in the World Court over the taking of U.S. hostages in Teheran—it withdrew from the proceedings. This broke a long-standing U.S. policy of official support for the court and its decisions and again suggested that tiny Nicaragua had found another forum where it could derive the full benefits of its sovereign equality and compete on equal terms against the pressure of the superpower to its north.

Nicaraguan faith in the ICJ and the fairness of international law was further vindicated when the World Court issued its ruling on the merits of the case in 1986. By twelve votes to three, the court decided that: "the United States of America, by training, arming, equipping, financing and supplying the contra forces or otherwise encouraging, supporting and aiding military and paramilitary activities in and against Nicaragua, has acted against the Republic of Nicaragua, in breach of its obligation under international law not to intervene in the affairs of another state" and that "by laying mines in the internal or territorial waters of the Republic of Nicaragua during the first months of 1984, the United States of America has acted against the Republic of Nicaragua, in breach of its obligations under customary international law not to use force against another state, not to intervene in its affairs, not to violate its sovereignty and not to interrupt peaceful maritime commerce."

By fourteen votes to one (Judge Schwebel of the United States dissenting), the court found "that the United States of America, by producing in 1983 a manual entitled 'Operaciones sicológicas en guerra de guerrillas' [Psychological operations in guerrilla warfare], and disseminating it to contra forces, has encouraged the commission by them of acts contrary to general principles of humanitarian law [the Geneva Conventions et al.]."[33]

This ruling helped to solidify Nicaragua's position before the nonaligned countries and the United Nations and clearly vindicated Nicaraguan faith in the possibilities for fair treatment in the international legal system. It also led to further isolation of the United States in its dispute with Nicaragua. Nicaragua continued to cultivate good relations with widely different nation-states and became a strong advocate of the use of international law before the Nonaligned Movement. Indeed, as it continued to push for a strengthened and refined international legal system as an instrument for peace and international security, Nicaragua was instrumental in organizing the June 1989 International Nonaligned Conference on Peace and International Law, in the Hague.[34] Likewise, on a Nicaraguan initiative, the final declaration of the 1989 Ninth Summit of the Nonaligned Movement included a proposal to the United Nations to declare the 1990s the Decade of Peace and International Law.[35]

Relations with Western Europe

Nicaragua experienced much initial success in its efforts to maintain good relations with Western Europe. This was manifest in the aid from the region that poured into Nicaragua. In the 1979–1981 period European donations to Nicaragua exceeded $61 million. The European Economic Community alone donated $16 million.[36] From 1979 to 1982, Western Europe provided 33 percent of all loans to Nicaragua.[37] Likewise, 28 percent of Nicaraguan exports were purchased by Europeans, who in turn accounted for 14 percent of Nicaragua's imports.[38] Moreover, on the level of people-to-people diplomacy, friendly ties with Nicaragua encouraged hundreds of public agencies and solidarity groups to send thousands of (mostly young) Europeans to see the Nicaraguan revolution and contribute to its success. On their return, these internationalists— as they were called by the Nicaraguans—helped to favorably inform their national publics about the Nicaraguan revolution and to mobilize greater support for it. Nicaraguan leaders also frequently made trips to European capitals to explain their country's position and seek economic and technical support.

Initially, all but the most conservative European policymakers were quite receptive. Thus in the July 1983 European Economic Community meeting in Stuttgart, ten EEC leaders seemed to affirm Nicaragua's position and criticize the Reagan administration Central American policies when they issued a statement that asserted that regional problems could not "be solved by military means but only by a solution springing from the region itself," called for "respect for the principles of non-interference and inviolability of frontiers," and endorsed the Contadora process.[39]

However, intense diplomatic pressure by the Reagan administration combined with growing European dissatisfaction with Nicaraguan actions to prompt the Europeans to reassess their position. The replacement of the Social Democrats by Helmut Kohl's Christian Democrats in West Germany in 1982 was also a key factor. Many Western European critics became quite concerned about what they perceived as Nicaragua's growing alignment with the Socialist Bloc, its encroachments on the private sector, and its limitation on political democracy. Even Nicaragua's friends, having expected an evolution toward social democracy, were somewhat intolerant of the strong measures the Sandinistas took to contain the contra threat. In addition, it soon became apparent that the Western European governments could not provide the increased level of economic aid that was necessary for Nicaragua to survive in light of the contra war, the cutoff of U.S. economic assistance, and the reduction and eventual cutoff of U.S. trade. Nor was Central America a high priority for most European governments. Although good diplomatic and economic relations continued, the Nicaraguans had to look elsewhere among their

diverse trading and diplomatic partners for additional support.⁴⁰ Petroleum
was supplied by Mexico and Venezuela, and other petroleum exporters
like Libya and Algeria contributed direct payments. However, by the
mid-1980s Cuba and the socialist states in Eastern Europe began to
play a much larger role in Nicaraguan economic and political relations.
This trend continued throughout the remainder of the 1980s.

True to their announced principles of diversity in foreign relations,
the Nicaraguans did avail themselves of trade and aid from socialist
states. They did not, however, diminish their initiatives toward Western
Europe. Indeed, to the extent possible, they tried to balance relations
with the two Europes, often—as President Ortega did in his controversial
trip to the USSR in 1985—making it a point to stop in capitals in
both Western and Eastern Europe whenever a trip was made to the
European continent. Thus Daniel Ortega, Tomás Borge, and other
Nicaraguan leaders continued to make frequent trips to the EEC capitals
and to take advantage of the Western European preference for change
through flexibility and negotiated solution in Central America. Even
after the U.S. trade embargo in 1985, the EEC continued to give aid
to Nicaragua and the other Central American countries. From 1984 to
1989 there were five meetings of the European governments on Central
America. For each year between 1984 and 1987, the EEC countries
gave between $40 and $80 million to the region. Nicaragua received
the largest portion (30 percent) of this aid for the entire period. Regional
aid was increased to $122 million in 1988.⁴¹

In 1987, relations with Western Europe were not so cordial as they
had been in the early 1980s, and when seven European foreign ministers
met in San José in February for their third annual European–Central
American encounter, Nicaragua was not even invited. Encouraged, if
not pressured, by the United States, the Europeans were anxious to
see more Western-style democratization in Nicaragua and were most
concerned that the long-awaited municipal elections had again been
postponed.⁴² That same month, Sandinista Comandante Bayardo Arce
traveled to Madrid to meet with prominent European representatives
of the Socialist International, an organization of Social Democratic
parties, mostly Western European, to reassure them that Nicaragua was,
indeed, practicing pluralist democracy.⁴³ He also asked the Socialist
International to act as lobbyist to secure additional political and financial
support and suggested that Nicaragua would in turn undertake a series
of actions that included scaling down State of Emergency measures,
allowing La Prensa to renew publication, and arranging for early municipal
elections.⁴⁴ Though receptive to the flexibility demonstrated by this
initiative, the Europeans were not yet totally convinced. Subsequent
events in Nicaragua would show just how committed the Sandinistas
were to open elections.

By the beginning of 1988, West Germany had ended all aid to Nicaragua, France and the Netherlands had cut back, and Italy had refused to increase its aid. Only Sweden promised that it would increase its support in 1988.[45] While maintaining good relations with other groups, Sandinista ambassadors and envoys vigorously lobbied the Christian and Social Democratic governments and even went as far as to convey the message that Managua was contemplating the possibility of inviting sectors of the opposition to form a coalition government.[46] In the short run, Nicaragua was forced to rely more heavily on friendly Socialist governments rather than do without. In the long run, the continuity of policy and vigor of such initiatives bore fruit.

In May 1989, President Daniel Ortega traveled to the Old World to woo the Europeans. In a major diplomatic effort, he met with François Mitterrand, Helmut Kohl, and even Margaret Thatcher to convince them that Nicaragua was earnest about democratization, that the 1990 elections would be impeccably clean, and that Nicaragua would scrupulously fulfill the provisions of the Esquipulas II peacekeeping accords.[47] Later that same month, Sweden hosted a two-day conference on aid to Nicaragua. At the end of what came to be called the Stockholm Conference and mindful of Nicaraguan initiatives and domestic concessions, the Western European nations finally increased their support. Sweden, Italy, and Spain would each put up $10 million in grants, and $20 million would be forthcoming from Norway, Finland, Denmark, the Netherlands, and the EEC.[48] In June 1989, the Nicaraguan government sent Bayardo Arce again to meet with the Socialist International. He succeeded in strengthening ties considerably and in a speech to the plenary session even invited the organization to send permanent observers to the upcoming Nicaraguan elections.[49] Only after many efforts and significant concessions concerning elections and political freedom was Nicaragua able to maintain generally cordial relations with Western Europe and continue to balance its political, trade, and aid ties among a wide variety of states. The resultant trade and economic support were, however, not enough to halt the generalized decline in Nicaraguan economic conditions.

The Socialist States

After the first few years of Sandinista rule, problems with the United States, the contra war, the developing economic crisis, and the difficulties engendered in maintaining good relations with Western Europe combined to necessitate a cautious policy of engagement with the socialist countries.[50] The Sandinistas' relations with Moscow and with Soviet-oriented orthodox Marxists had not always been good. The Sandinistas had been in conflict with Nicaragua's pro-Moscow orthodox Marxist party, the

Nicaraguan Socialist party (PSN), for some time. The PSN was in favor of waiting for economic conditions to induce political action, rather than focusing on political action immediately. Thus the party played almost no role in the revolution, and the Soviet Union initially paid little attention to Nicaraguan events even after the Sandinistas had taken power.[51] Indeed, the 1979 victory "was a sharp political defeat for the Soviet Union . . . [because it] showed how wrong the Moscow sponsored strategy of the peaceful road had been."[52] Furthermore, the PSN had for many years considered Sandino nothing more than a bourgeois nationalist. Thus even Sandinista leaders who were Marxist were very critical of orthodox Communist parties in Latin America and berated them for their lack of nationalism.[53]

Most of the Sandinistas did, however, still consider themselves socialists of some kind and had chafed for years under the old Somocista policy of not maintaining diplomatic relations with any socialist states and of prohibiting Nicaraguan citizens from traveling to them. Given Nicaragua's newly declared independence in foreign relations, it was thus an expression of sovereignty to establish such diplomatic ties.[54] Nicaragua, like other nonaligned states, wanted to have diplomatic and commercial relations with both East and West as well as with a wide diversity of Third World states. Establishing such relations further differentiated the new government's foreign policy from that of other Latin American nations that were so attuned to the old U.S.-dominated Inter-American system that they feared even the most minimal relations with socialist states.

But Nicaragua's changing relations were only part of a larger picture. Indeed, in *Partners in Conflict: The United States and Latin America,* Abraham Lowenthal underscored the growing diversification in trade and diplomatic relations in Latin America as a whole.[55] By the 1980s, more of the Latin nations, including Venezuela in 1989, had become members of the Nonaligned Movement and had established relations with Cuba and the Eastern European countries. Indeed, by the mid-1980s, the USSR had diplomatic relations with nineteen Latin American nations. There was also increased trade with Eastern European states. For example, even while it was still under military rule, Argentina's grain sales to the USSR had increased dramatically. As this trend increased, the Soviet Union eventually became Argentina's primary trading partner.[56]

Of all the socialist states, Cuba maintained the closest ties with Nicaragua. Cuban aid and political ties to the Sandinistas were strong even before the end of the dictatorship. Throughout the first decade of Sandinista rule, relations between Managua and Havana remained warm and Cuba continued to supply substantial amounts of technical support and economic and military aid.

However, significant support from the Soviet Union was much slower in coming. The first economic-technical pacts were not signed until almost two years after the Sandinistas came to power and only after the Reagan administration had begun its punitive economic policies.[57] Early U.S. efforts to begin the organization of a counterrevolutionary army no doubt also influenced this decision.[58] Soviet assistance increased dramatically only after the contra war had begun in earnest in 1982.[59] For instance, during the 1979 to 1982 period only 18.5 percent of the loans to Nicaragua came from the socialist countries.[60] Trade statistics are even more telling. During this period, a scant 12 percent of Nicaragua's imports came from the socialist countries (as compared to 19 percent from the United States) and only 2 percent of Nicaragua's exports went to socialist countries.[61]

Even though Nicaragua wanted to maintain a balance in its economic and diplomatic relations, the military exigencies of the contra war and the economic exigencies that resulted from the total trade embargo the Reagan administration imposed in 1985 forced it to rely more heavily on the socialist nations. The United States had been Nicaragua's principal trade partner, so the embargo was a particularly severe blow to the Nicaraguan economy. As suggested above, the Western Europeans were not prepared to increase trade or aid sufficiently to offset the losses. Moreover, in 1980 the United States refused military aid to Nicaragua. Thereafter, other Western governments were pressured not to sell to the Sandinistas or if they had done so (as had France), to cancel all or part of the order and/or delay shipment.[62] In 1985 and 1986 the revolutionary state was in desperate need of aid and other trade outlets. The Nicaraguan response to this situation is seen clearly in the words of a prominent Foreign Ministry official: "When we asked for aid it was the socialist countries that gave us unconditional cooperation."[63] In this same interview he went on to note that it was once again the socialists who offered arms to defend the revolution when it was under attack.[64]

Although the initial plan had been to diversify Nicaragua's dependence by spreading it among several states from different blocs, external military and economic pressures combined with internal problems arising from Sandinista mismanagement and low productivity in the private sector to force the Nicaraguan government to strengthen its ties with the socialist countries and to become more dependent on them. Indeed, "in many ways, Reagan himself was responsible for the quantitative leap in [Nicaragua's] relations with the socialists."[65]

Apparently foreseeing just such a possibility, Daniel Ortega had been careful to maintain cordial ties with Moscow and had continued to visit the USSR annually. Thus he visited Leonid Brezhnev in 1982, Yuri Andropov in 1983, Konstantin Chernenko in 1984, and Mikhail Gorbachev in 1985.[66] After the United States imposed the economic embargo in 1985, the USSR increased its levels of aid and trade to make up for some of the shortfall. It should be noted, however, that according to the Nicaraguan Ministry of Foreign Cooperation, donated aid from all the socialist countries (including Cuba) totaled only $214.6 million for the period 1979 to 1986, whereas the donated aid received from the Western countries, private Western organizations, and the United Nations came to $365 million.[67] Deteriorating conditions in Nicaragua prompted the Soviet Union to increase its overall aid to $200 million for the 1986–1987 period and to supply more and more of Nicaragua's petroleum needs.[68] However, even after such drastic increases, the USSR was only able to pick up about one-half of the 70 percent of Nicaraguan exports that had gone to the United States before the trade embargo.[69] Indeed, according to the International Monetary Fund, imports from the Soviet Union and other nonmember (socialist) states increased only 5 percent in 1985 and in 1986 and an additional 10 percent in 1987. Exports to those states increased by the same percentages respectively for those years.[70]

By 1985 the USSR was supplying virtually all of Nicaragua's crude petroleum.[71] Mexico and Venezuela had been Nicaragua's primary suppliers in the early 1980s but had eventually suspended shipments because of U.S. pressure and Nicaragua's inability to pay. The Soviet Union continued this level of petroleum support through 1986 and into 1987. It should also be noted that such trade and aid arrangements between the USSR and Nicaragua were only a small fraction of those extended to Cuba. Furthermore, such aid was mostly in the form of concessionary trade credits, technical assistance, and development project aid.[72] The Soviet Union had little hard currency itself and would increasingly need to focus its economic resources on meeting growing demand for economic change internally. This and persistent questions about the way in which the economy was being run in Nicaragua precipitated a reevaluation of Soviet and Eastern European support beginning in 1987.

In June 1987, the USSR announced that it intended to limit the amount of crude petroleum that it would supply to Nicaragua. This forced Nicaragua to negotiate with Mexico and Venezuela over terms for additional petroleum.[73] The socialist states did continue to supply relatively high levels of military aid to Nicaragua (estimated by the U.S. Department of Defense to run over $500 million annually for 1986, 1987, and 1988).[74] As the contras were defeated militarily by late 1987 and the first part of 1988, the socialist countries felt even less obliged to continue to subsidize Nicaragua (whose economy was far from the type of directed economy they favored) with their economic support. Indeed, Soviet government officials were highly critical of the Nicaraguan economy.[75] Likewise, in private conversations, Sandinista leaders frequently criticized the Soviets for being unresponsive to popular needs and shackled by dogma.[76] The 1987 Soviet announcement to limit Soviet petroleum supplies to 40 percent of Nicaragua's needs may well have been symbolic of the postcontra period in Nicaraguan-Soviet relations. When crucial for Nicaragua's survival, military supplies were forthcoming. Increased (though not unlimited) economic support was available during a time of military attack. However, once the revolutionary state was no longer directly threatened militarily, economic aid was reduced and Nicaragua was encouraged to become more self-reliant economically and to remedy the production, management, distribution, and monetary problems that continued to plague its efforts at economic stabilization. Once a regional peace agreement guaranteed Nicaragua against continuing attack, military support would be reduced. Indeed, in January 1989 direct Soviet arms shipments were suspended altogether pending the outcome of the Central American peace process. Consistent with Gorbachev's evolving foreign policy initiatives, the USSR wanted to diffuse a tense situation in Central America and reverse a trend whereby it was supplying an ever-increasing share of Nicaragua's economic needs (in 1988 it gave $384 million in aid to Nicaragua).[77]

This message seems to have been communicated to President Daniel Ortega when he visited Moscow in November 1987. The Soviet administration continued to be highly critical of the Nicaraguan economy and proved much less amenable to continue subsidies to maintain it. The Soviets also reportedly put pressure on Nicaragua to rely less on them and more on natural allies in the region like Mexico and Venezuela.[78] Soon after returning to Managua, President Ortega reversed a longstanding policy by announcing that Nicaragua would meet directly with the contras.

Indeed, by mid-1988 the Soviets had begun to press the Sandinistas to seek greater economic and financial support in the West. In a foreign policy change that was consistent with reducing regional tensions and aligning its policy with traditional international law, the USSR viewed all governments in Central America as legitimate, regardless of regime type.[79] In addition, in 1989 the Nicaraguans were being encouraged to follow the Soviet example and try to make their economic production more efficient.[80] By the time of the February 1990 election, the Soviet Union and East Germany had both already begun to reduce aid to Nicaragua. Nor did events in Eastern Europe suggest that more aid would be forthcoming, even if the Sandinistas had won the election.

Meanwhile, relations with Cuba (which seemed to ignore Soviet suggestions about economic and political restructuring) continued to be good through the tenth anniversary of the Sandinista victory. Cuba also continued to supply needed military supplies and economic aid, and—like other socialist states—to pay above world (capitalist) market prices for Nicaraguan primary products.

Relations in Latin America

When the Sandinistas came to power in 1979, they experienced a great deal of Latin American support and goodwill. Costa Rica, Panama, Venezuela, Cuba, and Mexico had all supported the Sandinistas in different ways before the victory and had joined with other Latin American states to fight a U.S. attempt to have the Organization of American States impose a solution that would have kept the National Guard intact and the Sandinistas out of power. During 1979 and 1980, relations with the Latin American nations not under right-wing military dictatorships remained good. Trade increased and Venezuela and Mexico began to supply Nicaragua's petroleum needs under very favorable terms. The Latin American nations applauded Nicaragua's firm stand in support of self-determination and national sovereignty. This was manifest in Managua's support for Argentina in the dispute over the Falkland Islands and occurred when the military government in Buenos Aires had advisers in Honduras who were setting up and training the contra army. In tacit acknowledgment of Nicaraguan support, the regime subsequently withdrew its advisers and relations warmed considerably.

Although the initial enthusiasm toward the Sandinistas cooled in some nations, the abiding respect for self-determination and nonintervention convinced most to maintain pragmatic, if not always supportive, relations with the Sandinistas.[81] As Peru's newly elected president said in 1985, "We are supporting Nicaragua because it is a symbol of an independent sovereignty and destiny for the continent."[82]

From 1981 on, the United States put substantial pressure on Latin American nations to diminish their trade and diplomatic relations with the revolutionary government in Managua. A cleverly orchestrated press campaign to discredit the Sandinistas and diminish domestic support for governments that dealt with them was also put into play by the United States. However, as U.S. policy toward Nicaragua became increasingly hostile after 1981, the Latin American nations realized the inherent danger in the protracted nature of the conflict that was developing and the fact that it was very destabilizing when added to the ongoing guerrilla wars in El Salvador and Guatemala. In January 1983, the foreign ministers of Venezuela, Colombia, Mexico, and Panama formulated their own Latin plan to achieve peace in Central America. It was called the Contadora process (see Chapter 18). By the end of the year these Central American nations were poised to sign a treaty making concrete the plan. Although supportive of a negotiated settlement, Nicaragua held out initially but surprised many by finally agreeing to sign the accord. This treaty clearly satisfied any legitimate security concerns that the United States or other Central American states had. It was not, however, consistent with the traditional hegemonic stance of the United States (it was, after all, the result of a Latin and not a U.S. initiative) and would have ended the contra war with less than a total victory for the U.S. proxies (the Sandinistas would not have to cry uncle). Thus the United States successfully pressed its most dependent allies (El Salvador and Honduras) and Costa Rica to reverse themselves and declare the treaty unacceptable. The United States declared its support for the Contadora process publicly but did everything it could behind the scenes to block it. This and similar Washington-inspired machinations prevented the Contadora process from ever implementing the accords. It was also indicative of the pressure that the United States was bringing to bear on other Latin American states that (like Mexico) continued cordial relations with the Sandinistas. Indeed, the economic crisis in the South and the need to restructure Western and international loan repayments made them increasingly susceptible to such pressure.

The Reagan administration continued to pressure its allies in and out of Latin America to minimize their diplomatic and economic relations with Managua. Nonetheless, most Latin American states (like Western European nations and Japan) continued to maintain normal (and in some cases cordial) diplomatic and economic relations. As was the case in 1985, the Nicaraguan president and vice president frequently made tours of the Latin capitals to maintain good relations and prevent diplomatic isolation. There was, however, a cooling in relations with nations like Venezuela and Costa Rica because of U.S. pressure and the perception that Nicaragua was becoming more authoritarian domestically and was relying too heavily on the East Bloc nations. The contra war had also sapped Nicaraguan foreign exchange so that payment for oil from Venezuela and Mexico and trade with other Latin nations became increasingly difficult. Indeed, Nicaraguan trade with Latin America continued to decline from 1982 to 1986. This trend was not reversed until 1987, and even then, Nicaraguan–Latin American trade was much below 1981 levels.[83] It was only after renewed economic conversations that Mexico finally agreed to a renewal of oil exports to Nicaragua in the latter part of 1987.

Nicaraguan efforts to bolster Latin autonomy did meet with some success. As the Central American states became increasingly concerned with the ongoing contra war and the blundering nature of U.S foreign policy for the region, they began to seize the initiative.

After President Arias won the Nobel Peace Prize for his diplomatic initiative, the Reagan administration was forced to praise the new peace process publicly. Nicaragua soon demonstrated that it took the accords seriously and led the other countries in implementing key provisions. Nicaragua continued to take the lead in implementing each new accord that the Central American peace process engendered[84] (see Chapter 18). Furthermore, the Nicaraguan leadership was even able to convince the

National Assembly to move up the time of the next elections from November to February 25, 1990, and to schedule the long-awaited municipal elections for the same day. Not only did this demonstrate Nicaragua's commitment to the peace process and internal democracy, it also was a direct response to calls by Venezuela and other members of the Group of Eight (the four Contadora nations plus Peru, Brazil, Uruguay, and Argentina) for more openness and domestic flexibility. As such, it served to strengthen Nicaraguan relations with the Latin American states even more, although these actions set the stage for the Sandinista electoral defeat on February 25, 1990.

Conclusion

From 1979 to early 1990, Nicaragua vigorously pursued its independent foreign policy through optimal utilization of good relations with a variety of different nations in the Nonaligned Movement, the United Nations, Western Europe, Canada, the socialist states, and Latin America. It also achieved a major victory in the World Court and utilized international law as an effective means of protecting smaller states against external aggression. By combining military defense with effective foreign policy, Nicaragua temporarily checked the Reagan administration's attempt to reimpose traditional U.S. hegemony in Central America. By 1989, it had become increasingly clear that many Latin American nations would increasingly seek solutions to their problems as Nicaragua had done. This newfound Latin independence was manifest in the February 1989 accord signed by all five Central American presidents. Such a solution guaranteed that domestic politics—and not external intervention—would be the primary determinant of who would rule in Managua, if not elsewhere in Central America.

Nicaragua had developed a foreign policy that was fresh, unique, and independent and that was able to protect the revolution from a very hostile U.S. policy for more than a decade. In the long run, it was not able to garner sufficient external economic support to compensate for the embargo and severe domestic economic problems or to obtain sufficient compliance with regional peace accords to disband the contras and stop their attacks. It was, however, able to achieve a framework that allowed the Nicaraguan government to sponsor the cleanest and most observed elections in Nicaraguan, if not Latin American, history.

Notes

1. Abraham Lowenthal, *Partners in Conflict: The United States and Latin America* (Baltimore: Johns Hopkins University Press, 1987), pp. 32–37.
   2. *Historic Program of the FSLN* (Managua: Departamento de Propaganda y Educación Política, 1981), pp. 27–28.

3. Statement of the National Government of Reconstruction, as cited in Denis Tórres Pérez, "La política exterior de la revolución popular Sandinista (Elementos para un balance)," *Cuadernos de Sociología* 9–10 (January-June 1989), p. 153.

4. See Article 15 of the original Charter of the OAS.

5. Thomas W. Walker, "Nicaraguan-U.S. Friction: The First Four Years," in Kenneth M. Coleman and George C. Herring, eds., *The Central American Crisis: Sources of Conflict and the Failure of U.S. Policy* (Wilmington: Scholarly Resources, 1985), pp. 157–158.

6. Walker, "Nicaraguan-U.S. Friction," pp. 157–158. Much of this section relies on H. Vanden and T. Walker, "Nicaraguan-U.S. Friction," in Kenneth M. Coleman and George C. Herring, eds., *The Central American Crisis: Sources of Conflict and the Failure of U.S. Policy*, 2nd ed. (Wilmington: Scholarly Resources, 1991).

7. Walker, "Nicaraguan-U.S. Friction," p. 158.

8. Walter LaFeber, "Introduction," in Coleman and Herring, eds., *The Central American Crisis* (1985 ed.), p. 1.

9. "President Asserts Goal Is to Remove Sandinista Regime," *New York Times*, February 22, 1985, p. 1.

10. See, for instance, Thomas W. Walker, ed., *Reagan Versus the Sandinistas: The Undeclared War on Nicaragua* (Boulder, Colo.: Westview, 1987); Holly Sklar, *Washington's War on Nicaragua* (Boston: South End Press, 1988); Leslie Cockburn, *Out of Control: The Story of the Reagan Administration's Secret War in Nicaragua, the Illegal Arms Pipeline and the Contra Drug Connection* (New York: Atlantic Monthly Press, 1987); and Jonathan Kwitny, *Crimes of Patriots: A True Tale of Dope, Dirty Money and the CIA* (New York: Norton, 1987).

11. Paul Kennedy, *The Rise and Fall of the Great Powers: Economic Change and Military Conflict From 1500 to 2000* (New York: Random House, 1987).

12. Mary B. Vanderlaan, *Revolution and Foreign Policy in Nicaragua* (Boulder, Colo.: Westview, 1986), p. 14.

13. "Nicaragua's Foreign Policy: Ten Years of Principles and Practice, An Interview with Alejandro Bendaña," *Envío* 8, no. 97 (August 1989), p. 27.

14. Ibid.

15. Daniel Ortega, Speech Before the Sixth Summit of the Nonaligned Movement, Havana, 1979, as quoted in A. Bendaña, "The Foreign Policy of the Nicaraguan Revolution," in Thomas Walker, ed., *Nicaragua in Revolution* (New York: Praeger, 1982), p. 320.

16. Waltrud Queiser Morales and Harry E. Vanden, "Relations with the Nonaligned Movement," in Thomas Walker, ed., *Nicaragua: The First Five Years* (New York: Praeger, 1985), pp. 470–471.

17. Ibid., pp. 472–473.

18. Ibid., p. 473.

19. "Pronunciamientos Referentes a América Latina Extraidos de Documentos de Conferencias y Reuniones Ministeriales Habidas desde 1961 a 1982," no date or source, working papers from the Ministry of Foreign Affairs, Managua, as cited in Morales and Vanden, "Relations with the Nonaligned Movement," p. 474.

20. Alan Riding, "Nonaligned Bloc Backs Nicaragua: 'Systematic Attacks' Against Sandinistas Are Denounced," *New York Times*, January 15, 1983.

21. Morales and Vanden, "Relations with the Nonaligned Movement," pp. 475–476.

22. Interview, UN Diplomat, New York, August 8, 1989.

23. Ibid. See also UN document, G.A. S.C., A/41/697, S/18392, October 14, 1986, which contains the proceedings of the meeting.

24. "Nonaligned Movement Supports Peace in Central America," *Barricada Internacional* 9, no. 301 (September 30, 1989), p. 3.

25. Torres Pérez, "La política exterior," p. 158.

26. "U.N. General Assembly Adopts Resolution Calling on U.S. to Comply with World Court Ruling," *New York Times*, October 26, 1988.

27. For a statement of Nicaragua's policy in regard to international mechanisms, see "Nicaragua's Foreign Policy: Ten Years of Principles and Practice," pp. 25–38.

28. Dennis Torres Pérez, "La política exterior de la revolución popular sandinista," a Ministerio de Relaciones Exterior document, Managua, 1989, pp. 6 and 12.

29. See Torres Pérez, "La política exterior" (*Cuadernos*), pp. 164–165, for a comprehensive listing of these positions.

30. Bendaña, p. 30.

31. The legal team that argued Nicaragua's case before the International Court of Justice included: Carlos Arguello Gómez, agent and counsel; Ian Brownly (Oxford University), Abram Chayes (Harvard Law School), Alain Pellet (University of Paris), and Paul S. Reichler, counsels and advocates; and Agusto Zamora Rodríguez (legal adviser to the Nicaraguan Foreign Ministry), Judith C. Applebaum (Reichler and Applebaum), and David Wippman (Reichler and Applebaum), counsel.

32. Cited in Louis Henkin et al., *International Law: Cases and Materials*, 2nd ed. (St. Paul, Minn.: West, 1987), p. 634.

33. Ibid., pp. 708–709. See also pp. 633–650 and 708–736. The judgment of the World Court against the United States also stated that "under general principles of humanitarian law, the United States was bound to refrain from encouragement of persons or groups engaged in conflict in Nicaragua to commit violations of common article 3 of the four Geneva Conventions of 12 August 1949" (p. 722). (Common Article 3 treats conflicts not of an international character and states that persons not taking part in the hostilities—civilians and the wounded—shall not be subject to (1) violence to life and person, including mutilation and torture, (2) being taken as a hostage, (3) outrages upon personal dignity, and (4) the passing of sentences and the carrying out of executions without previous judgment pronounced by a regularly constituted court.)

34. Torres Pérez, "La política exterior" (*Cuadernos*), p. 15.

35. "Nonaligned Movement Supports Peace in Central America," p. 3.

36. Nadia Malley, "Relations with Western Europe and the Socialist International," in Walker, ed., *Nicaragua: The First Five Years*, p. 487.

37. Harry E. Vanden and Waltrud Queiser Morales, "Nicaragua's Relations with the Nonaligned," *Journal of InterAmerican Studies and World Affairs* 27, no. 3 (Fall 1985), p. 159.

38. Malley, "Relations with Western Europe," p. 487.

39. Ibid.

40. Ibid., pp. 493–496.

41. "Nicaragua's Foreign Policy: Ten Years of Principles and Practice," p. 20. It should, however, be pointed out that the trends I noted—particularly U.S. pressure and the election of more-conservative governments in West Germany and Holland—led to a decrease in the Nicaraguan proportion of such Central American aid. See, for instance, Latin American Weekly Report, February 12, 1987, p. 8; and Solon Barraclough et al. Nicaragua: desarrollo y supervivencia (Amsterdam: Transnational Institute, 1988), p. 112. Nicaragua received 50 percent of such aid from 1981 to 1984 (p. 114).

42. Latin American Weekly Report, February 19, 1989, p. 5.

43. Ibid., p. 6.

44. Ibid., March 26, 1987, p. 11.

45. Ibid., January 15, 1988, p. 8.

46. Ibid., July 14, 1988, pp. 6–7.

47. Ibid., May 4, 1989, pp. 10–11.

48. Ibid., May 25, 1989, p. 7.

49. "FSLN Broadens Relations with the Socialist International," Envío 8, no. 97 (August 1989), p. 21.

50. I would like to thank Patricia Grace Wilson for sharing her insights and making important research materials available for this section.

51. Cole Blasier, The Giant's Rival: The USSR and Latin America, 2nd ed. (Pittsburgh: University of Pittsburgh Press, 1987), p. 140.

52. Ibid., p. 144.

53. Interview, Tomás Borge, Managua, December 7, 1984.

54. "Nicaragua's Foreign Policy: Ten Years of Principles and Practice," p. 38.

55. Lowenthal, Partners in Conflict, p. 35.

56. Ibid.

57. Theodore Schwab and Harold Sims, "Relations with the Communist States," in Walker, ed., Nicaragua: The First Five Years, p. 452.

58. See H. Vanden, "State Policy and the Cult of Terror in Central America," in Paul Wilkinson and Alasdair M. Stewart, eds., Contemporary Research on Terrorism (Aberdeen: Aberdeen University Press, 1987), p. 264; and Christopher Dickey, With the Contras (New York: Simon and Schuster, 1985).

59. Schwab and Sims, "Relations with the Communist States," p. 452.

60. Vanden and Morales, "Nicaragua's Relations with the Nonaligned," p. 159.

61. Ibid.

62. Robert Mathews, "The Limits of Friendship: Nicaragua and the West," NACLA: Report on the Americas 19, no. 3 (May/June 1985), p. 23. This issue of NACLA is devoted to Sandinista foreign policy.

63. "Nicaragua's Foreign Policy: Ten Years of Principles and Practice," p. 33.

64. Ibid., p. 34.

65. Ibid.

66. Blasier, The Giant's Rival, p. 145.

67. Baraclough et al., Nicaragua: Desarrollo y supervivencia, Appendix 2. Long- and medium-term loans and credits from the socialist countries for this period totaled $1.57 billion.

68. Latin American Weekly Report, January 14, 1987, p. 8.

69. Ibid., p. 9.

70. International Monetary Fund, Direction of Trade Statistics, *Yearbook 1988, International Monetary Fund* (Washington, D.C.: International Monetary Fund, 1988), p. 302.

71. *Latin American Weekly Report*, June 11, 1987, p. 4.

72. Blasier, *The Giant's Rival*, pp. 146–147.

73. *Latin American Weekly Report*, June 11, 1987, p. 4.

74. U.S. Department of Defense, "Trends in Soviet Bloc Aid to Nicaragua," provided by U.S. State Department in interview, Washington, August 3, 1989.

75. *Latin American Weekly Report*, November 19, 1987, p. 2.

76. Blasier, *The Giant's Rival*, p. 145.

77. *Latin American Weekly Report*, October 26, 1989, p. 11.

78. Ibid., November 19, 1987, p. 2.

79. Ibid., July 14, 1988, pp. 6–7.

80. Interview, UN diplomat, New York, August 8, 1989.

81. Vanderlaan, *Revolution and Foreign Policy*, p. 242.

82. Alan Garcia, as quoted in ibid., p. 242.

83. International Monetary Fund, *Yearbook 1988*, p. 302.

84. See Carlos Tunnermann B., "Nicaragua cumplió: ¿Lo harán los otros?" *Pensamiento Propio* 4, no. 60 (May 1989), pp. 12–17.

PART III

The Counterrevolution

The two chapters in this section examine the counterrevolution. Chapter 15 is by Peter Kornbluh of the National Security Archive, the Washington-based research institute that played the central role in uncovering and documenting the Iran-contra scandal. After describing in detail the character of the low-intensity conflict the United States orchestrated against Nicaragua, Kornbluh documents the tremendous human and material loss it inflicted and concludes that "although the Sandinista government survived the external violence of the Colossus of the North, internally the 'full impact' of U.S. policy translated into a resounding political defeat [of the FSLN] at the polls." Angharad Valdivia (Chapter 16) focuses on the narrower, but very important, topic of U.S. manipulation of the Nicaraguan and other Latin American media. She shows how U.S. government agencies and front institutions bought influence in regional and Nicaraguan media outlets—particularly Violeta de Chamorro's La Prensa—and used the media in a propaganda campaign to discredit the Sandinistas within Nicaragua, in the region, and in the United States.

FIFTEEN

The U.S. Role in the Counterrevolution

PETER KORNBLUH

The U.S. campaign to undermine the Nicaraguan revolution began even before the overthrow of the Somoza dictatorship on July 19, 1979. The Carter administration tried desperately to block the triumph of the Sandinista-led insurrection. The Reagan administration deployed every conceivable weapon of war—short of an overt military incursion—in a protracted effort to roll back the revolution. The Bush White House, which could not continue its predecessor's contra policy because of domestic political constraints, resorted to quieter, subtler methods of intervention. Yet throughout the decade of U.S.-Nicaraguan relations beginning in 1979, Washington's overall objective remained the same— to force the Sandinistas from power.

Carter Confronts the Revolution

The Carter administration's policy toward the Nicaraguan revolution was based on the same "hegemonic presumption" that has dominated the posture of U.S. presidents since the early nineteenth century.[1] Despite a reformist approach to U.S. relations with the Third World, uncontrolled change in Central America remained anathema to U.S. officials, who were wedded to the notion that Washington had a historical imperative to dictate events in its traditional sphere of influence. During strategy discussions on how to handle the growing insurrection in Nicaragua, National Security Council (NSC) Adviser Zbigniew Brzezinski echoed the language of the 1823 Monroe Doctrine: "We have to demonstrate that we are still the decisive force in determining the political outcomes in Central America and that we will not permit others to intervene," he told President Carter.[2]

Carter officials recognized that the Somoza regime had become a catalyst for radicalization and instability. "In a nutshell, what exists [in Nicaragua] is very widespread opposition to the continuation of Somoza in power . . . an opposition that spreads across the spectrum from conservative businessmen to leftist extremists," Assistant Secretary of State for Inter-American Affairs Viron Vaky informed the Senate Foreign Relations Committee in a classified executive session as early as September 19, 1978. "Perhaps," Vaky told the senators, "some outside catalyst might be able to promote this process so that the choice does not develop into that radical polarization of just Somoza on one side and the extremists, who are willing to take violent action, on the other."[3]

Nevertheless, the administration delayed in exercising Washington's traditional dominion over Nicaraguan politics until mid-1979, when the Sandinista Front for National Liberation (FSLN) was on the verge of taking power. Having placed the first Somoza in power in 1932, the United States informed his son on June 28, 1979, that the dynasty was over. U.S. Ambassador to Managua Lawrence Pezzullo cabled Washington that he had met with Somoza and "suggested we design a scenario for his resignation."[4]

The Carter administration's "scenario" for a transition of power in Nicaragua called for creating a provisional government of moderates that excluded the FSLN. At the same time, the White House sought to salvage the Nicaraguan National Guard, as Assistant Secretary Vaky instructed Ambassador Pezzullo, "to avoid leaving the FSLN as the only organized military force."

Indeed, preserving the very military institution created by U.S. Marines to counter nationalist leader Augusto Sandino in the 1920s became the cornerstone of U.S. strategy to stop the revolutionary movement that bore his name more than fifty years later. Even as Somoza's widely despised praetorian army rampaged through civilian sectors of Nicaragua, indiscriminately killing teenage boys and girls, U.S. officials labored to find a means to save the National Guard. "Some national security forces must remain to maintain order after Somoza's departure," Ambassador Pezzullo wrote in a June 30, 1979, cable entitled "National Guard Survival." "Otherwise the vacuum we all wish to avoid will be filled by the FSLN, with all the negative consequences that would bring." With "careful orchestration we have a better than even chance of preserving enough of the GN to maintain order and hold the FSLN in check after Somoza resigns."[5]

Despite Washington's orchestrations—which included an effort to enlist an OAS multilateral peacekeeping force to intervene in Nicaragua and prolonging the bloodshed by using Somoza's departure date as a bargaining chip in a futile effort to change the composition of the Sandinistas' interim government—the Carter administration's frantic efforts to alter the course of Nicaraguan history failed. The National Guard totally disintegrated within hours of Somoza's departure for Miami on July 17. Two days later, Sandinista troops marched, unopposed, into Managua, and the revolution was complete.

Attempting to salvage what influence it could in the face of a Sandinista victory, the Carter administration shifted from a policy of counterrevolution to cautious accommodation. Employing economic aid as a carrot to moderate the course of the revolution, the administration advanced $15 million in emergency reconstruction aid and pushed a $75 million assistance package through Congress. In September 1979, the Sandinista *comandantes* even received an invitation to meet with Jimmy Carter at the White House.

The Reagan Doctrine of Rollback

Ronald Reagan came into office predisposed to replace President Carter's carrot with a heavy stick. Achieving a modus vivendi with the FSLN was all but ruled out from the beginning. Instead, the new president and the ideological cold warriors around him decided to make Nicaragua a test case of the Reagan Doctrine of taking the offensive against revolution in the Third World.[6]

For the new team in Washington, the Sandinista revolution was a symbol of Washington's post-Vietnam loss of preeminence—not only in Central America but also around the globe. "We had just witnessed a five-year period where the Soviet Union tried out a strategem of sponsoring guerrilla movements that would topple moderate regimes, and install their own totalitarian successor, and they had phenomenal success . . . in Angola, Ethiopia, South Yemen, Cambodia, Afghanistan, Mozambique, [and] Nicaragua," as Robert McFarlane, former national security adviser, said later in explaining the impetus for applying the Reagan Doctrine in Nicaragua. Failure to react so close to home, administration officials believed, would jeopardize Washington's ability to dictate events elsewhere in the world. "If we could not muster an effective counter to Cuban-Sandinista strategy in our own backyard, it was far less likely that we could do so in the years ahead in more distant locations," McFarlane continued. "*We had to win this one.*"[7]

Unlike in the earlier era of "gunboat diplomacy," however, a U.S. president in the 1980s could no longer simply dispatch the marines to Central America to install the government of his choice. The Vietnam Syndrome—a widespread public resistance to having America's young people fighting and dying in a distant Third World conflict—constrained Reagan and his advisers as they plotted their Nicaragua strategy. Therefore, U.S. officials turned to an emerging strategic doctrine known as low-intensity conflict (LIC) for post-Vietnam intervention in the Third World.

In a February 1981 "Covert Action Proposal for Central America," one of the earliest documents concerning the Reagan administration's plans to counter revolution in the region, McFarlane presented the case for a multifront assault short of direct military intervention. "The key point to be made now is that while we must move promptly, we must assure that our political, economic, diplomatic, propaganda, military, and covert actions are well coordinated."[8] This approach reflected a new reliance on the LIC doctrine, which, according to Pentagon manuals, called for the "synergistic application of comprehensive political, social, economic and psychological efforts." By combining various methods of intervention short of overt military deployment, the United States could engage in what one LIC proponent called "total war at the grassroots level," presumably without the domestic and international political backlash that a conventional war would provoke.[9] In Nicaragua, this "total war" strategy called for four main fronts.

Paramilitary Operations

Between 1981 and 1988, the centerpiece of the Reagan administration's low-intensity-warfare strategy was a program of direct paramilitary attacks. Conducted by a proxy force of exiles supplemented by specially trained U.S. operatives, these operations were, ironically, meant to be the covert side of Reagan's policy. Instead, the so-called contra war became the most notorious symbol of U.S. intervention in Nicaragua.

For the so-called bleeders (those willing to wage a bloody war of attrition to undermine the Sandinistas) in the Reagan White House, building and directing a surrogate force of counterrevolutionaries proved the perfect instrument for a policy of punishment designed to undermine Nicaragua's fragile revolutionary economic and social reconstruction. What U.S. officials depicted as a campaign to harass and pressure the Sandinistas into halting their alleged export of revolution into neighboring El Salvador in practice translated into vicious attacks on small villages, state-owned agricultural cooperatives, rural health clinics, economic infrastructure, and, finally, civilian noncombatants. Indeed, CIA training manuals explicitly advised the contras on how to "neutralize carefully selected and planned targets"—an intelligence euphemism for assassinating court judges, magistrates, police, and state security officials.[10]

Even with contra forces pillaging the Nicaraguan countryside, U.S. paramilitary strategies called for ever-more-dramatic and devastating assaults against the Sandinistas. "Let's make them sweat," CIA director William Casey repeatedly urged his CIA managers of the covert war. "Let's make the bastards sweat."[11] Accordingly, the CIA, and later the National Security Council, took a direct operational role in special paramilitary attacks on Nicaraguan installations. Economic sabotage focused on oil storage tanks and pipelines, port facilities, communication centers, and military depots, causing hundreds of millions of dollars in damages. As a propaganda ploy, the contras claimed credit for these attacks; in reality they played no part.

Economic Destabilization

Paramilitary sabotage on the ground was supplemented from abroad by a concerted program of punitive economic sanctions. First, bilateral aid and, later, all economic trade was terminated. In addition, U.S. officials orchestrated an "invisible blockade" of multilateral bank credits to Nicaragua. Some loans from World Bank or the Inter-American Development Bank (IDB) were simply vetoed; where a U.S. veto was not possible, U.S. officials quietly moved "to persuade the Managements of the [multilateral development banks—MDBs] not to bring these loans forward," according to internal Treasury Department memoranda. After September 1983, Nicaragua received no further loans from the World Bank or the IDB.

The Reagan administration also attempted to pressure U.S. allies in Europe and Latin America to halt their economic trade and aid to Nicaragua. "We were very active in trying to reduce Western financial flows," admitted one former NSC official.[12] One July 1983 NSC "action plan" called on Secretary of State George Shultz to "press Western European governments at the highest level to cease financial support for the Sandinistas." National Security Decision Directive 124, signed by President Reagan in February 1984, authorized U.S. national security agencies to "intensify diplomatic efforts with the Mexican government to reduce its . . . economic and diplomatic support for the Nicaraguan government" because of its role in the Contadora peace negotiations and its substantial exports of oil to Nicaragua.[13]

Military Operations

The Pentagon, in addition to the CIA and U.S. monetary agencies, played a key—and largely unreported—role in the Reagan administration's LIC strategy of destabilizing the economy and political situation without actually sending U.S. troops. On July 12, 1983, President Reagan directed Secretary of Defense Caspar Weinberger to aid the CIA's contra war: "The Department of Defense will provide maximum possible assistance to the Director of [Central Intelligence] in improving support to the Nicaraguan resistance forces."[14] The Pentagon's assistance to the covert war took a number of forms: In 1983 and 1984, the Department of Defense collaborated with the CIA on Operation Tipped Kettle, a joint covert project to acquire armaments captured by Israel from the PLO during the siege of Lebanon and transfer them to the contras.[15] During the same time period, the Pentagon conducted Operation Elephant Herd, a covert program to help the CIA circumvent congressional budget restrictions on the contra war by transferring "surplus" Department of Defense planes and other equipment to the agency free of charge.[16] U.S. special operations forces conducted support operations on behalf of the contras, and in 1986 the Pentagon began training contra commanders in tactical insurgency warfare at military bases in the United States.

An unprecedented U.S. military buildup in Central America, undertaken as part of a series of highly visible military maneuvers around Nicaragua's coasts and near its borders, represented the largest Pentagon contribution to the U.S. war. The maneuvers constituted a grandiose psychological operations program designed to instill uncertainty among Sandinista officials about U.S. intentions. Among Pentagon psy-ops specialists, this program was known as Perception Management. According to a top-secret Defense Department action plan prepared for President Reagan, "a perception management program . . . will be coupled with the activities of Ahuas Tara II," one of the large military exercises.[17] "One of the central purposes is to create fear of an invasion, to push very close to the border, deliberately, to set off all the alarms," as one U.S. official explained.[18] With Sandinista government coffers already drained from the fight against the contras and the economic blockade, the constant threat of direct U.S. military intervention forced Nicaraguan leaders to divert personnel and resources from social programs into preparing for the worst-case war scenario.

A Propaganda War

A July 1983 presidential directive also called for a "public affairs action plan . . . to educate and heighten the perception of the American people regarding the situation in Central America and the dangers posed by the Marxist/Leninist government of Nicaragua."[19] To implement this plan, and wage the important fight for U.S. public opinion, the Reagan White House created a sophisticated propaganda apparatus that employed Orwellian tactics to reshape perceptions of the conflict in Central America. This campaign resembled the type of covert propaganda operations the CIA routinely engages in against foreign nations but is prohibited from undertaking at home. Indeed, a senior CIA propaganda specialist, transferred to the National Security Council in 1982, oversaw the administration's "public diplomacy" effort.[20] Moreover, U.S. military psychological operations specialists, skilled in "persuasive communications," were detailed to Washington from the 4th Psychological Operations Group at Fort Bragg, North Carolina, to "prepare studies, papers, speeches and memoranda to support [public diplomacy] activities" and to look for "exploitable themes and trends," according to internal public diplomacy documents. "We have enough to keep them busy until the Contras march into Managua," joked one Pentagon official in another memoranda.[21]

The institutional arm of the public diplomacy operations was the Office of Public Diplomacy for Latin America and the Caribbean. Housed in the State Department, the Office of Public Diplomacy actually reported to NSC officials, including Lt. Col. Oliver North. The activities of the office were reviewed at weekly Public Diplomacy Working Group meetings attended by North, as well as CIA, Department of Defense (DOD), U.S. Information Agency (USIA), and State Department representatives.

A confidential-sensitive strategy paper, drafted by the Office of Public Diplomacy deputy director, Col. Daniel Jacobowitz, himself a Pentagon psy-ops specialist, described the office's thematic approach to influencing media and public perceptions of the war in Nicaragua. He noted, "Overall theme: The Nicaraguan Freedom Fighters are fighters for freedom in the American tradition, FSLN [Sandinistas] are evil." The contras would be depicted as "the good guys . . . the underdogs," by public diplomacy efforts that would emphasize their "religious" and "anti-Somoza credentials." The Sandinista government, on the other hand, would be cast as "an outpost of the Soviet Empire" and the public diplomacy campaign would highlight "subthemes" that included Nicaragua's military buildup, "the drug connection," and human rights violations.[22]

The Office of Public Diplomacy peddled these "themes" to journalists, editors, academics, conservative constituent groups, Congress, and the public-at-large through a variety of mechanisms. Glossy publications were disseminated en masse, and public diplomacy officials selectively leaked stories to the TV networks and other press outlets in an effort to galvanize support for contra aid. Public diplomacy tactics also incorporated what internal documents called "White Propaganda Operations"—sponsoring stories and opinion columns in the press but disguising any government connection—and promoting misinformation, as in the case of the 1984 mythical "MIGs crisis." Private-sector lobbyists were paid to shepherd contra leaders around the country, with particular focus on the districts of swing Democrats whose votes were needed to win contra aid in Congress. Public diplomacy, concluded the congressional authors of the report, *Iran Contra Affair*, "turned out to mean public-relations lobbying, all at taxpayers' expense."[23]

The Counterrevolution Begins

Within weeks of Ronald Reagan's inauguration, White House officials began to contemplate a "destabilization program" in Nicaragua. Their long-term plan called for Washington to undermine Nicaragua's fragile economy—still recovering from Somoza's destructive efforts to stay in power—by ending U.S. assistance, blocking multilateral bank loans, and pressuring other nations to isolate the Sandinistas. The resultant social and economic distress, it was hoped, would incite internal opposition and evolve into a widespread insurrection led by U.S.-backed contras invading from Honduras and Costa Rica.[24]

Nothwithstanding the failure of the contras to overthrow the Sandinistas, U.S. policy between 1981 and 1988 closely followed this scenario.

On March 9, 1981, Reagan signed his first "Finding," authorizing $19.5 million for expanding CIA operations throughout Central America; on April 1, bilateral economic assistance was terminated. In short order, the administration denied Nicaragua U.S. Export-Import Bank trade credits—needed by industrialists, merchants, and farmers to import U.S. manufactured goods—and Overseas Private Investment Corporation guarantees, which underwrite U.S. corporate investments in the Third World. The first threatening military maneuvers off Nicaragua's coast, Halcon Vista, were conducted in August 1981. And on November 27, the president signed National Security Decision Directive (NSDD) 17, authorizing the instigation of the CIA/contra covert war program.

"I hereby find that the following operation in a foreign country (including all support necessary to such operation) is important to the national security of the United States . . . : Support and conduct [CIA] paramilitary operations against Nicaragua," stated President Reagan's December 1, 1981, Finding, which accompanied NSDD 17.[25] From then on, proxy warfare in the form of a counterrevolutionary army of Nicaraguan exiles became the vanguard of U.S. strategy toward Nicaragua. The CIA moved quickly to expand relations with former Nicaraguan National Guard officials, Honduran military officers, and Argentine operatives already training small bands of contras—relations that had been established even before Reagan signed NSDD 17. As early as August 1981, Duane "Dewey" Clarridge, the head of the CIA's Latin American section, traveled to Honduras to meet with the Honduran generals. "I speak in the name of President Ronald Reagan," he told them. "We want to support this effort to change the government of Nicaragua."[26] After Reagan authorized $19.95 million for the covert war in November, the CIA began funneling large sums of money and equipment through the Hondurans and Argentines to set up training facilities and bases along the Nicaraguan-Honduran border.

But the U.S. role went far beyond financing the contra campaign. A CIA "scope paper" that accompanied NSDD 17 stated that the CIA would "work with foreign governments as appropriate," a provision that enabled the CIA to collaborate with Honduras and Argentina and later to approach more than a dozen other nations to assist the contra war. The plan also specified that "in some instances CIA might (possibly using U.S. personnel) take unilateral paramilitary action"—which portended direct CIA attacks on Nicaraguan targets.[27] A subsequent secret "scope paper" stated, "Arms and other support will be provided to Nicaraguan paramilitary forces operating inside Nicaragua [and] instructors will train these forces to attack targets inside Nicaragua." In addition, the scope paper identified CIA "Propaganda and Civic Action" as an important part of the contra operation: "guidance and media assistance will be provided to Nicaraguan opposition elements and paramilitary forces."[28]

In fall 1981 the contras constituted a force of 250 men, most of them remnants of Anastasio Somoza's personal army, the National Guard. Ragtag bands roamed the Honduran-Nicaraguan border, resorting to random violence and chicken theft in order to survive.[29] Under CIA direction, these groups were transformed into paramilitary forces equipped with trucks, planes, automatic weapons, and artillery. With the influx of U.S. funds, equipment, and personnel, the frequency and destructiveness of the contra attack increased rapidly.

The war on the ground, supplemented by escalating U.S. trade sanctions from abroad, quickly took a discernible toll on Nicaragua's government, social order, and economy. "The contra activity has some heavy costs for the Sandinistas," Ambassador Anthony Quainton reported in a classified October 1982 cable, "Assessment of Recent Counterrevolutionary Activity." The contras "compell the GRN [Government of the Republic of Nicaragua] to divert an increasing portion of its meager resources to security. In addition, they serve to provide encouragement to those opponents of the regime who are convinced the survivability of the GRN is at risk."[30] In another confidential cable, titled "The Economic Costs of the Counterrevolution," Ambassador Quainton described the direct and indirect economic damage wrought by the CIA/contra war:

Over the past eighteen months, the ebb and flow of anti-government guerrilla activity on two fronts has forced the GRN to devote substantially greater resources to its internal defense. While direct military costs have risen, the country has also paid an increasing price in damage done to crops, productive equipment and infrastructure. By devoting the time and effort of several thousand active young men to the military struggle, Nicaragua has forgone the productive benefit of their work, while land has remained idle simply because the ongoing military struggle has made it impossible to work in some areas. The economic costs are real.[31]

Moreover, the brutal character of the contra war became apparent within months of its initiation. "In a 100 day period from 14 March to 21 June, at least 106 insurgent incidents occurred within Nicaragua," the Defense Intelligence Agency reported in July 1982. Attacks during this period included: sabotage of highway bridges, sniper fire on small military patrols, the burning of customs warehouses and crops, and "the assassination of minor government officials."[32] By mid-1982 the assassination of civilians and wanton acts of terrorism against nonmilitary targets that would come to characterize the reality of the contra operations were already well recognized within the U.S. national security agencies.

The Contras: Myths and Realities

The CIA's campaign to build the contras into a fighting army was accompanied by a parallel political campaign—conducted in large part by the public diplomacy apparatus—to obscure their origins and falsify their purpose. Contra mythology included initially depicting the rebels as a "interdiction force" and later as "freedom fighters." The purpose of sponsoring a violent counterrevolution, President Reagan and his top advisers avowed, was to force the Sandinistas to negotiate with their internal opposition and regional neighbors. According to the president, the Sandinistas would "come to the negotiating table only when they see the carrot of peaceful settlement backed up by the stick of a well-equipped armed opposition."[33]

Initially, the contras broke down into three general groupings: those forces operating in the north, along the Honduran-Nicaraguan border; those operating in the south, along the Costa Rican–Nicaraguan border; and Mískito Indian contra organizations, rebelling against the Sandinista encroachment on indigenous rights in the Atlantic Coast region. The Mískito contras divided their allegiance between the first two groups.

The Nicaraguan Democratic Force (FDN) became the vanguard contra organization. Forged in August 1981 through the efforts of the CIA and Argentina to unify several small exile groups, it operated out of Honduras. From the beginning, the FDN was dominated by former officers of Somoza's National Guard. A classified Defense Intelligence Agency report described the FDN as "led by Col. Enrique Bermudez—former GN member and last Nicaraguan military attache to the US under the government of President Anastasio Somoza—and other ex-GN officers" and as "the largest, best organized and most effective of the anti-government insurgent groups."[34] Until 1988, when military aid to the contras was finally terminated, the FDN would receive the bulk of U.S. resources and attention; throughout the war it was the most active of the various contra armies.

Nevertheless, CIA officials recognized early on that former National Guard officers who filled the FDN command made it difficult to cast the contras as a nationalist force of democrats. Accordingly, in 1982 Duane Clarridge recruited the famous former Sandinista "Comandante Zero"—Edén Pastora—to the contra ranks. In February, the CIA flew Pastora to Acapulco to meet with Clarridge; in March and again in May, Clarridge brought Pastora to Washington to meet with CIA Director Casey. By then Pastora had formed the Democratic Revolutionary Alliance (ARDE), based in Costa Rica, and joined with a former member of the revolutionary junta, Alfonso Robelo, in establishing a Southern Front in the war against the Sandinistas.

ARDE served CIA purposes for two key reasons: First, because Pastora was a former Sandinista commander, his nationalism could not be challenged. As a CIA intelligence report noted, ARDE had "stronger anti-Somoza credentials than the Nicaraguan Democratic Force."[35] Second, a viable Southern Front was necessary in order to provide a strategic war plan of contra attacks from the north and south. Soon, ARDE forces were receiving approximately $400,000 a month through CIA intermediaries.[36]

For anyone with a sense of Central American geography, covert U.S. assistance to Costa Rican–based contras exposed the first major myth of the contra war—the CIA's initial claim to Congress that the rebels were an "interdiction force" that was to block Cuban/Sandinista arms shipments flowing northward from Nicaragua to leftist rebels in El Salvador. As legislators became increasingly edgy about the purpose of these covert operations and the character of the exile forces, the Reagan administration mounted a concerted propaganda campaign to depict the contras as a nationalist force—"freedom fighters," as President Reagan was fond of repeating—whose goals of democracy were worthy of U.S. support. The contras were "indigenous Nicaraguans fighting for their cause," argued one resource paper put out by the Office of Public Diplomacy. They were "the moral equivalent of our founding fathers," Reagan intoned in February 1985.

Such hyperbole struck even contra members and their closest U.S. advisers as absurd. FDN leaders were "liars and greed and power motivated. . . . They are not the people to build a new Nicaragua," concluded Oliver North's personal liaison with the contras, Robert Owen, in a classified memorandum.[37] "It was reminiscent of Orwell's doublespeak," wrote Edgar Chamorro, former FDN directorate member. "Counterrevolutionaries hand-picked by the CIA were compared to founding fathers." The main reason the contras failed, argued Chamorro, was precisely because they were not a nationalist, independent force: "We were a proxy army, directed, funded, receiving all intelligence and suggestions, from the CIA. We had no plan for Nicaragua, we were working for American goals."[38]

Indeed, according to documentation now available, U.S. national security agencies, including the CIA, NSC, and Department of State, governed every facet of the contras' political and military operations. The same "control mentality" that dictated broader U.S. policy in the region manifested itself in the micromanagement of the contra war.

Starting with the FDN in August 1981, every major contra coalition formed over the next seven years was "made in the USA." "CIA promoters of the contras use[d] all the repackaging techniques for marketing a new product," noted Chamorro in his book *Packaging the Contras.*[39] In December 1982, before the first major vote in Congress on contra aid, the CIA brought together seven prominent anti-Sandinista exiles to create a new FDN ostensibly controlled by civilians who had

opposed Somoza. This directorate was designed to offset charges that
the FDN was commanded by Somocista national guardsmen who wanted
to restore the old order. At their first press conference, CIA officials
counseled the new directorate members to say that they were not trying
to overthrow the Sandinistas but instead were "creating the conditions
for democracy."⁴⁰ Two months later, the CIA hired a Miami-based public
relations firm—paying $2 million over the next two years—to "publicize
the FDN and the FDN directorate in specific target countries," according
to the contract, and "to project your organization and its goals in a
very positive manner."⁴¹

Similarly, before a critical vote on nonlethal aid to the contras in
June 1985, NSC officials brought together Adolfo Calero, Alfonso Robelo,
and Arturo Cruz—the "Triple A" as they were known—to form yet
another "new" organization, the Unified Nicaraguan Opposition (UNO).
"UNO is a creation of the USG [U.S. government] to garner support
from Congress," noted a candid "eyes only" memo written to Oliver
North by Robert Owen. "Almost everything it has accomplished is
because the hand of the USG [U.S. government] has been there directing
and manipulating."⁴²

The main contra leaders, including the three men who made up the
leadership of UNO, were on the CIA/NSC payroll. Calero, the FDN's
political chieftain, was reported to be a longtime CIA asset.⁴³ (Through
1988, this relationship would protect Calero from multiple efforts by
more moderate contra factions to oust him as the contras' preeminent
political leader.) In 1985 and 1986, National Security Council operatives
funneled more than $100,000 to Robelo to finance his Southern Front
political activities. Cruz, the most moderate civilian leader—and the
most respected on Capitol Hill—was actually transferred from the CIA
payroll to the covert account controlled by Oliver North after the House
Permanent Select Committee on Intelligence objected to the illegality
of his lobbying while being paid by the CIA.⁴⁴

In a February 27, 1985, memorandum aptly entitled "Cruz Control,"
Oliver North reported to Robert McFarlane that Cruz had been a "CIA
asset for several months" and that certain members of Congress were
threatening to expose his CIA connections if Cruz was not removed
from the payroll or did not stop lobbying. "I told director Casey that
[Cruz's] costs and retainer fees could be paid for by another source so
that both [Cruz] and the Agency could honestly say he is not 'on the
payroll,'" North advised. "After some deliberation, Casey decided that
they would prefer to keep him. Their rationale is based on being able
to control [Cruz] because he is, as you know, the key to our [deleted]
program."⁴⁵ Subsequently, however, Cruz was transferred to a covert
NSC slush fund; North arranged to have approximately $6,200 per
month deposited in the contra leader's bank account to secure his
continuing cooperation.

U.S. officials also participated in the drafting of all major political/ diplomatic statements released by the contras. The FDN's first "peace initiative," published in January 1983, was put together by CIA officials for release by the new FDN civilian directorate.[46] The more famous San José Declaration, signed by dozens of exile organizations and contra leaders and released in Costa Rica on March 1, 1985, was actually drafted at the direction of Lieutenant Colonel North in Miami several months earlier. "The document was written by Calero, Cruz and North in my hotel room on January 29 and 30," North reported to his superiors. "All agreed that the objective was . . . to galvanize the internal opposition and convince the U.S. Congress that the opposition was led by reasonable men."[47]

U.S. control over the contras extended into the military sphere as well. From the start, the CIA supplied the funds, purchased the weapons, established logistical infrastructure, provided intelligence and target lists, coordinated the training programs—in short, ran the paramilitary war. Rather than an independent, nationalist force, the result was a contra operation wholly dependent on the United States, unable to sustain itself without U.S. support. "When the CIA left there was no structure left behind for these people to get their own supplies," one operative brought in by the NSC to assist the contras after Congress cut off CIA funding testified at Oliver North's trial. "I don't think they knew where to go to buy anything because everything had been given to them up to that point."[48]

Even North admitted the abject surrogacy of the contras, although he blamed it on the CIA's inability to train them sufficiently. "To this date," he wrote in a secret January 1986 memorandum for John Poindexter, "the CIA has been unable to produce a coherent military strategy, the tactics to support such a strategy, or to adequately train the [contra] force to accomplish either."[49]

The contras did prove adept at carrying out U.S. guerrilla warfare strategies, supplied in the CIA training manuals, which advised them to "neutralize" civilian leaders, incite mob violence, and attack "soft" targets such as agricultural cooperatives. But all major acts of sabotage inside Nicaragua were conducted by the CIA itself. These attacks were designed as much to foster the myth of the contras as a viable paramilitary force as they were to wreak havoc on the Nicaraguan economy. Although the contras publicly took credit for these attacks, in reality they played no role whatsoever.

These attacks began in September 1983 when the CIA initiated a campaign of destruction, using their own personnel and unilaterally controlled Latino assets (UCLAs). In response to direct orders from Director William Casey, on September 8, CIA assets launched a major sabotage attack on oil pipeline and dock facilities at Puerto Sandino.

On October 10, operatives set an oil storage facility ablaze, forcing the evacuation of the city of Corinto.[50]

In early 1984, these attacks escalated with the authority of President Reagan. "Our objective should be to bring the Nicaragua situation to a head in 1984," a Special Interagency Working Group reported to McFarlane in January of that year. At a January 6 meeting of the National Security Policy Group (NSPG), the most elite foreign policy-making body of the Reagan administration, the president approved his advisers' recommendation that the "covert action program should proceed with stepped up intensity."[51]

According to a "secret/sensitive" CIA "Chronology of Salient Para-military Actions and Related Developments," between January 1 and April 24, the agency, UCLAs, and, infrequently, contra personnel conducted twenty-two direct attacks on Nicaraguan economic targets, including the laying of mines.[52] Using a "mother ship" anchored in international waters as an operational base, the CIA launched helicopter gunship attacks, "Q (quick motorized) boat" assaults, and mine-laying missions against Nicaraguan boats, oil facilities, communications centers, military bases, and international shipping. CIA agents crewed the "mother ship" and flew the intelligence support planes and the lead helicopters used in the attacks, while the "Q boats" were commanded by "3rd country nationals and manned by personnel from Central America."[53]

On a number of occasions, these attacks resulted in direct military confrontations between agency personnel and Sandinista troops. In the March 27, 1984, mining of Corinto harbor, for example, the CIA reported: "Six mines placed in shipping channel (major clash). One British tanker damaged; one Japanese freighter damaged. Four Nicaraguan patrol boats hit; two sunk, two damaged. Clash damaged one Nicaraguan patrol boat; one KIA, one WIA.[54]

The explicit purpose of the mining operations, Oliver North and his NSC colleague Constantine Menges reported to McFarlane in a top-secret March 2, 1984, memorandum titled "Special Activities in Nica-ragua" was "to severely disrupt the flow of shipping essential to Nicaraguan trade during the peak export period." In order to "advance our overall goal of applying stringent economic pressure" and to "further impair the already critical fuel capacity in Nicaragua," they recommended an even more dramatic operation—to sink an oil tanker in a Nicaraguan harbor. "It is entirely likely that once a ship has been sunk, no insurers will cover ships calling in Nicaraguan ports," effectively ending Nicaragua's access to Western petroleum, stated the memorandum.[55]

McFarlane authorized the plan and briefed President Reagan on March 5. But the operation never came to fruition, perhaps because the CIA's mining of Nicaragua's harbors exploded into an international scandal three weeks later. Even with the public outcry against such operations, however, the Reagan administration continued its unilateral sabotage campaign. In December 1984, North contracted with a former member of the British Special Air Service, Maj. David Walker, to engage in "special operations" inside Nicaragua. Walker's saboteurs, aided by Panamanian agents of Gen. Manual Noriega, undertook the March 6, 1985, bombing of a downtown Managua military complex that included a hospital. This successful mission, North noted in a report to McFarlane, was one of a series of "highly visible operations" scheduled to influence a pending vote in Congress to renew contra aid.[56]

And more spectacular sabotage operations were being planned when the Iran-Contra scandal intervened. In August 1986 North met with an emissary of General Noriega who offered Panamanian support to "assassinate the Sandinista leadership for the U.S. government" and conduct other sabotage operations if the NSC would help "clean up" Noriega's drug-tainted image. In a memorandum to Poindexter, North reported that "Noriega had the capabilities that he had proffered." The United States "could not be involved in assassination, but Panamanian assistance with sabotage would be another story," Poindexter responded. In September North met personally with Noriega in London and, according to documents introduced at the North trial, reported back to Poindexter that "Noriega would take immediate actions against the Sandinistas and offered a list of priorities including an oil refinery, an airport, and the Puerto Sandino off-load facility."[57]

The very nature of these operations exposed what was perhaps the biggest myth of the contra war—that the U.S. objective was not to overthrow the Nicaraguan government but rather to "pressure" the Sandinistas to halt the "export of revolution" and into a negotiated settlement for a more democratic society. "Let us be clear as to the American attitude toward the Government of Nicaragua. We do not seek its overthrow," President Reagan declared to the nation in April 1983.[58] "The United States does not seek to destabilize or overthrow the Government of Nicaragua," the president reiterated in an April 1984 letter to Senator Howard Baker. "We are trying, among other things, to bring the Sandinistas into meaningful negotiations and constructive, verifiable agreements with their neighbors on peace in the region."[59]

Such pronouncements contradicted what the CIA was telling the contras on the battlefield. In agency-written manuals, the rebels were exhorted to "participate in the final fight" and to "work for the moment when the overthrow can be achieved and our revolution can become an open one."[60] As early as November 1984, North and the CIA's Central American Task Force director, Alan Fiers, reviewed "the prospects for a liberation government in which [Arturo] Cruz and [Adolfo] Calero would share authority," according to one NSC document.[61]

After the National Security Council took over operational control of the contra war, ousting the Sandinistas remained the final solution of the war, according to a July 1985 planning paper titled "U.S. Political/ Military Strategy for Nicaragua." Drafted by Oliver North, this strategy paper is worth quoting at length since it is the only extant copy of an explicit U.S. plan to overthrow the Sandinista government. In it, North laid out an incremental scenario whereby the contras would erode the Sandinistas' political, economic, and military strength and ultimately oust them from power. "This strategy is divided into three phases," he wrote. "The first phase consists primarily of a continuation of the efforts already in progress with the following objectives," among them:

☐ Development of a sound FDN logistics support base in Honduras.
☐ Development of an FDN operational base in Nicaragua so that support distances can be reduced. . . .
☐ Development of a secondary Costa Rican front. . . .
☐ Establishment of an aerial resupply system for both fronts.
☐ Near-term FDN urban guerrilla capability to demonstrate an active FDN presence in the urban centers.
☐ Development of a robust FDN psychological warfare capability.[62]

Phase 2 would be what North described as "the offensive phase" of the strategy, with the following goals:

☐ To repeatedly but temporarily disrupt the economic infrastructure of Nicaragua with priority to the electrical grid, water, transportation, and communications systems. (A show of force action with maximum psychological benefit.)
☐ To establish a strong political presence in the urban centers focusing on graffiti, leaflets, selective targeting of known FSLN population control groups. . . .
☐ To attack the regular Sandinista security forces to force them into a defensive posture. . . .
☐ To treat the Nicaraguan people much better than the Sandinista forces.
☐ To destroy the legitimacy of the Sandinista Government.
☐ To control more and more of the country by gradually and systematically replacing the Sandinista control with UNO/FDN control.[63]

Finally, according to North's scenario, the contras would overthrow the Nicaraguan government, the revolution's social programs would be dismantled, all North Americans in Nicaragua who were sympathetic to the Sandinistas would be expelled, and U.S. assistance would flow to a new contra government. "The third and final phase," he wrote, "would have the following objectives":

☐ The defeat and demobilization of Sandinista armed forces.

☐ Implementation of the UNO/FDN political program.
☐ Repatriation of all foreign advisers and foreign supporters (to include the Sandinista [sic] Americans).
☐ Immediate implementation of U.S. and foreign economic aid, social assistance . . . , and military assistance to establish a professional, nonpolitical [armed forces].[64]

Through North's courier, Robert Owen, this plan was provided to contra leaders for evaluation.

The Iran-Contra Resupply Operations

As U.S. support for the contras escalated, accompanied by such major political scandals as the CIA "assassination" manual and the mining of Nicaragua's harbors, Congress became increasingly skeptical of continuing the Reagan administration's covert war policy. As early as December 1982, legislators passed the first "Boland amendment"—named for Rep. Edward Boland, then chairman of the House Permanent Select Committee on Intelligence—which authorized CIA support for the contras to "interdict" arms. The bill explicitly stated that funds could not be expended for the purpose of overthrowing the Sandinista government. But by May 1983, the Intelligence Committee had concluded that the law was being violated. Anyone "with any sense," stated Representative Boland, "would have to come to the conclusion that the operation is illegal, [and] that the purpose and mission of the operation is to overthrow the government in Nicaragua."[65]

In July 1983, the House of Representatives passed a bill banning all covert CIA assistance to the contras and appropriating overt aid for the mythical arms interdiction program. The Senate, however, supported continuing aid to the contra program. In a compromise, Congress passed legislation appropriating $24 million for the contra effort in December but stipulated that no other funds could be used. When the $24 million ran out—it was expected to last six months—the CIA would have to terminate the contra operations.

This law set in motion the creation of an "alternative," extra-official system to sustain the contra war. At the highest levels of the Reagan administration, strategies evolved to fulfill the President's order to "keep the contras together, in body and in soul," until Congress could be convinced to vote more funding. Operational command was progressively transferred from the CIA to the NSC; CIA Director William Casey designated NSC staff member Oliver North as the manager of day-to-day of the contra program. To provide the administration with "plausible deniability," former covert operatives, most notably Richard Secord, a retired major general, were enlisted to facilitate the financing, weapons procurement, transport, logistics, training, and resupply of the contras.

As the $24 million began to run out in spring 1984, U.S. officials began covertly soliciting their counterparts in other countries for contra funds. "I am in full agreement that you should explore funding alternatives with the Israelis and perhaps others," William Casey wrote in a March 27 memo to McFarlane. The CIA, he noted, was already "exploring . . . the procurement of assistance from South Africa."[66] Besides Israel and South Africa, U.S. officials or their private-sector intermediaries would subsequently approach Saudi Arabia, China, Taiwan, South Korea, Singapore, Brunei, Chile, Guatemala, El Salvador, Honduras, Costa Rica, Panama, Venezuela, and Great Britain for monetary, logistical, or matériel support for the contra war. Saudi Arabia responded with the largest financial contribution, agreeing to deposit $1 million per month in a contra bank account beginning in July 1984. Eventually Saudi Arabia's contra donations totaled $32 million.

In the aftermath of the harbor-mining scandal, Representative Boland won passage of a second amendment, this one explicitly banning all U.S. support for the contras. The legislative language, passed in October 1984, was unambiguous:

> During fiscal year 1985, no funds available to the Central Intelligence Agency, the Department of Defense, or any other agency or entity of the United States involved in intelligence activities may be obligated or expended for the purpose or which would have the effect of supporting, directly or indirectly, military or paramilitary operations in Nicaragua by any nation, group, organization, movement, or individual.[67]

Since President Reagan's own Executive Order 12333 described the NSC as "the highest Executive Branch entity" involved in intelligence activities, the second Boland amendment clearly appeared to cover the activities of McFarlane, North, and other NSC officials.[68] In the words of Representative Boland, "the law clearly ends U.S. support for the war in Nicaragua."[69]

Yet by the time that Boland prohibition on contra funding was passed, the NSC-directed system to circumvent Congress and sustain the covert war was already in place. As Oliver North later testified, "General Secord had been engaged and money had started to flow to the Nicaraguan Resistance from outside forces."[70] Within weeks of the congressional ban becoming law, the "Enterprise" set up by Secord and his business partner, Albert Hakim, and directed out of North's NSC office, was using false Guatemalan end-user certificates—a document required for international arms transactions—to purchase hundreds of tons of arms from China and Portugal. By early spring 1985, air and boat shipments of weapons were arriving in Honduras for transshipment to contra camps.

To secure Honduran cooperation, without which the resupply operations could not take place, President Reagan authorized "an approach to the Hondurans" that "provides incentives for them to persist in aiding the freedom fighters." The now famous quid pro quo plan included expediting U.S. security assistance, increasing economic aid, and $4.5 million in CIA covert operations that reportedly included direct payoffs to Honduran military officials.[71] "We believe that Honduran wavering and uncertainty will be [a] continuing problem at least until the 'contra funding' issue is resolved, and that the measures described above can be helpful in shoring up a nervous ally during this period," Assistant Secretary of State for Inter-American Affairs Langhorne Motley reported to Secretary Shultz in a secret memorandum titled "Honduran Actions with Respect to Nicaraguan Resistance Forces."[72]

Initially, the Enterprise acted as a broker and shipper of arms, acquiring more than $11 million worth of rifles, mortars, rockets, grenades, and bullets for the contras; in mid-1985, however, Lieutenant Colonel North decided to expand to full-scale resupply operations, complete with a transshipment and warehouse base in El Salvador, cargo planes and crews for airdrops inside Nicaragua, and a handful of shell corporations created to launder money and provide a cover for the contra resupply operations.[73] Through retired CIA agent, Felix Rodriguez, the NSC secured the cooperation of the Salvadoran military to use Ilopango air base, outside of San Salvador, as the center of the resupply operations. In collaboration with CIA Station Chief Joseph Fernandez, land was purchased and a clandestine airstrip was constructed in northern Costa Rica to facilitate an arms airlift to the Southern Front. "The cover for the operation is a company, owned by a few 'crazy' gringos, wanting to lease the land for agricultural experimentation and for running cattle," Rob Owen wrote to North after visiting the airstrip site.[74]

Beginning with the first major airdrop of weapons on April 11, 1986, the NSC-run resupply operations delivered thousands of tons of equipment to contra positions inside Nicaragua. These operations enabled the Reagan administration to sustain the contras as a viable paramilitary force until the public diplomacy apparatus, also run out of the NSC, could convince Congress to renew official funding in summer 1986. On June 25, 1986, the House of Representatives reversed its previous position and passed Reagan's request for $100 million in funds for CIA/Pentagon support for the contras. "We can be proud that we as a people have embraced the struggle of the freedom fighters in Nicaragua," President Reagan exulted. "Today, their cause is our cause."[75]

Yet, the administration's political victory was short-lived. On October 5, as the CIA prepared to disburse the $100 million in new funding, an antiquated cargo plane used by the Enterprise was shot down over southern Nicaragua. The story told by the survivor, Eugene Hasenfus, coupled with the discovery of a memorandum in Oliver North's files that stated that $12 million in "residual funds" from the sale of arms to Iran "will be used to purchase critically needed supplies for the Nicaraguan Democratic Resistance Forces," led to the now-famous Iran-Contra Scandal and the denouement of the official contra program.[76] Through 1987, as congressional investigators uncovered the ugly evidence of "pervasive dishonesty" and "disdain for the law" by high U.S. officials, the Reagan administration repeatedly postponed returning to Capitol Hill for more contra assistance. Finally, in a vote on February 8, 1988, the House of Representatives narrowly rejected the White House request for $36.2 million in new war funds. Although Congress agreed to continue nonlethal assistance to the contras, official military aid came to an end, as did the administration's obsessive hopes for a clear-cut Reagan Doctrine victory.

The Bush Administration
and the Internal Front

The new administration of George Bush chose to make virtue out of necessity: Congressional opposition to aiding the contras was impossible to overcome; therefore, the Bush White House turned to the more promising path of fostering an internal front against the Sandinistas as Nicaragua prepared for elections in February 1990. Old-guard contra leaders for whom, according to a Rob Owen report to Oliver North, "the war ha[d] become a business" were removed from the payroll as Bush officials closed down contra offices in Washington and Miami.[77] While the Bush administration maintained the contra option through a bipartisan agreement with Congress to send $66 million in nonlethal assistance to the contras in 1989, the new assistant secretary of state for inter-American affairs, Bernard Aronson, informed contra commanders that after the February 25 elections only repatriation aid would be available.[78]

U.S. officials "realized early on that you had to have a complementary effort of the internal opposition to the contras if we were going to get anywhere," one State Department officer explained in August 1988.[79] Indeed, fostering an internal opposition to the Sandinistas had long been a quiet but critical component of U.S. policy toward Nicaragua. As early as 1980, President Carter had authorized a $1 million CIA program to support opposition political parties, labor unions, and the media covertly—a program similar to the one the agency had conducted against the Allende government in Chile ten years before.[80]

President Reagan's contra war authorizations also included a clandestine internal influence program. A "Scope of CIA Activities" summary that accompanied Reagan's September 19, 1983, "Finding" on covert operations against Nicaragua included a section on internal "political actions": "Financial and material support will be provided to Nicaraguan opposition leaders and organizations to enable them to deal with the Sandinistas from a position of political strength and to continue to exert political pressure on the Sandinistas."[81]

These operations included funding for the Nicaraguan Catholic church, the main opposition newspaper *La Prensa*, and the promotion of political agitation against the government. According to a report in *Newsweek*, the Nicaraguan Catholic church, led by Cardinal Miguel Obando y Bravo, "may have received hundreds of thousands of dollars in covert aid from the United States—from the CIA until 1985 and . . . from Oliver North's rogue elephant operation in the White House basement."[82] During the Carter administration, *La Prensa* covertly received "newsprint and funds to keep the newspaper . . . alive," noted Bob Woodward's authoritative book on the CIA, *Veil*.[83] And after a major anti-Sandinista rally that was broken up by Nicaraguan security forces, the speaker of the House, James Wright, told reporters that "we have received clear testimony from CIA people that they have deliberately done things to provoke an overreaction on the part of the government of Nicaragua. . . . Agents of our government have assisted in organizing the kinds of anti-government demonstration that have been calculated to stimulate and provoke arrests."[84]

During the Reagan administration, the CIA reportedly spent $10 to $12 million from a political account earmarked for the internal opposition.[85] The administration also advanced the internal front through overt funding, primarily the National Endowment for Democracy (NED), a quasi-private agency created as part of President Reagan's "project democracy." Through NED programs, closely supervised by the NSC's public diplomacy specialists, the administration funneled over $5.6 million to favored elements of the Nicaraguan opposition. *La Prensa* was a key recipient, receiving grants totaling $282,500.[86]

During President Bush's first year in office, both covert and overt aid to the opposition became key elements of U.S. policy. Nicaragua's electoral process provided a golden opportunity for clandestine U.S. intervention. During the 1984 elections, U.S. policy had been for the opposition to avoid participation, rendering the process illegitimate; toward that goal, the CIA paid off opposition candidates to withdraw from the race.[87] Given Nicaragua's dire economic condition in 1990 and the distinct possibility that the opposition could win a fair election, U.S. strategists took a different approach. Contra leaders were urged to return to Nicaragua and participate. U.S. advisers worked closely with the National Opposition Union (UNO), fashioning an electoral strategy and designing the campaign for presidential candidate Violeta Chamorro and her running mate, Virgilio Godoy.

In mid-1989, the CIA drew up a major covert plan to influence the election, only to meet with stiff resistance from the House Intelligence Committee. White House officials made it clear that they reserved the option to funnel covert funds to the political opposition, even as they agreed with Congress to send $9 million in overt assistance through NED. Since NED is prohibited from spending money to finance the campaigns of candidates for public office, the Bush administration claimed the funds were intended to assist "political organizations, alliances, independent elements of the media, independent labor unions, and business, civic and professional groups . . . to ensure the conduct of free, fair and open elections."[88]

Extensive U.S. efforts to install a new government through the electoral process came to fruition on February 25, 1990. Led by Chamorro, the UNO coalition scored an upset 55 to 41 percent victory over the Sandinista incumbant, Daniel Ortega, in a vote that international monitors, including a delegation led by former U.S. president Jimmy Carter, judged free and fair. Given the catastrophic economic crisis wrought by ten years of U.S. low-intensity warfare against Nicaragua, the Sandinista loss was hardly surprising. Indeed, while White House officials lauded the opposition for its democratic victory—and even complimented the Sandinistas on the conduct of the elections—the vote represented nothing less than the successful culmination of a decade of concerted U.S. efforts to roll back the Nicaraguan revolution and unseat the Sandinista government.

The opposition victory marked a turning point in U.S.-Nicaraguan relations. While the Sandinistas retained control over the military, the international and domestic legitimacy of the revolution they had led was gone. The Bush administration moved quickly to restore normal bilateral and multilateral economic relations and to provide $300 million in financial assistance to bolster the new Chamorro coalition government.

U.S. Low-Intensity Warfare
Against Nicaragua: A Postmortem

As a decade of U.S. low-intensity warfare against Nicaragua came to a close, some lessons were clear. Beyond a doubt, Washington proved once again that it could wreak death and destruction upon a small Third World nation. Indeed, by the tenth anniversary of the overthrow of Somoza, U.S. policy had successfully rolled back the gains, albeit not the spirit, of the Nicaraguan revolution.

In human and economic terms, the price of U.S. intervention was appalling. Between 1980 and 1989, the total death toll—Nicaraguan military, contra, and civilian—was officially put at 30,865.[89] Tens of thousands more were wounded, orphaned, or left homeless. As of 1987, property destruction from CIA/contra attacks totaled $221.6 million; production losses, $984.5 million.[90] Nicaraguan economists estimated monetary losses due to the trade embargo at $254 million and the loss of development potential from the war at $2.5 billion.

Even as the Nicaraguan government requested $12.8 billion dollars in damages, it noted that the human suffering could never be quantified, let alone repaid: "No such reparation can revive the human lives lost, or repair the physical and psychological injuries suffered by a population that has endured an unrelenting campaign of armed attacks and economic strangulation," according to the Nicaraguan government's Memorial on Compensation submitted to the World Court in March 1988. "The full impact of such a policy on a small, impoverished nation is simply incalculable."[91]

But although the Sandinista government survived the external violence of the Colossus of the North, internally the "full impact" of U.S. policy translated into a resounding political defeat at the polls. To be sure, the failure of the contras to force the Sandinistas to "say uncle" had demonstrated that no amount of Reagan rhetoric or CIA manuals could transform terrorists into "freedom fighters"—that despite the expenditure of hundreds of millions of dollars, an imperial war could not be recreated as a legitimate war of national liberation. Nevertheless, the Bush administration's ultimate success in fostering an internal front out of the destruction left by Reagan's war reflected Washington's continuing ability to exercise its presumption of hegemony in Central America.

Even so, a decade of U.S. intervention in Nicaragua offered an ominous warning for the North American public. The policy demonstrated that even a low-intensity war abroad carried with it a high price at home. The contra scandals, and their paralytic effect on U.S. politics, suggested that the quest to win hegemony in the Third World through a coordinated strategy of paramilitary, political, and economic warfare could only result in a loss of prestige, credibility, and constitutional strength for the U.S. system of government itself. In the end, Washington's policy of rolling back Third World revolution became subversive of the very ends it was meant to serve.

Notes

U.S. government documents cited here, unless otherwise noted, are part of the National Security Archive's microfiche documents collection *The Iran-Contra Affair: The Making of a Scandal, 1983–1988*. These documents were declassified as part of the Iran-contra investigations and the trial of Oliver North.

1. See Abraham Lowenthal, "The United States and Latin America: Ending the Hegemonic Presumption," *Foreign Affairs*, October 1976.

2. Brzezinski's argument is recorded in Robert Pastor, *Condemned to Repetition: The United States and Nicaragua* (Princeton: Princeton University Press, 1987), p. 162.

3. Vaky is quoted in a declassified "Administration Briefing on the Current Situation in Nicaragua," United States Senate, Committee on Foreign Relations, September 13, 1978, pp. 6, 9.

4. See Pezzullo cable to Secretary of State, "First Visit to Somoza," June 28, 1979.

5. Just as Washington had selected the first Somoza to head the National Guard in 1932, U.S. policymakers again drew up a list of candidates to lead the "new" National Guard in 1979. "What follows is a first out at putting together a list of officers who might be considered for taking command of the GN . . . following the departure of Somoza," Pezzullo cabled on June 30. At the top of the list was the name of Colonel Enrique Bermúdez, then Somoza's military attaché to Washington. Subsequently, Bermúdez became the commander of the Nicaraguan Democratic Force, the largest contra group, and the one most closely associated with the CIA. See Pezzullo cable to Department of State, "National Guard Survival," June 30, 1979.

6. For an overview of the Reagan administration's policy toward the Sandinistas, see Peter Kornbluh, *Nicaragua: The Price of Intervention* (Washington, D.C.: Institute for Policy Studies, 1987). See also Thomas Walker (ed.), *Reagan Versus the Sandinistas* (Boulder, Colo.: Westview, 1987).

7. McFarlane is quoted from his testimony before the Iran-contra committees on May 11, 1987. See U.S. Congress, Senate, Select Committee on Secret Military Assistance to Iran and the Nicaraguan Opposition, and House, Select Committee to Investigate Covert Arms Transactions with Iran, *Joint Hearings on the Iran-Contra Investigation, May 5–August 6, 1987*, 100th Cong., 1st sess., 1988, vol. 100-2 (emphasis added).

8. McFarlane memorandum to Secretary of State Haig, "Covert Action Proposal for Central America," February 27, 1981.

9. These quotes and a broader assessment of LIC strategy in Nicaragua are contained in Kornbluh, *Nicaragua*, p. 4.

10. See, for example, the 1983 CIA manual *Psychological Operations in Guerrilla Warfare*, which was published in book form by Vintage Press in 1985.

11. See Bob Woodward, *Veil: The Secret Wars of the CIA* (New York: Simon and Schuster, 1987), p. 281.

12. See Peter Kornbluh, "Uncle Sam's Money War Against the Sandinistas," *Washington Post Outlook*, August 27, 1989.

13. Ibid.

14. This directive is contained in the *Report of the Congressional Committees Investigating the Iran-Contra Affair* (Washington: GPO, 1988), appendix A, vol. 1, p. 55.

15. Operation Tipped Kettle is described in a forty-two-page summary of U.S. approaches to other nations on behalf of the contras released at the trial of Oliver North. See "The United States Vs. Oliver L. North, Stipulation of Facts," March 10, 1989, p. 1 [Hereafter referred to as "The Stipulation"].

16. Operation Elephant Herd is cited in the U.S. Congress, Senate, *Report of the Congressional Committees Investigating the Iran-Contra Affair, with Sup-*

plemental, Minority, and Additional Views, November, 1987, 100th Cong., 1st sess., 1987, pp. 34, 35 [hereafter referred to as the Iran-Contra Affair].

17. Weinberger memorandum for the President, "Central American Initiatives," July 13, 1983.

18. Quoted in the New York Times, March 30, 1985.

19. See "Central America Public Affairs/Legislative Action Plan," July 12, 1983.

20. For an exposé of the public diplomacy operations, see Robert Parry and Peter Kornbluh, "Iran-Contras' Untold Story," Foreign Policy, Fall 1988.

21. Col. Daniel Jacobowitz to S/LPD director Otto Reich, "Duties of TDY Military Personnel," May 30, 1985.

22. This document is quoted in Peter Kornbluh, "Propaganda and Public Diplomacy: Selling Reagan's Nicaragua Policy," in Fairness and Accuracy in Media (FAIR), Human Rights and the Media, Summer 1989, p. 20.

23. See Iran-Contra Affair, p. 34.

24. This plan was laid out in the first published story on the planned contra war. See Morton Kondracke and Nicolas Kotz, "How to Avoid Another Bay of Pigs," New Republic, June 20, 1981.

25. Presidential Finding on Central America, December 1, 1981.

26. Quoted in Roy Gutman, Banana Diplomacy: The Making of American Policy in Nicaragua, 1981–1987 (New York: Simon and Schuster, 1988), p. 57.

27. The first CIA scope paper is described in the Washington Post, May 8, 1983.

28. "Scope of CIA Activities Under the Nicaraguan Finding," September 19, 1983.

29. Author interview with a member of the original contra force, called the September 15 Legion.

30. Quainton cable to the Secretary of State, "Assessment of Recent Counterrevolutionary Activity," October 20, 1982.

31. Quainton cable to the Secretary of State, "The Economic Costs of the Counterrevolution," July 6, 1983.

32. Defense Intelligence Agency, "Weekly Intelligence Summary," July 16, 1982.

33. Reagan is quoted in the Washington Post, March 15, 1986.

34. Defense Intelligence Agency, "Weekly Intelligence Summary."

35. CIA, "Nicaragua: Significant Political Actors and Their Interaction," September 30, 1984, p. 16.

36. This figure was reported on the ABC News "Weekend Report," April 22, 1984.

37. Owen "Eyes Only" memorandum to Oliver North, "Overall Perspective," March 17, 1986.

38. See Edgar Chamorro, Packaging the Contras: A Case of CIA Disinformation (New York: Institute for Media Analysis, 1987), pp. 49, 57.

39. Ibid., p. 57.

40. Ibid., p. 11.

41. This document is reprinted in Kornbluh, Nicaragua, p. 37.

42. Owen to North, "Overall Perspective," March 17, 1986.

43. See New York Times, March 6, 1986.

44. See North to McFarlane, "Cruz Control," February 27, 1985.

45. Ibid.
46. "The CIA instructed us step-by-step how to draft it," according to Edgar Chamorro, who was involved in releasing the document. See Chamorro, *Packaging the Contras*, p. 15.
47. North memorandum to McFarlane, "Using the March 1 San Jose Declaration to Support the Vote on the Funding for the Nicaraguan Resistance," April 1, 1985.
48. See testimony of Rafael Quintero at the trial of Oliver North, p. 2959 of court transcript.
49. North to Poindexter, "Meeting with General Jack Galvin, USSouthCom," January 15, 1986.
50. See *Washington Post*, April 18, 1984.
51. The Special Interagency Report and the NSPG meeting are cited in *Iran-Contra Affair*, p. 36.
52. United States, Central Intelligence Agency, "Chronology of Salient Paramilitary Actions and Related Developments: 1 January–24 April 1984." This document remains classified.
53. Ibid.
54. Ibid.
55. North and Menges action memorandum to McFarlane, "Special Activities in Nicaragua," March 2, 1984.
56. North memorandum to McFarlane, "FDN Military Operations," April 11, 1985.
57. For descriptions of the Noriega meetings, see the "Stipulation," pp. 38, 40.
58. Reagan's speech is reprinted in *New York Times*, April 28, 1983.
59. Quoted in Kornbluh, *Nicaragua*, pp. 179–180.
60. See the introductions to the CIA's *Freedom Fighters Manual* and *Psychological Operations in Guerrilla Warfare*, circa October 1983.
61. North memorandum to McFarlane, "Clarifying Who Said What to Whom," November 7, 1984.
62. "U.S. Political/Military Strategy for Nicaragua," circa July 15, 1985, p. 1.
63. Ibid., p. 2.
64. Ibid., p. 3.
65. Quoted in Kornbluh, *Nicaragua*, p. 57.
66. Casey memorandum to McFarlane, "Supplemental Assistance to Nicaragua Program," March 27, 1984.
67. The Boland amendment ban is officially recorded as Public Law 98-473, Section 8066 [A], October 12, 1984.
68. See Reagan's Executive Order 12333, signed December 4, 1981.
69. Representative Boland's opinion is quoted in *Iran-Contra Affair*, p. 41.
70. North's testimony is quoted in ibid., p. 42.
71. See McFarlane's decision memorandum to Reagan, initiated by the President, "Approach to the Hondurans regarding the Nicaraguan Resistance," February 19, 1985.
72. Motley to Shultz, "Honduran Actions with Respect to Nicaraguan Resistance Forces," February 7, 1985.

73. For a full account of the Enterprise contra operations, see Chapter 3 of *Iran-Contra Affair*, "The Enterprise Assumes Control of Contra Support," pp. 59–84.

74. Owen report to North, "August 25, 1985, Trip," August 26, 1985.

75. Quoted in *Iran-Contra Affair*, p. 72.

76. The famous "diversion memo" was actually a five-page report, written on April 4, 1986, by Oliver North to John Poindexter, on the "Status of American Hostages in Beirut." In one paragraph on the last page, North reported that "residual profits" from arms sales to Iran would be used to purchase arms for the contras.

77. See Owen to North, "Overall Perspective," March 17, 1986. For press coverage on the closing of the contra offices see *Newsday*, July 15, 1989.

78. See *Washington Post*, January 12, 1990.

79. The U.S. official is quoted in a United Press International wire story, "Policy Shifts to Support Internal Nicaraguan Opposition," August 7, 1988.

80. President Carter's program is reported in *Wall Street Journal*, March 5, 1985.

81. "Scope of CIA Activities Under the Nicaragua Finding," September 19, 1983.

82. See "Covert Aid and the Church," *Newsweek*, June 15, 1987.

83. Woodward, *Veil*, p. 113.

84. Wright's statement is quoted in *Washington Times*, September 22, 1988.

85. This figure is cited in United Press International, "Policy Shifts."

86. For a discussion of *La Prensa* and NED grants, see John Spicer Nichols, "La Prensa: The CIA Connection," *Columbia Journalism Review*, July/August 1988.

87. Evidence of CIA involvement with opposition candidates is cited in the Report of the Latin American Studies Association Delegation to Observe the Nicaraguan General Election of November 4, 1984, *The Electoral Process in Nicaragua: Domestic and International Influences*, November 19, 1984.

88. For this description and a breakdown of how the money was spent, see the United States, Agency for International Development, *Report to Congress* (P.L. 101-119), "A.I.D. Grant to the National Endowment for Democracy (NED) and Summary of NED's Intended Subgrants," December 4, 1989. For an account of the NED money and the 1990 Nicaraguan elections, see John Spicer Nichols, "Get the N.E.D. out of Nicaragua," *Nation*, February 26, 1990.

89. These official statistics were provided by the Nicaraguan Ministry of the Presidency, January 1990.

90. Republic of Nicaragua, *Memorial on Compensation*, Submitted to the World Court, March 29, 1988, p. 42.

91. Ibid., pp. 4, 5.

SIXTEEN

The U.S. Intervention in Nicaraguan and Other Latin American Media

ANGHARAD N. VALDIVIA

The war has changed from the military front
to the political and ideological one,
and the media are the chief battle ground.

—Sofiá Montenegro

The role of the mass communications system in a society undergoing a process of structural and ideological change has been hotly debated in recent decades. The issue is quite complex because technologies as well as distribution systems are often in the hands of transnational enterprises, which have little respect for national sovereignty. Furthermore, the accepted narrative conventions in both entertainment and news are rooted in Western models; often the media in other cultures feel forced to imitate those models or risk losing their audience. Finally, Western theory of the press,[1] especially the component that deals with the government's role vis-à-vis press operations, labels most options chosen by developing countries as "authoritarian" or "Communist."

When a society has been pegged as authoritarian and/or Communist, the "defenders of world democracy" may feel the need to intervene covertly or overtly. Countries within the sphere of influence of a world power, because their actions may be considered a material and ideological threat to existing economic and political arrangements, fear the possibility of intervention. Consequently, a country seeking to regain influence over its mass media system faces challenges both internationally for proposing an alternative model and domestically from opposition forces who can increase their leverage by becoming allies of international players. The July 19, 1979, triumph, which made Nicaragua a revolutionary society, also made the country a target for international, mainly U.S., intervention. Therefore, Nicaragua provides a good example of the perils of attempting to rechart a course for a mass communications system.

The U.S. government labeled the Sandinistas both authoritarian and Communist and acted accordingly. Although the United States stopped short of invading Nicaragua, it engaged in a strategic destabilization campaign. Coordinated low-level military activities and the fomenting of opposition civilian forces formed the core of a low-intensity effort designed to win over the Nicaraguan population. The plan was to cause a shift in local and regional opinion from pro-Sandinista to counter-revolutionary sentiments in order to bring about the toppling of the Sandinista government.

A crucial component of the low-intensity effort during Nicaragua's revolutionary period was the emphasis placed on the Central American region's mass media systems, especially print and broadcast news. Much of the activity in the overt war of ideas took place in Costa Rica and Honduras, and to a lesser extent in El Salvador, with covert funding sources linked to the CIA. Within Nicaragua, the debate centered on government censorship of La Prensa, the opposition daily, as well as its possible links to U.S. funding sources. The latter charge, made by Nicaraguan government officials, linked La Prensa to the elaborate Iran-Contra Scandal. There was also external input into the broadcasting diet of the Nicaraguans. Here again, charges of CIA intervention were frequently made by official Nicaraguan sources. This chapter will study both the regional disinformation tactics and the situation within Nicaragua's borders during the revolutionary period and will examine allegations of undercover funding sources.

Central American Disinformation Tactics

Throughout the revolutionary period, changes in counterrevolutionary tactics were matched by the increased understanding of the importance of the media by members of the Sandinista government. Although leading Sandinistas such as Tomás Borge and Ernesto Cardenal were acutely aware of the importance of the mass media system in a changing society, they were largely unable to control activities outside Nicaragua's borders. It was precisely from this arena that the counterrevolution operated.

Although the counterrevolution was active within Nicaragua, its military arm as well as its civilian directorate were organized and trained outside of national borders in neighboring countries. Honduras, which borders Nicaragua to the north, and Costa Rica, Nicaragua's southern neighbor, provided little resistance to the establishment of contra military bases. Additionally, members of the press within these countries were linked to contra-funding sources. From 1981 through 1984 when a "close U.S. ally and vehemently anti-communist"[2] general ruled the country, Honduras forbade journalists to mention contra presence within its borders. After that, leaks from the government to the press served the interests of the Honduran regime by blaming contra forces for Honduran intelligence forces' wrongdoings. However, the Honduran government was not the only source of misinformation about the contras. Although Costa Rica remained officially neutral in regard to the U.S.-Nicaragua conflict, it served as the ground for both military and press support for contra forces.

The CIA, which provided much of the funding and probably the original impetus for the contras, was also deeply involved in both the Honduran and Costa Rican press. Whereas military assistance to the contras rested on shaky legal grounds, there was no U.S. statute prohibiting the CIA from employing foreign journalists or from allowing agency operators to pose as such. This operation appeared to be one of the most cost effective in the Central American region. For roughly $330 a month, the CIA could nearly double a local journalist's salary and generate "press stories, commentaries, or editorials attacking Nicaragua and sympathetic to the Contras."[3] Payments could be made directly by the CIA to journalists or handled more covertly through contra accounts. Carlos Morales, a prominent Costa Rican professor and journalist, revealed that at least eight of his former students received these monthly stipends. Three of these journalists were "top editors."[4] Edgar Chamorro, a former spokesperson for the Nicaraguan Democratic Force (FDN) who became a critic of the counterrevolutionary effort, claimed that he was personally involved in a similar campaign in Honduras that included "approximately 15 Honduran journalists and broadcasters . . . and our influence was thereby extended to every major Honduran newspaper and radio and television station."[5]

In addition to the contribution made by friendly press personnel to anti-Sandinista sentiments, there were related mass communications activities wherein counterrevolutionary forces, with CIA help, made their presence felt through the news and political systems of the Central American region. Newspaper supplements written by contra supporters, official spokespeople of the anti-Sandinista forces, and fictitious stories contributed to the elaborate CIA propaganda scheme. For example, the public relations office of the FDN in San José, Costa Rica, produced a weekly supplement that was carried by La Nación, one of the most influential Costa Rican newspapers, as well as by newspapers in six other Latin American countries.[6] Nicaragua Hoy (Nicaragua today), while being openly anti-Sandinista, was not equally open about its funding source, the FDN, or about the FDN's funding source, the CIA.[7]

More damaging to the CIA's disinformation program was Edgar Chamorro's incriminating testimony before the World Court. Chamorro testified that CIA contacts urged him to publicly claim FDN responsibility for mining Nicaragua's harbors, bombing the Managua airport, and destroying other Nicaraguan infrastructural facilities.[8] He added that he found out about these acts after the CIA had carried them out and did not even get to formulate the press releases, which were, in fact, manufactured by the CIA. Chamorro added that the CIA trained contra leaders to handle news conferences in the United States, to lobby in Congress, and even gave them names of prominent people in the United States who would in turn influence their government representatives. Chamorro's testimony suggested that an entire public relations campaign package was created by the CIA in violation of the statutes that prohibit the agency from participating in U.S. politics. Chamorro's testimony was corroborated by charges made by another prominent member of the Nicaraguan opposition. Edén Pastora, then head of ARDE, another contra group, claimed he was also asked by a CIA contact to take credit for the mining of harbors and did so only after revisions to a press release written by the CIA.[9] Both Chamorro and Pastora eventually resigned their posts because of the strong influence of the CIA on the counterrevolutionary agenda.

Fake press releases by contra officials were compounded by fictitious or slanted stories by journalists on the CIA payroll. Dery Dyer, a Costa Rican reporter, claimed that fictitious stories were so commonplace in the region that, besides adding to the prevailing disinformation campaign, these stories sidetracked reporters who might have otherwise spent their time and meager resources covering real events.[10] This charge applied just as easily to broadcast services.

Although these newspaper tactics were important, the special qualities of broadcasting technology made the electronic media even more influential. Listening to radio is much more widespread than reading newspapers throughout most of the developing world. Low literacy levels in the Central American region, with the exception of Costa Rica and, to a lesser extent, Nicaragua, made the potential radio audience much larger than that of newspapers. Battery-powered radio receivers were widely available even in remote regions. Moreover, one should not discount the impact of television. It is true that there are few sets per capita in Third World countries, but the high ratio of viewers per set makes television a powerful and influential medium in densely populated areas. Finally, broadcast signals do not stop at national borders, and since the Central American region is fairly small, powerful transmitters provided the counterrevolution with a powerful and relatively inexpensive propaganda tool that could reach Nicaraguans as well as citizens of every country in the region.

As with the print journalists, many broadcast journalists in both Honduras and Costa Rica were paid supplementary salaries by the CIA and its contra operatives to disseminate anti-Sandinista and procontra news.[11] The difference was that the radio and television messages were well heard and viewed within Nicaraguan borders, sometimes even better than nationally broadcast material.[12] El Salvador, whose printed press is nearly nonexistent, also compounded the electronic barrage by joining Costa Rica and Honduras in beaming messages to Nicaraguans. Furthermore, Nicaragua's own telecommunications system suffered from a shortage of trained personnel, spare parts, and powerful transmitters. In many areas residents had access only to foreign television stations. Although prior to the revolution, the content of Nicaraguan and neighboring countries' stations were quite similar, later the situation changed: "In contrast to foreign entertainment programs . . . foreign television news often had content directed at Nicaragua. All these channels frequently covered U.S. intervention and the Nicaraguan counterrevolution in a sympathetic fashion. Furthermore, when the SSTV (Sandinista television system) news aired at 8 P.M., these stations often placed their best programs against it."[13]

Radio allowed for even more influence. Since radio technology is cheaper and more mobile than television technology, opposition forces operated entire mobile clandestine stations. While commercial stations of foreign countries indirectly touted the wonders of democracies such as theirs, clandestine stations in Nicaragua incited violence and the overthrow of the current government by giving both blueprints for insurrection and by fabricating stories designed to outrage the Nicaraguan population. Clandestine contra stations, like the rest of the contra movement, received their funding from undisclosed sources, which were widely believed to be financed by the CIA and similarly minded wealthy donors. Edgar Chamorro's World Court deposition included information about the CIA's funneling of money to Venezuelan investors to buy Radio Impacto, a powerful radio station based in San José, Costa Rica.[14] An analysis of Costa Rican stations heard in Nicaragua revealed that Radio Impacto did not openly disclose its ownership by contra forces and that its content was "especially biased against the Nicaraguan revolution . . . [and was] viewed by the Sandinistas as a vehicle for Contra disinformation."[15] Yet another participant in the war of ideas was the Voice of America (VOA), which transmitted news with a Washington slant, one that became more anti-Sandinista as time passed. Thus the VOA was a component in a diversified, well-funded, and externally organized disinformation campaign within the Central American region.

Broadcast, and to a lesser extent print, material reached not only the Nicaraguan population but also the entire Central American region, creating widespread negative feelings toward the Nicaraguan revolution. The disinformation campaign, however, had graver ramifications. In a process that has been termed "blowback," much of this disinformation was picked up as legitimate news by policy analysts in the United States. Thus CIA-fabricated material became part of the information collected by the agency itself and by other U.S. government bodies, most significantly the State Department, which in turn used this information to formulate foreign policy in the Central American region.[16] Compounded with the domestic tactics to influence U.S. government representatives, this disinformation campaign reached U.S. residents and thus had an effect on public opinion and mass media output within U.S. borders.

Former CIA officials and government critics noted that these tactics were very similar, and indeed some of the rhetoric was identical, to those used in previous CIA campaigns in Vietnam, Chile, and Angola.[17] The target country, in this case Nicaragua, was usually unable to counter this international propaganda campaign. Internally, however, Nicaragua sought to maintain influence over its mass communications system. In doing so, it used its knowledge of the revolutions in which the CIA had actively intervened. For example, after Salvador Allende was elected to the presidency of Chile in 1970, the United States embarked on a destabilization campaign designed to topple the left-of-center Popular Unity government. Among other measures was the dissemination of antigovernment news through Chile's best-known daily, El Mercurio. El Mercurio's pre-1970 style merited the label of "the Times of Chile." However, within months of Allende's election, its content rapidly changed from mere opposition to Allende's policies to outright incitement to overthrow the democratically elected government.[18] Subsequent U.S. Senate investigations documented CIA influence and funding in both media and larger political and economic campaigns.[19] Specifically: "The CIA subsidized news services, provided money for a TV station, paid journalists to plant false and distorted stories about the government in national and international media, and poured $1.5 million into El Mercurio."[20]

The Allende government was forced to counter a mass media system that was largely based on U.S. models and sometimes owned and controlled by foreign interests. Nevertheless, keeping its word to uphold democratic structures, the government did not impose any press sanctions and thus allowed itself to be attacked from within. Local media personnel and scholars had no models to follow, and their theoretical formulations did not translate into practice in time to counter the opposition's efforts.[21] El Mercurio's stories provided a forum for and inspired those members of the opposition who eventually participated in the overthrow of the Allende government. News stories were also picked up as "facts" by international news service and intelligence-gathering bodies, thus contributing to the formulation of worldwide public opinion and foreign policy.

The Chilean experience led leftist activists and scholars to grapple with the theoretical contradiction between a bourgeois media system and a government in the process of planned social change. Both revolutionary and counterrevolutionary forces could refer to the Chilean experiment in preparing strategy to use when the next socialist country faced the dilemma of freedom of the press. Revolutionary Nicaragua's attempt at a mixed economy, which included the media, made the Chilean lesson all the more relevant and provided an opportunity to put the theoretical formulations into practical use.

Media Intervention in Nicaragua

Learning from previous experiences, Sandinistas devoted their attention to media issues from the early days of the new government. The provisional media law, decreed in August 1979, noted that news and information services were not purely for profit and that the media ought to help in the reconstruction process.[22] To carry out this mission, the Sandinistas inherited Somoza's broadcasting assets, which included radio stations and the two national television networks.

In order to complement their broadcast assets with print outlets, within a week of the revolutionary victory the FSLN founded a newspaper, La Barricada, which became the official organ of the FSLN and, for a short time, was the only major newspaper published in Nicaragua. Barricada took a vanguard approach to journalism. Its editorial board eschewed notions of objectivity and openly acknowledged that "journalism is a weapon placed at the service of a [political] cause."[23] Its original shrill style was gradually tempered once Carlos Chamorro, martyred La Prensa editor Pedro Joaquín Chamorro's youngest son, was appointed managing editor. However, the political spectrum allowable during the reconstruction period would prove less than limitless. A short-lived El Pueblo, politically to the left of the Sandinistas, was censored and eventually closed by the Sandinista government after taking too radical a stance on issues of national reconstruction. The true test for the permissiveness of the new government in regard to freedom of the press would come once La Prensa returned to business.

La Prensa, the perennial voice of opposition during the rule of the Somozas, was back in print by early August 1979 (after recovering from bombings and attacks on its personnel suffered during the final days of the insurrection). Initially Barricada welcomed La Prensa's return with open arms. In a front-page editorial dedicated to La Prensa's return, Barricada offered the following words:

We trust that La Prensa, a newspaper characterized by its traditional criterion of independence, will know how to follow this process with the patriotism which it has so often demonstrated. . . . La Prensa reappears and it receives the greetings of its colleagues at Barricada. . . . It is a pleasure to be able to say, with legitimate satisfaction, that among one of the first achievements of the Sandinista revolution is the reappearance of *La Prensa*.[24]

As expected by *Barricada* journalists, *La Prensa* originally provided supportive coverage of the new government. Although each newspaper had its own "real hero" of the revolution (Augusto César Sandino for *Barricada* and Pedro Joaquín Chamorro for *La Prensa*), they did not disagree about initial government policy. Both newspapers focused on the immense task of reconstruction, and both devoted much space to the many people who contributed to the overthrow of the Somoza regime. During that time Violeta Barrios de Chamorro, Pedro's widow, served on the provisional junta that ruled the country. However, the short journalistic honeymoon ended roughly at the same time that Violeta resigned her government post for health reasons.[25] Violeta's return to *La Prensa* marked that newspaper's return to its traditional opposition stance and precipitated a struggle between the newspaper's owners and workers. Violeta's value as a powerful symbol had been realized by the Sandinistas long before she shifted allegiance to the counterrevolution.

During April 1980, the division between *La Prensa*'s two internal factions became permanent. One faction, less numerous but controlling most of the assets, favored increased criticism of the Sandinista regime and the need for a public voice for the private sector. The other faction favored constructive but supportive criticism of the new government, thus contributing to the building of socialism. As a result, Pedro Chamorro's brother Xavier, together with most of *La Prensa*'s personnel and with 25 percent of its assets, founded a rival paper, *El Nuevo Diario* (The new newspaper). Thus in 1980 Nicaragua had three major dailies, none of which had existed prior to the revolution, except in name, and all of which were headed by a member of the Chamorro family.

Although *La Prensa* remained in business, it was not the same paper that the National Guard had once bombed. Most of the people who had worked for *La Prensa* moved to one of the other newspapers, broadcast operations, or into government posts. The new *La Prensa* inherited the name and opposition reputation of its former self, along with some of the material assets, but few of its former journalists. In style, *La Prensa* adhered to the traditional U.S. model of newspapers with international, sports, and entertainment sections. Nevertheless, its avowed anti-Sandinista stance made it a recipient of many domestic and external donations and grants from forces wishing to "preserve democracy." Indeed, covert funding may have existed from the time of the new *La Prensa*'s inception. Some scholars have wondered whether the split itself did not allow CIA personnel to "infiltrate its own people on the *La Prensa* staff," especially since the paper did not then hire new personnel.[26] Widespread rumors of CIA funding as well as unmitigated opposition content led to frequent bouts with censorship and closings of La Prensa by the Sandinista government.

During the Somoza years, La Prensa had suffered constant censorship, ending with its editor's death and the bombing of its physical plant. The Somoza dynasty had faced a losing proposition vis-à-vis the opposition newspaper: It either allowed distribution of inflammatory material, fueling growing internal discontent, or it closed the paper, risking international disapproval, especially from its most important ally, the United States. After the split between conservative and revolutionary forces within La Prensa, the Sandinista government faced basically the same challenge. Continued publication placed the revolutionary effort at risk, and attempts at censorship generated support within the United States for continued funding of the contras. The initial enthusiasm with which the reopening of La Prensa was greeted by Barricada, and therefore the government, inevitably soured.

The resulting cycle became hard to avoid. Increased contra funding led to attacks on the Nicaraguan population. The first major wave of warfare, in March 1982, led the government to declare a State of Emergency, with censorship of the press, including La Prensa.[27] The newspaper had been suspended in the past when it made false accusations of government corruption or abuse of power, which were easily and quickly disproved by verification of sources.[28] Beginning in 1980, La Prensa allied itself with and provided ample coverage of the Catholic church hierarchy (pitting Christians against Sandinistas as if they were mutually exclusive), sponsored antigovernment rallies, gave more space to the British royal wedding than to the first anniversary of the revolution, and, most important, blamed all Nicaragua's problems on the Sandinistas instead of acknowledging the fifty years of the Somozas' plundering policies and the effects of the U.S. economic embargo.

Scare stories running the gamut from alleged massacres and the importation of tainted food from socialist countries were repeatedly shown to be false. Yet the disclaimers were not so visible, locally or internationally, as the original stories. Censorship continued in the form of short closings or deleted statements. From 1980 until June 1986 the government did nothing to stop La Prensa's distribution of precensored copies to various embassies and international bodies in Managua. In 1986 La Prensa was closed for over a year, following yet another victory for contra funding in the U.S. Congress.

After the Arias peace plan resulted in the beginning of a tortuous dialogue process between the Sandinistas and contra forces, La Prensa was allowed to reappear in October 1987. Despite making "little effort to disguise its role as agency of U.S. propaganda, dedicated to overthrowing the government of Nicaragua by force,"[29] it enjoyed a period of relatively unhindered publication until July 1988. During those nine months, *La Prensa* continued to offer false and misleading reports. For example, a reported mobilization of Sandinistas for totalitarian purposes (May 1988) turned out to be related to the swift change of currency that left many contras with worthless heaps of money. In addition to assertions that the people "unanimously" opposed the Sandinistas (November 6, 1987), *La Prensa* quite openly identified itself with the contra forces (December 12, 1987), often interviewing its leaders (e.g., Adolfo Calero, Pedro Joaquín Chamorro, Jr.), some of whom still served as codirectors of the newspaper.[30]

These incidents peaked in July 1988 when the newspaper was closed again for three weeks. The closure followed a month-long period of incitement to overthrow the government, which included calls to violence and allegations of the arrival of a Soviet nuclear submarine—in reality, a ship full of donated cornmeal.[31] *La Prensa's* reporters referred to contra forces as "the democratic opposition" and demanded a dialogue between the government and the counterrevolution, as if they were both equally legitimate. *La Prensa* also demonstrated an amazingly slavish pro-U.S. attitude through its absolute refusal to cover, as news, the downing of an Iranian civilian airliner by the USS *Vincennes* that same month. Instead, while the other two dailies ran front-page stories, it printed only an editorial that, in fact, attempted to absolve the United States of all responsibility. During this same period, the U.S. embassy in Managua provided barely covert assistance to internal opposition forces (widely reported in the local media except *La Prensa*), which resulted in the expulsion, for the first time in Nicaragua's history, of the U.S. ambassador.

It was against this background of provocative behavior by *La Prensa* and escalating tensions created in large part by the apparently well-coordinated activities of the U.S.-financed opposition that *La Prensa* was finally closed for three weeks. This, and the other measures taken, allowed the ninth anniversary of the revolution to be celebrated in relative peace. Though the *La Prensa* closure created scandal in the U.S. media, little or no notice was paid by the latter to the fact that at the end of that short period, *La Prensa* was allowed to resume publication and continued thereafter to behave in the same manner that had caused it to be closed in the first place. Until the end of the revolutionary period, *La Prensa's* role in the U.S.-organized low-intensity war on Nicaragua remained unchanged.

This history leaves much unsaid and unexplored. First is the fact that the U.S. government in 1980 saw in the success of *La Prensa's* conservative faction the opportunity to influence both the Nicaraguan population and world opinion about "democracy" in the new society. By focusing on *La Prensa's* troubles, the Reagan administration set into motion the following logic: "(1) Repression of the media is bad. (2) The

Sandinista government of Nicaragua frequently censors *La Prensa* and suspended it from publication for over a year in 1986 and 1987. (3) Therefore, the Sandinistas are bad and deserve to be overthrown."[32]

This logic ignored other government actions within the first decade. *El Pueblo*'s experience, which involved temporary prison sentences for some of the members of the collective as well as permanent closure, was seldom mentioned. The fact that *El Pueblo* was politically to the left of the Sandinistas illustrated the relatively centrist position of the new government. Other publications also were closed, albeit temporarily. A March 8, 1988 (International Women's Day), cartoon of a woman in *La Semana Cómica*, a somewhat risqué Marxist weekly, was so loudly protested by local feminists that the government closed the periodical for a short time. *El Nuevo Diario*'s reprint of the same cartoon evoked the same response from the Sandinista government.

These examples indicate that although *La Prensa* was the newspaper most often censored, other print media outlets were also occasionally silenced. Moreover, violently repressive measures violating freedom of the press in other countries in Central America (notably El Salvador and Guatemala), where opposition papers were shut down permanently and where journalists were routinely killed, were conveniently ignored. Such incidents received little or no coverage in the U.S. mainstream media, nor did they prompt the U.S. government to suspend foreign aid to those countries. The high standards of freedom of the press to which the U.S. government held the Nicaraguan government were not consistent with U.S. practice during wartime periods, when there has been press censorship. Again, the many articles in the U.S. media that criticized Nicaragua's handling of *La Prensa*, an opposition voice in a country at war, failed to mention U.S. censorship. They also ignored the issue of objectivity and press autonomy from the U.S. administration line. A case study of the U.S. press revealed that "the press substantially replicated Washington biases covering over or distorting Nicaraguan political dynamics in the process."[33] Finally, the mainstream U.S. press myopically focused on *La Prensa*'s woes and only cryptically and apologetically referred to some of its funding sources, precisely where the Sandinista government's major objections to the opposition paper lay.

Although CIA ties to *La Prensa* had been widely rumored since early 1980, it took several years for firm evidence of this link to surface. *La Prensa* spokespersons vehemently denied the charge, which in turn, was denounced as pure demagoguery by the U.S. State Department and in the U.S. mainstream press. Yet as has been shown by the Chilean experience, the CIA has a history of foreign intervention, which includes funding of the opposition press. The many assertions and testimonies of CIA control and funding of contra forces, including those of Edén

Pastora and Edgar Chamorro, further strained the credibility of both *La Prensa*'s and the CIA's denials. The consecutive scandals of the CIA-distributed manual designed to inspire an overthrow of the Nicaraguan government and the Iran-contra affair added fuel to the allegations and inspired both journalists and scholars to continue research into the possible funding sources.

Using material acquired through the Freedom of Information Act (FOIA) and congressional evidence as a result of the Iran-Contra Scandal, John Spicer Nichols obtained evidence of some of the darker moments in *La Prensa*'s history.[34] Nichols linked *La Prensa* to both the CIA and Oliver North's intricate network of government and private organizations. Funding began during the Carter administration when "the CIA used third parties . . . to send printing equipment and other supplies needed to rebuild *La Prensa*'s plant."[35] Although the Reagan administration's own expanded activities in Nicaragua revealed no direct funding to *La Prensa*, in 1984 "private foundations linked to North's covert network and to the Contras began to supply *La Prensa* with newsprint and other materials."[36] Nichols disclosed that *La Prensa* received considerable financial support from the National Endowment for Democracy (NED), an agency created by the U.S. Congress in 1981, which "became closely linked both to the National Security Council (NSC) and to the surrogate funding network for the Contras."[37] Nichols's findings corroborated previous allegations that a concerted public relations campaign, which culminated in procontra op-ed pieces in U.S. newspapers, also was covertly funded by U.S. sources, in this case the State Department. Other ostensibly private U.S. organizations involved in North's network included AmeriCares, PRODEMCA, and Delphi Research Associates. Nichols concluded that "the record clearly shows that most U.S. aid to *La Prensa* was an integral part of a campaign to help the Contras overthrow the Sandinista government."[38]

The Nicaraguan press was not the sole target of covert counterrevolutionary activity. The Nicaraguan air waves were also influenced by external forces. Besides the many radio and television programs broadcast from neighboring countries available to Nicaraguans, national voices also preached dissent. Whereas television was government controlled, many radio stations remained in private hands, part of the mixed economy envisioned by the Sandinistas. One particularly problematic radio network was Radio Católica. Echoing much of the *La Prensa* line and adding pseudoreligious teaching that pitted the Sandinistas against Christianity, Radio Católica also suffered from occasional bouts of censorship, and its director, Father Bismarck Carballo, was exiled temporarily. The impact of this station was considerable because most Nicaraguans consider themselves Catholic and the radio station capitalized on this identification.

Like *La Prensa*, Radio Católica was also accused of receiving covert CIA funds.[39] In the familiar pattern, covert aid until 1985 came from the CIA. From then on it was connected to Oliver North's operation. Although Cardinal Miguel Obando y Bravo denied knowledge of funding sources, receipts with his signature prompted the accusations.[40]

Conclusion

The continuous and extensive U.S. funding of the mass media in the Central American region was carried out in hopes of generating anti-Sandinista sentiment among Nicaraguans, Central Americans, and the U.S. public. Although accusations of CIA ties and other U.S.-sponsored covert funding sources for the counterrevolutionary media were initially dismissed by the mainstream U.S. press, most of these allegations proved to be well founded. The long history of CIA intervention in revolutionary situations repeated itself, this time with a well-coordinated regional strategy combined with U.S. public opinion campaigns. Although the Sandinistas were aware of counterrevolutionary history, they were virtually powerless to stop the Central American propaganda blitz.

Domestically the Sandinistas exercised a bit more influence, but their control was by no means total. In particular, *La Prensa*'s existence and its counterrevolutionary rhetoric contributed to the polarization of Nicaraguan politics. In the process, however, its credibility, due to its unabashed pro-U.S. and procontra orientation, was badly damaged. Many Nicaraguans expressed their wishes that they could have a "real" opposition newspaper, as it was obvious that *La Prensa* was externally manipulated and full of half-truths.

The most important effect of the counterrevolutionary mass media strategy was that much of the fabricated information became part of the news and "conventional wisdom" in the United States and therefore contributed to a U.S. foreign policy that translated into high numbers of civilian deaths and displacement and a badly battered economy in Nicaragua. On a practical level, the symbolic struggle contributed to real death and destruction and thus should not be seen as a peripheral part of the counterrevolutionary aggression. This death and destruction in turn contributed to the election results of 1990, which unseated Sandinista President Daniel Ortega and fulfilled a major goal of the counterrevolution. Finally, U.S. support of Violeta de Chamorro's successful presidential bid was not unrelated to her *La Prensa* connections.

On a theoretical and academic level, the mass media situation brought up a host of questions and considerations. The need for defining freedom of the press in the Nicaraguan context was underscored during the revolutionary period. How much freedom can be allowed during a time of war? Furthermore, should a press organ that is externally funded by forces seeking to overthrow the government be allowed to continue publication? These questions are seldom asked in a media system that assumes that freedom of the press is an absolute without historical and situational variations.

Additionally, the U.S. media focus on La Prensa's woes ignored other important media developments occurring within Nicaragua that demonstrated the government's commitment to a more democratic communications system. Among these developments were the growth of popular radio stations operating at a grass-roots level and an increase in the number of publications of mass organizations. Local grass-roots Christian organizations also produced widely read material that posited the combination of Christianity and socialist ideas as a compatible ideology. The increase in the number of periodicals also allowed groups that were previously silent to gain access to the symbolic arena. In particular, women rose to a high status within the Nicaraguan press. Their participation gradually changed the character of news: Instead of relying on political and governmental sources, journalists turned to the everyday experiences of the people. Communications scholars have long theorized that this kind of development is more democratic and participatory.[41]

Thus the concentration on La Prensa served only anti-Sandinista forces. Although it was important for scholars to document La Prensa's shady history, their avoidance of other important media issues obscured efforts to form a more democratic symbolic environment. By continuing to focus on La Prensa, many communications scholars contributed to the very dilemma that they were studying. We were following the false agenda set by the U.S. government and ignoring a rich and multifaceted reality.

Notes

1. The work most often cited in this regard is Fred S. Siebert, Theodore Peterson, and Wilbur Schramm, Four Theories of the Press (Urbana: University of Illinois Press, 1959). Although recent debates in the field of mass communications have questioned both the basic assumptions and the misinterpretation of classical liberal theorists in Four Theories, the book continues to be used in journalism departments and quoted in scholarly works.

2. Anne-Marie O'Connor, "Dateline: Honduras; Subject: The Contras," Columbia Journalism Review, May/June 1987, p. 39.

3. Martha Honey, "Contra Coverage—Paid For by the CIA," Columbia Journalism Review, March/April 1987, p. 31.

4. Ibid.

5. Jacqueline Sharkey, "Back in Control," Common Cause Magazine, September/October 1986, p. 29.

6. Ibid., p. 33.

7. Sharkey conceded that neither the CIA nor the FDN had admitted to this link. Yet Edén Pastora and other former contras claimed "everyone knows the CIA funds it [the newspaper]." Ibid., p. 32.

8. Ibid.

9. Honey, "Contra Coverage."

10. Ibid.

11. See ibid.; Sharkey, "Back in Control"; and O'Connor, "Dateline: Honduras."

12. Much of this section on broadcasting is based on Howard H. Frederick's "Electronic Penetration," in Reagan Versus the Sandinistas, ed. Thomas W. Walker (Boulder: Westview Press, 1987).

13. Ibid., p. 129.

14. Sharkey, "Back in Control," p. 32.

15. Frederick, "Electronic Penetration," p. 135.

16. Sharkey, "Back in Control."

17. Ibid.

18. Michelle Mattèlart documented El Mercurio's shift from so-called objective reporting in times of bourgeois stability to class warfare during the Allende years in Women, Media, and Crisis (London: Comedia, 1986).

19. United States Senate, Select Committee to Study Governmental Operations with Respect to Intelligence Activities, Covert Action in Chile: 1963–1973 (Washington, D.C.: USGPO, 1975).

20. Sharkey, "Back in Control," p. 35.

21. The best sources on this subject are Armand Mattèlart and Michelle Mattèlart, both of whom lived through the Chilean experience as scholars and practitioners. M. Mattèlart, Women, Media, and Crisis, includes several related articles on the subject. Armand Mattèlart's works include "Communication Ideology and Class Practice," in Communication and Class Struggle (New York: International General, 1979), as well as numerous interviews in Cuadernos del Periodismo, a Managua-based journal. He has also edited Communicating in Popular Nicaragua (New York: International General, 1986). His work in Chile made him a valued scholar in Nicaraguan mass media circles, yet another indicator of the germaneness of the Chilean experience to revolutionary Nicaraguans.

22. Doris Lapple Wagenhals, A New Development Model—A New Communication Policy? (New York: Peter Lang, 1984).

23. "Reaparece La Prensa en Nicaragua sandinista," Barricada, August 16, 1979, p. 1.

24. Ibid.

25. It was widely known that Violeta's reasons for resigning had much more to do with the increasing schism between the Sandinistas and the bourgeoisie than with health considerations.

26. David Kunzle, "Nicaragua's La Prensa: Capitalist Thorn in Socialist Flesh," in Communicating in Popular Nicaragua, ed. A. Mattèlart, p. 56.

27. John S. Nichols, "U.S. Government Funding of La Prensa: Uses and Abuses of the Nicaraguan Opposition Paper," paper presented to the 14th International Congress of the Latin American Studies Association, New Orleans, March 17, 1988, p. 4.

28. In this section I rely heavily on Kunzle's "Nicaragua's La Prensa."

29. Noam Chomsky, *Thought Control in Democratic Societies* (Boston: South End Press, 1989), p. 325.

30. Ibid., pp. 324–337.

31. These incidents were reported daily in *La Prensa*'s front pages from mid-June until its closure in mid-July.

32. Nichols, "U.S. Government Funding," p. 1.

33. Jack Spence, "The U.S. Media: Covering (Over) Nicaragua," in *Reagan Versus the Sandinistas*, ed. Walker, p. 199.

34. The material in this section relies heavily on John S. Nichols, "*La Prensa*: The CIA Connection," *Columbia Journalism Review*, July/August 1988, pp. 34–35, as well as his previously mentioned "U.S. Government Funding." See also the vehement rebuttals by those implicated by Nichols's article as well as his counterrebuttal in "Unfinished Business," *Columbia Journalism Review*, September/October 1988, pp. 66, 68.

35. Nichols, "*La Prensa*: The CIA Connection," p. 34.

36. Ibid.

37. Ibid.

38. Ibid., p. 35.

39. "Covert Aid and the Church: Did the CIA and Ollie North Help a Cardinal?" *Newsweek*, June 15, 1987, pp. 27–28.

40. Ibid.

41. For example, see A. Mattèlart in his introductory essay to *Communication in Popular Nicaragua*.

PART IV

The Search for Peace

The single chapter in this last section examines the complicated search for peace in Central America, particularly Nicaragua, which began in the early 1980s. In Chapter 17, William Goodfellow and James Morrell of the Washington-based Center for International Policy describe the process through which four, then eight, and finally ten or twelve Latin American countries cooperated—in the face of great offstage pressure and resistance from the U.S. government—to push for a peaceful solution to all of the region's conflicts. Providing the factual basis for a clear understanding of the various stages in the process—Contadora, Esquipulas, Sapoá, Tela—the chapter also highlights some of the great ironies of the affair: (1) Once the first peace accords were signed, Nicaragua, the country that consistently made the greatest effort to comply, became the focal point of world attention and pressure for compliance even as the cosignatory U.S. client states of northern Central America were violating the accords with great abandon. (2) The lopsided attention and pressure on Nicaragua forced that country to make electoral law concessions to the opposition, such as allowing foreign financing of parties and candidates, which few countries (certainly not the United States, the major source of such funds) would allow in their elections. Though they note that the elections were held "under conditions of gravely impaired national sovereignty," Goodfellow and Morrell conclude on a guardedly optimistic note, stressing that, as of the time they were writing, a tentative peace had come to Nicaragua.

SEVENTEEN

From Contadora to Esquipulas to Sapoá and Beyond

WILLIAM GOODFELLOW & JAMES MORRELL

The overwhelming reality the Sandinistas faced in their foreign relations was the reflexive, ideologically driven hostility of the United States toward any sort of nationalistic, autonomous, especially leftist, stirrings in the Third World. This U.S. hostility is ultimately traceable to the postwar consensus among mainstream U.S. politicians for an open-trading world order in which U.S. interests could operate unhindered by tariff, currency, or other statist restrictions, whether imposed by nationalist-minded businessmen or leftist revolutionaries. Although the diverse challenges from Korea and Guatemala to the Dominican Republic, Vietnam, El Salvador, and Nicaragua had minor economic significance individually, Washington invested each of them with an enormous symbolic importance to the point that by the mid-1980s Reagan appointee Jeane Kirkpatrick could seriously argue that Central America was "the most important place in the world for the United States." With equal earnestness, her Democratic predecessors had assigned remote Vietnam the same importance.[1]

U.S. hostility and a huge disparity of forces, therefore, were givens, and the Sandinistas had to take them into account in their diplomatic strategy. They tried every expedient from direct negotiations with the United States to marshaling regional support and seeking European and Socialist Bloc aid, but after the setback of the revolutionaries in El Salvador during 1980–1983, Nicaragua was politically isolated and geo-graphically vulnerable on the Central American isthmus. The enormous popular enthusiasm that sustained the Sandinistas at the beginning of the decade steadily waned as the war and economic isolation took their toll.

In one way or another, any diplomatic strategy the Sandinistas undertook had to register these power realities. Diplomacy had the great benefit of mobilizing allies and making Washington's vindictive campaign politically difficult—most notably in 1988 when the House of Representatives voted to cut off military aid to the contras. Nevertheless, any real negotiation—whether directly with the U.S. administration or, as ultimately occurred, via surrogates with Congress—risked becoming an engine of unrequited concessions that could ultimately drive the Sandinistas from power. As their objective position slowly deteriorated over the decade, they routinely accepted one-sided terms they had earlier dismissed out of hand, just to keep the diplomatic process going. Finally, in a maximum effort to use the peace process to deflect Washington's hostility, they agreed to an election whose purpose was less to pick a government than to please outsiders. That being the purpose, it was, in hindsight, no surprise when the majority voted accordingly.

Diplomacy Begins: The Enders Round

Such an electoral debacle was the last thing in the Sandinistas' minds as they confronted the new Reagan administration in 1981. It would take some months after the Reagan inauguration before the less-confrontational Carter policy would give way to a virulent right-wing approach. Professional State Department officers knew well that the immediate difficulties between the United States and Nicaragua could be negotiated, and accordingly Thomas Enders, then assistant secretary of state for Latin America, tried to strike a deal with the Sandinistas. On August 12, 1981, he arrived in Managua to restate U.S. opposition to the Nicaraguan arms flow to El Salvador and called for an end to Nicaragua's own Soviet Bloc–aided arms buildup. In return, Enders said that the United States would enforce U.S. neutrality laws against Nicaraguan exiles training in Florida, would publicly commit itself not to use force against Nicaragua, and would resume economic aid.

The terms of the Enders deal, which did not touch internal Nicaraguan matters, were better than terms Nicaragua would later routinely accept in regional negotiations. Nicaragua never responded to Enders and let various side issues, such as his allegedly threatening tone or the launching of a small U.S.-Honduran naval and air exercise in October, distract it from pursuing the deal. "We were not so pragmatic in those days," a Nicaraguan official admitted later.[2] The Sandinistas in 1981 were still buoyed up by the national enthusiasm for their 1979 revolution and may have overestimated their strength vis-à-vis Washington.

However, Nicaragua also had good reason to doubt that Enders's deal would be the final one. The right wing in Washington kept pushing forward new demands, such as recrating and sending back Nicaragua's Soviet tanks. As Lawrence Pezzullo, former U.S. ambassador to Nicaragua, put it, "No matter what you do, you are always going to get a new approach by the right that will shoot you down. Because all the people in this administration are people who shoot down negotiations rather than people who negotiate."³ After the collapse of these talks, the Reagan administration in November began funding the contras with $19.95 million.

The Quainton Eight Points

Congressional approval of the contras, however, depended on how convincingly the administration was pursuing a negotiated solution. Accordingly, on April 8, 1982, the Reagan administration had Ambassador Anthony Quainton in Managua hand an eight-point proposal to the government of Nicaragua. The new point in this proposal was to elevate internal Nicaraguan affairs to the status of "essential elements" in future relation with the United States; specifically, Nicaragua would have to respect political pluralism and hold free elections. Although Foreign Minister Miguel d'Escoto rejected this demand as "an inexcusable position of interference in matters which are of Nicaragua's sole and exclusive competence," it was a demand that would not go away.

Launching Contadora

The collapse of these negotiations in 1981–1982 and the funding of the contras motivated Mexico to convene a meeting of its foreign minister and those of Colombia, Panama, and Venezuela on Contadora Island in January 1983. The basic concept of the Contadora group was to guide the five Central American countries to a peace agreement among themselves that would limit superpower, mainly U.S., intervention in the region. The guiding philosophy of the Contadora countries was Third World neutralism and nonalignment. The group's function was to fill the diplomatic void left by the United States. Because the Reagan administration refused to negotiate, Contadora would arrange a regional settlement and confront the United States with the result.

The motivation was not merely altruistic. As a later Mexican Foreign Ministry internal document on Central America put it, "The failure to reach agreements endangers not only regional order but the security and the preservation of values and principles that are in the national interest of the Latin American countries, particularly the neighboring countries like Mexico."⁴

Contadora was a major step forward, if only because it put in the lead countries that genuinely wanted to negotiate instead of, as before, a country that wanted to "shoot down" negotiations. Moreover, Contadora cobbled together a negotiating group and a forum—the five Central American countries—that in this context had not previously existed. A previous meeting of Costa Rica, El Salvador, and Honduras with the United States, the "San José Forum for Peace and Democracy," on

October 4, 1982, had been notable chiefly for the exclusion of Guatemala and Nicaragua.

By September 9, 1983, Contadora produced a lofty "Document of Objectives" that everybody, including the United States, could endorse. Next came the hard work of reducing these objectives to legally binding commitments. When that document was finished, it would be apparent who was really for or against a peace agreement. By June 1984 Contadora and the Central Americans had finished a first draft.

Nicaragua had been predictably leery of the provisions about internal democratization that smacked of foreign interference, and Secretary of State George Shultz made the most of this inflexibility. Nicaragua, he charged, "has rejected key elements of the draft, including those dealing with binding obligations to internal democratization and to reductions in arms and troop levels."[5]

But Nicaragua had learned from its two years of negotiations with the United States and Contadora. On September 21 Nicaraguan President Daniel Ortega shocked Washington with this reply to Contadora: "We inform you of the Nicaraguan government's decision to accept in its totality, immediately and without modifications, the revised proposal submitted on September 7 by the Contadora group."

All a flabbergasted State Department official could say was, "It's not at all clear to me that in the long run Nicaragua won't come to regret its precipitous action." Nicaragua's offer to sign he dismissed as a "good negotiations ploy," but one that would "come back and haunt them. . . . So it remains to be seen who will get the last laugh on this one."[6]

Nicaragua's response was highly significant. For the first time, one of the major parties had truly embraced a negotiated solution. It would take until October 30 before the National Security Council staff could report, "We have trumped the latest Nicaraguan/Mexican efforts to rush signature of an unsatisfactory Contadora agreement."[7]

> We have effectively blocked Contadora group efforts to impose the second draft of the Revised Contadora Act. Following intensive U.S. consultations with El Salvador, Honduras, and Costa Rica, the Central Americans submitted a counterdraft to the Contadora states on October 20, 1984. It reflects many of our concerns and shifts the focus within Contadora to a document broadly consistent with U.S. interests. . . . Contadora spokesmen have become notably subdued recently on prospects for an early signing.[8]

Although the administration had indeed sidetracked Contadora, there remained one nagging problem in its efforts to weld the other Central American countries (the "Core Four") into an anti-Sandinista bloc: "The uncertain support of Guatemala for the Core Four is a continuing problem. Continuing personality problems . . . continue to hamper efforts to keep the Core Four together. We will continue to exert strong pressure on Guatemala to support the basic Core Four position."[9] The United States never did prod Guatemala back into the fold. And its diplomatic strategy would completely collapse when, far from recruiting Guatemala, it would lose Costa Rica as well.

This loss was still a matter of the future. The failure of Costa Rica, El Salvador, and Honduras to sign the revised Contadora draft in 1984 put negotiations into a tailspin. These three countries met in Tegucigalpa on October 19, 1984, to produce a counterdraft allowing U.S. military bases, exercises, and advisers in the region.

Manzanillo Talks

George Shultz, secretary of state in the Reagan administration, initiated a new attempt at negotiation with Managua in spring 1984, which President Reagan reluctantly let go forward because Congress was balking at aid to the contras. For the president the only point was how to get support in Congress for the contras. He saw no hope in negotiations but told his advisers, "Our participation is important from that standpoint, to get support from the Congress."[10]

Shultz met Ortega at the Managua airport to propose bilateral talks, which began in Manzanillo, Mexico, in June. By August, the U.S. negotiator finally had clearance to present a proposal, left incomplete by action of the Right in Washington. In return for Nicaragua's expelling all Soviet and Cuban military advisers, the United States promised only to "take Nicaraguan actions into consideration." An earlier version with actual reciprocal actions had been vetoed by the hard-line Right. The U.S. draft proposal did agree to cease support of the contras if Nicaragua did the same to the Salvadoran guerrillas. It finessed the issue of U.S. interference in Nicaragua's internal affairs by requiring free elections in El Salvador. In a later stage, it restored U.S. aid to Nicaragua.

Even though Nicaragua's point man in the negotiations, Deputy Foreign Minister Víctor Tinoco, was ready and willing to deal, the lack of reciprocity was too much to take. Next to the highly articulated Contadora agreement, it looked at first reading like a "proposal of surrender." He declined comment and took it back to Managua, where the comandantes resented its emphasis on the internal affairs of Nicaragua. On security matters, the proposal asked Nicaragua to take specific steps but did not offer anything clear in return.

The Sandinistas came back in October with a counteroffer, which was based on the Contadora agreement. Their position thus incorporated the many concessions they had made in accepting that agreement, such as sending home Soviet and Cuban advisers, excluding a Soviet base in Nicaragua, limiting Nicaragua's army, and verification. But the United

States rejected Contadora's ban on U.S. bases and exercises and sought to direct the discussion onto internal Nicaraguan politics. With Reagan safely reelected, the U.S. side broke off the talks for good in January 1985.[11]

Contadora Second Draft

The Manzanillo failure again left the field to Contadora, and in September 1985 the group produced a new draft incorporating some of the Tegucigalpa counterdraft positions. For example, it let the United States keep its exercises and bases in Honduras, albeit under restrictions. Now it was Nicaragua's turn to balk, as it rebelled against the logic that its concessions should lead only to demands for more concessions.

Meanwhile, in August 1985 the Contadora four were joined by a "support group" of Argentina, Brazil, Peru, and Uruguay. Together the eight represented nearly 90 percent of Latin America's economy and population. Foreign ministers of the eight met in Caraballeda, Venezuela, and on January 12, 1986, issued the rousing Caraballeda Message, which insisted on simultaneous, parallel work on signing Contadora and preparing the conditions (i.e., stopping aid to the contras). Three days later, the Central American presidents found themselves together in Guatemala City for the inauguration of President Vinicio Cerezo. An energetic politician, Cerezo corralled them all into endorsing the Caraballeda Message. New meetings and deadlines were set, and the Contadora foreign ministers went to Washington to appeal unsuccessfully for an end to aid to the contras.

The Contadora and Central American foreign ministers met in Panama City on April 5–6, 1986, to set a date for the signing. Mexico and Nicaragua failed to persuade the other Central American countries to issue a declaration against the contras, and Nicaragua refused to agree to sign the Contadora pact without that. President Ortega soon found himself opening an almost-peremptory letter from Presidents Alán García of Peru and Julio Sanguinetti of Uruguay urging him to sign anyway on June 6, the date Contadora had set as the "final" deadline.

Esquipulas Process Begins

Meanwhile, in late May 1986, Guatemala's Cerezo reconvened his four colleagues at Esquipulas, Guatemala. He intended at this meeting to clear out the last obstacles to Contadora's signing in June and to launch his pet project of a Central American parliament. It soon became evident, however, that the other presidents had come to argue, and the meeting achieved nothing except the establishment of a new, high-level negotiating forum.

When the foreign ministers convened again in Panama on June 6, 1986, for the signing, the old game of musical chairs resumed. Nicaragua and Guatemala apparently would have signed, but the traditional trio of Costa Rica, El Salvador, and Honduras demurred. The agreement went unsigned.

The twin failures of Esquipulas and Contadora, coming one month apart, cleared the way for the Reagan administration to get the Democratic-controlled House of Representatives to vote military aid to the contras. Although that decision failed to overthrow the Sandinistas, it added prodigiously to the body count in rural Nicaragua.

These June days marked the nadir of the Central American peace process. After three and half years' labor, Contadora had reaped merely a total breakdown in the dialogue and $100 million in aid to the contras. The Reagan administration felt it was no longer necessary even to accord lip service to the attempt. The United States was adamantly opposed to "any lousy, fake, sham Contadora treaty," a State Department official said.[12] Even if the treaty were signed, the United States would not abide by it. "We are committed to the Nicaraguan resistance," a secret State Department briefing paper said. "Our support will not slacken whatever the results in Contadora."[13]

Contadora saw the vote for the $100 million a "historic mistake that may damage inter-American relations," as Mexico's foreign minister put it. "Peace is still possible," the Contadora ministers declared in October 1986 at the United Nations.[14] Since the Central Americans would not talk to each other, the ministers decided to go to all five Central American countries themselves to jump start the negotiations. The secretaries-general of the UN and OAS joined them. But the Central American presidents lacked the political will to end the war, UN Secretary-General Javier Pérez de Cuellar sadly concluded at the end of the trip in January 1987.

The Arias Plan

Genesis

One of the greatest ironies of the Central American peace effort is that at just this juncture, when the process seemed to scrape bottom, it was poised for its greatest leap forward. Contadora had failed; military aid was pouring in to the contras; and President Arias was calling a meeting that excluded Nicaragua. The meeting, to be held in San José on February 15, 1987, appeared about to inaugurate Nicaragua's isolation. Instead, what the meeting produced was a plan for Nicaragua's salvation.

This was the Arias plan, in all essential respects the same plan as that finally signed by all five presidents in August 1987. The practical thrust of the plan was to relegitimize Nicaragua enough, through association with the other Central American countries, to persuade Congress to stop aid to the contras. Most of the plan's provisions dealt with internal democratization measures to be traded off for an end to external support for rebels.

The presidents of El Salvador and Honduras came to San José expecting something far different. As a Salvadoran official laid out the scenario: (1) presentation of the plan by President Arias to his three counterparts; (2) approval of the plan by these four; (3) approval by Contadora, the United States, and the European Economic Community; (4) discussion of the plan with Nicaragua "in an effort to make that country restore its democracy and establish good relations with its neighbors"; and (5) recommendation of political and diplomatic sanctions against the Sandinistas for "rejecting the peace plan, not complying with the Contadora document," and showing that it was a regime "with which one cannot coexist."

The presidents of El Salvador, Honduras, and Guatemala arrived in San José and read the plan for the first time. It had the democratization clauses that they thought Nicaragua would reject. But it also had Contadora's clear prohibition of aid and sanctuary to regional rebels like the contras. These were clauses that would be difficult for virtual U.S. client states like El Salvador and Honduras to sign.

Suddenly, the rough talk about using the plan to isolate Nicaragua evaporated. Instead, there were only lame references to the plan as a mere "working document." It is "senseless to say that we fully endorse it," the Honduran Foreign Ministry said. "We only learned about the proposal two days before the meeting."[15] The presidents failed to approve the binding language of the plan, and the minisummit, which was to have presented a united front to Nicaragua, broke up in disarray. El Salvador's President José Napoleón Duarte said, "If I sign this plan, you might as well shoot me here, because I will be shot when I return."

Meanwhile, in Managua President Ortega was fuming, furious at President Arias for excluding him. Costa Rica was a "neocolony" and a "traitor," he snapped. But he quickly forgot his harsh words when President Cerezo stopped off in Managua on his way back from San José and briefed him on the summit. By February 18, Ortega found much in the Arias plan worthy of study and agreed to go to the next Esquipulas meeting. The same game of musical chairs that had gone on so long within the Contadora group began again. As Nicaragua swung in favor of a peace plan, the unconditional U.S. allies turned against it.

Such was the confused, tumultuous birth of the Arias plan. A Costa Rican diplomat noted the irony: "At first we did not reveal the plan. So the people who should not be in agreement with the plan did agree with it, and those who should agree with it did not."[16]

Apart from its intrinsic logic, the plan was a face-saving device by which Costa Rica could leave the Tegucigalpa bloc and join the peace-makers. By May, the plan was threatening a diplomatic disaster to the Reagan policy. Both Nicaragua and Guatemala were lining up in support, making a majority of three to two. "The Americans are scared to death of the talks," a Nicaraguan official chuckled, "because they know we might walk in the door and say it's a great peace plan, then pull out our pen and offer to sign it immediately."[17]

Arias still voiced the rhetoric of Washington. But simply by asserting the fundamental premise of diplomacy—concessions by both sides—he had wandered far off the reservation. Rhetoric aside, the Reagan administration had made no concessions at all in the Contadora negotiations, and the one offer the State Department had made, contained in a letter by Special Ambassador Philip Habib on April 1986—a promise to cut off the contras if Contadora were signed—had been repudiated by the White House a month later. Nicaragua, on the other hand, had gotten used to making concessions in the Contadora talks. By voicing Washington's stated position and proceeding in workmanlike fashion to implement it, Arias thought he had found a formula for bridging the gap.

Congressional Endorsement

A quick endorsement came from the U.S. Congress. Arias's rhetoric was tailor-made for both sides of the debate, which accepted as a given that the Sandinistas were suppressing democracy in Nicaragua. On March 12, the Senate passed, ninety-seven to one, Sen. Terry Sanford's resolution supporting the Arias plan, strongly signaling the administration that its majority for contra aid was once again eroding.

Contadora's endorsement followed in April. Perhaps it first saw the Arias plan as a competitor. But Contadora above all wanted to resume dialogue among the Central Americans, and Arias's plan made that possible.

U.S. Position

On June 17 Arias, who was on a private trip to the United States, was invited to the White House. President Reagan lambasted the plan as too lenient toward Nicaragua. "The greatest concern is the need for the Sandinistas to act on genuine democratization before pressure on the regime is removed in any way," Reagan told Arias. The Costa Rican stood his ground, vainly trying to convince the president to give his peace plan a chance.[18]

In the region, Honduras kept finding new problems with the plan. Twice the summit meeting of the five presidents was postponed, as Salvadoran President Duarte kept remembering last-minute appointments in Europe. At last the five foreign ministers agreed to meet in Tegucigalpa at a session mediated by the Contadora ministers to set the agenda for the summit meeting in Guatemala a few days later.

Arrival in Tegucigalpa

The change was visible as the foreign ministers arrived in the Honduran capital. The Hondurans started by issuing an entirely new peace plan text—in effect, another counterdraft requiring many months more of negotiations. But in introducing the plan under the icy gaze of Mexican Foreign Minister Bernardo Sepúlveda, Honduran Foreign Minister Carlos López Contreras insisted that he had merely offered a series of suggestions, which the meeting could consider as it chose. The meeting promptly disregarded them and went straight onto a discussion of the Arias plan. Nicaragua's d'Escoto suggested that Contadora collect all the amendments to the Arias plan, reconcile them the best it could, add its own suggestions, and put all into a draft that the ministers could take to their presidents. That was done.

Overall, the changes were minor, but they tightened up the Arias plan in two crucial respects. First, the original Arias plan merely called on the governments to declare a cease-fire. The Hondurans argued successfully that there was no sense in the governments declaring a cease-fire, since they were not fighting each other. The cease-fire needed to be worked out between the government and the guerrillas of each afflicted country, even though this meant Nicaragua would have to talk to the contras. Contadora agreed to this suggestion and put it into the revised draft. Although this change did not explicitly require face-to-face talks, it was nevertheless the genesis of the many rounds of later cease-fire talks.

Second, Contadora also tightened up the original Arias language against aiding the region's rebels. From suspension of aid it went to cessation and from military aid it went to all aid except that for repatriation or resettlement.

Guatemala Agreement

The five presidents arrived in Guatemala City. The momentum for an agreement was palpable. When on August 5, just as the summit meeting began, the White House released its own peace plan for the region that it had worked out with House Speaker Jim Wright, the Central Americans took it in stride. With a broad grin, President Cerezo told reporters, "We welcome plans from any quarter, from the United States, from Europe, from the Soviet Union or even the Middle East. But we are here to sign the Central American Peace Plan, and that is what we are going to do."[19]

Arias held them to the task. When some of the presidents prepared to quit for dinner—for them, a three-to-four-hour undertaking—Arias insisted on calling room service. When Duarte suggested that a ninety-day deadline for compliance would be more realistic than Arias's thirty days, Arias immediately agreed and Ortega, after huddling with his advisers, agreed as well. When Honduran president José Azcona showed signs of getting cold feet, Arias's aides called Speaker Wright in Washington to announce that agreement was imminent. Just as Salvadoran President Duarte finally tired of canceling summit meetings, now Azcona did not want to be singled out as the spoiler. And all of them were sick of the region's wars.

The Signing

Miraculously, then, all five presidents walked up the aisle of the Guatemalan National Palace to sign the plan. Heralded by a drumroll and a fanfare from a brass band, the five presidents strode into the ornate reception hall, listened to their national anthems, watched President Arias read his peace text, and then signed the Procedure for a Firm and Lasting Peace in Central America.

The sublime moment, four and one-half years after the first meeting of the Contadora group, was not only a key victory for patient Sandinista diplomacy but also an important marker in all Central America's political modernization. The five presidents agreed, above all, that they were in charge of their five countries—they, not the military, not the guerrillas, not the Americans. They were the constitutional authorities in their countries and would not tolerate endemic guerrilla warfare, the "Lebanonization" of the region. The presidents had frequently talked about Central America becoming another Beirut.

The historic agreement pledged the five countries to take the following actions in ninety days: (1) to decree amnesty for irregular forces (who would also be obligated to release their prisoners); (2) to vehemently call for a cease-fire in countries where armed conflicts were under way; (3) to promote a pluralistic, participatory democracy, without outside interference, guaranteeing complete press freedom, and assuring access of all political parties of every persuasion to the press, radio, and television; (4) to call on the governments within and without the region to cease all aid, whether military, logistical, financial, or even propagandistic, to all irregular forces or insurrectional movements, with the exception of aid for repatriation or relocation; and (5) to prevent irregular forces from using the territory of any Central American state to attack other Central American states or as bases of supply.

After the signing of the accord, the Nicaraguan government moved the most quickly to implement it. It was the first country to set up a National Reconciliation Commission required by the accord. President

Ortega appointed Cardinal Miguel Obando y Bravo, an outspoken critic of the regime, as the commission's chairman. La Prensa and Radio Católica reopened. Political opposition rallies took place, although one opposition leader was arrested. The government and opposition met in the "national dialogue."

The more difficult provisions of the plan came later. President Ortega waited the full ninety days but on November 5, 1987, announced to the gasps of his audience the beginning of indirect talks with the contras on a cease-fire. The Sandinistas had vowed for five years never to talk to them. The talks sputtered through two rounds in Santo Domingo in November and December, with Cardinal Obando relaying messages back and forth between the two delegations. The government side struggled to keep the talks on technical aspects of a cease-fire. The contra side sought to introduce political issues. The talks were deadlocked almost as soon as they began.

In Sweden, the Nobel Prize committee named President Arias the winner of the 1987 peace prize. Arias appeared before an unofficial joint session of the U.S. Congress in October. In El Salvador, meetings between the government and guerrillas were set, and in Madrid, the first meeting in twenty-five years of conflict was held between the Guatemalan government and the guerrillas.

Verification Commission

Throughout the region, governments and opposition figures made their moves, but as yet no guerrillas had agreed to stop fighting. The plan had established a verification commission composed of the five Central American and eight Contadora and Support Group foreign ministers and UN and OAS representatives to evaluate compliance 120 days after signature. The significance of the verification commission was that, with its Contadora and UN-OAS membership, it was the final mechanism to assure that the plan would be applied evenhandedly instead of unilaterally on Nicaragua, as the power realities would dictate.

The commission's work was first hobbled by Honduras, which refused it the right of on-site inspection, which would expose the country's illegal harboring of the contras. Then, as the commission toured Central American capitals conducting its interviews, El Salvador, Guatemala, Honduras, and even Costa Rica bridled under the criticism that they knew would be coming.

Under their pressure, the commission watered down but did not totally weaken its 118-page report, which was never made public. Completed January 14, 1988, the report was signed by all five Central American foreign ministers, but with reservations by some. It called a cutoff of aid to the contras an indispensable requirement for peace. It found continuing human rights problems in El Salvador and Guatemala.

In Nicaragua it found both restrictions and the beginnings of a democratic process.

Alajuela Summit

Since July the peace process had been going well, but at the beginning of 1988 seemed again on the brink of failure. No new aid had gone to the contras, but the war continued; Nicaragua had liberalized, but restrictions remained; Honduras had pledged nonuse of its territory, but the contras remained; El Salvador had promised democracy, but the death squads remained.

The presidents had agreed to meet in a new summit, held in Alajuela, near San José, on January 16, 1988. The issue before them was whether they could agree at all on a common statement when the plan so far had failed to stop the region's wars. Much was hanging on the outcome, as the U.S. administration had asked Congress for $270 million for the contras.

Alajuela would clarify the true dynamics of the Arias plan, which the evenhandedness of the bare text only masked. Nicaragua benefited chiefly by being included at all. It got the benefit of a certain safety in numbers, a pale reflected legitimacy, in biased U.S. eyes, by being associated with its four conservative neighbors in a process that included a call for the end to aid to the contras, even though one of those neighbors continued to harbor the very same contras.

On the debit side was the fact, now starkly revealed, that all the rigors of the Arias plan were being applied to Nicaragua alone. Apart from Costa Rica, where democratic procedure was already in place, only Nicaragua was doing anything to comply.

Thus, Ortega arrived at this summit already outnumbered four to one. He could argue and defy, as he had at Esquipulas I; then the summit would break up in discord and Reagan would get his money. Or he could accept the double standard. He chose the latter, announcing a series of unilateral concessions at the summit. The five presidents issued a statement pledging themselves to full compliance immediately, unilaterally, and "without excuses." The latter phrase, inserted by Arias, was widely seen as aimed at Nicaragua. And as if to ratify the abandonment of evenhandedness, the verification commission was dropped.

Decisive Test in Congress

Whatever its weaknesses, the joint declaration also reiterated the call for an end to contra aid. This issue was now finally coming onto the U.S. congressional agenda for decision. Assistant Secretary of State for Inter-American Affairs Elliott Abrams had begun 1987 by confidently predicting Congress would vote the aid because it had no alternative. Now it had an alternative in the Arias plan.

For some of the sixty undecided "moderates" in the House, who held the balance, the progress of the Arias plan was decisive. In a situation so evenly balanced, President Ortega's concessions on January 16 and impetus toward a cease-fire nudged the debate in the direction of the Arias plan. The House leadership also promised wavering members, if military aid was defeated, the chance to vote for nonlethal sustenance aid, misnamed "humanitarian." This way they could uphold Arias yet avoid "abandoning" the contras.

During the last week of January, Congress was subjected to a public barrage it had rarely experienced on any issue in the 1980s. Calls came in overwhelmingly against contra aid from around the country. Even in conservative, rural districts of the undecided, in states like North Carolina and Oklahoma, calls usually ran at least two to one against the aid. The administration so feared this onslaught that it reduced its request from $270 million to $36 million.

Nevertheless, the progress of the Arias plan, the leadership's adroit strategy, and the indignation of millions of ordinary Americans combined at the same moment. The administration had jockeyed itself into a position of opposing a diplomatic solution. On February 3, the House voted to deny the administration's request for military aid to the contras; the margin of victory was eight votes. Twelve Republicans voted against aid; nearly sixty southern Democrats went with the administration.

Definitive Affirmation

This February 3 vote was the House of Representatives' definitive affirmation of the Arias plan. The confusion over passage of sustenance aid a month later was anticlimactic. Still insisting on military aid, the administration urged the Republicans to vote on March 3 against anything less than that. Fourteen liberals adamantly opposed to any contra aid also voted against sustenance aid, and the bill went down in defeat. President Reagan rejoiced, but the contra leadership felt abandoned. First military aid was lost, and then because of the administration's maneuvering, all aid was lost. The contras showed their resentment of the cutoff by going on strike. In their rebellion, the contras showed a perverse sense of Latin pride.

The Alajuela summit and the House vote set the stage. Acting on his commitment at Alajuela and sensing that the contras were ready to move, Ortega instituted direct talks between them and the Sandinistas. At the February 1988 talks in Guatemala, the positions narrowed markedly; both sides accepted the proposal of Cardinal Obando, the mediator, "in principle." Then the appointment of higher-ranking delegations and the proposal to hold the talks on Nicaraguan soil directly without a mediator brought the top players together in mid-March 1988. The contras, beaten in both Congress and the field, embraced the logic of the Arias plan. The government, by reopening *La Prensa*, lifting the State of Emergency, and releasing prisoners, had already done so.

Sapoá Cease-Fire Agreement

After the February House vote, the agreement signed between the government and contras at Sapoá, Nicaragua, on March 21 was the Arias plan's greatest triumph, the first true agreement between the warring factions. However, it only suspended the war. The contras were to retain their weapons during the sixty-day negotiating period that began on April 1. During this period a permanent cease-fire was to be sought. The contras were to relocate in zones. More prisoners were to be amnestied. Sustenance aid recently passed by Congress was allowed for the contras. They were invited to join the national dialogue and rejoin political parties.

The successful outcome of the Alajuela summit, the House vote against military aid to the contras, and the Sapoá cease-fire vindicated President Ortega's strategy of concessions designed to keep negotiations going. The momentum toward massive aid to the contras, regional war, and U.S. intervention had been completely upset. Ortega pocketed the lesson for future application and turned to the talks with the contras to make the cease-fire permanent.

On April 17 the government made a comprehensive proposal for a permanent cease-fire, building on the Sapoá agreement. It was immediately rejected by the contras, but, meanwhile, contra leader Alfredo César initiated back-channel talks with government negotiators Paul Reichler and Gen. Humberto Ortega. César gave Reichler a list of political concessions that, if accepted, César said would enable him and other members of the directorate to sign an accord.

At the penultimate May 26–28 round in Managua, the government formally accepted all these points, completely abandoning its previous position that political questions were to be negotiated with the internal opposition, not illegal rebels. Nevertheless, César and the others did not sign but insisted on the extreme demands of the faction headed by former National Guard colonel Enrique Bermúdez.

June 9 Round in Managua

The contras returned to Managua in June 1988 with their extreme demands, and at noon on June 9, the last day, piled on a new series of demands, including: the right of draftees simply to leave the army any time they chose, forced resignation of the Supreme Court, restoration of confiscated property that had been distributed to smallholders or cooperatives, and the opening of contra offices in Managua. The government would have to carry out these actions while the contra army remained armed and in its enclaves; they would take until January 31,

1989, to disarm. The contras gave the government an ultimatum: It had two hours to accept these demands or they would walk out.

César denied that these were new demands; he was merely "putting into effect and implementing the points" made in their previous proposal, he said at the press conference. "But whenever the Resistance tries to move to a discussion of written accords the government avoids making this type of commitment," César charged. "The democratic reforms should be clearly laid out and written into the accord with specific dates, and if they are not put into effect the Resistance cannot proceed with reintegrating itself into the political life of the country."[20] It was this sort of exaggeration by César that outraged government negotiator Reichler on June 9 and prompted him to go public with the back-channel negotiations, where he had met César's demands for written accords on democratic reforms.

The contras had persistently escalated their demands each time agreement seemed near. Their walkout from the June 1988 Managua negotiations was intended to force a crisis that would trigger new U.S. military aid, one of their leaders later admitted.[21] The walkout effectively ended the government-contra talks for the year, although the two sides would meet in September 1988 in Guatemala for an afternoon of talks that failed to yield agreement even on the site of the next negotiating round.

Esquipulas Process Resumes

Nevertheless, the peace process was not dead. Just as Contadora had resumed when U.S.-Nicaraguan talks collapsed, now the Esquipulas process cranked up again after the contra talks petered out. Finding themselves together at the Mexican presidential inauguration on November 30, 1988, the Central American foreign ministers drafted a letter to Secretary-General Pérez de Cuellar asking the United Nations to set up a peacekeeping operation, soon to be termed ONUCA (for the Spanish initials for United Nations Observers in Central America), using personnel from Canada, Spain, and West Germany to patrol the borders against the flow of arms and provision of territorial sanctuary to armed groups. The call for a UN peacekeeping operation was a blow to the contras, and once again mobilized international support for efforts against them.

Meanwhile, President Reagan left office, and ten days later the senior Latin American statesman Carlos Andrés Pérez was inaugurated as president of Venezuela. Four Central American presidents—all except the ailing Duarte—converged on Caracas, as did Fidel Castro, Alán García of Perú, and Felipe González of Spain. Pérez got all of them together in a hotel room on February 2 and hammered out with them a full peace agenda for 1989.

It was there that President Ortega made the fateful decision to apply fully the strategy of concessions that had worked so well to date—to stake his entire rule on an election wholly designed to fulfill the letter and spirit of the Arias plan, end all questions of the legitimacy of the government, and deprive the United States of grounds for continual attack. With Castro nodding his assent, Ortega agreed to forgo various advantages of incumbency the Election Law gave him, while braving the protest vote that was the natural disadvantage of incumbency. Only such elections with international observers and credibility would reopen international aid flows and ease U.S. hostility, the assembled social democrats told Ortega. When Ortega said he doubted the opposition would even run, they promised to apply their full powers of persuasion. In return for this extraordinary concession by Ortega, the other presidents promised to move diplomatically against the contras.

Leaving Caracas, the presidents had a solid, full agenda for their first summit in more than a year, which they held forthwith in El Salvador on February 13–14, 1989.

El Salvador Summit

Each president arrived with a wish list. The Guatemalans wanted progress toward regional peace and avoidance of criticism of their human rights record. El Salvador similarly wanted to avoid such criticism and as the host wanted a smooth meeting. Honduras's Azcona wanted to move to demobilize the contras, yet with enough vagueness so as to avoid collision with the United States.

President Arias most of all wanted to see his plan succeed. Unlike the other four presidents, the plan did not affect his country, for Costa Rica was fully in compliance. Yet his country could not escape the region's turmoil. Costa Rica was in a depression, and its diplomats maintained that they were playing host to 200,000 refugees from Nicaragua. Moreover, Costa Rican businessmen could no longer safely ship products overland through Nicaragua; they had to send them around Nicaragua by ship, a slow and costly route. Investment was down, and the strain on relations with the United States over President Arias's opposition to the contras had cost Costa Rica much-needed U.S. foreign aid.

Nicaragua saw the summit as an opportunity to demobilize the contras and finally come to terms with the United States by holding an internationally verified election. The accession of a new, apparently more pragmatic administration in Washington seemed to offer the hope that the eight-year war of survival with the Reagan administration finally was over. However, Nicaragua was hearing from Democrats in Congress what it had just heard in Caracas: An end to the U.S. trade embargo and the credit embargo that had prevented Nicaragua from getting any funds from the Inter-American Development Bank, the World Bank, and the International Monetary Fund would come only after Nicaragua had held the election. Given the high priority of rebuilding its war-shattered economy, Nicaragua's leadership went to the summit with plans to announce that not only the municipal elections, but elections for president, vice president, the legislature, and the Central American Parliament would be moved up to February 25, 1990, fully eight months earlier than required by Nicaragua's constitution.

The Washington debate over Nicaragua had hinged over how best to encourage Nicaragua to democratize. The Reagan administration and its allies in Congress, Republicans and hard-line southern Democrats, insisted that the Nicaraguan government would respond only to force. On the other hand, the Democratic leadership in both the House and Senate, and President Arias and most of America's Latin and European allies, argued that a combination of diplomatic pressure and economic enticements would best draw the Nicaraguans into the democratic camp. The summit would be the first real test of the carrot approach.

Demobilization Plan

For Washington, the summit's most startling development was the news that the five presidents had asked their foreign ministers to come up with a plan within ninety days to disarm and resettle the contras. Nicaragua had been hoping for a bilateral agreement with Honduras but considered it a long shot. Now Honduras decided it was safest to make the plan multilateral.

The contras were the big losers at the summit. Although they held a nonstop press conference right across the street from the presidents' meeting, they were ignored by the presidents and most of the press. The presidents' clearly stated opposition to any aid that did not disarm and relocate the contras made it much harder for the Bush administration to keep the contras encamped indefinitely in Honduras.

The new Bush administration had not drawn up its own wish list in time for the conference. This vacuum would not last forever. However, by moving decisively to demobilize the contras, the Central American presidents limited the Bush administration's options. Moreover, by re-scheduling their elections, releasing the ex-guardsmen, and opening further their political system, the Nicaraguan government hoped to remove any arguments the new administration in Washington might make for a resumption of the Reagan administration's war against them.

It was, nevertheless, a measure of how deeply the U.S. onslaught had impaired Nicaraguan sovereignty that Ortega would agree to negotiate with foreigners wholesale changes to a national electoral law and invite in a virtual UN supervision of his election. That was unprecedented in any sovereign country and verged on an admission that the government was incapable of conducting a fair election on its own, which was manifestly untrue. Reputable observers reported that the 1984 election had been fairly conducted and was marred mainly by the opposition's boycott. The decision to use what is the most intimate exercise of national sovereignty for purposes of international legitimation was to have unforeseen consequences.

Adjusting to the Bush Administration

After the encouraging start at Caracas and the El Salvador summit, the peace process went into a holding pattern from March to August 1989 as the various actors oriented themselves to the new administration. Honduras reverted to a familiar pattern of backsliding, Congress approved new logistical aid to the contras, and Arias struggled to find a point of balance.

Honduras. Moving to get the Hondurans back in line, the Bush administration sent an official to Tegucigalpa in March with a request to leave the contras alone until February 1990—the Nicaraguan election. When the Central American foreign ministers met in San José at the end of March, Honduras's López Contreras stalled on the demobilization plan and attached a crippling reservation to the UN peacekeepers' force as well.

Congress. Turning to Congress in April for the contras' money, Secretary of State James Baker tried to move beyond the usual rancorous debate by yielding on questions of principle. Given the makeup of Congress, he had no doubt he could push through nonmilitary aid, but he wanted an agreement with the Democratic leadership as well—a "bipartisan accord." The administration pledged itself to support the peace process, refuse money to contras who launched offensive operations, make the money also available for contra demobilization, and submit to a midterm review at which Congress could block further money if the administration were found in noncompliance. The Democratic leadership agreed, and Congress voted $55 million in sustenance aid to the contras. The effect was to give the administration a free hand. The trade embargo and anti-Nicaraguan rhetoric continued.

Thus when in late April Nicaragua made its first electoral changes, giving those who had boycotted the 1984 elections equal standing with those who had run, the State Department immediately belittled the concessions, as did various commissions set up by U.S. right-wing foundations. The Nicaraguan Electoral Law they criticized was entirely modeled on those of other Latin American countries, as a series of studies by the United Nations, OAS, U.S. Library of Congress, and the Venezuelan electoral commission all confirmed. Nevertheless, the media and Congress faithfully echoed the administration's complaints.

With contra demobilization and UN peacekeepers already stalled by Honduras, the cacophony against the electoral reforms also jeopardized the third plank of the presidents' El Salvador program.

Arias. The poisoned atmosphere also made Arias worry about whether the opposition would indeed boycott the election, as they had in 1984. At the El Salvador summit in February he had foreseen that a mere perfunctory reform by Nicaragua, combined with an adamant opposition stance, could lead to such a boycott. He asked the Nicaraguans then to give him powers to impose binding arbitration, but they refused. He began in May to pressure President Ortega for more concessions. In June Ortega appointed a balanced Supreme Electoral Council—a key issue he had discussed with Arias and Pérez in Caracas. Although according to the results of the 1984 elections, the Sandinistas were entitled to put three Sandinistas on the five-person board, they gave up their majority. The opposition, which had wanted to name four of the five members, predictably complained, but Arias and his advisers found the council acceptable.

Arias still was not finished. In a seven-hour face-to-face session in San José on July 14, 1989, he extracted Ortega's agreement to further overtures toward the opposition. Ortega agreed to try again to open a national dialogue with the opposition parties together, instead of meeting with them individually as he had been doing.

National Political Dialogue

This last decision immediately yielded a twofold result. On August 3–4, Ortega held a marathon twenty-two-hour televised public dialogue with twenty opposition parties. It produced the first-ever agreement between the Sandinista government and the opposition parties. It also helped weld the squabbling oppositionists together into a formidable bloc that they appeared incapable of achieving on their own.

In the dialogue, the opposition finally agreed to participate in the February 1990 elections and the government agreed to further concessions such as abolishing a mild public-order law and advancing the date for turnover of power to the winner of the elections. It also agreed to suspend the military draft until after the elections.

The opposition made another stride toward a common Nicaraguan position: It joined in a declaration calling on the Central American presidents in their upcoming summit in Honduras to demobilize the contras and asked foreign countries not to channel covert aid to the electoral campaign. With this political accord, one of the last essential pieces of the Arias plan fell into place.

Tela Summit

The political accord within Nicaragua cleared the way for the five presidents to end the stagnation and push the process forward. Abandoning all previous reservations, they now formally put into motion all three planks agreed on in their previous El Salvador meeting: endorsement of Nicaragua's electoral preparations, deployment of the ONUCA peacekeepers, and dismantlement of the contras. This last was to be carried out by a newly created International Commission for Support and Verification (CIAV), made up of the UN and OAS secretaries-general. The CIAV was to visit the contra camps, collect their weapons (a function later turned over to ONUCA), conduct returnees to Nicaragua, and guarantee their rights and livelihood. It was to "take control to the extent possible" of the $4 million a month in so-called humanitarian aid Congress had voted to the contras. Much of the aid was in fact field equipment to outfit the contras for their forays into Nicaragua: fatigues, boots, ponchos, field packs, canteens, and mess kits.[22] Since the Bush administration refused either to stop or to relinquish control of the aid, the results of the Tela summit gave the Democratic leadership in Congress full grounds to freeze the aid at the midterm review provided for in the bipartisan accord. The leadership, in meetings with concerned citizens in April 1989, had promised it would do exactly that if the accord's terms were violated.

Undermining the Tela Accord

For the contras, the Tela accord was the signal to reinfiltrate into Nicaragua, both to avoid demobilization and to attack an election that they feared would render them irrelevant. From August to October 1989 they sent 2,300 fighters back in, stepping up attacks on remote roads and farms. Most victims were civilians, but on October 21 the contras scored a lucky hit and killed eighteen reservists on a road that was supposed to have been covered by the army.

Furious, President Ortega resolved to draw attention to the unfolding violence through the only means open to him—he canceled the unilateral cease-fire with the contras, which was the remaining achievement of the Sapoá accord. U.S. newspapers, which had scarcely reported the step-up in contra attacks, gave front-page coverage to the cancellation. Even though the contras were engaging in offensive operations, Congress did not activate the provision in the law cutting off their aid but instead passed more resolutions against Ortega.

At the root of the Democrats' inaction was not only a change in personnel—Speaker Jim Wright had resigned, succeeded by Tom Foley—but also a calculation based on domestic politics. Once the administration had ceased confronting Congress with incessant contra aid requests, Congress simply disengaged. Confrontation with the administration over a volatile, unpredictable issue such as Nicaragua was to be avoided.

Reviving the Diplomatic Process

Called together by CIAV, the Nicaraguan government and contras met in New York and Washington on November 9–21 to attempt to renew the cease-fire, but sustained by the continued flow of aid, the contras refused either to demobilize or to withdraw from Nicaragua. Deputy Foreign Minister Tinoco entered the talks with a position based on the Tela accords and with carefully prepared fallback positions to demonstrate flexibility. The strategy almost worked when the contras threatened to walk out entirely, thus taking the blame, but they returned. Tinoco then retreated to his final fallback position by accepting a compromise proposal of CIAV to evacuate only those contras who had reinfiltrated since Tela. But the contras refused to move a single person. By the end, Tinoco and his fellow-negotiator Paul Reichler joked that they had been "negotiating against ourselves." The remark well summarizes Nicaragua's entire diplomatic experience with the United States and contras.

San Isidro Emergency Summit

What the contra negotiations did produce, however, was an exhaustive record of Sandinista attempts to resolve the problem peacefully. Nicaragua urgently called for a new meeting of Central American presidents to consider the situation the contras had created. Not only had the cease-fire broken down and the deadline for demobilization passed, but also the offensive launched by the rebels in the Farabundo Martí Liberation Front (FMLN) made sure that the question of El Salvador would be high on the summit agenda. Ortega apparently let the FMLN use Nicaragua as a base for arms shipments and flights—whether inadvertently or in a deliberate effort to gain greater leverage for removal of the contras, it was unclear. But El Salvador's President Alfredo Cristiani refused to go to the summit unless the presidents endorsed him and called for demobilization of the FMLN. As he said, Nicaragua had extracted all the benefits of the peace process and he wanted them for El Salvador as well. The Salvadoran army's murder of six prominent Jesuit clergymen in November revealed how dreadfully far El Salvador had yet to go in even minimal compliance with the plan, whose benefits Cristiani now demanded cost free.

Until that point, the Central American peace process had scarcely dealt with El Salvador, although formally the provisions of the agreement applied to all five countries equally. In fact, President Arias believed the plan had to work in Nicaragua before it could be applied to El Salvador. The emergency meeting that the five presidents held in San Isidro de Coronado, outside of San José, on December 10–12, 1989, was their most difficult since Alajuela. On the one hand, they could scarcely fail to meet after offensives in two of their countries. On the other hand, the disputes among them were severe. Cristiani's price for attendance was high, and Ortega paid it with utmost reluctance in order to eke out progress on the contras. The presidents agreed to demand that all remaining aid to the contras be immediately transferred to CIAV, the commission they had set up in August. They also agreed to expand ONUCA's mandate.

The results of the San Isidro emergency meeting were consistent with the entire record of Sandinista diplomacy since their unexpected acceptance of Contadora in 1984: Make extensive concessions in order to extract progress. It hurt Ortega, and damaged the peace process, to make a completely unbalanced pronouncement on El Salvador, but this was the price of progress on Nicaragua.

Enigma of the Arias Plan

By the beginning of 1990, the election in Nicaragua had become the centerpiece of the peace process—the supreme regional effort to transfer its raging disputes from the military to the political arena. By conducting a credible election under the auspices of a regional diplomacy that mobilized all five countries and the UN and OAS as guarantors, Nicaragua rendered the contras irrelevant despite their continued funding from Washington.

Nevertheless, to hold elections under conditions of gravely impaired national sovereignty, and to use the elections for international purposes, created unpredictable dynamics. Left to themselves, the Nicaraguan miniparties would have boycotted and squabbled. It took the combined efforts of the Sandinistas and foreigners to persuade them to run in the elections and come together into a formidable bloc. The Sandinistas, who had previously refused even to discuss electoral matters with the United States, now allowed open U.S. government aid to the opposition. So fundamental had the economic issue become that this aid, which few countries in the world would have tolerated, had less the effect of tarring the opposition as collaborators than of advertising them as the ones who could deliver U.S. largesse. Invited to participate in an election held to please foreigners, the majority voted in exactly the way indicated.

The unexpected outcome of the election removed from power the most dedicated proponents of the regional peace plan and cast a shadow over the revolution's social achievements in a region that desperately needed successful examples of closing the social chasm. But the same pragmatism and moderation that the opposition first showed at the Managua political dialogue just before Tela it now displayed in victory. Indeed, Violeta Chamorro best captured the spirit of the times with her statement that reconciliation was more beautiful than victory. Her team negotiated demobilization accords with the contras and left re-distributed land in the hands of the peasantry.

It had been a long and winding road from the beginning of Contadora. Mexico and the other countries that had begun the process were only spectators at the end. But President Arias's plan had tentatively silenced the cannons in Nicaragua. It had enabled the Sandinistas to give an example of concessions in a country used to conflict and of moderation in a country used to absolutism. Although there would inevitably be more frustration and setbacks in the process, from here the road led upward.

Notes

All unpublished documents referred to here are in the files of the Center for International Policy, Washington, D.C.

1. Gabriel Kolko, in *Confronting the Third World: United States Foreign Policy, 1945–80* (New York: Pantheon, 1988), stressed that not only leftist revolutionaries but also quite conservative Third World businessmen intent on raising tariff or currency barriers consistently aroused bitter U.S. opposition in the postwar period.

2. For a comprehensive account of Reagan era diplomacy in Nicaragua, see Roy Gutman, *Banana Diplomacy: The Making of American Foreign Policy in Nicaragua, 1981–1987* (New York: Simon and Schuster, 1988), from which this quote is drawn (p. 72).

3. Ibid., p. 78.

4. Mexico, Ministry of Foreign Affairs, "Estado Actual y Perspecticas de la Negociación en America Central," November 1986 (internal memorandum).

5. Unpublished cable from U.S. Secretary of State George Shultz to European Economic Community, September 7, 1984.

6. State Department official L. Craig Johnstone, unpublished press briefing, October 1, 1984.

7. U.S. National Security Council internal memorandum, October 20, 1984, first revealed in *Washington Post*, November 6, 1984.

8. Ibid.

9. Ibid.

10. National Security Planning Group Meeting, June 25, 1984, unpublished document made available by the National Security Archive, Washington, D.C. We are grateful to Peter Kornbluh for drawing this passage to our attention.

11. Further discussion in Gutman, *Banana Diplomacy*, pp. 207–232, 260–266.

12. The official insisted on remaining unidentified, although few could doubt that it was Elliott Abrams.

13. Richard H. Melton to Elliott Abrams, Memorandum: Secret/Sensitive, May 22, 1986, declassified in Iran-contra trials and kindly made available by the National Security Archive. Melton was the head of the State Department's Central America desk.

14. "Peace Is Still Possible in Central America," Declaration of the Foreign Ministers of the Contadora and Support Groups, New York, October 1, 1986.

15. Radio Voz de Honduras, Tegucigalpa, March 24, 26, as quoted in [U.S. Central Intelligence Agency], Foreign Broadcast Information Service Daily Report: Latin America (distributed by U.S. Department of Commerce, National Technical Information Service, Springfield, Va., May 12, 1986), p. P1.

16. Interview of Melvin Saenz, an adviser to Costa Rican Foreign Minister Rodrigo Madrigal Nieto, by Lidwien Michiels, of the Oficina por la Paz en Centroamerica in Managua on May 14, 1987.

17. New York Times, June 16, 1987.

18. New York Times, June 18, 1987.

19. Authors' notes, President Cerezo's press conference, Camino Real Hotel, Guatemala City, August 6, 1987.

20. Statement by Alfredo César at press conference in Managua, June 9, 1988.

21. Roy Gutman, "Contra Peace-Talks Ploy Disclosed," Newsday, July 5, 1988.

22. U.S. Agency for International Development, "Status Report of the Task Force on Humanitarian Assistance in Central America: Report on Phase III, May 1–August 31, 1989," September 27, 1989, p. 8. We are grateful to James Matlock of the American Friends' Service Committee for drawing our attention to this report.

Abbreviations and Acronyms

ADAL Association of Cotton Growers of León
AMNLAE Luisa Amanda Espinoza Association of Nicaraguan Women
AMPRONAC Association of Women Confronting the National Problem
ANC Conservative National Action
ANDEN National Association of Educators of Nicaragua
ANS Association of Sandinista Children
APP Area of People's Property
ARDE Democratic Revolutionary Alliance
ATC Rural Workers' Association
BCL light hunter battalion
BLI irregular warfare battalion
CACM Central American Common Market
CARIN Central America Research Institute
CAS Sandinista Agricultural Cooperative
CAUS Confederation of Union Action and Unity
CAV Antonio Valdivieso Center
CCS credit and service cooperative
CDC Civil Defense Committee (before 1979 triumph)
CDC Community Development Committee (after 1988)
CDD "certificate of exchange availability"
CDN Nicaraguan Democratic Coordinator
CDS Sandinista Defense Committee (until 1988)
CEB ecclesiastical base community
CELAM Council of Latin American Bishops
CEP Popular Education Collective
CEPAD Evangelical Committee to Aid the Destitute; later, Evangelical Committee for Aid to Development
CETRA Center for Labor Studies
CGT General Confederation of Independent Workers
CIA Central Intelligence Agency
CIAV International Commission for Support and Verification
CIERA Center for the Investigation and Study of the Agrarian Reform
CNASP Nicaraguan Council for Friendship, Solidarity, and Peace
CNMPT National Center of People's Traditional Medicine
CNPPDH National Commission for the Promotion and Protection of Human Rights
CONAPRO National Confederation of Professionals
COPETES permanent territorial companies
COSEP Superior Council of Private Enterprise
CPI consumer price index
CSE Supreme Electoral Council
CST Sandinista Workers' Federation

CUS Confederation of Union Unity
DBs primary leaders
DIs intermediate leaders
DNC Joint National Directorate
DOD Department of Defense
DSs higher leaders
EAP economically active population
EEC European Economic Community
ENABAS National Foodstuffs Enterprise
EPS Sandinista People's Army
FAO Broad Opposition Front
FDN Nicaraguan Democratic Force
FER Student Revolutionary Front
FETSALUD Federation of Health Workers
FMLN Farabundo Martí National Liberation Front
FO Workers' Front
FOIA Freedom of Information Act
FSLN Sandinista Front for National Liberation
GDP gross domestic product
GN National Guard
GPP Prolonged Popular War
GRN Government of the Republic of Nicaragua
HUAC House Un-American Activities Committee
ICJ International Court of Justice
IDB Inter-American Development Bank
IMF International Monetary Fund
INSSBI Nicaraguan Institute of Social Security and Social Welfare
JGRN Governing Junta of National Reconstruction
JS Sandinista Youth
LASPAU Latin American Scholarship Program of American Universities
LIC low-intensity conflict
MAP-ML Marxist-Leninist Popular Action Movement; later, Marxist Leninist party
MBS Ministry of Social Welfare
MDBs multilateral development banks
MED Ministry of Education
MEIC Ministry of Economy, Industry, and Commerce
MIDINRA Ministry of Agricultural Development and Agrarian Reform
MILPAS People's Anti-Somocista Militia
MINSA Ministry of Health
MINVAH Ministry of Housing and Human Settlements
MIPLAN Ministry of Planning
MISURA Mískitos, Sumus, and Ramas
MISURASATA Mískito, Sumu, Rama, and Sandinistas Working Together
MPS Sandinista People's Militias
MPU United People's Movement
MUR Movement for Revolutionary Unity
NAM Nonaligned Movement
NCA National Constituent Assembly
NED National Endowment for Democracy
NSC National Security Council
NSDD National Security Decision Directive
NSPG National Security Policy Group
OAS Organization of American States
OLM Women's Legal Office

ONUCA United Nations Observers in Central America
OPs grass-roots organization
PAHO Pan American Health Organization
PCD Democratic Conservative party
PCdeN Communist Party of Nicaragua
PIP Program of Public Investments
PLC Constitutional Liberal party
PLI Independent Liberal party
PLIUN Liberal Party of National Unity
PLN Liberal Nationalist party
PLO Palestine Liberation Organization
PNC National Conservative party
PPSC Popular Social Christian party
PRODEMCA Citizens' Committee for the Pro-Democratic Forces in Central America
PRT Revolutionary Workers' party
PS Sandinista Police
PSC Social Christian party
PSD Social Democratic party
PSN Nicaraguan Socialist party
SDN Secretariat of the National Directorate
SMP Patriotic Military Service
SNOTS National System of Wages and Labor
SNUS National Unified Health System
SPA Sandinista People's Army
TIMAL Tipitapa-Malcatoya
TP Proletarian Tendency
TPA People's Anti-Somocista Tribunal
UCLAs unilaterally controlled Latino assets
UDEL Democratic Union of Liberation
UNAG National Union of Farmers and Ranchers
UNAN National Autonomous University of Nicaragua
UNE National Union of Employees
UNO National Opposition Union (to 1990)
UNO Unified Nicaraguan Opposition (after 1990)
UPANIC Union of Nicaraguan Farmers
USAID United States Agency for International Development
USIA U.S. Information Agency
VOA Voice of America

About the Book

A comprehensive overview of the Sandinista revolution in Nicaragua, this book offers an interdisciplinary study of the domestic and foreign challenges that faced the Sandinista government during its ten years in power. Based on extensive research in Nicaragua during the revolution, the essays examine important aspects of both the revolution and the U.S.-orchestrated counter-revolution that brought it to an end.

After an introduction to the historical background of the revolutionary period, contributors offer an overview of specific groups and institutions within the revolution, such as women, grass-roots organizations, and the armed forces, and provide a balanced assessment of Sandinista public policy and performance in such areas as agrarian reform, health care, education, and housing. The impact and implications of the *contra* war, financed by the United States, are also analyzed, as well as efforts made over the years to promote a negotiated peace.

About the Editor
and Contributors

The Contributing Editor

THOMAS W. WALKER is professor of political science and director of Latin American Studies at Ohio University. He holds a B.A. in political science from Brown University and an M.A. (Latin American Studies) and Ph.D. (Political Science) from the University of New Mexico. Walker is the author of *The Christian Democratic Movement in Nicaragua* and *Nicaragua: The Land of Sandino*; the coauthor, with John Booth, of *Understanding Central America*; and the editor/coauthor of *Nicaragua in Revolution, Nicaragua: The First Five Years*, and *Reagan Versus the Sandinistas: The Undeclared War on Nicaragua*. From 1983 to 1984 he served as founding cochair of the Latin American Studies Association's Task Force on Scholarly Relations with Nicaragua. He was a member of the LASA teams that observed the Nicaraguan elections in 1984 and 1990.

The Chapter Authors

WILLIAM BARNES holds a Ph.D. in political science from the University of Michigan. He taught political theory and comparative politics at the University of Michigan, Ohio State University, Montana State University, and California Polytechnic State University at San Luis Obispo for ten years before taking a law degree at Boalt Hall, the University of California at Berkeley. He began interviewing Nicaraguan politicians and intellectuals in 1986 and was an adviser to the Boston-based election-monitoring organization Hemisphere Initiatives during the 1989–1990 Nicaraguan election campaign. He was also a member of the Commission on Nicaraguan Pre-election Polls and is a principal author of the commission's report. He practices law in Oakland.

EDUARDO BAUMEISTER, an Argentine sociologist, is a research associate at the Central American University (UCA), Managua. He holds a B.A. from the University of Buenos Aires and an M.A. from CLASCO. Until 1987, he was a researcher at the Center for the Investigation and Study of the Agrarian Reform (CIERA), also in Managua. Baumeister has published widely in the area of rural sociology in *Estudios Sociales Centroamericanos, Desarrollo Económico, Estudios Rurales Latinoamericanos*, and *Nueva Sociedad*. He has also contributed chapters to several books.

PATRICIA M. CHUCHRYK is associate professor and chair of sociology at the University of Lethbridge in Lethbridge, Alberta, Canada. She has published widely on feminist movements in Latin America and has conducted extensive research on women's groups in Chile during the period of military dictatorship. She is presently a fellow of the Center for Research on Latin America and the Caribbean at York University. Chuchryk holds a B.A. from Glendon College of York University, an M.A. from the University of Regina, and a Ph.D. in sociology from York University in Toronto, Canada.

MICHAEL DODSON is professor of political science at Texas Christian University, Fort Worth, Texas. He has published extensively on religion and politics in Latin America. His articles have appeared in the *Latin American Research Review*, *Polity*, and the *Journal of Latin American Studies*, and he is coauthor, with Laura O'Shaughnessy, of *Nicaragua's Other Revolution: Religious Faith and Political Struggle*. Dodson holds a B.A. from the University of South Dakota, an M.A. from the University of New Mexico, and a Ph.D. from Indiana University.

WILLIAM GOODFELLOW is director of the Center for International Policy in Washington, D.C. In that capacity, he traveled frequently to Central America and was deeply involved in covering the Central American peace process. In addition to numerous articles authored or coauthored by him in the center's *International Policy Report*, he has also published in the *New York Times*, *Washington Post*, *Los Angeles Times*, and *Newsday*. Goodfellow holds a B.A. in political science from Boston University and an M.A. from Goddard College.

PETER KORNBLUH is a senior analyst at the National Security Archive, a nongovernmental research library in Washington, D.C. Kornbluh holds a B.A. in Latin American Studies from Brandeis University and an M.A. in International Relations from George Washington University. Before joining the National Security Archive, he was a fellow at the Institute for Policy Studies, also in Washington, D.C. He is the author of *Nicaragua: The Price of Intervention* and coeditor of *Low Intensity Warfare: Counterinsurgency, Proinsurgency, and Antiterrorism in the Eighties* and *The Iran-Contra Affair: The Making of a Scandal, 1983-1988*.

MICHAEL LINFIELD practices law in Los Angeles. Prior to 1986, he served variously as chief lobbyist for the United Farm Workers Union, liaison to the Governor of California on Pension Investment issues, and Vice President of the American Civil Liberties Union of Southern California. Linfield is the author of *Freedom Under Fire: U.S. Civil Liberties in Times of War* and *Investments of California's Public-Sector Pension Funds* as well as reviews that have appeared in the *Harvard Civil Rights-Civil Liberties Law Review* and the *Harvard Human Rights Yearbook*. He received a B.A. in philosophy from the University of California, Los Angeles, and a J.D. from Harvard Law School. While at Harvard, he received a Ferguson Fellowship to study human rights in Nicaragua where, during the summer of 1987, he served as the intern to the chief justice of the Nicaraguan Supreme Court. Two trips there in the late 1980s were funded by the Harvard Law School Human Rights Program.

JAMES MORRELL is director of research at the Center for International Policy (CIP), Washington, D.C. He holds a B.A. and a Ph.D. in history from Carleton College and Harvard University, respectively. Before coming to the CIP, he taught at the Boston School of Adult Education, Harvard University, and Johnson State College, in Johnson, Vermont. In addition to twenty-eight articles in CIP's *International Policy Report*, he has published in over twenty prominent newspapers and magazines and has testified before committees of the United Nations, the U.S. Congress, and the Canadian Parliament.

GARY PREVOST is professor of government at St. John's University in Collegeville, Minnesota. He has written extensively on the politics of Spain, Central America, and the Caribbean. He is coeditor of *Politics and Change in Spain* and *Cuba—A Different America*. He has just completed a coauthored manuscript on contemporary Nicaraguan politics and has received a Fulbright award for research on the FSLN. Prevost holds a B.A. from Union College and an M.A. and Ph.D. from the University of Minnesota.

ANDREW A. REDING is senior fellow for hemispheric affairs at the World Policy Institute in New York. He has engaged in extensive on-site research and analysis of democratic processes and human rights in Mexico and Central America, including the drafting of the Nicaraguan constitution of 1987. He is the author of *Christianity and Revolution;* articles in several dozen major magazines, journals, and newspapers; and chapters in *The Nicaragua Reader* and *The Nicaraguan Constitution of 1987: English Translation and Commentary*. Reding holds a B.A. from Middlebury College and a Masters in Public Affairs from the Woodrow Wilson School of Public and International Affairs at Princeton University.

JOSEPH RICCIARDI is assistant professor of economics at Babson College, Wellesley, Massachusetts. During 1988, he was visiting assistant professor of Economics and Latin American Studies at the University of Texas, Austin, and taught in the postgraduate program at the Central American University (UCA) in Managua. He has worked as a research economist in Peru and Central America. In 1987 and 1988, he worked at the Central Bank of Nicaragua and co-founded EcoNica, an organization of economists working in Nicaragua. His studies have been published in *Research in Political Economy, The International Journal of Political Economy, Dollars and Sense,* and *Against the Current*. His current research includes an analysis of financial distortions in mixed economies. Ricciardi holds a B.A. from the State University of New York College at Purchase, and a Ph.D. from the University of Texas, Austin.

LUIS HECTOR SERRA, an Argentine, is professor of sociology at the Central American University (UCA) in Managua. Since 1979, he has resided in Nicaragua where he has worked variously in the Literacy Crusade, with the Christian revolutionary movement, and with peasant popular education. In this respect, in the late 1980s he worked as an assessor to the National Union of Farmers and Ranchers (UNAG), the grass-roots organization of small and medium landholders. He is a graduate in law and history from the National University of Buenos Aires. He also holds M.A.s in international affairs and political science from Ohio University and in sociology from Louvaine la Neuve in

Belgium where he is currently completing a doctorate in sociology. His recent works include "Educación Popular y Revolución en América Latina" and (with Laura O'Shaughnessy) *The Church and Revolution in Nicaragua.*

ANGHARAD N. VALDIVIA is assistant professor of communications at Pennsylvania State University. She has researched mass communications issues in Chile, Peru, and Nicaragua. Valdivia holds a B.A. from the University of California at San Diego and a Ph.D. from the University of Illinois at Champaign-Urbana.

HARRY E. VANDEN is professor of political science at the University of South Florida. In the 1970s he was a Fulbright scholar in Peru, where he stayed on to work in the National Institute of Public Administration. In addition to a number of articles, he has produced such books as *National Marxism in Latin America: José Carlos Mariategui's Thought and Politics* and *A Bibliography of Latin American Marxism.* Having focused his recent research on Nicaragua and Central America, he is currently preparing a book on democracy and socialism in Nicaragua. Vanden completed his undergraduate work at Albright College and the University of Madrid. He holds an M.A. and Certificate in Latin American Studies from the Maxwell School of Syracuse University and a Ph.D. from the New School for Social Research.

KIRSI VIISAINEN is a Ph.D. candidate in public health at the University of Helsinki, Finland. She holds an M.D. degree from the same institution plus an M.A. degree in medical anthropology from McGill University, Montreal. Her chapter is based on extensive research she conducted in Nicaragua in 1989 for her master's thesis, "Nicaraguan Midwives, Integration of Indigenous Prac- titioners into Official Health Care."

ERIC WEAVER is a founder of the Central American Research Institute (CARIN) of Berkeley, California, and was managing editor of the CARIN's *Central American Bulletin* throughout most of the 1980s. He has traveled extensively in Central America and began interviewing Nicaraguan political figures in 1984. He is the coauthor of *Honduras: Pieza Clave en la Política de los Estados Unidos en Centro América* and editor of the bilingual edition of Roque Dalton's *Poemas Clandestinas.* A graduate of the University of San Francisco Law School, he currently practices law in Berkeley.

HARVEY WILLIAMS is professor of sociology and chair of sociology and anthropology at the University of the Pacific, Stockton, California, where he joined the faculty in 1977. He has published widely on Latin American topics including several chapters on social-sector programs that have appeared in *Nicaragua in Revolution, Nicaragua: The First Five Years, Reagan Versus the Sandinistas: The Undeclared War on Nicaragua* and *Third World Medicine and Social Change.* Williams holds a B.A. from the University of California, Berkeley, and an M.A. and Ph.D. from Vanderbilt University.

Index

Abortion, 31, 59, 67, 153, 154, 156, 159, 202. *See also* Women
Abrams, Elliott, 381, 393(n12)
Acquired Immune Deficiency Syndrome. *See* AIDS
ADAL. *See* Association of Cotton Growers of León
Adult Education Centers, 203
Africa, 296, 305
Agee, Philip, 80
Agrarian reform. *See* Land reform
Agrarian Reform Law, 22
Agrarian Reform Tribunals, 23
Agricultural Reform Law (1981), 62
Agricultural Self-Defense Cooperatives, 89, 94
Aguirre, Danilo, 30, 38
Ahuas Tara II, 328
AIDS, 202
Algeria, 296
Allende, Salvador, 77, 80, 106, 279, 299, 342, 356
Alliance for Progress, 236
Amanecer, 21
American Convention on Human Rights (San José Pact), 30, 37, 290(n2)
AmeriCares, 362
Americas Watch, 278
Amnesty International, 276, 283, 288, 291(n4)
AMNLAE. *See* Luisa Amanda Espinoza Association of Nicaraguan Women
Amparo, 16, 31, 37–38
AMPRONAC. *See* Association of Women Confronting the National Problem
ANC. *See* Conservative National Action
ANDEN. *See* National Association of Educators of Nicaragua
Andropov, Yuri, 311
Angola, 356
ANS. *See* Association of Sandinista Children
Antonio Valdivieso Ecumenical Center (CAV), 21, 172
APP. *See* Area of People's Property
Applebaum, Judith, 305, 318(n31)
Arab countries, 82, 86
Arbenz Guzmán, Jacobo, 80, 92, 237, 299
Arbizú, Ramón, 37
Arce, Bayardo, 20, 32, 63, 103–104, 108, 109, 308, 309
ARDE. *See* Democratic Revolutionary Alliance

Area of People's Property (APP), 251, 252, 253, 255. *See also* Land reform
Arévalo, Juan José, 80
Argentina, 2, 3, 93, 271(n25), 374
and contra war, 314, 330, 332
foreign policy, 298, 310, 314
See also Peace negotiations
Argüello, Carlos, 318(n31)
Argüello, Leonel, 41
Argüello, Roberto, 21
Arias, Oscar, 39, 134, 135–136, 182, 280, 315, 380, 388. *See also* Peace negotiations, Arias peace plan
Armed forces, 31, 77–96
benign behavior of, 80, 82, 97(n9)
buildup, 13, 85–88, 94, 98(n20), 175
and grass-roots organizations, 54
loyalty to Sandinistas, 9–10, 81, 132, 137
and 1990 transfer of power, 44, 91, 92–93, 96
and opposition parties, 132
origins of, 17, 77–80
posttriumph consolidation, 81–84, 123
and U.S. propaganda, 85, 93–95, 98(n20)
women in, 143, 145, 154, 158, 161(n11)
See also Foreign arms assistance; Military draft; National Guard; Sandinista Defense Committees
Army Intelligence Survey (1984) (U.S. Army), 86, 90, 95, 98(n20)
Aronson, Bernard, 342
Association of Cotton Growers of León (ADAL), 232
Association of Sandinista Children (ANS), 67
Association of Women Confronting the National Problem (AMPRONAC), 122, 144–145, 146. *See also* Luisa Amanda Espinoza Association of Nicaraguan Women
ATC. *See* Rural Workers' Association
Atlantic coast minorities, 31, 179, 205
and contra war, 33, 90, 174, 194, 332
education, 33, 191, 198
and 1990 elections, 38–39, 42–43
regional autonomy, 32–35, 90, 104
Austerity program, 38, 58, 90–91, 102, 247, 248, 259–267
and armed forces, 90–91
and capital investment, 240, 241

405

Vaky, Viron, 323–324
Valdivia, Angharad, 321
Vanden, Harry, 185
Vatican, 129, 172, 173–174, 181, 182
Vega, Pablo Antonio, 129, 176, 178, 182
Veil (Woodward), 343
Velasco Alvarado, Juan, 237
Venezuela, 2, 82, 298, 310
  as model for Sandinista government, 26, 31, 37, 45(n3)
  petroleum trade, 267, 312, 314, 315
  See also Peace negotiations
Verification Commission. See International Commission for Support and Verification
Vice Ministry of Adult Education, 194
Vietnam, 296, 356, 369
Vietnam Syndrome, 325
Vigil, Miguel Ernesto, 21
Viisainen, Kirsi, 186
Vilas, Carlos, 161(n10), 197, 264
VOA. See Voice of America
Voice of America (VOA), 355
Voluntary Police, 54

Walker, David, 337
Walker, William, 6, 296
Wall Street Journal, 27
War of Liberation. See Prerevolution insurgency
War of the Communeros, 7
Washington Post, 95, 125
Weaver, Eric, 13–14
Western Europe, 36, 282, 283, 287, 290, 314, 376
  and constitution, 29
  economic assistance, 45, 266, 267, 307, 308, 309, 311, 319(n41), 327
  and 1984 elections, 26, 28
  and 1990 elections, 42
  and peace negotiations, 307, 309
  public opinion, 301
  Sandinista relations with, 45, 259, 301, 307–309
West Germany, 36, 307, 309, 319(n41)
Wheelock, Jaime, 20, 103, 106, 108–109

WHO. See World Health Organization
Williams, Harvey, 185
Wippman, David, 318(n31)
Witness for Peace, 41
Women, 14, 143–160
  in armed forces, 143, 145, 154, 158, 161(nn 10, 11)
  and constitution, 30–31, 131, 159
  and economic situation, 143, 148, 152
  family roles, 56, 145–147, 148, 149, 151, 152–153, 155
  FSLN policies, 68, 69, 143, 144, 147, 155–156, 157–158
  in grass-roots organizations, 56, 57, 59, 66, 67, 68–69
  labor force participation, 143, 144, 148–152, 155, 163(n56)
  in labor unions, 69, 143, 148–149
  and media, 364
  in War of Liberation, 143–146, 161(nn 10, 11)
  See also Abortion; Child care; Social programs
Women's Government Office, 147
Women's Legal Office (OLM), 147, 153
Women's Program, 147
Woodward, Bob, 343
Workers' Front (FO), 62, 75(n15)
World Bank, 201, 251, 270(n10), 327, 386
World Court, 21, 197, 301, 304, 305–306, 318(nn 31, 33)
  Edgar Chamorro testimony, 353–354, 355
  Memorial on Compensation, 345
World Health Organization (WHO), 194
World Parliamentary Union, 305
Wright, James, 301, 343, 378, 379, 389

Yatama, 43, 118
Yoquepierdismo, 73
Young Conservative movement, 120
Youth, 54, 80, 88–89, 132, 169. See also Sandinista Youth

Zamora Rodríguez, Agusto, 318(n31)
Zelaya, José Santos, 6, 119
Zeledón, Benjamín, 7